National Thea 2

NEW PLAYS FOR YOUNG PEOPLE

Class

The Sad Club

Flesh

Variations

Salt

Ageless

terra/earth

Chaos

The Small Hours

Stuff

With introductions by

HOLLY ASTON and TOM LYONS

methuen | drama

LONDON • NEW YORK • OXFORD • NEW DELHI • SYDNEY

METHUEN DRAMA
Bloomsbury Publishing Plc
50 Bedford Square, London, WC1B 3DP, UK
1385 Broadway, New York, NY 10018, USA

BLOOMSBURY, METHUEN DRAMA and the Methuen Drama logo are
trademarks of Bloomsbury Publishing Plc

First published in Great Britain 2019

A catalogue record for this book is available from the British Library.

A catalog record for this book is available from the Library of Congress.

ISBN: PB: 978-1-3501-0837-0
       ePDF: 978-1-3501-0839-4
       ePub: 978-1-3501-0838-7

Series: Modern Plays

Typeset by RefineCatch Limited, Bungay, Suffolk
Printed and bound in Great Britain

To find out more about our authors and books visit www.bloomsbury.com
and sign up for our newsletters.

Contents

National Theatre Connections

Connections is the National Theatre's annual, nationwide youth theatre festival and is a celebration of new writing, partnership, and above all the importance of access for young people to the arts. Each year Connections offers a unique opportunity for youth theatres and school theatre groups to stage new plays written specifically for young people by some of the most exciting playwrights writing today, and then to perform them in leading theatres across the UK.

New plays are at the heart of Connections – newly commissioned scripts that are for and about young people, and that are challenging and relevant. Ten new plays are commissioned each year, building up a repertoire permanently available to schools, colleges and youth theatres.

At the beginning of the rehearsal process, the National Theatre hosts the Connections Directors' Weekend – an opportunity for the directors of all the companies in the Connections programme to work with the playwright of their chosen play and a leading theatre director. Notes from these workshops accompany each of the plays in this anthology, giving an insight into the playwrights' intentions, creative inspiration and practical suggestions for text exploration.

In 2019, 300 companies from across the UK took the challenge of staging a brand new Connections play – that's over 7,000 young people, aged 13 to 19, involved in every aspect of theatre-making. Connections is not just the National Theatre's programme: it is run in collaboration with theatres across the UK who are equally passionate about youth theatre. This year we are collaborating with 30 brilliant partner theatres who will help us to support every company to develop and transfer their production, meaning every young person taking part will have the opportunity to work on a professional stage.

One production of each play is invited to perform at the National Theatre in a week-long Connections Festival which celebrates new writing and the next generation of theatre-makers.

Through Connections, young people work together, establishing trust, building confidence and creating empathy. Young people say they find somewhere they belong and it can be a transformative experience. As one participant remarked: 'Learning compassion and learning things that come with understanding of others – theatre will save the world.'

Holly Aston, Connections Producer
National Theatre, 2019
For more information and to get involved visit:
www.connections.nationaltheatre.org.uk

Introduction

The Connections 2019 anthology is much more than simply a collection of ten plays. These are stories of collaboration, stories about collaboration and stories born out of collaboration. Stories of working together to find unity, or create order in chaos, or to arrange a really good party sit alongside creative collaborations between playwrights, choreographers, composers and scientists.

It is the scale and range of creative collaboration inherent in theatre that sits at the very heart of National Theatre Connections. This begins with the writers and creators of these plays and immediately extends to the hundreds of brilliant young people from across the UK who have helped to shape these ideas and texts through development workshops. It extends further with the 300 directors who participate in the Connections Directors' Weekend to explore and workshop the plays.

Yet more links are added to the creative chain as actors, designers, stage managers and musicians join their creative teams. Like sculptors, all of their fingerprints can be seen on each piece of work.

Theatre, arguably more than almost any other art form, is a collaboration – a shared activity. You might sit and read these plays alone, but your mind will undoubtedly jump to 'who might play Alice', 'who could choreograph Terra's dance', 'who will play the drums in the Sad Club band', a steady stream of creative collaborators surrounding you.

This collection of ten plays is both the result of collaborations between artists and creative young people from across the UK and the provocation for thousands more creative collaborations.

The Plays

Class *by Ben Bailey Smith and Lajaune Lincoln*

It's school election time and, while most of the school is busy enjoying their lunchbreak, a deadlock is taking place amongst the members of the school council. Bitter rivalries, secret alliances and false promises are laid bare. As a ruthless battle ensues, who will win and does anyone really care? A play about politics, populism and the 'ping' of a text message.

The Sad Club *by Luke Barnes with music by Adam Pleeth*

This is a musical about depression and anxiety. It's a collection of monologues, duologues and songs from all over time and space, exploring what about living in this world stops us from being happy and how we might go about tackling those problems. When you're feeling your most trapped and alone, The Sad Club has a live band and free entry. A play with songs about depression, fears and hope.

Flesh *by Rob Drummond*

A group of teenagers wake up in a forest with no clue how they got there. They find themselves separated into two different coloured teams but have no idea what game they are expected to play. With no food, no water and seemingly no chance of escape, it's only a matter of time before things start to get drastic. But whose side are you on and how far would you go to survive? This is a play about human nature, the tribes we create and cannibalism.

Variations *by Katie Hims*

Thirteen-year-old Alice wishes her life was completely different. Then one morning she wakes up and it is. Alice is taken through a series of parallel universes, reliving the same ten minutes over and over again. Maybe different isn't all it's cracked up to be, but once you've started on a path can you go back to normality? A play about family, string theory and breakfast.

Salt *by Dawn King*

Life is never plain sailing, but when a new government initiative comes into place offering young people the opportunity to train and learn skills overseas, droves of teens jump at the chance to secure their future. Once on board the transport ship, the promises of the glossy advert seem a far cry from what lies ahead. A play about generations, choices and hope.

Ageless *by Benjamin Kuffuor*

In a not-too-distant future, the Temples pharmaceutical corporation has quite literally changed the face of aging. Their miracle drug keeps its users looking perpetually young. With an ever-youthful population, how can society support those who are genuinely young? A play that questions what it means to be young and what happens when generations collide.

terra/earth *by Nell Leyshon with choreography by Anthony Missen*

A contemporary narrative dance piece. A group of classmates are torn apart by the opportunity to perform their own dance. As they disagree and bicker, two distinct physical groups emerge and separate into opposing teams. When a strange outsider appears – out of step with everyone else – the divide is disrupted. A piece about individuality, community and heritage.

Chaos *by Laura Lomas*

A girl is locked in a room; a boy brings another boy flowers; a girl has tied herself to a railing; a boy doesn't know who he is; a girl worries about catastrophe; a woman jumps in front of a train; a boy's heart falls out his chest; a butterfly has a broken wing. *Chaos* is a symphony of dislocated and interconnected scenes. A series of characters search for meaning in a complicated and unstable world. Bouncing through physics and the cosmos, love and violence, they find order in the mess of each other.

The Small Hours *by Katherine Soper*

It's the middle of the night, and Peebs and Epi are the only students left at school over half-term. At the end of their night, Red and Jazz are former step-siblings trying to navigate their reunion. With only a couple of hours till morning, Jaffa is trying to help Keesh finish an essay. As day breaks, Wolfie is getting up the courage to confess a secret to VJ at a party. Their choices are small yet momentous. The hours are small but feel very, very long. And when the night finally ends, the future is waiting: all of it.

Stuff *by Tom Wells*

Vinny's organising a surprise birthday party for his mate Anita – she needs cheering up and Vinny can't think of any better way to do that. It's not going well. His choice of venue is a bit misguided, Anita's not keen on leaving the house and everyone else has their own stuff going on. Maybe a surprise party wasn't the best idea? A play about trying (but not really managing) to help.

Tom Lyons, 2019

Class

by Ben Bailey Smith and Lajaune Lincoln

It's school election time and, while most of the school is busy enjoying their lunchbreak, a deadlock is taking place amongst the members of the school council. Bitter rivalries, secret alliances and false promises are laid bare. As a ruthless battle ensues, who will win and does anyone really care? A play about politics, populism and the 'ping' of a text message.

Cast size
14–30

Ben Bailey Smith was known as the underground rapper Doc Brown before moving into mainstream TV and film acting, stand-up comedy, playwriting, screenwriting and children's books. He has a host of notable television and film performances under his belt including ITV's *Law & Order* and *Brief Encounters*, Channel 4's *The Inbetweeners* and *Derek*, and the 2016 Ricky Gervais film *David Brent: Life on the Road*. He has also written music for the movies *Attack the Block* and *Quartet*. Smith boasts a wide following amongst children, starring in and writing for the cult animation *Strange Hill High* and creating and co-writing the BAFTA-winning *Four O'Clock Club*, now into its fifth series, both for CBBC. His first children's book, the Walker/Candlewick-published *I Am Bear*, is on sale worldwide and has been an instant hit with critics and readers alike. The follow-up, *Bear Moves*, will be released in February 2019. He has a third picture book called *Get a Move On!* due to be released by Bloomsbury in 2019 and is currently working on a novel for eight- to eleven-year-olds. *Class* is Ben's second commission for the stage. He previously wrote a monologue for the Arinzé Kene project *One Voice* at the Old Vic, to mark the hundredth anniversary of the end of the First World War.

Lajaune Lincoln is a London-based screenwriter. In 2009 he co-directed his second written feature *Other Side of the Game* which played at several festivals before an international release in the US, Canada and Australia. His current slate includes the neo-noir *Real Eyes* and industry satire *The One That Got Away* featured in both *Screen International* and *The Hollywood Reporter*. Alongside his writing partner, Ben Bailey Smith, he is now working on a number of television shows for their production company Bust-A-Gut. *Class* is his first foray into writing for the stage.

Note to companies

For the first two acts of the play characters exchange private online text messages in a 'WhatsApp' mould, betraying many of their secrets and feelings. Utilising additional cast to portray these moments physically and verbally will provide the piece with an ensemble cast. How this is staged is open to directors' interpretation.

It is essential, however, that there is a clear distinction between the live and online versions of the same character. This could be reflected by pushing the physicality of performers and changes in lighting states to create a theatrical 'other-worldly' feel. Numbers allowing, it is advised that two different actors portray the live and online personas of a character. A suggestion for staging is as follows:

A classroom is set up on the stage. Behind this is a raised platform above which hangs a large screen. This platform is the setting for the online characters' communication. The sound of a text message arriving will signal the start of an online exchange.

Online personas will then appear from behind the screen when different performers playing their live counterparts are sending or responding to a message on their phones.

The online personas will vocalise the online dialogue exchanged between their live counterparts then return behind the screen when their dialogue has ended.

During this, live characters will continue with their actions (we'll notice them checking their devices and reacting to messages) but will perform on mute so the audience can hear the online personas. A maximum of two online personas will appear at any one time. They will each be distinctively dressed in the same costume as their live character.

Unless otherwise indicated, transitions between live and online action should be seamless and swift – an intricate but fluid weaving of the two worlds.

Characters *(all seventeen/eighteen years old)*

Jason, *from the hood, popular and straight talking, with a sharp street edge*

Chloe, *monied, arrogant yet incredibly charming, witty, cool and calm*

Oli, *clever guy, but not that smart, with big aspirations*

Melissa, *Chloe's best friend – forever?*

Abigail, *Chloe's older and much, much, much wiser sister*

Tammy, *Abigail's doormat, but also quietly heroic and ready for a revolt*

Debs, *clued-up classmate*

Sol, *very well spoken, mummy's 'little gangsta'*

Rash, *solid and straight-up*

Rachel, *reluctant messenger*

Mark, *key voter and Lane's passionate boyfriend*

Lane, *key voter and Mark's passionate girlfriend/boyfriend*

Noel, *moany voter*

Shay, *key voter*

'Online' characters can be played by different actors:

Online Jason

Online Chloe

Online Oli

Online Melissa

Online Abigail

Online Tammy

Other Students *(ideally no fewer than seven performers – but this is subject to the size of the company)*

Interior of a classroom set up in typical fashion: students' desks and chairs lined up in rows; tutor's desk at the front, whiteboard on the wall behind it. Your quintessential, academically inspirational learning environment . . .

From behind the screen a young man appears.

Online Jason   Yo, Oli, you blocked me or something? Hit me up, man. (*Waits. Disappears.*)

Online Abigail *appears.*

Online Abigail   Are you on your way, Chloe?

Online Chloe *appears.*

Online Chloe   Just chill.

Online Abigail   You do know what time you were supposed to be here?

Online Chloe   Yep, five minutes ago.

Online Abigail   And that doesn't bother you at all does it?

Online Chloe   Don't worry, big sis. I'm the one who's late, not you. Your rep will remain intact. Unless I'm another ten minutes late of course. Ha ha.

Online Abigail   Grow up.

Online Abigail *disappears.*

Online Chloe   You there yet, Mel?

Online Melissa *appears.*

Online Melissa   Where are you?

Online Chloe   Two minutes.

Online Melissa   Late. Always. Loser. Oli's here already.

Online Chloe   Ha. He reckons being early will get him more votes.

Online Melissa (*laughs*)   That loser needs all the help he can get.

They both disappear. **Online Jason** *appears.*

Online Jason   Don't need to keep blanking me, man. I told you. That thing with your moped was nothing to do with me. (*Waits.*) Yo. (*Waits.*)

Online Jason *disappears.*

The live characters appear outside the classroom. The noisy group of twenty or so students file in and sit in their various cliques. We recognise **Abigail** *and* **Melissa** *from the clothes they are wearing that match those of their online personas.* **Abigail** *looks around and nabs* **Melissa**.

Abigail   Mel, do you know where my sister is?

Melissa   Literally, she'll be here any second.

Abigail   I'm so sick of having to look out for her – just constantly. Like looking after a two-year-old.

She storms off in a huff. **Melissa** *catches the attention of a boy walking past.*

Melissa   Oli! Good luck! (*Talks loudly to make sure she is heard.*) You know if you were up against anybody else but Chloe you'd get my vote.

Oli (*winks conspiratorially*)   Who knows, still might get your vote, innit . . .

Melissa *looks around then giggles and punches* **Oli** *on his arm.*

Oli *walks off and approaches two boys. Before he gets there he is stopped by another girl –* **Debs**.

Debs (*shy and sincere*)   Oli, my mum says thanks again for those flowers.

Oli   No worries. Tell her get well soon, yeah?

Debs *smiles gratefully and walks off.* **Oli** *gets to the two guys –* **Sol** *and* **Rash**.

Sol   Alright, Ol.

Rash   Yes, mate! How's it going?

Oli   Feeling good! Your votes are gonna make a big difference today.

Sol   The only difference I want to see is with our science lessons. You got that covered, right?

Oli   Sorted. Trust.

Rash   Be good to get some other bits and pieces though. Been talking about getting proper lockers –

Sol (*interrupts*)   – in the changing rooms, *and* getting better food in the canteen *and* blah-de-blah-de-shut the hell up. We heard it the hundred and eighth time you said it.

Oli   I'm on it, Rash, don't worry.

Rash   About time. We need a president who's gonna care about more than just the shade of their lipstick or something.

Sol   Exactly. Eyeliner's just as important.

They all crack up.

Rash   Oh yeah, Ol, can you give me a lift home later?

Oli   No, uh . . . I didn't ride in today.

Rash   How come?

Oli   Uhhh . . . it wouldn't start this morning.

Sol   Gutted. I thought it was new?

Oli (*ultra glum*)   Yeah, I know.

Rash *and* **Sol** *wave to* **Jason** *as he enters.* **Oli** *looks up and he and* **Jason** *exchange a glance.* **Jason** *nods a hello but* **Oli** *blanks him and turns back to his cronies.* **Jason** *pulls out his phone and begins to text.*

Online Jason *appears from behind the screen.*

Online Jason   You really want to go there? I'm not that guy, bruv!!!!!

Oli *pulls out his phone.*

Online Oli *appears.*

Online Oli   After what you did, you're the one getting angry with me?

Online Jason   I. WAS. NOT. INVOLVED.

Online Oli   Liar. Play it how you want, I don't care.

Online Jason *and* **Online Oli** *disappear.*

Abigail *and her reluctant sidekick* **Tammy** *walk over to* **Jason**.

Abigail (*sarcastic*)   Comrade Jason! Thought you weren't coming back?

Jason   And miss this pantomime? Nah I want a front-row seat for this. (*Looks around.*) And I mean, it's not exactly the most diverse group is it? You might need people who actually have their own opinion.

Abigail   It's all a big joke to you isn't it?

Jason   To be honest, the way it's been run the past few years, it has been. It's not like things have got much better for the students who actually need some support.

Abigail   If you're talking about your 'crew', I don't think they're that interested in politics, Jason.

Jason   My crew? (*Laughs to himself.*) Yeah, you're right, I don't think the student population from my endz of the social scale *are* that interested in politics, we're more interested in systems that will actually achieve something.

Abigail (*to* **Tammy**)   You see, Tammy, there he goes again. (*To* **Jason**,) We can really do without your crap this time, okay? Some of us take this seriously.

Jason   Then you should understand I'm doing you a favour by being here. Being an elitist wouldn't look good on your CV. (*Cheeky.*) Or in your case, maybe it would.

Tammy *starts laughing.* **Abigail** *gives her an evil glare.*

Abigail   Something funny?

Tammy *chokes back her laughter.*

Jason (*smiles*)   No need to feel threatened, Abi. I'm just a 'humble observer'.

Abigail   Oh, I'd love to see that.

Jason *turns to walk off.*

Jason   This is your lucky day then, innit?

Behind them, **Chloe** *enters the classroom without a care in the world. It is clear she is popular with some of the* **Other Students**.

Tammy *taps* **Abigail**.

Tammy   Your sister's here.

Abigail   So the silly cow has decided to show up.

She approaches **Chloe** *with a face like thunder.* **Tammy** *trails behind her.*

Chloe (*puts on a voice to annoy* **Abigail**)   Wassup, homie? (*Smiles at* **Tammy**, *normal tone.*) Hey, Tam Tam.

Tammy *scowls.* **Abigail** *pulls* **Chloe** *aside to talk in private.*

Abigail   Are you nuts? How do you think it makes us both look with you turning up this late for your own election?

Chloe   *My* election? (*Faux shock.*) So my victory is a foregone conclusion?

Abigail   Well, it wouldn't be if you didn't have me helping you out.

Chloe   I really don't think I need your help.

Abigail   I wouldn't think too much. It doesn't suit you.

Chloe   Oh screw you, Abby!

Abigail   You can tell Daddy how mean I was when you become the new student president.

Chloe   You can tell Daddy . . .

Abigail   Exactly. (*Walks off to front of class.*)

Chloe *flops down irritatedly in a chair next to* **Melissa**.

Melissa   Where you been?

Chloe   I just had an interrogation from Abby, thanks. I swear she thinks the world revolves around her. Anyway, how do I look? Big moment coming up.

Melissa   Is that new lipstick? You weren't wearing it earlier.

Jason *walks past.*

Jason   Yes, Mel. How you doin', Chloe?

Melissa   Hey, Jason. (*Gives him a genuine and warm smile.*)

Chloe (*offhand*)   Oh hi, J. You alright?

Jason (*equally offhand*)   Cool.

Jason *and* **Chloe** *barely exchange a glance.* **Jason** *sits at a table nearby. Casual. A couple of flirtatious girls join him.*

Chloe *looks at him quickly then turns away.*

Melissa   What's that about?

Chloe   What?

Melissa   You two.

Chloe   Who two?

Melissa (*playful nudge*)   You and Jason!

Chloe (*confused*)   What are you talking about?

Abigail *is standing at the tutor's desk.*

Abigail   Okay, everybody. Can I . . . can I get your attention please. Everybody. (*Waits for people to gather and be quiet.*) Mark. Lane.

Mark *and* **Lane** *stop their canoodling in the corner.*

Abigail   Tammy, come here please.

The long-suffering **Tammy** *slowly walks over to stand just behind* **Abigail***.*

Abigail   Thank you all. Thank you. Well, first of all I just want to say it's been an honour to be your student president for the past two years and to work with all of you as part of the student council.

Already losing a few. The natives are restless . . .

I know it's our lunch break but it's important that we take voting seriously, so if we want to eat, let's all work together and get this done.

Mark   When are we going to talk about the prom?

Noel   Yeah, the teachers are saying it might have to be in the gym even though we have to pay for tickets. I'd rather stay at home and watch *Corrie* with me mam!

Class laughs.

Mark   We want a proper rave-up, especially if we're paying for it!

Abigail   Is that the only reason you're here?

Lane (*snuggles up to* **Mark**)   Some of us are looking forward to the slow jams . . .

The class 'Woooooooos'.

Abigail (*raises eyebrow at the loved-up* **Mark** *and* **Lane**)   Mmm. Anyway, all of that will get sorted out after voting. We can decide on a venue and DJs and stuff and then the first act of the new president will be to get the Principal to stump up more money. But before all that . . . (*Inhales and holds herself regally.*) . . . let me just say a few words . . . (*Ignores the rolled eyes of the class and carries on in mute as . . .*)

Online Oli *appears.*

Online Oli   So what you got for me?

Online Melissa *appears*

Online Melissa   Huh?

Online Oli   Any more dirt?

Online Melissa   Don't say it like that.

Online Oli   Okay. Anything to help a noble cause, m'lady?

Online Melissa (*laughs*)   You're such a loser.

Online Oli   Not for long.

Online Oli *and* **Online Melissa** *disappear.*

In the classroom **Melissa** *laughs out loud and disturbs* **Abigail***'s speech. Everybody looks at* **Melissa** *and* **Abigail** *gives her a cold glare then continues talking.*

Abigail   As I was saying – (*Back to mute.*)

Online Chloe *appears.*

Online Chloe   What was so funny?

Online Melissa *appears. Pause.*

Onlne Chloe   Helloooooooo.

Online Melissa   Nothing. Your sister is just such a loser.

Online Chloe   She thinks she's something special right?

Online Chloe *and* **Online Melissa** *disappear.*

Abigail *is hitting her stride.*

Abigail   . . . So going forward our priorities as a student council must be ensuring that every student is valued as an individual! Respected as a person! We must –

Online Chloe *appears.*

Online Chloe   How long is this going to go on for?

Online Tammy *appears.*

Online Tammy   How should I know?

Online Chloe (*sarcastic*)   Well, Miss Vice-President, you should know these things. Didn't you write her speech for her?

Online Tammy   Leave me alone.

Online Chloe *and* **Tammy** *disappear.*

Abigail *continues with her speech.*

Abigail   So with campaigning over, our two candidates will now give their final speeches.

Online Melissa *appears.*

Online Melissa   Kill it!!!!

Online Chloe   Get my Oscar ready.

Online Chloe *and* **Online Melissa** *disappear.*

Noel   Oh come *on*, do we have to sit through more speeches?

Abigail   No, Noel, you don't. The door's that way.

The class 'Ooooohs'.

Noel   Alright, alright, I was just asking.

Sol   And you got told!

Abigail (*to* **Chloe** *and* **Oli**)   So, strict rules. You talk for one minute. I'll keep time on my phone. (*Pulls out phone, looks at screen and acts surprised.*) Oh wow! This is amazing. My dad – and Chloe's as well of course – just sent a text to say he'll cover our venue hire. He'll pay for that pleasure-boat cruise we were looking at. The one that Mr Francis said was too expensive. Listen to this: 'To the student council – great achievements this past year. "Smooth sailing" (*Laughs.*) for the year ahead. Very best, Henry Worthington, QC.' Isn't that amazing?

Some of the people in the room look excited and begin to whoop and clap. Others just roll their eyes. **Oli** *and his friends look annoyed.*

Abigail   And I'm sure that with the savings we make, members of the school council can get free tickets.

Noel   I'll drink to that!

Jason   And everybody else that maybe can't afford it still has to pay, right? Jokers!

Abigail   Thank you, *humble observer*. Okay, everyone. Let's do this. (*Lets this settle in with everybody for a moment.*) Tammy, could you set the ground rules please?

Tammy (*sarcastic*)   Sure, Abigail. Thanks. (*To class.*) Okay, so after the speeches you'll all come up here and cast your votes into our ballot box. (*Taps box on the desk.*) After that, we'll – (*continues in mute as:*)

Chloe *pulls out her phone.*

Online Chloe *appears.*

Online Chloe   You are such a bitch!!! You had to go and make this the bloody 'Abigail show'!

Online Abigail *appears.*

Online Abigail   Daddy did this for you.

Online Chloe   I don't need help from you or him!

Online Abigail   Whatever. Just don't do or say anything stupid. Play it safe and this is all yours.

Online Chloe *and* **Online Abigail** *disappear.*

Tammy   – simple and fair. Okay?

Abigail   Good job, Tammy. Have a seat now. Chloe, Oli, up to the front please?

Chloe *and* **Oli** *walk up as the* **Other Students** *applaud.*

Abigail   Right, strict rules. One minute each, no more okay? Let's keep it clean.

Chloe *takes centre stage. She is all smiles.*

Chloe   First of all can I say a huge thanks to Abigail. I'm sure she's really tried to do her best for the past two years. But now it's time for a fresh start. I'm focused on creating a real school community. And the most important way to achieve this is to have more activities like our prom where we can really come together and bond. Knowing that we can count on each other and support each other as students. We don't need outside help – not from teachers, and not from those that think they're superior or know better than us. (*Lovely warm smile to her lovely sister.*) This is our time now. Let's make the changes we want to see as a community for our community.

Led by **Melissa**, *applause has already begun.*

Chloe   First and foremost, this is about us.

Applause continues although some students aren't clapping at all. **Chloe** *steps back, demure but triumphant.*

Online Melissa *appears.*

Online Melissa   And the award for best actress goes . . .

Online Chloe *appears.*

Online Chloe   Oh, you're too kind, darling!!!

Online Chloe *and* **Online Melissa** *disappear.*

Oli *steps forward and waits for the applause to die down.*

Oli   I truly believe in the power we have as a student council, and that's why I agree with Chloe. Change does need to happen. But it needs to be the right change in the right way. Yeah, the social side is important, but long-term action is better. We all want a great end of year bash, but what about afterwards? We need to get a better academic environment around here and more opportunities so that we can get to where we want to be in life. Universities and employers want to see achievements on our CVs, not Instagram posts from a boat. To do this we need to establish a better working relationship with our teachers. We need their input and there are some of them that really want to help. This isn't about me. It's not even about us in this room. It's about everybody and all of our futures. Thank you.

Moment's silence. then hearty and sustained applause.

Chloe *and* **Abigail** *look worried.*

Abigail *steps forward.*

Abigail   Thank you, both. Great speeches. Makes me wish I were able to stand for election again . . . (*Quick glance at* **Oli**.) and really give you some competition. Okay . . . Let's vote!

All the students apart from **Jason** *get up from their seat and line up in front of the desk.* **Abigail** *gives him a pointed look. He stands reluctantly.*

An impatient, athletic student bursts into the classroom – **Rachel**. *She is dressed in a football kit.*

Rachel   Hey, Abigail, Francis asked me to come and get you. He wants to speak to you right now.

Abigail   What are you talking about?

Rachel   Aren't you the school president or something?

Abigail   Yes.

Rachel   Then why you so dumb? Francis. His office. Now.

Abigail   Er, are you blind? I'm busy.

Rachel   And I'm supposed to be on the pitch. Not running around trying to find you.

Abigail   Well, now you found me you can go back and tell Francis –

Rachel (*interrupting*)   I'm not your minion. Listen, Abigail, this whole 'school president, alpha-bitch attitude' really doesn't do it for me. Just get to his office or not only him but my whole team are going to be on your case. *Again!*

She lunges menacingly towards **Abigail***, who flinches backwards.*

Abigail (*embarrassed*)   The lot of you are a bunch of cows.

Rachel (*laughs*)   That's right.

She turns to walk out the door. She spots **Rash**.

Rachel   Hey, Rash, you working on getting those lockers sorted?

Rash   Yeah, well, Oli said he'd look into it.

Rachel   Whatever. Same old.

She leaves. **Abigail** *gathers herself.*

Abigail   Guys, I'm gonna have to pop out for five minutes. Yet again, another case of teachers interfering with what we're trying to do. So the vote will have to wait until I get back.

The group grumbles.

Sol   That's long.

Lane   We're starving and it's chicken nuggets today.

Noel   My mum's outside. I gotta go dentist.

Abigail   No vote. No student president. No one to sort out the prom.

Noel (*on his way out of the room*)   Your dad said he was going to pay for it. What's to sort out?

Abigail   Tammy, do me a huge favour, please. Make a note of everybody that leaves the room whilst I'm not here. They're obviously giving up their free tickets to the prom.

Noel *sits back down in a hurry.*

Noel   Alright, alright, just hurry up then.

Tammy (*to* **Abigail**)   I can get everybody to fill out the cards at least.

Abigail   No, Tammy. As President, I'll take care of everything when I get back. But you can make sure there's no more campaigning or speeches. Okay?

Tammy *says nothing. Sulks.*

Abigail   Okay?

Tammy   Yes. Fine, *boss*.

Abigail   What?

Tammy   Nothing.

Abigail   Okay, everybody. Everybody. Just talk amongst yourselves. (*To* **Chloe** *and* **Oli**.) But no campaigning, Tammy's in charge.

Tammy   For once.

Abigail   I'm sure my hearing's going. Did you say something, Tammy?

Tammy   Nope.

Abigail *strides from the room.* **Tammy** *addresses the room.*

Tammy   Well, that's it, folks. We'll just wait for her to come back and take charge.

Sol   How long is she gonna be?

Tammy   Ask Abigail. I'm sure she'll be able to hear you.

She goes to sit by herself, frustrated. The rest of the class start their own conversations. **Jason** *sits by himself, but people constantly approach him – he's like a magnet.* **Melissa** *flits from student to student.*

Online Abigail *appears.*

Online Abigail   Watch out for Oli. Could actually give us a bit of trouble.

Online Chloe *appears.*

Online Chloe   Us? You mean me. You're old news. What's Francis want?

Online Abigail   Does it need to be anything? You know I hate his guts. And for some reason he's got it in for me.

Online Abigail *and* **Online Chloe** *disappear.*

Oli *approaches* **Chloe**. *They smile at each other although the smiles are not entirely genuine.* **Oli** *seems just a touch on edge.*

Oli   Great speech.

Chloe   Thanks. Yours was good as well I thought.

Oli   Well. You know.

Chloe   Seriously. It really made me think about things from a different perspective.

Oli   That's good. I mean it's useful for us to see things from another point of view.

Chloe   Uh-huh.

Oli   You really got across how much you care about people.

Chloe   That's important. And you too. We might be going in different directions but ultimately we want the same thing.

Oli   True.

Silence. They stare at each other. **Chloe** *is calm and confident.* **Oli** *is a bit embarrassed. He looks away.*

From opposite ends of the room **Jason** *and* **Melissa** *are watching them.*

Oli *looks up at* **Chloe.** *Plays it cocky.*

Oli   Anyway . . . whatever happens, I just want you to know it's nothing personal. (*Smug grin.*)

Chloe   Oh really? That's so sweet of you. And what I said to you the other day. That wasn't personal either.

Oli (*grin drops – defensive*)   Well . . . Uhh . . . That was just . . .

Chloe   It's fine, Oli. Let's move on. Forgotten, okay?

Oli   Sure. All right. Well umm . . . Good luck.

Chloe (*smiles the sweetest of smiles*)   You too.

Oli *moves in for a polite hug and peck on the cheek.* **Chloe** *steps back and holds out her hand to shake* **Oli** *'s.*

Chloe   Easy, tiger . . . don't want to give you the wrong idea. Again.

Oli *is ultra-embarrassed. He shakes* **Chloe** *'s hand awkwardly, then walks off.* **Jason** *is watching.*

Online Jason *appears.*

Online Jason   You wanna talk about me being two-faced. Look at you. 'She's so stuck up.' 'She's so arrogant.' Yeah, right.

Oli *pulls out his phone.*

Online Oli *appears. Pause.* **Online Oli** *disappears.*

Oli *puts his phone away and then puts as much distance as possible between himself and* **Jason**.

Chloe *walks up to* **Debs**.

Chloe   Oh, Debs – How's your mum at the moment? She's out of hospital now isn't she?

Debs   Yeah, well the –

Online Melissa *appears*

Online Melissa   What did Oli say?

Debs   – and with the medication –

Chloe (*has her phone out – interrupts*)   Sorry. One second.

Online Chloe *appears*

Online Chloe   Nothing.

Online Melissa   Looked like you two were getting veeeeeeery friendly . . .

Online Chloe   As if. He's an idiot. I'm going to walk this election.

Online Melissa   With Abigail helping you at every step.

Online Chloe   Puhleeeease.

Online Chloe *and* **Online Melissa** *disappear.*

Debs   What was that?

Chloe   Nothing.

Debs   Look, Chloe, I'm going to be honest with you okay. I'm not voting for you.

Chloe   What? Why?

Debs   I don't really want to go into it.

Chloe   It's fine, Debs. Honestly.

Debs   Well. Oli's sincere.

Chloe   And I'm not?

Debs   Did you actually listen to your speech? I did.

Chloe   And every single word was true.

Debs   There's a big difference between being honest and being sincere.

Chloe   Meaning?

Debs   C'mon, Chloe. I've known you for years.

Chloe   Exactly!

Debs   And you haven't changed. Even a minute ago, I'm trying to tell you about my mum and all you care about is your phone. There's always something more important and it's usually you.

Chloe   Okay, thanks, Deborah. Really good to know my friends are on my side. Especially since the last time I spoke with them they said they'd be voting for me.

Debs   That's just it then isn't it? You shouldn't be so sure about who you can trust. People don't always say what they mean. Right?

She walks off. **Chloe** *watches her go.* **Mark** *and* **Lane** *pass by.*

Mark (*to* **Chloe**)   Top speech.

Lane   Can't wait for that boat party. Your dad's a legend!

Mark   'Oli who', right?

They both laugh and continue on. **Chloe** *watches them, then can't believe it as they start talking and laughing with* **Oli**. *She becomes nervous. Pulls out her phone.*

Online Chloe *appears.*

Online Chloe   Hey, hun.

Online Jason *appears.*

Online Jason   Sup, babe?

Online Chloe   I know you said you weren't going to talk about it, but you are going to vote for me right?

Online Jason   If I did vote, it would have to be for your amazing opponent.

Online Chloe   So what we just did in the toilets meant nothing?

Online Jason   I've had better.

Online Chloe   Ohhhhh. So that's why you're voting for Oli, more your type.

Online Jason (*laughs*)   Idiot.

Online Chloe   You know you love me. Just vote for me as well.

Online Chloe *disappears.*

Sol *and* **Rash** *approach* **Jason**. **Jason** *quickly puts his phone away.*

Online Jason *disappears.*

Rash   Sorry, J, you got a minute.

Jason   Don't be stupid, man, of course. How you both doing? Ain't seen you in ages.

Rash   Studies, bro. Killing us.

Sol   Francis is a prick. No let-up. You think you're doing okay and then bam! Man slaps you with a D. I worked mad hard for that test.

Rash   He's a proper knob.

Sol   Yeah, man. Proper. You get me. (*This use of slang sounds entirely wrong.*)

Jason   I hear you. Your parents must be screwing as well with that D. I know those weekend tutors don't come cheap.

Sol *looks embarrassed as* **Jason** *and* **Rash** *burst into laughter.*

Sol   That was just that one time. It's not like I have them every week.

Jason   Chill, man. Just joking, innit.

Sol (*to* **Rash**)   Rah, one tutor session and man's on me fam'. Swear down.

Jason   Oh seen, they provide elocution lessons as well? (*Posh voice.*) By Jove I think he's got it!

Rash *laughs.*

Sol   Alright, J.

Jason   Sorry, man.

Sol   What did you think of the speeches anyway?

Jason   Sounded exactly the same. 'Vote for me.'

Rash *laughs again.*

Sol   Well, we're going for Oli obviously.

Jason   Why obviously?

Rash   Aren't you voting for him?

Sol   Yeah, we thought you were.

Jason   I'm asking why *you* are.

Sol   Well, we're tired of Chloe and her sister thinking they own the school.

Jason   Is that it?

Sol   No. Oli said he'd speak to the teachers about negotiating reduced elements of the curriculum. (*Checks himself.*) Get me.

Jason   Is that right? What does that mean anyway?

Sol   Well, you know, I suppose just making our lives a bit easier.

Jason   Really . . . Okay . . .

Rash   And he said he'd be looking at getting all the other stuff sorted, like the lockers, and the –

Jason (*interrupts*)   – yeah, Rash, we know.

Rash   Alright, alright. But still.

Sol   Aren't you going to vote for him though?

Jason   What difference does that make to you?

Sol   Nothing.

Jason   Exactly. You want to vote. Vote. Whatever I'm doing is just me.

Sol   But I bet you're bang on the prom now though. Free tickets . . . (*Trails off.*)

Jason   Meaning?

Sol   Nothing.

Pause. **Jason** *looks hard at* **Sol***.* **Sol** *looks awkward.*

Jason   Boys, I'm leaving you to it, yeah. Catch up in a bit.

Sol   Alright, bruv, (*Slang still sounds wrong.*)

Jason *shakes his head and walks off.*

Rash   You're such an idiot.

Sol   What?

Rash   You know what. Embarrassing him about the tickets. And all that. (*Imitates* **Sol***.*) 'You get me, bruv! Yeah, man, wicked!' What you trying to prove?

Sol *ignores him.*

Jason *approaches* **Oli** *who is talking to another student –* **Shay**.

Jason   You got a second?

Oli   I'm busy. Later, yeah.

Jason   Why you going there?

Cold stand-off.

Shay   Hey it's cool. You two talk.

Oli   You sure?

Shay   Course. Just remember about getting those toilet seats fixed in the Girls, yeah?

Oli   Done.

Shay *walks off to another group.*

Jason   Sounds like you're promising the world to everyone. You gonna be able to pay up?

Oli   Yeah, well, I'm a man of my word. Got ethics. Unlike some.

Jason   Grow up, bruv.

Oli   Get out my face!

Jason   You've got things so twisted it's a joke.

Oli   Me? Your friends rob me and you're still saying you didn't know what they were going to do.

Jason   First of all, yeah, they're not my friends. Just cos they live on my estate don't mean we're buddies, right. Second, if you're gonna come round on your 'ped, bigging yourself up and running your mouth off, what do you expect? If people see an opportunity they're gonna take it.

Oli   People like you.

Jason   Seen. Is that how you're going on? 'People like me' now? (*Cold. Dangerous.*) Yeah you're right. Us 'people', we're all the same.

Oli (*nervous*)   I didn't mean it like that.

Jason   For real? Break it down for me then, man.

Oli   I meant, you know, people that are just in it for themselves and don't care about the consequences for others. How much did all of you get for my moped? Enough to pay for boat-party tickets?

Jason   Have you actually stopped and listened to yourself? You're a smart guy so how come you end up adding two and two and coming up with foolishness?

Oli   You wanted to go to the prom though didn't you? Doing that, you could afford to go.

Jason   This stupid prom! Really? You think I'd set up my boy to get robbed for that? Neither of us are that dumb. (*Pause.*) Sol and Rash maybe.

Brief silence. Then **Oli** *quietly laughs. The tension eases.*

Jason   What's going on, man? I know this is about something else. You holding some grudge against me?

Oli (*too defensive*)   No! Something else like what?

Jason   You tell me. (*Eyes* **Oli** *suspiciously,*) What's been going on with you this past week? You gunning Chloe the other day for no reason and now getting all pally-pally with her. And then you blaming me for all this madness with your 'ped. What's gwarnin'?

Oli   Times change. Not like you've been around that much either. Anything you want to tell me?

Silence. The two guys stare at each other.

Jason   Just been busy planning how to rob my friends.

Oli (*smiles*)   Joker.

They smile at each for a second . . . and then the moment is gone. It becomes awkward again.

Jason   So uhh, listen, Sol the 'Original G' was telling me about how you're gonna convince Francis to ease up on timetables or something.

Oli (*evasive*)   Well, things are hectic at the moment. We need all the help we can get.

Jason   Yeah? (*Questioning look.*) How is your work going? Five A levels is a lot.

Oli   Tell me about it.

Jason   Did you get the grades you needed?

Oli   It's complicated.

Jason   Yeah?

Oli   Look, J, I got a lot to focus on right now. Need to get me some votes. I got yours though, yeah? (*Stares pointedly at* **Jason**.) No reason for you to vote for Chloe, right?

Jason   You gave a good speech. (*Smiles.*) You've got *some* principles.

Oli (*forces a smile*)   I uhh . . . I appreciate that, man.

Jason   Anyway, you go chat to your *people*. Later.

He walks off.

Online Melissa *appears.*

Online Melissa   We need to talk.

Online Chloe *appears.*

Online Chloe   Give me one minute.

Online Melissa   No. Right now.

Online Chloe *and* **Online Melissa** *disappear.*

Chloe *drags herself away from two students she is talking to and makes her way to* **Melissa** *who is waiting in a corner.*

Melissa   I'm not sure this election is going to be that easy. A lot of people seem to be going for Oli.

Chloe   Whatever. I'll always be more popular.

Melissa   Well, maybe that's it. Suppose this isn't a popularity contest, and people actually want someone who's going to stand up for them and make a difference.

Chloe   Well, what's Abigail done for the past year? If they voted for her then they'll definitely vote for me. I'll be a much better president.

Melissa   You know you don't need to constantly compare yourself to her. She's such a loser.

Chloe   Who's comparing?

Melissa   That's all you do.

Chloe   What do you mean?

Melissa (*sighs*)   Nothing, Chloe.

Chloe   No, go on. Say it.

Melissa   Well, it's just like you think you're in a competition with her or something.

Chloe   Which I'd win.

Melissa   You see? Just forget it.

Chloe   She's the one who tries to be like me.

Melissa   And maybe that's exactly why people want to vote for Oli. They don't want more of the same.

Chloe   Since when did you become a political analyst?

Melissa   Yeah, right. I'm just saying you'd be better off distancing yourself from your sister. She isn't doing you any favours.

Chloe   It's not like I'm asking for her help. And even if I was, people are happy to stick with more of the same, as long as the same works for them. If people aren't going to vote for me it must be something else.

Melissa   If I find out what, I'll let you know.

She walks off. **Chloe** *watches her thoughtfully then pulls out her phone.*

Online Chloe *appears.*

Online Chloe   You told anyone about us?

Online Jason *appears.*

Online Jason   No. Why?

Online Chloe   Nothing. Doesn't matter.

Online Jason   You're really worried about this election, innit?

Online Chloe   Well, apparently people aren't voting for me.

Online Jason   Hold up. Is that why you're asking if I told people about us seeing each other? You worried about what people might think?

Pause.

Is it?

Online Chloe   It's not even like that.

Online Jason   Doesn't need to be. Doesn't matter if it is.

Online Chloe   We both said we wanted to keep this a secret.

Online Jason *disappears.*

Online Chloe   Jason?

Online Chloe *disappears.*

Chloe *looks over at* **Jason**. *He purposefully walks over to the girls* **Chloe** *was previously chatting with. They appear intimate.*

Chloe *looks upset.*

She takes her phone out.

Online Chloe *appears.*

Online Chloe   Abby, where are you? I really want to talk. (*Pause.*) Please, Abby.

Silence stretches uncomfortably.

(*Angry.*) Fine!

Online Chloe *disappears.*

Chloe *gathers herself together and walks over to* **Tammy**.

Chloe   Hey, Tam Tam.

Tammy   You know I hate being called that.

Chloe   Yeah, I know.

Tammy   So why do it?

Chloe   How's things going? Abi still being a cow?

Tammy   You'd know better than me. Seeing as how you're both so similar.

Chloe (*loses her cool*)   Really, Tammy? I'm just saying hello.

Pause.

Tammy   Okay, sorry. I guess –

Chloe   I know what she's like. And I'm not her. Alright!

Tammy   Geez, okay, I said sorry.

Chloe (*calms down*)   Have you heard from her?

Tammy   No.

Chloe People are getting a bit restless. This is their lunchtime they're giving up . . .

Tammy Not much we can do.

Chloe So we just have to sit here and wait?

Tammy *Rules is rules.*

Chloe I mean, can't I even stand up and say a few words or something?

Tammy Nope. Looks like you've been keeping yourself busy anyway.

Chloe I'm not the one going around campaigning still. You should have a word with Oli.

Tammy He already had words with me. (*Smirks.*) Very interesting. (*Walks off.*) Good luck with the votes.

Online Abigail *appears.*

Online Abigail Just got your message. Everything okay?

Online Chloe *appears.*

Online Chloe This whole election. Starting to wonder if it's all worth it.

Online Abigail All of what?

Online Chloe The whole act. 'Hey, everybody, it's Miss Perfect. Vote for me and all your dreams will come true.'

Online Abigail Have you gone crazy?

Online Chloe What's taking you so long?

Online Abigail You would not believe.

Online Chloe Try me.

Online Abigail I already booked the boat using the student council account, and now Francis is talking about misappropriation of school funds. Fraud.

Online Chloe Are you serious?

Online Abigail He is.

Online Chloe Why didn't you ask Francis first?

Online Abigail Because I knew Daddy would just pay it back later.

Online Chloe So what are you going to do? Do you need me?

Online Abigail   It'll be fine. Gotta go.

Online Abigail *and* **Online *Chloe*** *disappear.*

Chloe *looks over at* **Jason**. *He is still talking with the two girls.* **Chloe** *walks over.*

Chloe   You don't mind if I interrupt?

Jason   Course not, let's make this a party.

Chloe   Actually, can we talk in private?

Jason (*acts shocked*)   Wow! (*To girls.*) You hear that. Our soon-to-be President actually wants to talk to me – alone. I must have done something right today.

Chloe (*pleads*)   Jason.

Pause.

Jason   Okay, okay.

He walks off with **Chloe**.

Chloe   You were the one who said you wanted to keep things a secret.

Jason   No. *You* said you didn't want anybody to know if it wasn't going to be serious.

Chloe   So what was all that about your 'boys finding out' and then cussing if they knew we were together?

Jason   That's just boys, innit. At least I'm not the one trying to hide it from their dad.

Chloe   That's just because he wants me to focus on my studies.

Jason   Oh for real? Is that why you're always cussing him and messing around in class? Because you care so much about what he wants you to do? Just be honest, you're not worried about your dad finding out you're going out with someone, just someone like me.

Chloe   Don't be stupid.

Jason   So I'm stupid now as well?

Chloe   You're acting like it. I didn't even want to have this discussion right now.

Beat. **Jason** *sees real concern in* **Chloe**. *He softens.*

Jason   This election is really getting to you isn't it?

Chloe   No it's just . . .

Jason   What?

Chloe   Well, I thought you might have some ideas or something.

Jason   Ideas?

Chloe   A lot of people look up to you, you know. Like Sol and Rash . . .

Jason   And you want me to get them to vote for you?

Chloe   Only if they want to.

Jason   Sure, babe. I'll do that for you. (*Pause.*) I mean, I'm not going to vote for you myself, but I'll see what they say.

Chloe   What do you mean you're not voting for me?

Jason   We need somebody who's actually going to do some good around here. Especially for the people that need help most, not just those that are interested in partying.

Chloe   Is that what you really think of me?

Jason   Honestly? When it comes to you I don't know what to think.

Chloe   So you and me meant nothing then?

Jason   It's really funny how you bring out the 'you and me' when it suits you. Let me tell you something. I never wanted to keep us a secret. I would have told the whole world about us.

Chloe   Yeah, right. What about your boys then?

Jason   D'you really believe I care what they think? I was making an excuse so I didn't look like some loved-up fool to you. (*Bitter laugh.*) And look at how that's turned out.

Melissa *walks up to them.*

Melissa   Hey, you two. (*Teasing.*) Now tell the truth. *What* is going on?

Jason   Your friend almost had me convinced she was the one. Proper had me fooled. Later.

He walks off. **Chloe** *watches him go and tries to conceal her upset.*

Melissa   So he's voting for Oli then?

Chloe (*watching* **Jason**)   Something like that.

Melissa   Anyway, another update. I just spoke to Mark and Lane and they were really cagey about who they were going to vote for.

Chloe   You're kidding. A minute ago they were telling me how excited they were about the boat!

Melissa   Well, that's what I thought you said. But then I got thinking, they don't actually need to vote for you to go to the prom do they? Your sister's already got it all sorted. No way she'd back out now.

Chloe *thinks.*

Chloe   Give me a minute, okay?

Melissa   Where you going?

Chloe *walks off to a quiet corner.* **Melissa** *watches her like a hawk.*

Online Oli *appears.*

Online Oli   Everything cool?

Online Melissa *appears.*

Online Melissa   She thinks everyone hates her. Gonna implode soon!

Online Oli   Crash and burn. Good work.

Online Oli *and* **Online Melissa** *disappear.*

Online Chloe *appears.*

Online Chloe   Hey, Tam Tam, I want to run something past you.

Online Tammy *appears.*

Online Tammy   Why you messaging me? I'm right here.

In the classroom **Tammy** *waves over at* **Chloe** *who looks up from her phone, ignores her and continues typing.*

Online Chloe   Better to talk on here.

Online Tammy   What d'you want?

Online Chloe   I think we should get things moving again. I'll say a few words.

Online Tammy   Hello? Campaigning's over.

Online Chloe   It's not campaigning.

Online Tammy   I don't think people would be too impressed with you trying to go behind Oli's back.

Online Chloe   And I don't think people would be too impressed if I told them a little something about you.

Pause.

Tammy   Something like what?

Chloe   Something that you shouldn't have told Abigail because she came and told me straight away.

Online Tammy   You bitch!

Online Tammy and **Online Chloe** *disappear.*

Chloe *looks over at* **Tammy** *who shakes her head in disgust.* **Chloe** *looks upset.* **Lane** *walks past her.*

Lane   Hey, you okay?

Chloe   I don't feel that great actually.

Lane   What is it?

Chloe   Nothing. It's my own fault.

Lane   D'you want some water or something? I've got some mints in my rucksack.

Chloe   Nah, I'll be okay. Thanks though.

Lane   That's what friends do. Look out for each other, right?

Tammy *reluctantly walks to the front of the classroom.*

Tammy   People. One second please.

Sol   When's Abigail back? This is some long ting! (*Gives* **Jason** *a knowing nod.*) Man like me got places to be, dred! (*Slang sounds embarrassing.*)

Jason   Oh yeah, you don't wanna be late for Roadman Club.

Everybody laughs. **Sol** *shrinks.*

Tammy   As Vice-President and currently in charge, can I ask Chloe to give everybody an update?

All heads swivel round to **Chloe**.

Chloe   Are you sure, Tammy?

Tammy   Oh yes, Miss Worthington. Absolutely, positively.

Chloe   Well I did get a text from Abigail, so it makes sense for me to fill you all in.

She walks to the front of the class.

Oli *takes out his phone.*

Online Oli *appears.*

Online Oli   What's going on?

Online Melissa *appears.*

Online Melissa   You're asking me? Do you think she knows?

Online Oli   Not unless you told her.

Online Melissa   Don't be stupid.

Online Oli *and* **Online *Melissa*** *disappear.*

Chloe *faces everyone with a charming smile.*

Chloe   Hey, everyone, I know we've been waiting for ages so I wanted to apologise on behalf of Abigail. She's actually been called in to see the Head. There's a problem with booking the boat . . .

The class groan and jeer.

Lane   That's so lame. Why?

Mark   Both of you are jokers.

Noel   You've made us sit in here all this time for nothing.

Chloe   Hold on. Hold on. The reason it *might* not go ahead is because of what Abigail did. I can make sure that it *definitely* happens.

Mark   How?

Melissa *turns from the group, who are all focused on* **Chloe.**

Online Melissa *appears.*

Online Melissa   You might wanna be here to see this. Chloe's saying the boat might not happen coz of you. People getting angry . . .

Online Melissa *disappears.*

Oli   Sorry, but I'm going to jump in here. I thought we weren't allowed to give any more campaign speeches.

Chloe   We're not.

Oli   So what were you just doing then?

Chloe   I'm updating everyone on the current state of affairs.

Oli   Sounded to me like you were making a last-minute effort to get votes. (*To* **Tammy**.) Are you seriously going to allow this, Tammy?

Tammy   Technically, it wasn't a speech.

Sol   Same old Chloe and Abigail. Rigging the system. Paigon business!

Chloe   I'm not rigging anything.

Oli   Tammy, if she's got the chance to give another speech I want one too.

Tammy   Oli, I'm really sorry about this. But rules are rules.

Jason (*loudly*)   This is bullshit!

Everyone turns to look at **Jason** *who is at the back of the room.*

Jason   I was gonna keep my mouth shut but I just gotta say it. Chloe might not have rigged the system, but she's playing it. Yep, yet again, same old people getting the same opportunities, whilst the rest of us don't have a chance. They already have a head start and then they still get help along the way. So where's that leave the rest of us that aren't related to the student president, or whose daddy can't put a little sweetener on the table? All this crap about equal opportunities. Everything's unequal from the start!

Oli   You hear that, Tammy? Jason's backing me.

Jason   I ain't backing anyone. I'm just sick of seeing certain people always getting what they want when they already have it all.

Chloe   Don't hold back, Jason. Anything else you want to add?

Jason   You know me, babe, full of *ideas*. Where d'you want me to start?

Oli   Am I going to get the chance to speak, Tammy?

Rash   Yeah, Tammy, if Chloe got the chance to campaign again so should Oli.

Debs   It's only fair, Tammy.

Tammy *looks around the room at everybody, under pressure. A steely determination washes over her.*

Tammy   Jason's right. The same people keep doing the same thing, and the only people it's helping is themselves. (*Turns to* **Oli**.) You get the floor, but we do it properly. Have a proper debate and get the truth out there. (*Turns to* **Chloe**.) That's only fair, right? Give everybody one last chance to really find out the kind of person they're voting for.

Chloe (*sweet smile*)   Fine by me.

Noel   More bloody speeches.

Online Melissa *appears.*

Online Melissa   Don't trust Tammy. She's up to something.

Online Chloe *appears.*

Online Chloe   Don't worry about it.

Online Chloe *disappears.*

Online Melissa   I think Chloe planned this all along.

Online Oli *appears.*

Online Oli   How?

Online Melissa   Don't know. What shall we do?

Online Oli   I'll work something out. She's done. Trust me.

Online Melissa   And you did mean what you said to me last night, didn't you?

Online Oli   Talk later. She's watching us.

Online Melissa *and* **Online Oli** *disappear.*

Melissa *nervously looks over at* **Chloe** *but she and* **Lane** *are talking.* **Melissa** *looks at* **Oli**, *puzzled. But he avoids her gaze.*

Tammy *finally takes charge.*

Tammy   Okay, guys, let's get all these desks and chairs moved.

The students begin to shift furniture around.

Online Abigail *appears.*

Online Abigail   What have you done?!!!!!

Online Chloe *appears.*

Online Chloe   Hey, sis, how's it going?

Online Abigail   You stupid cow. I told you not to do anything crazy.

Online Chloe   What?

Online Abigail   Lying about me and the boat.

Online Chloe   I needed the votes.

Online Abigail   So just ruin my reputation in the process? Wait till I tell Daddy.

Online Chloe   Tell him what you want. Sometimes you have to make a stand.

Online Abigail   You sound like that idiot Jason.

Online Chloe   He's not an idiot.

Online Abigail   He shouldn't even be on the council. Guys like him. No class.

Online Chloe   No class, or wrong class?

Online Abigail   Same difference.

Online Chloe (*offended*)   Sometimes I can't believe we're actually related.

Online Abigail   Tell me about it.

Online Chloe   Jason's a decent guy. More intelligent than you'll ever be.

Online Abigail   Intelligence doesn't get you anywhere. Knowing the right people does. Anyway, I haven't got time for a heart to heart right now. I'll be back soon.

Online Chloe   Fine. By that time I would have been a cow to everybody, lied to my friends and forced people to do things they don't want to do. I can really see why you loved being President.

Online Abigail   I know. It's great. Oh and whilst we're on the subject of lying to your friends, tell Mel thanks for keeping me in the loop about what you did.

Chloe *shoots a look at* **Melissa**.

Online Abigail *disappears.*

Silence stretches.

Online Chloe *disappears.*

The students have moved the desks and chairs into two rows facing each other. The tutor's desk is at the head of the rows. The room now resembles the House of Commons.

Oli *positions himself on one row with his key followers beside him –* **Sol**, **Rash**, **Debs** *and a couple of others.*

Chloe *sits on a chair on the opposite row along with her supporters –* **Melissa**, **Mark**, **Lane** *and a few others.*

The overall numbers on each side are very even.

Jason *stands by himself away from it all.*

Tammy *stands at the tutor's desk. She is on the phone having a conversation with somebody.*

Melissa (*to* **Chloe**)   Exciting.

Chloe (*cold*)   Is it?

Melissa   You got a plan?

Chloe   Not really. I'm just thinking it's about time we were all honest with each other. Right?

Melissa *laughs nervously.*

Oli   Hey, Tammy, you ready?

Tammy *gets off the phone, stares at* **Chloe** *and shakes her head in disbelief.*

Oli   Tammy.

Tammy   Okay, yeah. Alright everyone, listen up. Oli will go –

Chloe   Wait a minute.

Tammy   What now?

Chloe   I think somebody else should moderate.

Tammy   I'm Vice-President.

Chloe   We need somebody neutral.

Tammy   Are you trying to say I'm not?

Chloe *and* **Tammy** *stare at each other.*

Tammy   Okay, fair enough.

Rash   I'd say the best person is Jason. He's always straight up.

Tammy   That's true.

Jason   You're better off getting someone else.

Rash   There isn't anybody.

Oli   Just leave him. Get somebody who actually cares.

This annoys **Jason**. *He looks long and hard at* **Oli**.

Jason   You know what? Count me in. It's time something different got done. (*To* **Oli**.) You cool with that?

Oli   Fine by me.

Tammy   What about you, Chloe?

Chloe   I'm all right with it.

Oli   Cool. We can get everything out in the open.

Online Chloe *appears.*

Online Chloe   I'm glad you agreed to help. You've got a lot to offer.

Online Jason *appears.*

Online Jason   If you're trying to get me on your side, I'm telling you now, it's not gonna happen.

Online Chloe   Oh forget it, Jason.

Online Jason *and* **Online Chloe** *disappear.*

Jason *walks to the front of the class.*

Jason   Before we start, can I make a suggestion?

Tammy   Go for it.

Jason   How do people feel if we lock the phones off? No texting or messaging. As Oli says, get everything out in the open.

Worried murmurs from the class.

Lane   I don't know, Jason . . .

Sol   Yeah, what if somebody wants to link, mans?

Jason   Mummy will know where to find you, Sol, don't worry.

Everybody laughs.

Seriously though, if there's anything anybody wants to say about this election, you should be able to say it in front of everyone, not hide behind some screen. What do you think, Chloe?

Chloe   Hundred per cent agree. Right, Mel?

Melissa (*awkward*)   Sure.

Jason   Oli?

Oli   Works for me.

Jason   Let's do it then.

The whole class take out their phones and collectively switch them off. Online personas collapse on their platforms. It is a momentous occasion.

Everybody is quiet for a second.

Jason   Okay. This is it now. Oli, what do you want to say?

Oli *stands.*

Oli   I don't think I'm alone when I say I've had enough of Chloe and Abigail. The pretentious, arrogant, walk-on-water act does my head in. All this talk about caring about others – as if! We all know they're just in it for themselves. Chloe doesn't care about you, doesn't care about me (*Slight pause.*), doesn't care about the school. And why should she. It's not important to her if she gets good grades or not. She already has her future sorted, all paid up, whatever she wants to do. Not like the rest of us. If we don't get our grades we're stuffed. But why should she worry. She's just a spoilt brat, who always gets her own way and throws a tantrum when she doesn't. It's about time somebody else came out on top.

He sits down. **Sol** *and some of the other guys next to* **Oli** *begin to cheer.* **Rash**, **Debs** *and the girls on* **Oli***'s side are taken aback.*

Lane, **Mark** *and the other people on* **Chloe***'s side begin to shout angrily.*

Lane   Idiots!

Mark   Shut up!

Sol   You shut up. You know Oli's right. Wasteman!

Mark   Your mum.

Sol   D'you want a slap, rudeboy?

The exchange of cusses and jeers hots up.

Jason   Okay, everyone, 'low it. Relax!

The cussing continues.

Jason (*shouts*)   Everyone, just chill!

The noise quietens down.

C'mon, man, what are you lot? We're supposed to be responsible people, not screaming and shouting up the place like little kids. What kind of example you setting? Fix up!

People look embarrassed.

But, Oli, I gotta tell you, man, it's interesting.

Oli   What?

Jason   I know we want the truth, but the truth about your mandate, not how you feel about Chloe.

Oli   People need to know the facts for them to decide who to vote for.

Jason   So your plan to get people to vote for you isn't to talk about the good stuff you're going to do, it's just to cuss your opponent?

Chloe   I'm glad somebody else noticed that.

Oli   I'm just saying how it is.

Chloe   No, you're saying what you think. And correct me if I'm wrong but you think I'm a spoilt brat and you're bitter that I've got plans for the future. Yeah, that would get my vote.

Oli   It would if you thought that everybody having the same opportunities as you was important.

Chloe   Oh give me a break *please*! You all complain about not having opportunities, and then when I'm offering them you're still moaning.

Oli   Some cheesy school disco with a crusty DJ and free 7 Up isn't exactly the same kind of opportunity as a guaranteed job in Daddy's law firm.

Jason   Alright, Oli, you made your point about Chloe. We get it. But let's get back to business. Why should any of us vote for you?

Oli   Well, like I've said a million times, I'm focused on us getting real power, making a real difference.

Jason   And you plan to do that how?

Oli   We need better relationships with the teachers. More dialogue and understanding would be good for everybody.

Jason   Any teachers in particular?

Oli   No. Not really. Mr Francis said he'd be interested in supporting us.

Jason   Francis?

Oli   Yeah.

Jason   Your science teacher? Who everyone thinks is a dick?

Oli   He's not a bad teacher. He just has high expectations.

Jason   I know I asked you before, but how are your grades going?

Oli (*pause*)   What's that got to do with anything?

Jason   I just wanna find out what's going on that's all.

Oli   So what you trying to say? That I'm trying to improve my grades by getting on Mr Francis's good side?

Jason   Are you?

Oli   No. But yeah if I was, what's wrong with students establishing a good working relationship with their teachers to ensure they reach their full potential?

Jason   That sounds like something Francis would say. Is it?

Oli   Can we move on? I thought you said this wasn't supposed to be some personal thing? That we should both be focusing on our presidential mandates?

Jason   Yeah, you're right. I'd love to talk about yours but I don't know if we've got time. From what I hear you've promised everything to everyone. Reduced study periods, new toilet seats in the Girls, even Rash is finally going to get his five-star, fur-lined lockers.

Everybody laughs.

So, yeah, you gave a good speech. Had me and a few of us thinking this is a guy who's got everybody's best interests at heart. But that's the thing. We need to unpick all these promises you've made. How you gonna do all this?

Oli   Well, Mr Francis has said he's happy to look at what he can do to help us.

Jason   For real? Francis has never come across as the type to want to help anybody apart from himself. What's he want in return?

Oli   Nothing.

Jason   Nothing?

Oli   Yeah. He's just happy to be able to advise us on the areas we should be focusing on as a student council.

Murmurs of discontent from the class.

Jason   And what does that mean?

Oli   Well, I'm not sure yet. He hasn't discussed that with me.

Jason   So let me get this straight. You want to come in here and just be some puppet for one of the worst teachers there is, so he can start controlling us from a distance?

Murmurs of discontent grow louder.

Oli   No. Not at all. He's really happy to come and sit in our meetings as well.

Sol   You muppet!

Debs   No way. We are not having that!

Oli   So how do you lot think we're going to get anything? You really think we've got any power ourselves? We need the support of the people that are really in charge. They help us, we help them, everybody's happy.

Chloe   And you get your grades.

Oli   Not everyone can afford to buy them like you.

Jason   So just sell everybody out. That's a good look.

Oli   At least what I'm doing will benefit the whole school, not just a select few.

Chloe   Oh listen to yourself, Oli. You're the one that just said we can't get anything done without the teachers. So what makes you think they'll let us do anything that they don't want us to. What I'm doing means we might not change the world, but at least we can get something for ourselves and do it on our own terms.

Oli   But if there's at least a chance we can change things shouldn't we take it?

Chloe   What kind of change? Change that the teachers want?

Oli   No. Not necessarily.

Chloe   Helloooooo. It is NOT. GOING. TO. HAPPEN. The system is what it is. I'd rather get a few things for some of us than nothing for everybody.

Oli   Well, I'd rather try and fail than do nothing.

Chloe   Is this a new tactic of yours? Make a stupid point just to disagree with everything I'm saying even though you know I'm right.

Rash   I'm not saying Chloe's right, yeah, but, Oli, we definitely don't want teachers coming in here and telling us what we should do. Especially Francis.

Debs   That's not what we signed up for.

Rash   Yeah. I'm not having Francis ordering me around everywhere. Even if that means we don't get our lockers.

Everyone looks at **Rash** *in surprise.*

Sol   Big tings!

Oli (*panicked*)   Okay, okay, look. I'll uhh . . . focus more on student power. Yeah, let's keep the teachers out of this. This is our council; *we* need to be in charge.

Chloe   That was quick. What happened to more dialogue and understanding with teachers?

Jason   Grow some balls, man. How can you change your entire position just like that? You interested in becoming President because you really believe in something, or you doing it for some power trip?

Chloe   We all heard what he said before. He's only doing this to get good grades for himself. Wouldn't surprise me if he says one thing now to get everybody's votes and then flips as soon as he gets into power.

Oli *smiles smugly as if this is the moment he has been waiting for.*

Oli   Oh, I see what's going on now. It had to happen eventually, didn't it? Is this actually supposed to be a debate, or is this all part of your and Jason's masterplan to do me over.

Jason   What you on about?

Oli   C'mon, man. The same way you set me up to get robbed, the same way you're setting me up now. You and Chloe working together to take me down and guarantee she gets voted student president.

Chloe   Are you crazy?

Oli   Are you gonna deny it?

Jason   Course.

Oli   So you're gonna deny that you and Chloe are going out as well?

Ripple of surprise amongst the class.

Jason   We're not going out.

Chloe   Where'd you get that idea?

Oli   Oh, so it's just casual booty calls? Get some wherever you can – in the toilets, at the back of Chicken Express, wherever's clever.

Mocking laughter from students.

Chloe (*to* **Jason**)   You just couldn't keep your mouth shut could you?

Jason (*to* **Chloe**)   I didn't say a word I swear! (*To* **Oli**, *cold and angry.*) You know what, bruv. This is you and me now, yeah.

Oli   So you gonna do me suttin' now, bredren?

Jason   'Low the slang, bruv. You ain't from the ends, yeah.

Students laugh. Apart from **Sol**.

Oli   I'm just telling the truth. Everybody needs to know this whole thing was a set-up between you and Chloe. The star-crossed lovers.

Chloe   Okay, Oli, you want to tell the truth? I reckon you're just jealous because I blanked you when you asked me out last week.

Another ripple of surprise amongst the students and mocking laughter.

Melissa (*complete shock*)   What? Oli, is that true?

Chloe   What did you say, Oli? That we were made for each other? Something lame like that.

Jason   So that's why you're screwing with me. You're just vex because you think me and Chloe are going out, not because you think I set you up to get robbed.

Chloe   And that's why you're trying to embarrass me in front of everybody.

Rash   Is this true, mate?

Oli (*to* **Chloe**)   Who embarrassed who? Blatantly leading me on when you're going out with my friend.

Chloe   I never led you on. Get real. If a girl can't smile at you without you thinking she's in love with you then you're in trouble.

Jason   And we are not going out, man. You let some girl come between us and for what? Chloe doesn't even care about me anyway and you're getting all jealous.

Oli   Well, she's yours now. You can keep her.

Chloe   Oh, he can keep me now can he? Screw both of you. I'm not some trophy that you can trade between you. (*Stands.*) You know what,

I've had it! I'm sick of being used like some pawn in other people's games so they can get what they want. I'm not 'some girl', I'm my own person and I'll do what I want and live my life on my own terms. Not to please my dad, or Abigail or even you two idiots. Whatever I decide to do will because I'm doing it for myself, not other people.

Everybody looks at **Chloe** *with newfound respect. Her supporters begin to clap and cheer.*

Lane   And that's why she's getting my vote.

Tammy   What a load of bollocks!

Everybody looks at **Tammy** *in shock.*

Tammy   Don't let her fool you and don't buy into all of this 'poor little, persecuted me' crap. Chloe, do you want to tell everyone how you blackmailed me so you could get the chance to campaign again. Or how you stabbed your own sister in the back to get more votes.

Lane   Oh my days!

Sol   Deep.

Tammy   Don't even think about denying it. I've got all the texts you sent me and I spoke with Abigail on the phone earlier and she says that the boat trip was always going to go ahead.

Chloe *looks around at everybody and takes a deep breath.*

Chloe   I'm not going to deny it.

Pause. A moment of real sincerity. She swallows.

I did lie. And I've been a right cow to people. Maybe I wanted this too much, but there's nothing I can say as an excuse.

Tammy   And you've just realised that have you?

Chloe (*looks at* **Jason** *and* **Debs**)   I've realised how crap it is when people take you for granted. I'm sorry. I'm really sorry.

Tammy   So you still expect people to vote for you?

The room is silent.

Melissa (*to* **Chloe**)   Didn't I tell you not to trust her? She is such a loser.

Chloe (*tired*)   Mel, please just shut up. Loser this, loser that. You're the loser. I know you told Abigail what was going on. What kind of friend are you?

They stare each other out . . . **Melissa** *backs down.*

Melissa (*quiet*)   I was just trying to help that's all.

Chloe   No. You're just two-faced.

Melissa   *Me* two-faced?

Chloe   Whatever. I'm fed up of it and I'm fed up of you.

Melissa   I'm glad I told Oli what was going on between you and Jason. You're the one who's two-faced. Lying to everybody, even yourself. And now everybody knows.

Lane   Whoa!

Chloe   How did you find out?

Jason   Is that who told you, Oli?

Oli   I don't want to get involved.

Jason   You are involved. Fool!

Chloe   So Melissa's been helping you out behind my back.

Oli   No.

Mark   You know what though. Chloe, I didn't want to say anything but Mel has been kinda badmouthing you a little bit. I mean it wasn't like, serious at the time but now . . .

Debs   Yeah, and she told me how you were saying how I should just get over my mum being ill and stuff. Sorry, I should have said something as well. Actually I'm not sorry, but you should know what your so-called friends are saying about you.

Chloe   So why were you doing this then, Mel? To help Oli get votes?

Oli   Hey, I didn't really know about any of this, okay?

Melissa   Really, Oli?

Oli (*to the class*)   Mel isn't doing anything for me.

Melissa   Wow! You've changed your tune since staying at mine last night.

'Oohs' from the class.

Yeah. I'm not ashamed to say it. I own it. I was really into you, Oli, but I guess you were just using me to get at Chloe. You know what? You're a slut.

Noel (*to* **Oli**)   That is kinda desperate, man.

Chloe (*to* **Oli**)   Not nice is it? To be embarrassed in front of everybody.

Oli   So out of everybody I'm the bad guy?

Melissa   No, you and Chloe are both liars.

Lane   Is this what happens when we switch off our phones? We should do it more often.

Rash   This is some kind of joke.

Tammy (*to* **Chloe** *and* **Oli**)   Are you two serious?

Everybody is getting angry. **Chloe** *and* **Oli** *stand isloated.*

Jason   I'm listening to everything and you know what, you two are messed up. You've just used us as stepping stones to achieve your own personal agendas. Yeah – we're just the suckers that get caught up in the middle of your crap. Look at me. I'm there thinking I'm a friend, a boyfriend, and all I am is just some punk that the both of you are using to get what you want. (*Pause. Looks at everybody.*) But in saying that, we're the ones to blame because we actually let it happen. We just watch whilst they blatantly lie and sacrifice any decency or principles they might have. And all that so they can stand up and say they're doing us a favour, whilst the only people benefiting are them and the people pulling their strings.

Chloe *and* **Oli** *stand alone.*

Jason (*to* **Oli** *and* **Chloe**)   The thing is, I'm not standing here right now asking for your understanding because you'll never get me. I'm not asking for your friendship or your charity. All I want, all any of us want, is your respect. Just act and treat us with a bit of decency, some honour, a bit of class you know. (*Stares at* **Chloe** *and* **Oli** *and then laughs to himself. At himself. He looks round at everybody.*) But this is the system and this is how it works. We all know that we can scream and shout but nothing's going to change. Right? So just get on with it. Vote for your next president and then you can all sail off on a boat party into the sunset. That's all you lot really care about, right? (*Picks up one of the voting cards. Looks at it.*) But you can count me out. (*Puts card down.*)

The **Other Students** *pick up their voting cards.*

Suddenly, **Abigail** *bursts into the classroom, sees everybody holding their cards.*

Abigail   Just in time. It's okay everybody, everything's sorted out. (*Looks around the room.*) Well, looks like you have been having fun. Anyway, I know what you've been told but it's all back on the track. The boat's secured, there's no need to worry. So let's get things back to normal. Let's vote. Is everybody ready?

Silence. People look at each other.

Rash   I don't know about all of you, but if we are going to vote, I'm definitely not voting for Oli. (*To* **Oli**.) Sorry, mate, Chloe isn't my favourite person in the world, but what you did was messed-up. At least with Chloe we know what we're going to get.

Oli   Yeah, a nice little disco.

Rash   No. Francis not taking over and telling us what to do in here as well.

Debs   What happened to you, Oli? You used to be the nicest guy.

Rash   Yeah, man, you lost it.

Oli (*to class*)   I was doing this for all of us.

Chloe   No you weren't. You can't even fool yourself into thinking you were doing it for yourself. (*Looks at* **Abigail**.) You were doing this for somebody else, and that's the worst place to be. Trust me.

Oli (*to class*)   So this is it, then. You're just gonna let Chloe and Abigail come out on top like they always do.

Sol   You done messed up, bredren.

Tammy   Sol's right, Oli. For once.

Oli   Fine, do what you want. (*Walks to door.*) Like Mr Francis said, I'm better than all of you put together. I don't need this.

Jason   You need to drop some of those A levels. The pressure's getting to you.

Oli   Yeah, yeah, yeah.

He leaves. Slams the door behind him.

The class watch him go in shock.

Rash   What a dick move.

Tammy (*to* **Chloe** *and* **Abigail**)   So that's it. You've won.

Abigail   No, no, no. We still have to vote. You just don't quite get it do you, Tammy? (*To class.*) People! Voting cards.

Chloe *walks to the desk and looks at the class. Everybody looks fed up.* **Jason** *doesn't look at her at all.*

Chloe *holds her voting card up. Rips it in half. Then drops it to the floor.*

Abigail (*frantic*)   What are you doing?

Chloe (*to class*)   Jason's right. You shouldn't vote for either of us. Oli because he wanted to be president for the wrong reason. And me because I don't want to be president at all.

The class look at each other in shock.

Abigail   She's just messing around. (*To* **Chloe**.) Right?

Chloe   No. (*To the class.*) We're all told what to do, what to think. Whether it's our parents, our sisters, what we see online. It's crazy. We need to start thinking for ourselves. This is our time now and if we want to do it, we can make a difference. (*Takes a moment then turns to face* **Jason** *directly.*) Jason, you're right about the system. It doesn't work, but let's change it. I might not know how exactly, but whatever we do, I want to do it together.

The **Other Students** *turn to* **Jason**.

Chloe   Jason?

Jason *stands up, holding his voting card. He stares at* **Chloe**, *smiles, then rips his voting card in half as well.*

Jason   Let's do it.

Moments pass. Then apart from **Abigail**, *every other student also stands and rips their card.*

Abigail   You've all gone mad. Taking away the system is how everything ends!

Jason   Exactly. And it's how everything else begins.

The End.

Class

BY BEN BAILEY SMITH AND LAJAUNE LINCOLN

*Notes on rehearsal and staging, drawn from a workshop with
the writers, held at the National Theatre, October 2018*

How Ben and Lajaune came to write the play

'We wanted to think of something that would connect to young people, but
also connect to adults. We wanted to engage people who typically wouldn't
be interested in or involved with theatre. We wanted to write something
realistic that would connect with young people, that would entertain but
also educate without being preachy. We went through a range of ideas and
something that was very present to us at the time was Trump in the United
States and Jeremy Corbyn over here; people who wouldn't normally be
interested in politics were paying attention to it but not understanding the
ins and outs. So we thought it would be interesting to play around with
that, but to make it portray politics in a way that young people would
understand without patronising them. We also wanted to look at social
media and the impact of that. Not only on individuals themselves but also
on politics. It is only in the last few years that we've really seen what
impact it has in shaping what people think they know. So again we wanted
to create something entertaining, that would educate, that was relevant and
that connected to young people on a variety of levels. Something very
important to us was to try to reflect where we were coming from in terms
of our own personal backgrounds, and to make sure that the play offered
opportunities to those who mightn't have them and to talk about that in the
play as well.'

WHAT DO YOU WANT THE AUDIENCE TO EXPERIENCE?

'It comes down to the types of audiences who potentially will be watching
the play. Whether it's young people who think that theatre isn't really for
them, or people who are used to more traditional types of theatre. I'm
hoping people will be able to reflect more on themselves; a lot of the play
is about relationships, how we connect with each other, how others view
us, how we decide to portray ourselves to other people. I can sit here right
now and appear professional and nice but on social media I can have a
more aggressive personality. So who are we in the flesh and who are we
online? On a much larger scale, hopefully for people to start thinking

about what is happening in the wider world in terms of politics. What is happening with austerity, the cuts? It is not a call to arms, but it's about us making a stand against the system. You do have a power individually or collectively to do something. We don't want people to feel preached at, but hopefully something will resonate on a personal level.'

Ben Bailey Smith and Lajaune Lincoln, 2018

Text and language

During the workshop a participant asked for advice on how to navigate the slang that is used by the characters. Lajaune explained that the play can easily be set in any area. Although the slang is particular to London, both writers were quick to point out that as long as you understand what is being communicated in a line, then you can work with the local vocabulary and slang of your area. In addition, another participant asked if element of ad-libbing could be added in terms of background classroom noise. Again the writers emphasised if it rings true for your company and doesn't deter from the story then you can add elements, in particular for the reality of the classroom, which is very rarely silent. Your job is to equalise the additions so that those actors improvising or adding lines do not deter from key lines or plot points.

NOTE: 'Paigon business' refers to someone who might be in a position of power that is full of rubbish.

Themes

Class reflects the dynamics and machinations of the current state of our political system. It highlights the impact of social media and the influence and creation of new social cultures. Essentially, it depicts how class still impacts on every element of our lives today.

Ben discussed how the conflict between Abigail and Jason in the play is about class and not race. Jason was originally written as a black character to emphasise his disenfranchisement; however, he can be a minority in other ways. The key element is that when we first meet him he stands alone. It is not necessary to cast someone who 'looks' different for that role.

The group discussed the representation of politics within the characters. Whilst the characters are very true to life, all the central characters appear to reflect different political outlooks. There was debate whether time should be spent on representing the political affiliations of each character. Ben would prefer for didactic elements to be shown and not told and the script is a guide to that. For example, Oli is a classic flip-flopper people-pleaser; Jason wants to stick to his guns; Chloe is the right-wing element that becomes unsure as plans stop working. Again the writers stressed that political identity and class representation are hugely important themes. Lead director Roy Alexander Weise added that it is important for the young people involved to get to know the political undertone, especially in the latter part of the play, and to find a way to serve the ambition of the play in educating their audience about politics or awakening them to systems and how they work.

For example, the student council in the play: if the system of the school is such that you can only be on the council if you have 100 per cent attendance, then people with caring responsibilities will never have their voices heard. Ben strongly stressed that Jason doesn't have answers in the play; he has anger and questions, and isn't willing to subdue the anger. He is hyper-aware that the people he has grown up with feel the same as him but don't say anything; it's knowing that something isn't fair. Ben and Lajaune referenced the riots in 2011 and how the government were very quick to de-politicise it by saying it was just kids looting, but something they were feeling bubbled over and they couldn't articulate it. If you are constantly taking away people's right to speak then they will find a way to get themselves heard. The play is about taking up space – like young people listening to loud music on the bus, there is defiance in that; they can't do it at home or in school, but on the bus you can't tell them not to.

Structure

Whilst the play is written as one act straight through it is still essentially a three-act play. The writers suggested the following to help distinguish the three acts when rehearsing:

Act 1 is up until Abigail leaves the room on p. 18.

Act 2 is the backstabbing and intrigue.

Act 3 begins when the furniture is moved to resemble the House of Commons.

Roy made the offer of using *units* and *events* to break up the scenes and to help focus the cast on the essential story plots and actions to be followed.

ROY'S GUIDE TO UNITS

Units are a useful way to break up a scene that otherwise appears to have no start or ending. Often someone entering or leaving is a simple way to create a unit. New units give new energy and focus. Give your units titles, then not only are you rehearsing a scene but everyone in it is playing towards making that element of the story very clear for the audience. These titles don't have to be artistic, just very clear in terms of what is happening in the scene. For example, on pp. 16–17, the unit begins when Rachel enters the classroom and ends when she leaves; the title could be 'The wrath of Rachel stops the vote'. A secondary benefit of the title is the actor playing Rachel is made to feel very important; especially as this is her only scene, it shows how important her part is to the overall plot and story line. The following unit ends when Abigail leaves the classroom on p. 18 and the title could be 'Abigail reclaims her power by making everyone wait for her return'.

ROY'S GUIDE TO EVENTS

An event is a moment on stage when everyone is changed by something that happens. An example suggested in the workshop could be if a mouse were to run through the centre of the room, everyone would be affected. If someone were to walk past the window, only those with a view of the window would be affected. Big events are vital to the plot. The first mention of the 'prom' on p. 12 is an event as everyone on the student council is affected by the prom. Stage directions can also be units and events.

Casting

Ben and Lajaune said that it's important that an authenticity of voice is found in casting and to work against preconceptions.

The play can be performed by all-male or all-female casts; both writers suggested making the location of the play a single-sex school to match if needed, and therefore having same-sex relationships. Roy emphasised it is about the young people and the truth they bring to the scenario. With this play every word is important, and the integrity of the story must be held.

One of the play's central themes is inclusiveness. Roy said that through looking at the story and pulling apart people's actions you may be able to bring a young actor closer to a story that might be out of their comfort zone.

For large companies, you could have additional students onstage representing the rest of the student council in the room. In schools you always have a real-life Greek chorus and Ben pointed out the opportunity with this play in creating drama and reality for what is happening onstage. Especially in the final act, there should be constant noise and response to what is going on.

Characters and characterisation

Encourage your actors to embrace the complexity of each character and consider the journeys they go on in the play.

JASON

From the hood. Popular and straight talking. Sharp street edge.

A confident guy who follows his own path. Firmly believes in social justice but through bitter past experience is sceptical about how much influence people in his social strata actually have. He truly cares about Chloe and, when it comes down to it, is surprised by the depths of his feelings for her. This means it hits him hard when he feels she has betrayed him.

CHLOE

Monied, incredibly charming, witty, cool and calm.

A genuinely lovely young woman who goes on a big journey of self-discovery in the play. However, having to constantly battle for her father's approval as well as feeling that the whole election is yet another chapter in the often savage feud between her and her sister Abigail causes her to act in a way that is at odds with her true nature. Just like Jason, she is also taken aback by how much affection she has for him and how much she has learnt from their relationship. It is through the respect that she has for him that she learns to respect herself and follow her own path.

OLI

Clever guy, but makes some stupid decisions. Big aspirations.

A nice guy, but ambition and envy sours his personality. He has his eye on joining the educational elite, but knows he doesn't have the kind of monied background or the family connections that will make things easy for him. On top of it all, he isn't getting the grades he needs. So although originally wanting to do good with the student presidency, he now sees it as vital for getting the extra credits for his university application. Chloe is in his sights as she is not only standing in his way, but has also spurned his romantic overtures and has all the privileges and opportunities he dreams of. He thinks he has to ruthlessly level the playing field to climb the slippery ladder of social mobility. He and Jason have known each other their whole lives; they have a shared history, but not a shared connection anymore.

MELISSA

Chloe's best friend. Forever?

Impulsive and sometimes brash. She and Chloe go way back but she gets fed up with the constant bickering and competition between Chloe and Abigail (Chloe's sister). She's also had enough of the spoilt Chloe taking everyone and everything for granted. She finds what she thinks is a kindred spirit in Oli and has also had a serious crush on him for the past year. This results in her betraying her best friend without fully thinking through the consequences. You could see her like Iago – she is the archetypal, pantomime baddy. In the end she comes into her own – especially with the slut-shaming. Remember school is a battleground – the Wild West – and you do everything you can to survive. A way to sympathise with someone like Melissa is to ask how you would survive in a room full of vipers.

ABIGAIL

Overly entitled, self-obsessed, driven.

There is a sense that she feels she has earned her role. She has been President for two years, which means she is doing something right. Her redeeming quality is that she believes what she is doing is right. She is also a product of her parenting, and the pressures applied to her. Was she always this way or did something make her become like this? There's a sense that Abigail is like Dad and Chloe is like Mum (Mum is never mentioned).

TAMMY

A pivotal person in the play in terms of her own shift. There is a huge knock on Tammy's confidence, with Abigail knowing a secret Tammy had shared with her and using it to control her. Through the play her confidence grows. It is hugely important to show her growth, going from a yes person to standing her own ground. (In reherarsal, help the actor playing Tammy make a decision on what their background is and the secret that has happened; you don't have to know what they decide but you will see it in their work.)

DEBS

Honest, old beyond her years.

She is essentially a plot-point character but her back story with her mum is very important, especially in how Oli and Chloe try to use it to their advantage or disadvantage. She is the first person to make Chloe pause: 'there is always something more important going on and it's usually you'. She has a huge back story with these massive emotional elements.

SOL

Comic relief of the story, but represents the fetishisation of the working classes. Sol wants to be like the 'cool' kids – he constantly fails to sound like he is one of them but he is a good guy and has a big heart. Throughout the play he is trying to be someone he isn't, but towards the end he clearly can see others doing it and then it leaves a terrible taste in his mouth.

RASH

A good guy, always honest, bangs on about the lockers at school but that's what he wants. Middle of the road and no 'side' to him. He's embarrassed by Sol's play-acting.

RACHEL

She is there to add colour to the pallet of personalities on stage, instead of exposition and direction, so there is lots for an actor to find in terms of who she is.

MARK AND LANE

They come as a comic pair or double act. Always visible and should always be doing something conspiring, canoodling, joking. Actors should have as much fun as possible in these roles.

NOEL

Greek chorus – when we hear from him, he is hopefully the voice of the audience in that moment. He is also the student that always just moans about something!

SHAY

She is from Jason's ends; there is a warmth and understanding between Shay and Jason.

NOTE: All the characters need to be won over by Oli and Chloe. They have power: Chloe and Jason must get their vote, must win their hearts and heads. There are very high stakes for the key characters in this story by way of the minor characters.

Production, staging and design

THE ONLINE/OFFLINE WORLD

The group discussed for some time the online/offline world presented in the play and various ways to attempt to stage it. Ben and Lajaune emphasised that anything is a possibility when depicting this. The online world is a concept, but it is not an empty concept; it adds to the story. So don't add concept on top of concept that will clutter or not add to the story. Make sure it fits in with what the writers are trying to do with the story. We see characters' online presence in order to see them without it at the end and to see them vulnerable.

Some considerations are:

- If using the same actors to play their online and offline selves, think about how to differentiate between the two worlds. Perhaps through a change of costume, a change of lighting or physicality?

- When the online world disappears it is meant to be unsettling for the characters. Think about how to present that on stage and for the audience. The game has changed.

- At times within the structure it is quite clear when the offline and online appear and other times it weaves between the structure like a dance.

- There is a choice to be made with regards to how a character says the line they are typing as their online self. Do they react to what they are saying, or show what they are thinking? Do they say the line as though in the moment they have decided to hit send, or play with uncertainty and the range of the emotion that lives in the moments of deciding what to type before they hit send?

- There are also choices to be made about how a character reacts to a text they receive.

- You can play with the style of acting in these moments as well. Is it a heightened version?

- Focus more on the acting and physicalising of creating the online world rather than creating props.

- Think carefully about the use of sounds for the online world. Phone pings could get annoying, so make sure any sound is there for dramatic effect. Perhaps you could start with something at the beginning, which is recognisable as an online notification but then distort it somehow, because online you don't see the reality. Remember the huge stress on teenagers caused by the constant notifications that come at them. How could you bring that into the play as well?

- If you have separate actors playing the online characters, when the phone is switched off you could have them all leave – this could be a very good visualisation for the audience of the separation and quietness when switched off. However, there are complications in how to use all those extra bodies. Remember that whatever choice you make it mustn't get in the way of the story, it must facilitate it.

The group were divided into two and asked for offerings of how to tackle staging the online/offline world. Some of the possibilities tried were:

- Have separate actors for the online versions. Have your online personas sitting in the front row of your audience and move to their 'offline' selves at particular moments.

- Have the same actors play their online and offline characters. Online represented by holding their phones in front of their faces and walking forwards. The eye line of the rest of the room must stay where they are – in reality – not in the online world.

- Different actors could be the animated (cartoon) online personas they have created for themselves, working at a different physical level on the stage.

- Online characters could be at the front with heads down and heads only raise when they speak. This becomes an audible version.

These offerings raised the following practicalities:

- Think about the time you have with your group and how quick they are at picking up direction, especially if it is highly detailed or choreographic. Remain with what makes it clear.

- Consider sight lines, number of bodies on the stage, physical placings for storytelling.
- Ben's instinct was to pick out the online moments with light or movement; you don't have to have them move. This could give actors more freedom as they can switch on and off in a split second.
- Do they even need to be holding phones? You could embrace this element of the play as hyper-real or slightly surreal. Audience will go with it if you really go for it.
- The grey area in staging the play is where the worlds actually collide. As Jason talks there is an online conversation happening. Debs calls Chloe out on texting when talking to her. You could play with the moment of when the phone is put back into the pocket or put away, which could help when finding the moments when these two worlds combine.
- Find a way to make it work without any technology, then you know it will be strong.
- Create the rules that are going to work for the different worlds and then you can break and expand the rules as you go.
- Whether you have two actors playing one character or whether it is one actor playing the online and offline, you need to make a decision based on your resources, the number of actors you have, and what you and your team want to draw out as the most important themes.

HOUSE OF COMMONS

Page 37: *'The students have moved the desks and chairs into two rows facing each other. The tutor's desk is at the head of the rows. The room now resembles the House of Commons.'*

Ben and Lajaune discussed how Act 3 is a satire of British politics as a whole; the endless cycle of it and its ridiculousness. With the movement of the chairs all subtlety should go out of the window, and the bullying and yelling should be played loud, bold and with high energy. It is about the childishness of their speech and highlighting the childishness of the House of Commons sessions. It is very important to watch a Commons session with your students in order to appreciate the absurdity. A lot of the time nothing happens: people are sleeping whilst someone is speaking, and then it explodes. These elected representatives of our society will start yelling and screaming at each other, while some backbenchers appear to just make loud braying noises. They throw barbed insults at each other that have to start with 'My Honourable Member for ...', and so on.

Tammy is the one who makes it democratic at the end. She becomes the Speaker of the House. Then Jason steps in and we begin to see his true intelligence. In the Commons, the Speaker tends to only get involved if they think someone is getting out of line. The writers have taken a liberty with Tammy and have added Jason in as though a cross-examiner. He is Guy Fawkes: the rebel running in saying 'this is ridiculous' and trying to blow everything up!

Roy suggested that there is something iconic in the imagery of the physical positions of the speakers and MPs when debating in the House of Commons. These positions could (and possibly should be) used when staging this part of the play. Ideally, the staging will be recognisable to many in the audience and will link directly to the House of Commons or, if not, then at least to political speaking. Rebels/troublemakers are always at the back of the room or a bit further off, while sycophants sit near who they agree with and just nod heavily. You can physicalise this scene based on footage from the House of Commons or be inspired by it. In the barrage of the arguments ensure the audience doesn't lose the elements of the story.

Exercises

EXERCISE: CASTING

To help with casting, you could ask your group to read the script a line at a time going around the room, to hear which voice suits each part.

EXERCISE: BUILD A MACHINE

Working as a team, one by one your actors should take a position in the middle of the room and perform one single repetitive gesture, such as lunging. Each person then creates their physical action in relation to the previous one created. Keep going until everyone is involved and is relating to each other. This is a really simple game that you could do as a warm-up with your young people; then you could integrate it into a scene to remind them to keep alert and relating to each other.

EXERCISE: CLICKS

Send a click around the group, first stationary in a circle and then moving. Play with speed and pace and ensure you don't go in the same direction. You must keep the energy up. Then start to play with the public and the private; explore having the click happen just between two, three, four people, before sending it back out and in again. Then start being specific with where that energy is coming from – head, heart, groin, bum, and so on, as well as maintaining the private and the public. This is useful to keep everyone on the ball and learn to pick up cues. You could change the click and make it any other gesture specific to your group. You could also use it to find ways to play out in the space as well as to each other and to navigate the space from rehearsal to stage, especially if moving to larger stages.

EXERCISE: FACTS AND QUESTIONS

To help explore language and the themes of the play. List and highlight anything that is a definitive FACT in the play. For example, a given time of 10.03 a.m. is a FACT, but if someone says something to dispute it, then it becomes a QUESTION. When working this exercise with your company keep it physical, such as inviting them to stand up to announce a FACT and raise their hands if a QUESTION.

The group examined the exchange between Abigail, Jason and Tammy on pp. 9–10, beginning with the stage direction '**Abigail** *and her reluctant sidekick* **Tammy** *walk over to* **Jason**' on p. 9, and ending on Abigail's line on p. 10: 'So the silly cow has decided to show up.'

The group discussed the questions as they arose and then replayed the scene. Ben commented how you can sense a history between Abigail and Jason, an exhaustion from Abigail of having to deal with him. For Jason there is an internal amusement as to how he sees Abigail and the student council.

Some FACTS and QUESTIONS that were discovered in this section:

QUESTION: Abigail's line: 'Comrade Jason! Thought you weren't coming back?'

- Where has he been? Why does she think he wouldn't come back? Why does she refer to him as 'Comrade'?

QUESTION: Jason's line: 'And I mean, it's not exactly the most diverse group is it?'

- What is the diversity of this group? This question can be answered by your casting.

QUESTION: Jason's lines: 'To be honest, the way it's been run the past few years, it has been. It's not like things have got much better for the students who actually need some support.'

- How has the student council been run before now? What has the council been providing, if anything, for the students? Which students have been benefitting from the council?

- Suggestion from the room: Jason believes that there has only been a singular voice running the council and that voice belongs to a privileged few, and they are the only ones who are benefiting.

QUESTION: Abigail's line: 'If you're talking about your "crew", I don't think they're that interested in politics, Jason.'

- Who does Abigail perceive to be in Jason's crew? Why the quote marks around the word 'crew'?
- Suggestion from the room: Jason's crew, as far as Abigail is concerned, are kids not at her level and should be dismissed. The quote marks show her opinion and that it is a straight 'stab to the chest' attack on him. This should help an actor energise the line.

QUESTION: Abigail's line: 'We can really do without your crap this time, okay?'

- What was Jason's previous 'crap' that Abigail wants to avoid?

The same line is also a FACT – she views Jason's 'wants' as crap.

FACT: *Tammy starts laughing. Abigail gives her an evil glare.*

- Whoever is playing Tammy has to laugh or the next section won't work. Also this is the first hint of Tammy starting to retaliate against Abigail.

Suggested references

MPs and the House of Commons:
www.parliament.uk/education/about-your-parliament/mps-lords-monarch/mps-in-the-house-of-commons/
Live from the House of Commons:
www.youtube.com/watch?v=pM7gLKTKh-Q

Prime Minister's Questions:
www.youtube.com/results?search_query=pmqs+this+week

From a workshop led by Roy Alexander Weise
with notes by Jemma Gross

The Sad Club

by Luke Barnes | music by Adam Pleeth

This is a musical about depression and anxiety. It's a collection of monologues, duologues and songs from all over time and space, exploring what about living in this world stops us from being happy and how we might go about tackling those problems. When you're feeling your most trapped and alone, the Sad Club has a live band and free entry. A play with songs about depression, fears and hope.

Cast size
12–20 (opportunity for additional singing chorus)

Luke Barnes' plays include: *All We Ever Wanted Was Everything* (Bush Theatre, Welly and Paines Plough Roundabout with Middle Child); *No One Will Tell Me How to Start a Revolution* (Hampstead Theatre); *Bottleneck* (Soho Theatre with HighTide); *Chapel Street* (Bush Theatre and Edinburgh); *Weekend Rockstars* (Battersea Arts Centre and Hull Truck with Middle Child); *Ten Storey Love Song* (Hull Truck with Middle Child); *The Saints* (Nuffield Theatre, Southampton); *Lost Boys New Town* (National Youth Theatre); *The Class* (Unicorn Theatre with National Youth Theatre); *Eisteddfod* (HighTide); *A Wondrous Place* (Manchester Royal Exchange); *Loki and Cassie* (Almeida Theatre); *The Jumper Factory*, *Fable* and *Men in Blue* (Young Vic, Taking Part). His television work includes *Minted in Manchester* (Channel 4).

Adam Pleeth is a composer, musician and performer. As composer past projects include: (as composer) *James and the Giant Peach* (West Yorkshire Playhouse); *Pitcairn* (Chichester Festival Theatre, Globe Theatre and UK tour for Out of Joint); *Entries on Love, Time Stands Still When I Think of You, This May Hurt a Bit* (Out of Joint). As composer/performer: *The Elephantom* (New London Theatre and National Theatre Shed); *The Adventures of Ganz the Curious* (Silent Tide); *Ballad of the Burning Star* (Theatre Ad Infinitum); *Juana in a Million* (Vicky Araico Casas). As performer: *Romeo and Juliet* (Rose Theatre, Kingston); *Something Very Far Away* (Make Mend and Do); *Cinderella* (Travelling Light); *Babel* (Wildworks); *Brief Encounter* (Kneehigh); The Heavy (live and studio).

Author's note

There are songs in this piece: if you can play the instruments live that's great. If not . . . also great.

The **bold** sections of songs are the 'truth' of the songs. There should be a change in lighting, or movement, or . . . anything you like!

In the 'Best Things in the World' section you can add a few of your own things if you feel that's appropriate.

There is a sign at the back saying 'Welcome to the Sad Club'.

Song: 'Here We Are, We're So Happy'

Here we are, again, right here
All together in the sun, today
Sitting in a field again, laughing at everything we say
And we are so happy.
The future's great you see, for us
All the people who are right here, right now
Sitting in the sun again, laughing at everything we say
And we are so happy
And we are so happy
I can't see us being anything other than happy like we are
For all our lives
When we are grown up so happy we'll be happy like we are
For all our lives.
I can't see us being anything other than happy like we are
For all our lives
When we are grown up so happy we'll be happy like we are
For all our lives.

This is temporary all this,
Thinking this will pass and I am scared
That this is the best it will ever be
I am so scared

I can't see us being anything other than happy like we are
For all our lives
When we are grown up so happy we'll be happy like we are
For all our lives.
I can't see us being anything other than happy like we are
For all our lives
When we are grown up so happy we'll be happy like we are
For all our lives.
We are so happy
Look we're so happy
We are so happy
Look we're so happy
We are so happy
Look we're so happy
Happy happy happy happy!

Competition

Craig *is in Speedos.*

Craig   I have spent every moment of the last six months thinking about nothing else but beating David Gairn and getting into the England junior swimming team. My *entire* life is a direct relation to how well he is doing. It's absolutely about competition. Swimming is the thing that I'm the best at in the whole world. I have been training for ten years to get to where I am today. Everything has been leading to this. I haven't, like, stopped living, I still have friends and a girlfriend and all that. Dad insists that I'm not obsessing all the time. When I'm in Maccies I hear his voice going, 'Is David eating shit?' When I'm at dinner with my family, Dad's asking if David would have a second dessert. When I'm going to play football, Dad's asking whether David would risk a broken leg. Dad says the most important thing in the world is being the best because anything but the best isn't worth it. That is what consumes me. That is what's important to me. And now is the moment where I find out whether all my worrying about him has been worth it.

Announcer   Ladies and gentlemen, welcome to the final of the (*Insert county name.*) swimming trials.

Hurrah.

And a big round of applause for David Gairn.

Hurrah.

They line up to race.

Announcer   Ok. The style is freestyle.

Craig *and* **David**   Yes.

Announcer   Great. On your marks. Get set. Go.

They race . . .

Race music plays.

David *wins.*

Craig   Fuck! The world around me smashes into pieces. In the stands I can see Mum and Dad disappointed. My coach can't look at me. Everyone's looking down and I'm waiting to see David Gairn flailing about laughing at me but he's not. He just walks over and he says, 'Well swam, mate,' and he gives me a hug. Fuck this. I'm so tired. I'm so tired of thinking about nothing but him and now it's over. I fucked it. I don't care. I don't feel anything. I have wasted so much time thinking about David Gairn and I'm not doing it anymore. I'm not spending my life worrying about what he thinks. Dad, I'm not doing it anymore. I want to have fun. He looks shocked. Like I've slapped him in the face with a fish. My shoulders become free . . . And for a second I feel like the world is laid out in front of me waiting for me to enjoy it. The world is waiting. I can't wait.

Things to Look Forward to: Space

Best Friend 1 I'm looking forward to meeting your children.

Best Friend 2 I'm looking forward to seeing your first bedroom that's not at home.

Best Friend 1 I'm looking forward to seeing what job you do.

Best Friend 2 I'm looking forward to seeing what degree you do.

Best Friend 1 I'm looking forward to sitting down and having dinner one day and remembering today.

Best Friend 2 I'm looking forward to meeting *your* children.

Best Friend 1 I'm looking forward to falling in love and telling you.

Best Friend 2 I'm looking forward to talking about the first time I have sex.

Best Friend 1 I'm looking forward to meeting for coffees when we're both busy and important.

Best Friend 2 I'm looking forward to Sunday dinners with our families.

Best Friend 1 I'm looking forward to you writing that book.

Best Friend 2 I'm looking forward to learning instruments and starting a band.

Best Friend 1 I'm looking forward to going on holiday together.

Best Friend 2 I'm looking forward to sharing books.

Best Friend 1 I'm looking forward to sharing music.

Best Friend 1 I'm looking forward to going to gigs.

Best Friend 1   I'm looking forward to seeing the world with you. As much as we can. All the little things and the big things and things that might seem stupid or small or little but will open up everything for us.

Best Friend 2   I'm looking forward to everything.

Best Friend 1   Everything.

Best Friend 2   Everything.

Best Friend 1   Everything.

Best Friend 2   Everything.

Best Friend 1   Everything.

Best Friend 2   Everything.

Best Friend 1   Everything.

Best Friend 2   Everything.

Best Friend 1   Everything.

Best Friend 2   Everything.

Best Friend 1   Everything.

Best Friend 2   Everything.

Best Friend 1   But right now. Let's go to the park.

Best Friend 2   I'd really like that. You're the best. Honestly. You're the best friend anyone could have.

Song: 'Things I Do When I'm Upset'

Things I do when I'm upset
Things I do when I'm upset
Things I do when I'm upset
Things I do when I'm upset
Things I do when I'm upset
Sometimes I get a hotty, get a bath when feeling rotty
Pet my lovely dog.
When I feel I want to scream, eat some Häagen-Dazs ice cream
Cry to my lovely mum.
Go for a run, things I think are fun
Give my mates a hug.

Yes, yes, it's here but not oh dear
We know what to do.
Cuddle up on my own, give my mates a phone,
Pray to whoever I like.
Go for a walk, have a little talk,
Listen to 'Here Comes the Sun'
Eat some good food, walk around in the nude
Watch feel-good TV
Read a good book, do a big cook,
Go to bed early.
Things I do when I'm upset
Things I do when I'm upset
Things I do when I'm upset
Things I do when I'm upset
Things I do when I'm upset
Things I do when I'm upset

The Internet: Australia

Terri   I saw her. Right there on the screen. In a little blue dress at the circus.

Michelle   What was she doing?

Terri   Smiling. She was smiling like with a big smile on her face.

Michelle   Are you ok?

Terri   Course I'm not ok, I'm devastated.

Michelle   Was she with him?

Terri   Yeah.

Michelle   Look. That doesn't mean she was happy.

Terri   What does it mean then?

Michelle   Well, I guess, like, you know . . . When you put a picture on the internet or whatever why do you put it on?

Terri   Because you look good.

Michelle   Yeah but that doesn't mean you feel good. She could be like putting it on hating herself but thinking she looks good so people, like, think she's happy.

Terri   You reckon?

Michelle   Yeah. It's not real is it? I mean if you think about it it's basically a bunch of people who think they're not good enough lying to a bunch of people who think they're not good enough by pretending they're good enough and making everyone else feel worse.

Terri   Doesn't make me feel any better.

Michelle   I know but it's just important to remember. Do you want a mango?

Partying

Stacey   I am a party girl and I don't care. I'm sixteen. Mum's sound with it so I get smashed and I'm not arsed what anyone thinks of it. I do not care. I go to every party whether it's my school, or the other schools, or the boys' school, or the girls' school, I'll gatecrash anything. Mum doesn't mind because she thinks I'm the best thing ever. I am her life. My ambition is simple. To get the most smashed there and to get off with the most lads I can get off with. I go to all the parties with Chloe. Chloe is like me but she's a bit more together but basically she likes to pretend she's like me by saying she's mad and doing mad stuff but really she's, like, always careful. This is where I come alive and tonight at John O'Shea's party I am alive. Me and Chloe arrive late, obviously, and we're already pissed because we've been drinking on the train. So we arrive and I am steaming like proper fucking steaming and my ex is there and he's got fat and that's great. There's a lad with a guitar and he's fit. He looks like Johnny Rotten but with Johnny Depp's head. I'm a really good singer. Everyone says I'm a really good singer and if there's a guitar out I'll sing a song like no problem I don't mind doing that because everyone looks at me and thinks I'm great. He's playing 'Wonderwall' and I love this song so I come in and I harmonise with him. And the boy smiles and I know I've planted a seed. I know I can come back for that later and it'll be waiting. I turn around and my ex is there.

Ex   You know no one can save you.

Stacey   YOU'RE SO WEIRD. What are you saying?

Ex   You know that no one can save you, you know that don't you.

Stacey   Go away, you ming, you stink of Babybels.

Ex   Gladly.

Stacey   I try to down a tin of Fosters to forget about it but it's a lot so I just down loads in little gulps until I feel just pissed and bloated enough to talk to people and not really care what I think. The boy with the guitar comes over. Hello, I say, doing my best smile like this – hello. I'm actually really smashed but I'm good at pretending that I'm listening and I think he's saying something like, 'I see you at these all the time', and I'm like, yeah, I know obviously because I come here all the time. He tells me he plays the guitar and he asks me what makes me happy. I dunno. Like. Fun. Getting smashed. Ha. Do you want to go upstairs? He tells me I look sad. I don't look sad. I'm not sad. He says he's got to go. He says goodbye and goes to talk to someone else. I can feel my ex smirking into my back and I turn and I say, what do you want?

Ex   Nothing.

Stacey   Then why are you looking at me?

Ex   I'm not.

Stacey   What's your problem?

Ex   I haven't got one.

Stacey   You dumped me, why are you being a dick?

Ex   I'm not.

Stacey   Tell me.

Ex   Tell you what?

Stacey   Whatever you're thinking, I can see your brain whirring like a fucking fan.

Ex   What do you think I want to tell you?

Stacey   That I'm running away from something.

Ex   Why are you saying that?

Stacey   I know you're going to say that I'm just a drunken little slag and that I haven't got anything going for me because I fucked up my exams.

Ex   I literally was just going to tell you your flies are undone.

Stacey   And he walks away

Best Things in the World

The following is to be spoken over music but in no particular rhythm:

Rainbows
Dogs
Kissing
Eating toast in bed whilst it's raining outside
Falling in love
Making up songs
Baking cakes
Eating cakes
Cakes
Finishing a good book
Sunday dinners
Popping bubble gum
Zipping up a tent from the inside
Getting into bed with your dog
Having dinner with your family
The future
Your best friend's future
Your best friend's wedding
Your best friend's birthday
Your best friend's children
Children
Christmas
Swimming in the sea
Falling in love

How to Help Someone You're Not Close With: Greenland – 1300s

Anyu *and* **Tuuq** *are fishing.*

Anyu   Stop looking at me. We're not friends. We're just neighbours.
You don't have to be bothered.

Tuuq   Are you ok?

Anyu   Yes I'm fine.

Tuuq   Do you want to talk?

Anyu   No.

Tuuq   Look. I'm just going to say one thing then I'll shut up.

Anyu   How about you just shut up.

Tuuq   Ok. But before I do let me say one thing. I don't know what's going on but I'm just going to say this. It's ok. I know your head's fallen off and I just want you to know everyone's has. Everyone's mind's all over the place as well and I know I don't know you very well and that you think no one can understand but I just want to say that the world is a better place when we all understand that we're all all over the place. I understand.

Anyu   Ok.

Tuuq   I'm sorry.

Anyu   Ok.

Tuuq   Shall we just quietly get on with fishing?

Anyu   Ok.

Tuuq   Ok.

Anyu   Thank you.

Fear of Judgement

Cassie   It's mufti day and we're all allowed to come in in our own clothes and obviously this makes me anxious. I'm here in a tartan skirt from Zara, I feel stupid. I used to be a smelly and I liked Slipknot and all that until Chelsea and Dominika made friends with me. Chelsea saw me in the changing rooms after PE and she went, 'Oh you've got a lovely figure', and I thought it was a bit lesbiany. But she did it and you know it's Chelsea so obviously I'm going to talk to her and obviously I'm going to be friends with her and obviously I'm going to let her dress me up like a fucking rag doll.

I'm not the leader of the group but I'm definitely also present and that's enough for me at the moment. But I don't belong. I can't explain it but something just isn't right and now that I'm sitting here in this weird Britney Spears homage uniform on mufti day and I'm listening to Chelsea and Dominika talk about how much they hate smellies because they smell. They just don't get it. They don't get the culture. When I hear that music I hear the pure rage of thousands of people come out, I feel the social rejection, I feel pure anger and hurt and it's cathartic and they will never get that. I feel like I'm living in a cocoon. Like I'm a butterfly walking around in the shell of a caterpillar and I hate it. I want to be me. I want to be loud. I want to fart and own it. I want to listen to Slipknot. The smellies are laughing in the corner. I wonder if they feel like they are caged birds. I'm not alive. I'm just pretending. And I don't want to pretend to be alive, I want to live. Do you mind if I go and sit with them? Just for today? And they look at me like I have just pooed on the floor.

'If you go over there we are never talking to you again.'

I know that this means stopping being invited to parties. I know that I'll never be allowed at Connor O'Neill's again. I know that it means no one will fancy me. But is it worth it? Is it worth all that just to feel like . . . like you're not real? Just because of what a handful of people who think that being thin is more important than tasting doughnuts think?

She tells the band to play or, if there is no band, tells the deputy stage manager to press play.

She gets a microphone.

Song: 'Rage'

ARGHHHHHHHHHHHHHHHHH
ARRRRGGGGGHHHHHHHHHHHH
ARGHHHHHHHHHHH

(If this is impossible, she can mosh around the stage, waving her hair around being the absolute most free person ever.)

Thank you.

She puts microphone back.

Song: 'I'm Great, Honest'

We're like gods, we don't get hurt
We don't feel anything
We carry on
We carry on
We're the ones that rule the night
We're going out
We're having fun
We're having fun
Let's go let's go let's go

Let's go let's go let's go
Let's go let's go let's go
Feels like the night was made for us
We're going to sing like the world exists for us
This world exists for us
We're going to laugh like it's all that we can do
Like it's all that we can do
We're going to live like we're only here now, like we'll die tomorrow
    somehow
We're going to sing like the world exists for us
This world exists for us.
I'm so scared, I'm so afraid
I feel an emptiness
I won't let it show
I'm so sad and I don't know why
I can't speak so I drag it down
I bury it inside.
We're like gods, we don't get hurt
We don't feel anything
We carry on
We carry on
We're the ones that rule the night
We're going out
We're having fun
We're having fun
Let's go let's go let's go
Let's go let's go let's go
Let's go let's go let's go
Feels like the night was made for us
Let's go let's go let's go
Let's go let's go let's go
Let's go let's go let's go
Feels like the night was made for us
We're going to sing like the world exists for us
This world exists for us
We're going to laugh like it's all that we can do
Like it's all that we can do
We're going to live like we're only here now, like we'll die tomorrow
    somehow
We're going to sing like the world exists for us
This world exists for us

What I Need from a Loved One: Russia

Vladimer   Look, you can't say cheer up, you're my best friend, you should know better than that.

Illiyana   Why not?

Vladimer   Because I can't just cheer up, that's not how it works! You know that!

Illiyana   I'm so sorry I don't know what to do. Just get up and get out of bed and we can do something. Go to the shops.

Vladimer   I honestly can't, that's too much, please just let me be here for a minute.

Illiyana   Pull yourself together!

Vladimer   I can't.

Illiyana   Vladimer. You have homework

Vladimer   Just fuck off. I hate you. You know I hate you. I hate you more than anything or anyone that's ever lived, just leave me alone. Please don't leave.

Iliyana   I don't know how to handle this.

Vladimer   I need another few days for my homework.

Iliyana   I'll ask your mum to ask.

Vladimer   I'm sorry.

Iliyana   It's ok. I don't know what to do.

Vladimer   You're doing everything right. I know it doesn't feel like it but you are. Don't take anything I say personally, you're my best friend. I just . . . I've been better before; I'll be better again. I'm sorry.

Iliyana   Do you want to play PlayStation?

Vladimer   Yes please.

Work/life Balance: Consistency of 'Bulger'

Michael   My family have very high expectations of me. The tension in my shoulders isn't a medical condition, it's more of a thing that is a manifestation of my work ethic. From the day I was born I was told that achievement is the most important thing. I'm too weak to be an athlete so that all came out in my work. Mr Bulger, my tutor, tells me I'm the best student he's ever had because I do everything I'm supposed to and more, and then more again and more again, and I read everything, I know everything about everything and more. And today's the day it's all been leading towards: GCSEs. I have worked so hard. I have made so many sacrifices. In Year 9 Sarah Spooner asked me out and I could have said yes. One night I got a message from Sarah saying her cat was sick and that I should come round and cuddle her. Now I can't tell you how much I would have loved to have gone and cuddled Sarah Spooner. I put my book down and I got dressed and I put on my coat and I went downstairs and I thought, fuck me, I am going to get to touch Sarah Spooner but then I thought – what if? What if I go? And I touch Sarah Spooner and I don't work tonight. What if I get addicted to touching girls and that becomes my only objective. So I don't. I don't go and touch Sarah Spooner. I sit down, I read about Walter Raleigh. When everyone else is out getting fucked I'm here reading, and working, because I'm scared of what happens next.

Mr Bulger   Morning, Michael.

Michael   And I say 'Good morning, sir' in my customary good morning fashion. He's smiling; he knows something I know and my parents know and that every other fucker knows and he passes me my brown envelope. My parents and I go and sit in the corner and we open it up and we sit there and as expected I've got all top grades, mostly 9s with a few 8s and Mum and Dad aren't happy – they just expected it of me.

Mr Bulger   Are you off to the party?

Michael   Party? What party?

Mr Bulger   Oh I assumed you knew about John O'Shea's party?

Michael   No.

Mr Bulger   Right, well, then don't mind me, bye.

Michael   John O'Shea never invited me to a party. I do some online stalking. Everyone's going. Everyone. Even the smellies. And no one's invited me.

I'm sitting in the back of the Volvo with Mum and Dad. I can't stop thinking why John O'Shea wouldn't invite me to his party. I start to imagine the party and what might be happening there. I start to imagine people talking and jokes and girls . . . I've never had that. Not since Sarah Spooner. What if that was a joke? What if no one likes me? Am I so out of the loop that I wouldn't even hear about a party that even the teachers knew about? What else have I missed out on? Have I been working too hard to live? I imagine life. Having a really good group of friends. Parties. Sex on tap from Sarah Spooner. Would I swap these grades for that? Just for a minute? I get up, I walk to the bathroom, I go in, I jump out of the window and I run down to John O'Shea's house and when I'm there it's kicking off. The whole world is there and he opens the door and he says, 'What do you want?' and I say –

'I'm here for my one night of fun. From now I'm going to have one night of fun a week.'

And he looks at me weirdly and I say, 'Get out of my way'. And I march in and I grab a beer. And I switch the music off and everyone's looking at me like they hate me. 'Listen. I know most of you don't know who I am but I've wasted most of my teenage years working too hard so I'm going to make up for it tonight. Can you all please chant my name. It's Michael.'

Everyone and the audience chant 'Michael'.

Thank you.

He downs a drink.

Ok, now music.

Music plays.

He does a full-on dance routine – the audience clap along with him.

When it's done . . .

All work and no play makes Mikey a dull bull. Let's party!

Song: 'How Can I Tell You the Truth about How I Feel?'

Taking time
We've got homework to do
We need to be alone now
Yes we do.
In our rooms
Doing what we need to
Yes we are
Taking time for homework.

It's time to do our homework.
Do our homework.
We can't tell you what it is.
It's time to do our homework.
Do our homework.
And we are fine
Everything is just fine.
Not coming out
Got family things to do.
That's the truth
My gran is ninety-two.
I'm staying in
It's not because of you
It's just that I
Have family things to do.
It's time to see our family.
See our family.
We can't tell you what is up.
It's time to see our family
See our family.
And we are fine
Everything is just fine.
I'm telling you
I've got homework to do
It's not true
I just can't tell the truth.
If I could
I'd tell my friends how I am
But I can't
Because you'll cast me out.
We can do our own thing
Do our own thing
Can't tell you what it is
We're doing us.
We can do our own thing
Do our own thing
But we seem fine
Everything is just fine.
We can do our own thing
Do our own thing
Can't tell you what it is
We're doing us.

Jealousy

Sarah   It's morning and I'm walking to school behind Stacey with her perfect hair and her face and her bum and her tits and I wish I was her – I would give anything to be as beautiful as Stacey, I would give anything to be noticed. People like me get cast as best friends and not love interests.

It's the middle of lunch. The football team are staring right through me whilst I try to catch their eye and sexily eat a peach. I'm doing it really slowly to hope that they see, hating myself for wanting their attention, and . . . Then it happens. Stacey has entered the room like Jesus coming to Jerusalem with all the boys throwing down palm leaves but instead of palm leaves it's just sexual frustration.

Why can't I be sexy? Maybe I will. Maybe I'll do something now that's so sexy the world will stop. Something that's so sexy I can be like Stacey. I'm going to do something. I mean I don't know what but I'm going to do something. I'm going to make everyone fancy me like they fancy Stacey. Right. Ok. Right. Here I go. I'm going to *Legally Blonde* them. I can't believe I'm doing this. Right. Yeah. Here I go. I roll my skirt up, just here, just a little bit, just a tiny little bit, just a tiny little bit, and I walk right past her, right past where all the boys are looking and I drop my pencil. And I say, 'Ooopsy', and I bend over to get it, and I let my skirt ride up a bit, just so all the boys can get a glimpse, just a glimpse and as I do . . . Oh no. I fart. And it's loud. And Stacey's face recoils like a snake as she goes, 'Urgh', and all the boys laugh and my face goes red. I'm paralysed and all I can smell is last night's broccoli. This has gone terribly.

In Chemistry everyone's giggling about me and in the corner of my ear I hear it. 'Urgh. She used to be fit.' I what?! I used to be fit?! Why did no one tell me?! My world collapses. Everything falls in on itself. I am worthless. No one talks to me. I open the chemistry book. I have literally never opened a chemistry book before. I start to read. I come across this idea. The idea is that the universe is slowly and slowly pulling away like stretching cling film over a jar and one day it will be pulled so tight that our earth will pull away from the sun and we will lose all the heat on the earth and we will die. And I think about death and about how when the world is dead there will be so many things I miss. Mum. Hot cross buns. Getting in bed when it's raining. Birds. Cake. All those things frozen in time and it makes me sad. I think about how much time I've wasted wanting to be Stacey and how many opportunities I've missed to enjoy it. And looking around this room, I wonder how many people have missed out on their lives, wishing they were someone else. If I'm going to be alone I'm going to live. I get a peach out of my bag. I eat it. Just for me. It tastes great.

Song: 'Things I Am Supposed to Be'

Things I am supposed to be
I'm supposed to be thin
I'm supposed to be funny; I'm supposed to be bouncing around like a
  bunny
I'm supposed to be fit
I'm supposed to good at footie; I'm supposed to throw away bread
  from my butties
I'm supposed to be sexual
I'm supposed to be strong; I'm supposed to never be wrong.
I'm supposed to be cute
I'm supposed to be hard; I'm supposed to never let down by guard
I'm supposed to be happy
I'm supposed to be free; I'm supposed to make nothing about me
I'm supposed to be unique
I'm supposed to not care; I'm supposed to have amazing hair
I'm supposed to be happy; I'm supposed to be happy; I'm supposed to
  be happy; I'm supposed to be happy
Things I am supposed to be

Advice to My Younger Self

You   Ok, so I don't know what to say to you.

Young You   You're the one from the future.

You   I know.

Young You   So aren't you supposed to have all the answers?

You   I'm still only fourteen I don't know anything really.

Young You   So why are we here, then?

You   I don't know.

Young You   What can you tell me?

You   I know you feel sad sometimes and I still feel like that sometimes as well. I know you'll find that really isolating but I do. That feels like it could be useful?

Young You   That's literally the one thing I wanted you not to say.

You   Well, yano . . . I don't know. I'm still here. So even when it's really bad you won't kill yourself.

Young You   Are you happy?

You   Now and then yeah. I dunno. Being young feels like you're sad a lot I think.

Young You   Then what's the point?

You   I dunno. I guess the moments when we are happy?

Young You   I want to always be happy.

You   We can't always be happy.

Young You   Your eyes look tired.

You   I'm tired.

Young You   Are you still a virgin?

You   Yes and that's fine.

Young You   Are you in love?

You   No but that's fine as well.

Young You   Oh so we break up with Jenny?

You   Yes but that was always going to happen.

Young You   Why?

You   Because we're both children and when you get to high school you change friends and some people have other friends.

Young You   Is love not real then?

You   Yes, just not with Jenny.

Young You   Are you in love?

You   You need to work on yourself before you can even think about love.

Young You   Is being as fat as you avoidable?

You   I dunno. Probably. I don't think about being fat much, there's more important things to think about.

Young You   What's more important than not being fat?

You   Loads of things.

Young You   Like what?

You   Like cake. Pizza with friends. Treating yourself to a chocolate bar. Why would you not eat chocolate bars?

Young You   Why are things bad?

You   I don't know.

Young You   Am I unpopular?

You   Erm . . . Not particularly

Young You   Am I popular?

You   Not particularly.

Young You   So I'm neither.

You   Not really no.

Young You   How do I become popular?

You   I dunno. If I knew, I'd be popular, but I've got more important things to things about.

Young You   What's the most important thing I've got to deal with?

You   I dunno. Life. Carrying on.

Young You   Why are you saying that?

You   Sometimes you think you won't want to.

Young You   What do you mean?

You   Well, sometimes you'll feel like you don't want to carry on. Sometimes you feel like you might just sort of end it.

Young You   Why?

You   I don't know.

Young You   So why don't you do it?

You   Because it gets better.

Young You   Does it ever end?

You   I don't think it does, no.

Young You   Is this something I'll have to do forever?

You   I think it might be.

Young You   So how do I cope?

You   I dunno. You just sort of. Work it out. There's lots to look forward to. Isn't there?

Relationships

David   You don't know what love is until you've made a sculpture out of jelly of someone. I'm telling you now that that's what love is. Love is me and Dee. We've been together now for three months and it's great. She is the best. I think I would die without her. We met on a wet break in room 42 because she was drawing a giant picture of Aladdin, whilst eating jelly, and I went over and said I'm a Genie and I instantly thought after I'd said it that I was being weird but I apologised on Messenger later and she said it was ok because it was nice to be talked to and the rest is history. Today is Valentine's Day and it's my first ever Valentine's Day with a girl so I've spent I'd say four hours sculpting Dee's face into jelly. Right now I'm standing outside her house and I ring the doorbell and her dad answers. I go in, the jelly concealed in a lunch box, and we sit down and she goes . . . 'Ok, I've got something . . .' and I'm, like, wait before you do it before you bloody show me what you've got let me show you what I've got and I open the box of jelly and I go, 'Happy Jellytines,' she cries and I have smashed it. I am the best boyfriend in the world. Are you ok? Her dad leaves the room, his belly shaking his way out with him. She looks up. These aren't happy tears. These aren't tears of years of pent-up jelly joy. She loves jelly. All she talks about is jelly. All she eats is jelly. All she ever dreams of is jelly. What's the matter?

Dee   I'm moving to Spain.

David   Spain? Spain? Spain? Why are you going to Spain?

Dee   Dad is opening an *Only Fools and Horses* themed bar in Benidorm after the divorce.

David   Well, where does that leave us? And neither of us know. We just sit in silence like two penguins who know they're going to different zoos. She's my everything. My whole life. She's the reason I get up in the morning. When are you leaving?

Dee   Tomorrow morning.

David   I did wonder where all the furniture was. I assumed you were getting redecorated. Can I stay over?

Dee   No. I think it's best we just cut the tether now and go our own ways.

David   And before I know it I'm outside and the next thing I know I find myself in bed. When I'm in bed I'm not even thinking I'm just staring so I text her and I get nothing back and I ring her and she ignores me and I can't sleep. And –

The company step in (lights up).

Company   Ok, there's no way to tell you this other than stepping in because it's going to take you ages to work out.

David   What do you mean?

Company   Here's what's going to happen now so you're ready for the next time.

David   Next time?

Company   Yes, the next time. So here's how it works. You feel awful for what feels like forever. Then you'll start to feel ok for a bit then, occasionally, you'll just, like, erupt into tears a bit and you won't know why, then you'll realise it's because you haven't dealt with it, then you'll just feel numb for a bit. Then one day you'll wake up and you'll feel like you again. Only not the you when you were with her, the you that was before her. Every time. It's been like that for teenagers since the dawn of time. So it's actually always fine. Ok?

David   Not really.

Company   Right. Well look at this.

Disgrace: Medieval England

Baron Earlsfied *has pissed himself.*

Baron Earlsfied   I just don't know what to do now I feel . . . I don't even know what I feel.

Lady Homerton   It's ok.

Baron Earlsfied   It's not though is it?

Lady Homerton   Don't worry.

Baron Earlsfied   Is this normal?

Lady Homerton   Yes.

Baron Earlsfied   I'm normally really happy. I normally sing songs and . . . yano. Do stuff. Not . . . Not this.

Lady Homerton   It's ok.

Baron Earlsfied   It's not ok.

Lady Homerton   Look, it is.

Baron Earlsfied   She's gone and I'm never going to love again.

Lady Homerton   You're being dramatic.

Baron Earlsfied   I'm not being dramatic. That's it. My social life is done.

Lady Homerton   Do you remember when Lord Harrington laughed milk out of his nose?

Baron Earlsfied   Yeah.

Lady Homerton   Is Lord Harrington popular?

Baron Earlsfied   Yeah.

Lady Homerton   Why did you get over Lord Harrington laughing milk out of his nose?

Baron Earlsfied   Because he's Lord Harrington.

Lady Homerton   Yeah but really.

Baron Earlsfied   I dunno. Just forgot.

Lady Homerton   Exactly. Everyone forgot. Because we all have our own lives and we all are busy doing our own things. We fall in love. We make tits out of ourselves. We work. We have family problems. We get ill . . . We have lives. We forget stuff like this. And eventually . . . Eventually you'll forget about it too. Because we always do.

Baron Earlsfied   So what do I do now?

Lady Homerton   I dunno. Eat an ice cream, do your homework, play tennis, try and think about it less and then get over it.

Baron Earlsfied   But what if I never love again.

Lady Homerton   You're fourteen, you're going to love again. You want some ice cream?

Company   See. It's always been this way. You'll be fine.

David   Yeah.

Company   Ok. Let's move on.

Song: 'Things This Feeling Feels Like'

This is what it feels like
Like quicksand and stinking
Like sinking
Like suffocating and barking painting
Like sour sweets
Like bitterness and dog treats
Like blackness and dark moods
Like burnt food
Like vinegar and not knowing where to go
Like vertigo
Like vomit and crash footage
Like porridge
Like sandpapers and prison doors
Your mother doing all your chores
Like screaming and slow-burning violence
Like deafening silence
Like wotsits and ketchup
Becoming a grown-up
Like cigarette smoke and artichokes
A sheep getting lost all alone
This is what it feels like
This is what it feels like
This is what it feels like
This is what it feels like

Zest

Chloe *is ill.*

Chloe   I'm sick. I've been sick for a long time. I'm not going to lie to you and tell you that I don't hate it and that I don't see all the dickheads in school walk past me that don't deserve health and wish this wasn't on them. I'm invisible. It's not even that everyone knows what's wrong with me, it's just that I know there's something wrong with me and I can't talk to people and because I don't talk to people no one knows I exist. I'm not pretty or clever or anything like that I just sort of happen to exist in the same space as these people. Even if I wanted to talk to them I couldn't because of . . . Because of what's going on with me I'm tired. I'm tired all the time. I can't go out. I can't make friends. I can't go to sports or clubs or anything. I can't . . . I go to school and I go to class and I go home straight away and that's my life. It's not what I'd chose, I hate it, I hate it I hate it I hate I hate it I hate it I hate it I hate it. I'm not living. I go home and I lie in my bed and my house backs onto these woods, well I say woods, but they're more like just some shrubs that sort of gather together to look like woods and at night when I'm too tired to do anything, I'm too tired to read, I'm too tired to watch TV, I'm too tired to do anything at all, I lie on my back and I just listen. Outside I can hear everyone I see in school laughing, not at me, they don't know I'm there, but they're just laughing, they're just feeling their way around being young and they're playing and kissing and falling in love and I can't . . . I can't . . . My body won't let me live. I put ear plugs in. I let my mind wander and although I can't help it, although I know the last thing I want is this, the last thing I want is any of this, I let my mind wander to things I'd do if I was healthy. I let my mind wander to things like running and walking and climbing trees and just going out. Just going to a nightclub and dancing and not even talking to anyone, just being there, just letting the music and the lights and sound run over me and I know, I know by the way that they walk down the corridor in their shitty tight skirts, in their shitty fucking trousers that they don't know what it is to have the opportunity to live. They don't know what it is to not be ok. When I fall asleep I dream of going home from school and going to the shop and buying fucking . . . Maoams. I dream of standing outside the shop with the sugary fucking spit rolling out of my mouth whilst laughing with some people whilst falling in love whilst looking at the sky whilst doing anything. But I can't. I'm here. And the worst thing is that I know that being here and thinking and dreaming and wondering has opened the universe up to me, full of wonder and magic and delight and fucking poetry but I can't use it and you can't see it. You don't even see it. All you see is your fucking problems and the inefficiencies and the fucking boring mundane shit and you don't live! You don't live and you have the choice to live and I can't live and that's what kills me. Because if I was you I'd eat a shit ton of berries and you think that sounds weird because you think that sounds fucking mundane but until you have done without you don't get to choose what freedom tastes like. I cannot be happy. I have all this *life* in me, all this *zest* and I want to live. If I was you I would live. I would eat berries and Maoams and they'd taste amazing. I would run. I would kiss people. I would do *everything* just to feel it. I would forget about your bullshit and live. So why don't you. I know you don't. Do it. I fucking dare you.

Song: 'Here We Are, We're So Happy': Reprise

You're not alone
We're in the club too
Let's go out tonight
You're not alone
We're in the club
Let's go out tonight
Everybody in the club, sing
Come on let's sing
Everybody in the club, sing
Come on, everybody, let's sing
Everybody in the club, sing
Come on let's sing
Everybody in the club, sing
Come on, everybody, let's sing
Here we are, again, right here
All together in the sun, today
Sitting in a field again, laughing at everything we say
And we are so happy
The future's great you see, for us
All the people who are right here, right now
Sitting in the sun again, laughing at everything we say
And we are so happy
And we are so happy
I can't see us being anything other than happy like we are
For all our lives
When we are grow up so happy we'll be happy like we are
For all our lives
I can't see us being anything other than happy like we are
For all our lives
When we are grow up so happy we'll be happy like we are
For all our lives
This is temporary all this,
Thinking this will pass and I am scared

That this is the best it will ever be
I am so scared
I can't see us being anything other than happy like we are
For all our lives
When we are grow up so happy we'll be happy like we are
For all our lives
I can't see us being anything other than happy like we are
For all our lives
When we are grow up so happy we'll be happy like we are
For all our lives
We are so happy
Look we're so happy
We are so happy
Look we're so happy
We are so happy
Look we're so happy
We are so happy
You're not alone
We're in the club too
Let's go out tonight
You're not alone
We're in the club
Let's go out tonight
Everybody in the club, sing
Come on let's sing
Everybody in the club, sing
Come on, everybody, let's sing
Everybody in the club, sing
Come on let's sing
Everybody in the club, sing
Come on, everybody, let's sing
You are not alone
Everyone is in the club
You are not alone
Everyone is in the club
You are not alone
Everyone is in the club
You are not alone
Everyone is in the club

The End.

Here We Are, We're So Happy

Luke Barnes

Adam Pleeth

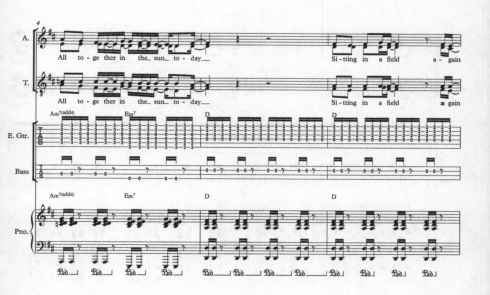

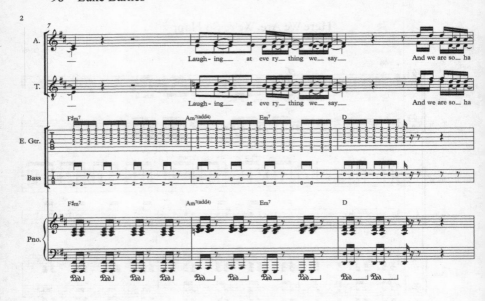

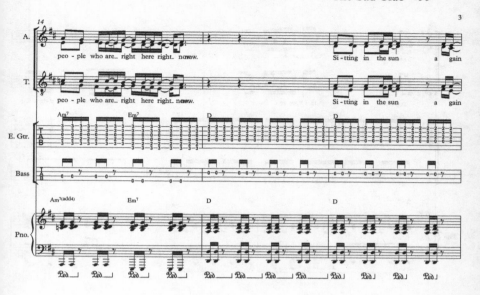

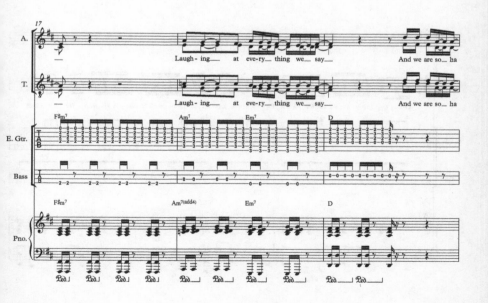

4

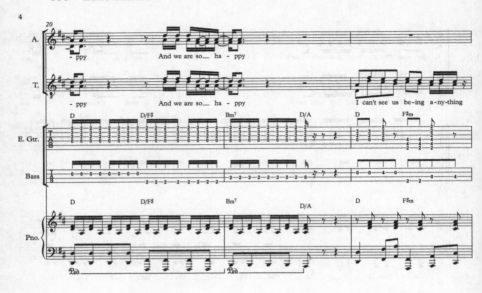

6

Swim Race/Dance

Adam Pleeth

Things I Do When I'm Upset

Luke Barnes

Adam Pleeth

2

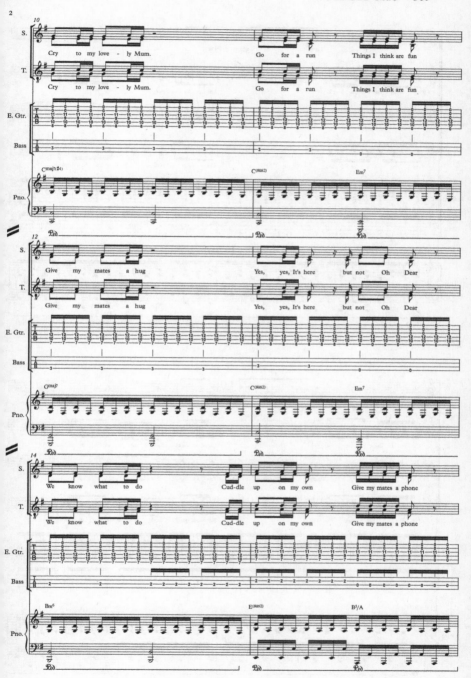

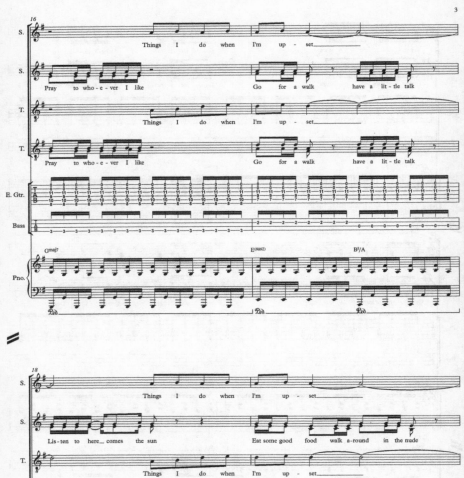

4

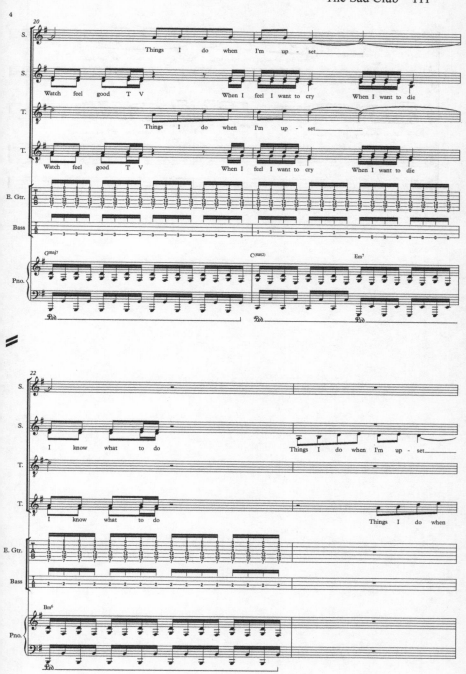

Best Things in the World

Adam Pleeth

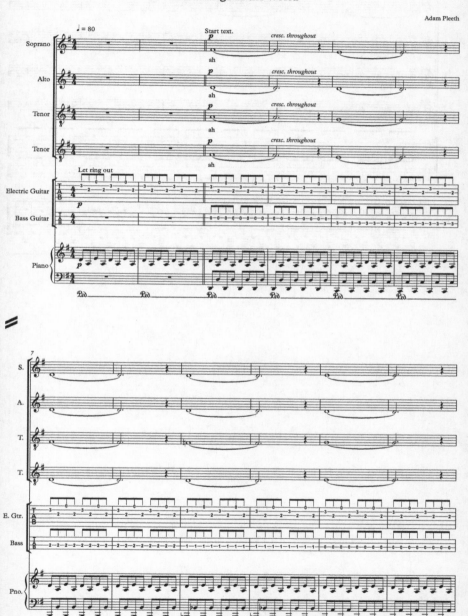

2

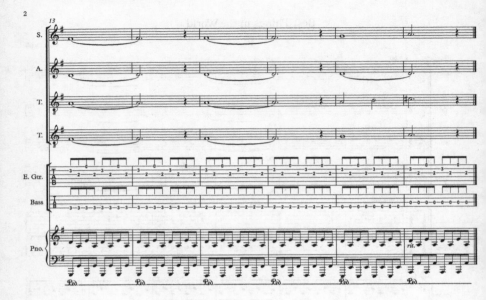

Rage

Adam Pleeth

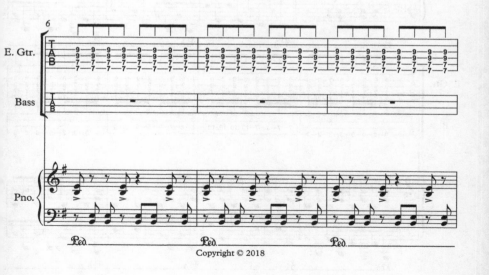

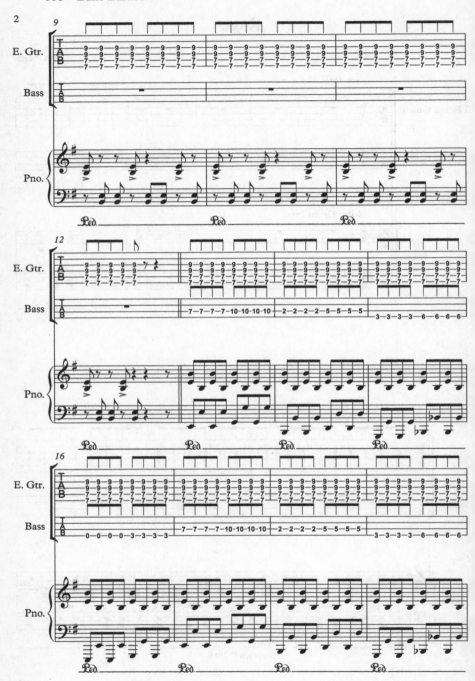

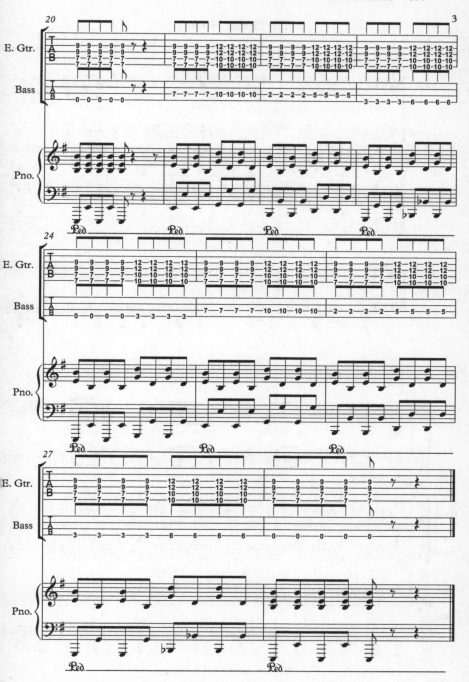

I'm Great, Honest

Luke Barnes

Adam Pleeth

2

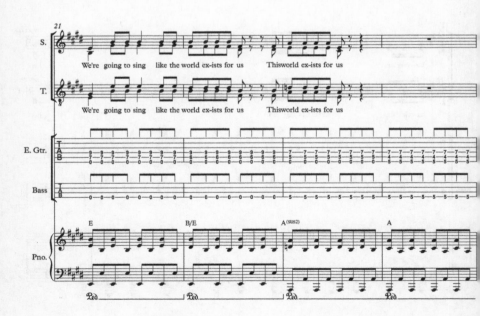

4

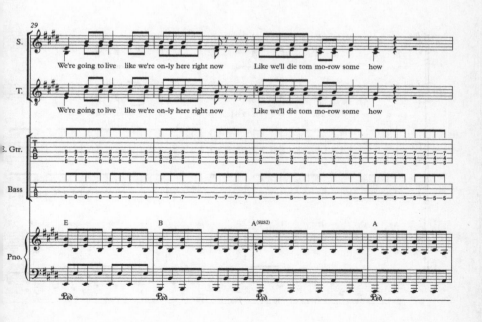

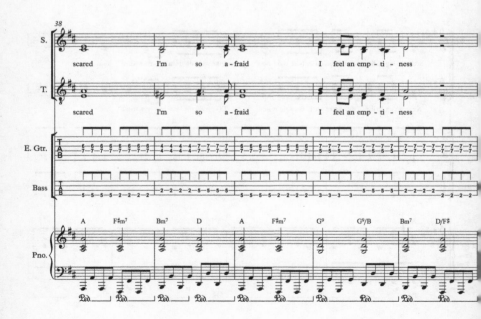

6

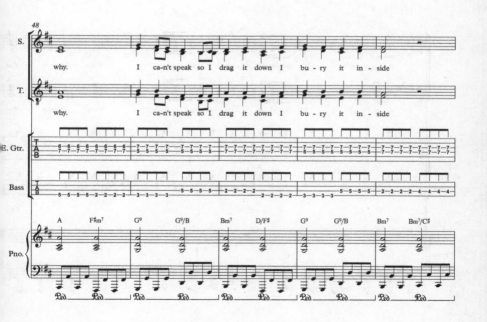

8

10

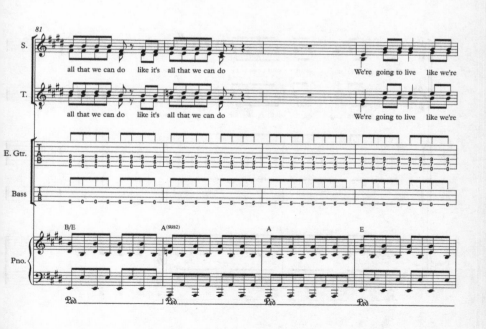

11

How Can I Tell You The Truth About How I Feel

Luke Barnes

Adam Pleeth

4

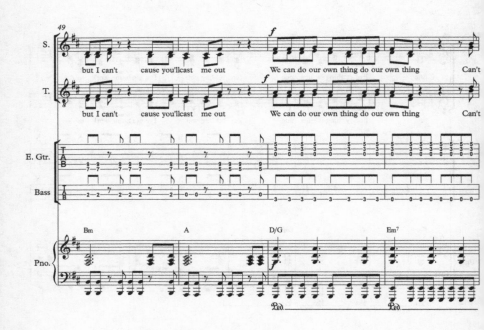

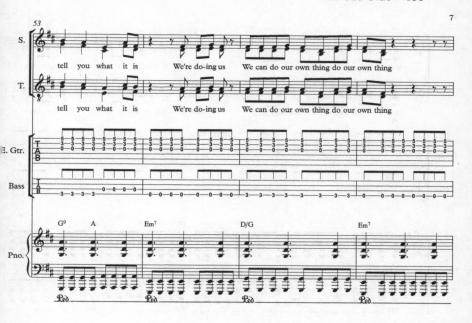

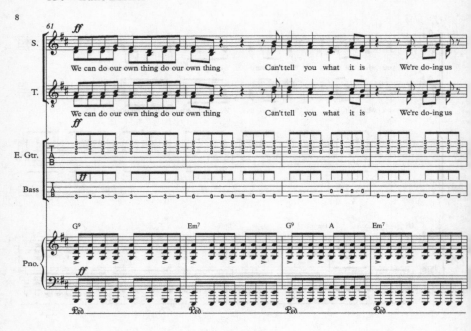

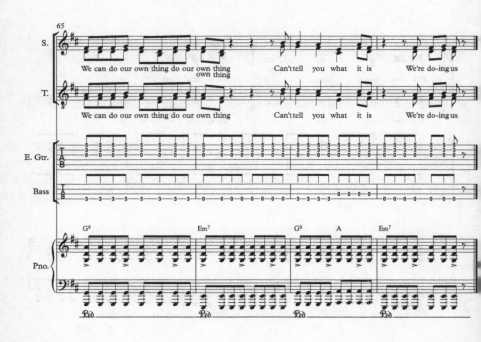

Things I Am Supposed To Be

Luke Barnes

Adam Pleeth

2

4

6

Things that this Feeling Feels Like

Luke Barnes

Adam Pleeth

144   Luke Barnes

4

Here We Are, We're So Happy: Reprise

Luke Barnes

Adam Pleeth

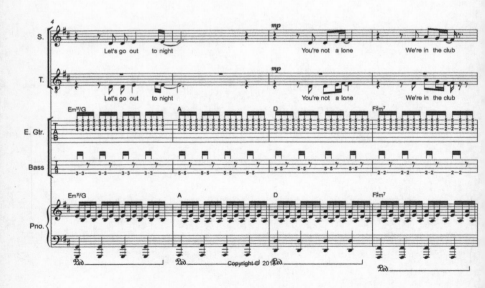

2

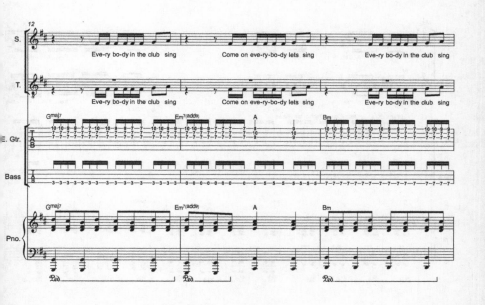

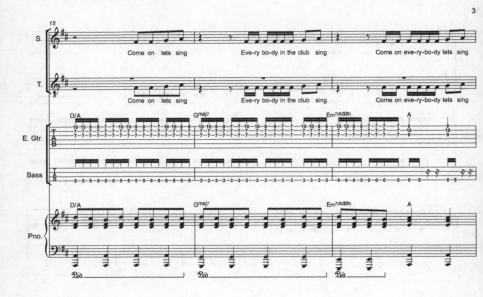

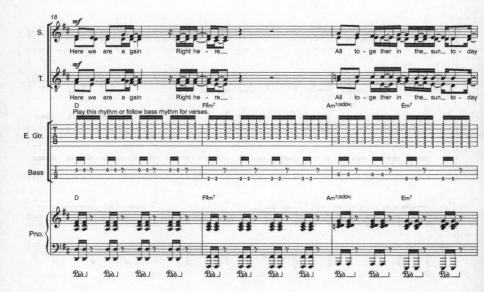

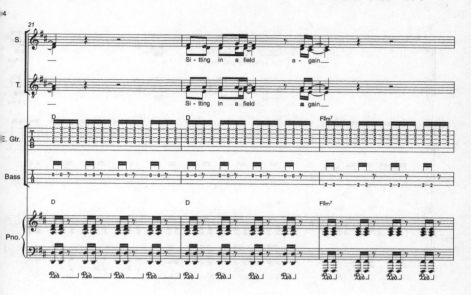

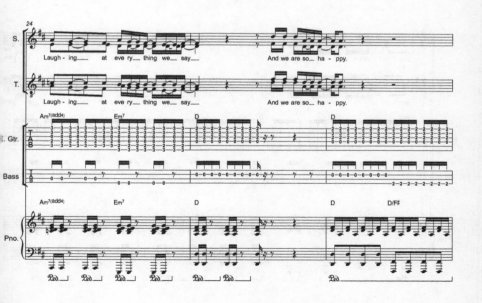

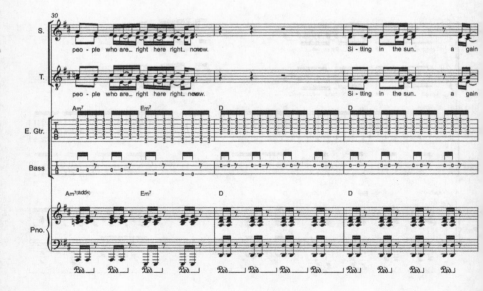

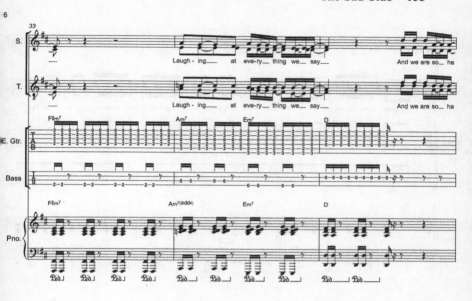

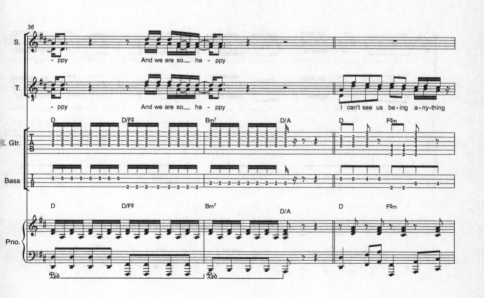

10

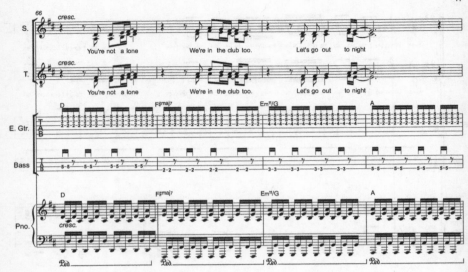

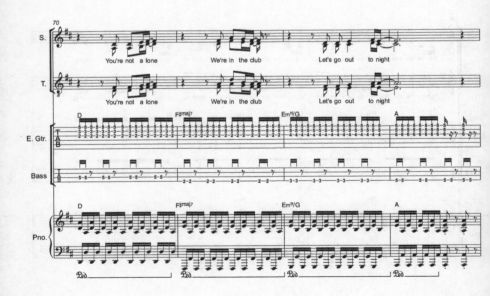

12

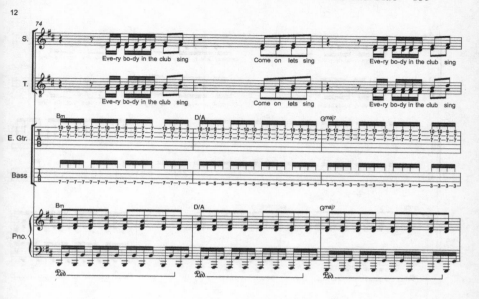

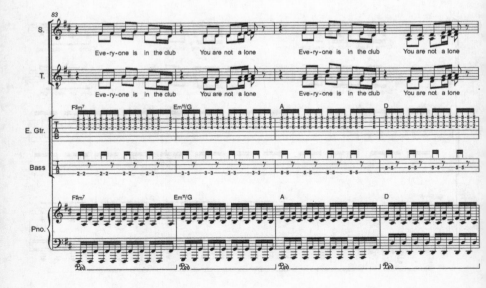

14

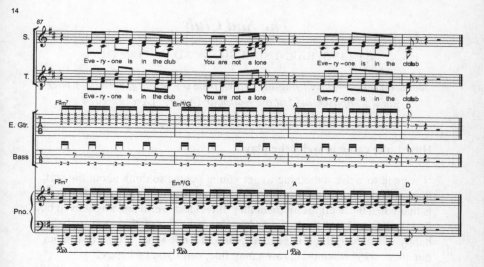

The Sad Club

BY LUKE BARNES, MUSIC BY ADAM PLEETH

Notes on rehearsal and staging, drawn from a workshop with the writer and composer, held at the National Theatre, October 2018

How Luke came to write the play

'I wanted to write something to get young people to think about the stuff that tripped me up in my twenties whilst they're at an earlier age. The hope is that when these things hit them they'll feel less weird and might even be better equipped to handle them. It's about the things that stop us being happy when everything is generally fine. It's not about illness or trauma, but about why, when things are going fine, can't you be happy?'

Luke Barnes, 2018

Approaching the play

Lead director Adele Thomas remarked that there are as many Sad Clubs as there are groups.

Is your Sad Club:

A band?

A self-help group?

A confrontation?

A provocation?

A cult?

A religious organisation?

A radical uprising?

She noted that the theatrical challenge of the piece is that there is no narrative or emotional build, and is instead a piece that is actively reaching out to the audience.

A playful exercise to do with your group: invite them to come up with their own metaphor to describe themselves. Highlights from the workshop included:

Amazingly tasty offcut chocolates
Sparky unbelievers
Electric wasps
Chaotic colourful sheep
Dodgems
A bag of revels

Themes

The group then created a list to give a collective sense of what the play might be about. Some suggestions were:

- What is stopping us from being happy?
- Living a life you don't believe in
- Failure
- Well-being
- Pressures of life
- Bravery
- Vulnerability
- The monster in your head
- The realisation you are not alone
- Timelessness
- Finding solace in others
- Accepting yourself
- The idea that life is difficult but that's okay
- The idea that the thing you hated about yourself when you were young can be the thing that shapes you
- The idea that things are more manageable when there is a club for it

Adele spoke a bit about the idea of failure as a social taboo, and suggested that the most radical thing is to admit failure.

'Everyone is a failure by definition in a capitalist world' – Luke Barnes.

Adele said that Arthur Miller would write one sentence that was at the heart of the play he was writing, as a mantra that he would stick above his typewriter. This forced him to constantly evaluate whether or not he was addressing that in his writing. Adele encouraged everyone to find the sentence that gets to the heart of what they want to do with their production of *The Sad Club*, write it out and stick it to the rehearsal room wall. Maybe that sentence is rewritten if, in rehearsal, you find that it's not quite right, but it will serve to give a focus to the work.

Adele also encouraged everyone to be selective about the palette they were using, avoiding the temptation to throw everything but the kitchen sink at the play. She elaborated on this in the Q and A that you can read later in these notes.

Warm-ups

MONSTER TAG

One person is the monster and holds their arms out in front of them, making monster sounds.

Everyone, including the monster, moves around the room at a walking speed.

If the monster catches you (by placing their hands on your shoulders) you are now the monster. You can protect yourself by hugging another person.

Only pairs can hug – you cannot hug an already formed pair to protect yourself.

Running is not allowed.

VOLLEYBALL

You will need a ball.

Divide the room in half using a row of chairs – this is your net.

There should be the same number of people on each side of the net.

Before you pass the ball across the net all of your team must have touched the ball.

You score points in the same way as volleyball; however, all touches of the ball including sending it over the net must be sending the ball in an upward direction.

SINGING

Adam Pleeth, the composer, led a vocal warm-up:
Everyone stands in a circle.

Turn so that you are facing the back of the person on your right.

Place your hand on their back.

Everyone starts to hum, feeling the vibration on the back of the person in front of them.

Move your hand to a different part of the back.

Move your hand to their neck.

Place your thumb on their cheek.

Then leaving the circle and working solo, continuing to hum. Using your fingertips feel the vibration on your neck, then on your cheeks, then on your lips.

The group then sang the following tongue twisters, ascending and descending an octave guided by a piano:

Dame Judi Dench

Benedict Cumberbatch

Richard Burbage

The group then explored the song 'This Is What It Feels Like'.

Adam stressed that though there are six harmonies available in the score, but groups do not have to use all of them. He pointed out that a lot of the songs start simple and then grow more complex. He noted that the challenge of the songs is the rhythm of the words and the fractured nature of the songs. The melody is quite simple in comparison to the rhythm.

Once the group had learned the song, Adele encouraged them to beware the tendency to slip into a polite received pronunciation (RP). Embrace your company's dialect and what their voices sound like; sing in a mosh-pit and embrace the possibility of failure. Explore and enjoy the wonkiness of the songs, the quick gearshifts and the way that the songs push you to contorted places. The exploration ended with the group moving around the room singing, with Adele encouraging them to move as if they were in a rock concert of their very own making.

Text analysis: how to help someone you're not close with

Adele led the group in exploring the scene 'How to Help Someone You're Not Close With' between Anyu and Tuuq.

READING THE SCENE

Instead of assigning characters to two of the group, to start off looking at the scene the group read the scene aloud in a circle, with each person reading one sentence before passing to the person next to them.

Adele pointed out that Luke has already given the scenes titles and that gives you a clue about the scene.

Adele suggested that it was often useful to think about the basics of space and time for each scene:

Space: Where are we?

Greenland.

What might that suggest atmospherically?

Frozen
Cold
Empty
Ice
White
Aurora Borealis
Stars
Vast whiteness
Water
A hole in the ice
Fishing
Calm

Adele reminded the group that what nobody is expecting is a literal representation of this environment, and it is worth considering how you might channel that atmosphere through the performances.

Time: When are we?

Two little people in the universe. The 1300s.

What might that suggest for the scene?

One of the group suggested that the fact it is the entire century as opposed to a specific year might tell us something about the glorious expanse of the scene. The idea was floated that there is a lot of time in this scene, even though on the page it is quite short. The act of fishing that holds the scene together is also a long-form sport which is often slow and silent.

Exercises for physical analysis of a scene

What follows are six exercises that can be done in pairs. You may find it useful to have other performers help by standing close by and feeding lines to the performers working on the scene, so that they don't have to worry about having scripts in their hands.

For each of the following exercises you will be able to read the directions given to the group, along with some of the reflections given after they had carried out the exercise.

EXERCISE 1: WHISPER

Directions

Stand facing each other. Make silent eye contact for around a minute. Start to whisper the scene to each other.

Reflections

Body language was noticed

A sense of intimacy

A sense of communion

A sense of cold, empty, isolation

Reminded that fishing has a dynamic of sitting side by side

A sense of having a secret

EXERCISE 2: PERSONAL PRONOUNS

Directions

Stand facing each other. Make silent eye contact for around a minute. Play the scene and make physical gestures on personal pronouns ('I', 'you', 'me', 'they', etc.). These should be big, bold gestures.

Reflections

The scene started really confrontational, then opened out to the world.

It felt passionately urgent.

Discovered that there is more going on with Tuuq – does Tuuq have something to share too?

Their relationship moves from cool to warm.

EXERCISE 3: FORWARD/BACK

Directions

Stand facing each other. Make silent eye contact for around a minute. Play the scene and with every sentence make the choice to move either forward or back. The size of the move is up to you – it can be a small step or a giant one.

Adele asked one pair to play the scene using this exercise and asked the rest of the group to raise their hands whenever they saw a decision that they felt could have been more interesting. She encouraged those working to take their time and reflect on the possibilities present in each choice.

Reflections

The slow tempo made words stand out.

This way of working allows a group to come to an agreement and challenge choices.

The exercise allows a shortcut to physical action without actors getting caught in their heads.

The exercise involves the ensemble in an active way in a two-hander scene.

EXERCISE 4: INTERRUPT

Directions

Stand facing each other. Make silent eye contact for around a minute. Play the scene and before A has finished speaking, B interrupts.

Reflections

There was a stronger feeling of urgency.

It felt contemporary.

There was a strong sense of attack.

Doesn't give space to each other to finish a sentence.

EXERCISE 5: I WANT TO BE HERE

Directions

Stand facing each other. Make silent eye contact for around a minute. Play the scene and before every sentence you speak, move to a new place, state

'I want to be here' and then speak the line. Don't be afraid to make big metaphorical choices that are expressive and bold.

Reflections

Breaking eye contact is powerful.

Allows dramatic, expressive choices – e.g. a tantrum on the floor.

Ability to make use of the entire physical environment of the space – e.g. pillars, levels.

Extreme choices allow the scene to be pushed to the max.

EXERCISE 6: PHYSICAL CONTACT

Directions

Stand facing each other. Make silent eye contact for around a minute. Play the scene and before every sentence you speak make physical contact, changing the contact point on every sentence. Your choice of physical dynamic should reflect your emotional connection.

Reflections

This exercise softens the relationship between characters.

Exploring contact versus distance is compelling.

The scene is intimate yet intrusive.

It's hard to make physical contact when you want to go away.

The exercise helps to shift the mood of the scene.

Discovery that eye contact is a full embrace.

This exercise is an antidote to find the subtlety and detail, following on from the previous exercise.

It's a way of exploring text that pushes it towards physical rather than literal expression.

Discovery that some of the scenes could be more physical and less naturalistic.

Objectives and obstacles

The group then moved on to look at the scene from both characters' perspectives.

1   What do they want – what is their objective – what are they trying to achieve?
2   What are the obstacles stopping them from achieving this goal?
3   These obstacles can be tangible physical obstacles or internally constructed emotional obstacles. What roadblocks do we create for ourselves?

The group settled on an objective and a list of obstacles for Anyu and Tuuq. In analysing the scene for yourself, you might settle on a slightly different objective, and identify other obstacles.

ANYU: OBJECTIVE AND OBSTACLES

Objective

To push away the nosey neighbour that won't stop staring at me

Obstacles

This is prime fishing space
Anyu does actually want to talk
Kindness in Tuuq's words
Shared knowledge that something has happened
Emotional leakage – Anyu's pain is palpable
They know each other
He doesn't trust that he won't crack
He's not ready to deal with it yet
He's trapped there

It might also be useful to write a list of any questions that come up. For example, a couple of questions that came up as they were thinking about obstacles were:

How long has Tuuq noticed this?
What has happened before the scene begins?

TUUQ: OBJECTIVE AND OBSTACLES

Objective

To reassure a fellow headless chicken

Obstacles

Inappropriate friendship level

Anyu does not want to play ball

The environment is hostile and stark

Tuuq doesn't know what they're bringing up

Feeling like this is a massive taboo

A shift in the nature of the relationship

Breaking the ice

Social boundaries

Can't fix it

Fear of being rejected by Anyu

Another major obstacle is the failure of language – Adele noted that we try and fail constantly to communicate and often the language we have is inadequate.

EXERCISE: PLAY THE SCENE

The text-work session ended with two performers playing Tuuq and Anyu. Before playing the scene, the group read the objective and list of obstacles for their characters to the performers so that they were fresh in their mind.

Best things in the world

After working with Adam on the music that underscores 'Best Things in the World', Adele split the group into smaller groups with a range of voices to devise a simple staging idea, striving for simplicity of the list over the angelic choral music.

Things they were asked to consider:

Are you going to use the title?

How do you use timing?

Proximity to audience?

Are the best things your best things or the audience's best things in the
    world?

One group shared a staging idea that involved the audience being invited to shout out the best things in the world prompted by numbers. There was a repetition of the scene title punctuating the piece. This felt like a genuine reaching-out gesture to the audience that provoked listening and simplicity.

Another group shared a staging idea in which one of the group was alone on stage while the others were speaking the best things in the world. It became 'reasons not to commit suicide'. They noticed when a narrative is built on top of the scene it loses something. It stops being an art gesture and distances the audience instead of drawing them into the conversation. It is also worth remembering that even when things are very moving, one thing that can take us off track is foregrounding the sombre versus the joy and rock and roll of the piece.

A third group shared a staging idea where they were lying down on the ground, looking up at the sky and spontaneously voicing the best things in the world. Adele remarked that it would have been amazing if there had been a way of inviting the audience to join them lying down.

There was an encouragement from Adele to try and find a way to share the love, always remembering that the gesture of the play is to change others.

Monologue work

As there are a number of monologues in the play, the group spent some time thinking about monologues and used the 'Party' monologue to dig a bit deeper into how to approach one. The group found the following three things scary about monologues:

1 They're long.
2 They're hard.
3 It's difficult to sustain audience engagement.

Adele pointed out that monologues are always dialogue and split the group into smaller groups for the following exercises to explore this idea further. For these exercises, one person in each group played Stacey and the other group members were the audience.

EXERCISE 1: PRIVATE CONVERSATION

Direction

Firstly, have a private conversation with just one of the group. The rest of the group just watch. Get into a comfortable position where you can have a genuine conversation.

Reflection

You get a reaction
You get to have a conversation
You're actively trying to change a person
Energy and tempo is of somebody offloading
You're waiting for someone to chip in
. The exercise unlocks natural rhythms

Adele pointed out that there is poetry in what Luke has written into the grammar. Obey the punctuation really clearly.

EXERCISE 2: TWO PEOPLE

Direction

Open out now so that you are including two people in the conversation

Reflection

There is a constant tension of winning over both of them
You have to keep two balls in the air
It provokes a challenge
Asides emerged
Alliances form with different people
There's more pressure to perform
Provoked a style of spouting words like Sick Boy from *Trainspotting*

EXERCISE 3: A GROUP

Direction

Rest of the group sitting in a row with Stacey performing to them all.

Reflection

Even more pressure to keep balls in the air
More desperation for the character
The lyric 'Save Me' jumped out
A sense of enlisting of the audience

Noticed how broken up the text is – it's not one through-line, there are
   lots of non sequiters

Audience connection in monologues

Through these exercises the group noticed how you can create compelling
work just by talking directly to someone. It is much more powerful when
you're genuinely trying to change someone rather than acting at them. In
working on the monologues in *The Sad Club* you should strive for a
genuine connection with the audience.

OFFSTAGE CHARACTERS

Stacey talks about her friend Chloe, who we never meet. It's important to
have a clear idea in your head about characters who are mentioned in the
text but never appear. Adele suggested finding a picture of them and
developing memories about them. The more extreme memories you can
create the better. Make them as visual and sensory as possible. State them
in your character's tone, boldly and unapologetically. These memories
should be fleshed out, spoken aloud to the group and be wildly contradictory.

OBJECTIVES AND OBSTACLES

In a similar way to the work on the Greenland scene, the group looked at
objectives and obstacles in the monologue.
   What is Stacey's objective in this monologue? Why does she want to
talk to us? What does she need from us?

Objective

To shock you with what a hardcore party girl I am

Obstacles

She's trying too hard

Her ex knows her fear

Desperation for human connection

All of her friendships are really fake

She's sixteen

Naïveté

Her mother – no sense of achieving rebellion

Terrified

Completely messed up her life

Doesn't know who she is

Loneliness in a crowd

Knows she is lying

Desperately needs to be liked

Wants any kind of reaction, if not love then something

Obstacles must remain obstacles – if we remove obstacles there is no drama.

MAKING A MONOLOGUE MORE MANAGEABLE

The group broke up the monologue into smaller chunks or units with more specific intentions and gave each unit a title like a newspaper headline. The first three units they came up with were:

1 Stacey shocks the audience with how much she doesn't give a damn.

2 Stacey amazes the audience.

3 Stacey outlines her life's mission.

You should make unit titles specific to your group. They become a scaffold to support them. Some of the titles will depend on decisions you make about the character, such as decisions you make about her relationship with Chloe. Uniting will give the intention shifts a structure and breaking a monologue into manageable chunks will also help with learning it.

Q and A with Luke Barnes ('LB') and Adam Pleeth ('AP'), talking to Adele Thomas ('AT')

AT   Luke said something interesting to me, which I thought was really profound and really brilliant . . . that he makes work for communities and not for approval. Is there anything further you want to say about that, Luke?

LB   I think that's exactly it. I think that one thing I'm really aware of in the work I make (and this is an exception because this play will be performed all over the country) but generally speaking we're doing it in a specific space, at a specific time, in a specific set of circumstances and all your choices should inform that – where you are, why you're doing it and who for. The place you are, it's inevitably for that community. *But* I'm not at all saying that anyone should listen to me, because one of the things I'm really keen in this play is that you do your version of it, as you find it, for that specific group that you think is cool.

AT   Well, it's so open, isn't it, this play? I think what I love about Connections more than anything else is (it sometimes happens in professional theatre but it happens so rarely) generally the reason people come together to make theatre professionally is because they're getting paid, maybe to have some status, there's kind of a time limit to gathering a group of people together to do a play and then they do it and sometimes that can be amazing, but more often than not it can feel professional. What I love about Connections (and when I think Connections works brilliantly) to elaborate on what you were saying is, it's not just a meeting of a group and the play but it's a meeting of a whole community and this play because that's what you have at your disposal. You've got the offcuts of a community – you've got the kids who are of a place and a space and are absolutely rooted there and when that whole community seeps into the play it's magic, absolutely magic – I'd urge all of you to say to your companies 'don't be perfect, be you' and embrace when someone isn't a very good singer and they're singing at the top of their voice and they don't care, because that will be so much more interesting than trying to get everyone to sing really beautifully. I've spent a lot of my time trying to get actors to do that and unfortunately they're professional so they're often too shiny and nice. All the rough edges are the best thing.

There seems to be a sort of thread that some characters are mentioned or some names are similar – how much of that would you like to be clear to the audience?

LB   I think it's entirely up to you. I'm afraid most of the answers to questions are going to be 'It's up to you' I think.

AT   For the medieval and Greenland scenes – do we have to do accents and authentic outfits?

LB   I think it's entirely up to you.

AT   And the character pissing himself on stage, is that up to us as well?

LB   Entirely up to you!

AT   There are so many ways you can deal with change of location, aren't there? It doesn't have to be literal. Or it could be entirely literal. It's completely up to you.

In general do you mind if things are gender fluid?

LB No I think it's fine. Definitely.

AT Are the two Davids that are mentioned the same David?

LB I think the monologue worlds connect and the other ones don't.

AT There are cycles of familiar stuff circling around and it's completely up to you whether you want that to be definitely nailed down to relationships or whether or not that's strange and palimpsestic: if it vaguely sounds familiar, but not the same.

LB I think in those monologues the world is linked slightly, overlapping, they're of the same shared place.

AT If you were to cast yourself as a monologue which one do you see yourself in and why?

LB All of them. Everything in this is me. Yeah it's all me. As I said the ambition of this piece was to get people thinking about things that I think messed me up and messed my friends up when I was in my twenties and get thinking about that earlier. That was the gesture really, so I think it's more felt than thought if that makes sense.

AT On page 72 with the Craig/David competition bit, can it be a different character that comes in to be the dad?

LB Assuming that I don't want anything is probably a good rule, because I genuinely have tried to make something that I want you to make your own and have fun with because I think the writer's job isn't to prescribe, I think genuinely it's trying to provoke people to make their aesthetic and their form for their place and their time. As a general rule unless I've said something specifically in the script, which I haven't, do what you want. And that's not me being flippant, you should see this as a provocation to go and do cool stuff rather than me saying, 'Go and stand stage left and take three steps, etc.'.

AT What would be your nightmare, and this is for music as well, what would be the worst thing that we could do with this play?

LB I genuinely don't think there's anything bad you could do with this. Do whatever feels natural and feels right for your group and, I think, take no guidelines from me because the worst version of it is me telling you what to do now. I genuinely mean that, I'm not a director, I have no idea how I'd stage this. I've got nothing in mind. Go forth.

AP [The worst thing would be] to not bring anything to it. It needs energy. The songs need energy. Overcomplicating it and losing the energy rather than strong and hard. Think simple and strong rather than overcomplicated and unsure of itself, which would undercut what we're trying to make. I would always opt for strong and simple.

AT   Do you want productions to keep the rawness of it?

AP   Yeah and there's a rawness to the whole thing. However you're going to do your own thing, there's still the energy of it.

AT   It's a 'Coco Chanel play', right? So Coco Chanel always said 'Put your outfit together, look in the mirror and then take something off' and it feels like if you can do this with one person standing there doing it, then think about 'What do I need to have for this to work?' This is a really good way to go about it. It makes it interestingly simple and devilishly complicated at the same time. Keep your palette limited.

There are songs that have got bold truths in them. How obvious do those changes, those shifts have to be?

AP   They've been orchestrated differently, they're quieter or they're louder, and also sometimes it might be that you just have to know that it's the truth of the song – as long as you know it then it will come through. There's not an orchestrated moment for it but as long as you know that's the truth of the song then that's the important thing.

AT   What does the phrase 'the smellies' mean?

LB   Those kids at school who were a bit grungy, who liked Nirvana and Slipknot.

AT   Mufty day?

LB   Non-uniform day.

AT   Can we change stuff like that to make it specific to our place?

LB   Yes. As long as you don't rewrite sentences and change vocab that's great with me. More than happy for that to happen. In fact I'd encourage it because then it feels like they're taking ownership of it for their place.

AT   Can we change names to fit gender?

LB   I'm happy with it in principle as long as it works in practice.

AT   Can we cut swearing if necessary?

LB   If it's inappropriate take it out. But just take it out, don't replace it. If you can't swear just take the swear word out.

AT   What about changing the lyrics in 'Best Things in the World' to get a sense of what they like?

AP   If you are lucky enough to have live instrumentation you can repeat it for as long as you like.

AT   Do you mind if we extend incidental music through the dialogue?

AP   We didn't write the play with that in mind. We wrote it to be episodic. That said, absolutely repeat sections, take elements of it and use your judgement.

AT   How should the song 'Rage' be performed?

AP   In our minds, someone is just screaming into a microphone. That's our idea for the scenario, but you might not have a microphone, you might not have the confidence of having someone scream and I don't know how many performances of this you will be doing and if someone can do it more than once without wrecking their voice. You could just move to it, you could do whatever you like. We put that in there as a release, and a moment, so do what you like but also don't force someone to scream if it will ruin their voice. Don't feel like we've said 'You have to make them scream in that moment' because that could be quite damaging.

AT   Is it OK if you want to repeat a scene?

LB   Great. Do the whole play twice! Why not?

From a workshop led by Adele Thomas
with notes by Alasdair Hunter

Flesh

by Rob Drummond

A group of teenagers wake up in a forest with no clue how they got there. They find themselves separated into two different coloured teams but have no idea what game they are expected to play. With no food, no water and seemingly no chance of escape, it's only a matter of time before things start to get drastic. But whose side are you on and how far would you go to survive? This is a play about human nature, the tribes we create and cannibalism.

Cast size
12–20

Rob Drummond is an award-winning playwright and performer who has worked with some of the most prestigious theatres in the UK. He is an associate artist at the Traverse Theatre, and his wide-ranging work includes *The Majority* (National Theatre), the multi-award-winning *Bullet Catch* (The Arches), the critically acclaimed thriller *Grain in the Blood* (Traverse) and dating show *In Fidelity* (HighTide), in which he helped audience members find love live on stage. At the time of publication, he is under commission to the Traverse, the National Theatre of Scotland, the Royal Court Theatre and the National Theatre, while in TV he has original series in development with World Productions and Synchronicity Films.

Author's note

This is a play for any number of performers. Characters are split into two teams – red and green. Lines written in standard text must be attributed to the greens while lines written in **bold** must go to the reds. Beyond this, it is up to the individual companies and directors to distribute the lines spoken as they see fit, finding and creating their own unique configuration of characters for each team.

At a certain point an older character, wearing yellow, whose lines will be <u>underlined,</u> will enter.

An effort has been made to make the parts gender neutral and pronouns may be added by directors to make these delineations more gender specific if desired.

Have fun!

Scene One: WTF

A number of teenagers lie sleeping in a clearing in some woods. Half are wearing red and the other half green.

One of the reds awakens. Holds their head.

Looks down at what they are wearing.

Looks around at the others.

Looks up to the sky.

A green awakens and looks across at the red. Holds their head.

Looks down at what they are wearing.

Gets up. Looks around.

The green and the red walk to meet in the centre of the clearing, stepping over the rest of the sleeping teens.

Together they say . . .

– **WTF**.

– WTF.

Scene Two: DNA

The teens are now awake and they stand surveying their surroundings. They stop as one and turn to face the audience.

– **Spill the tea.**

– There is a theory . . .

– **Put forward by . . .**

– Sociologists?

– **That the reason we will never solve any of the major human catastrophes that we face . . .**

– Is built into our DNA.

– **Our animal past has us by the throat . . .**

– And won't let us go.

– **See, back in the day . . .**

– When the world was one massive supercontinent . . .

– **Pangea . . .**

– Knowledge!

– **And we were closer to animal than human . . .**

– Which is really a distinction . . .

– **Without a difference.**

– Real talk.

– **Shots fired.**

– We are animals.

– **We are built to survive from day to day.**

– It wasn't useful to think long term.

– **It wasn't helpful to plan for thirty years . . .**

– A hundred years . . .

– **A thousand years' time.**

– All that mattered was . . .

– **Now.**

– Get food for my family.

– **Now.**

– Protect my family.

– **Now.**

– Make more family.

– **Now.**

– Thinking about our great . . .

– **Great . . .**

– Great . . .

– Grandkids . . .

– And what would be good for them . . .

– Was about as useful . . .

– As a knitted condom.

– The animals who had the DNA for long-term planning . . .

– They were too busy thinking.

– And they got munched.

– Zayum!

– And they didn't pass on their DNA.

– But the animals who got the job fucking done.

– BOOM!

– Their DNA was defs . . .

– Totes . . .

– Passed the fuck on.

– To us.

– So when someone says . . .

– The fundamental changes I'm suggesting are not a quick fix and will take thirty or forty years to show a return . . .

– People be like . . .

– BORING.

– Fail.

– No chill!

– OM gosh.

– We're suffering now.

– Ay?

– We need to fix it now.

– Ay?

– It's why politicians are re-elected every five years.

– Instead of twenty.

– **I mean who can save the country in five years?**

– Lol.

– **And so we split into tribes. Tribes who think one quick fix is the answer.**

– Savage!

– **And tribes who think another quick fix is the answer.**

– It's all g.

– **And the question remains.**

– Ninety-nine per cent of species who ever existed are now extinct.

– **What makes us think we're special?**

Scene Three: OMG

The fourth wall goes back up.

– **Does anyone remember how we got here?**

– What's that?

– **What?**

– Up there.

– **It's just fog.**

– Mist.

– **It's just fucking clouds.**

– My phone's missing.

– **Mine too.**

– That's so no chill.

– **Does anyone have their phone?**

– Fuck.

– Where are we anyway?

– **Looks like a forest.**

– You think?

– **Don't throw shade at me, you salty bitch.**

– I'm just saying. It's obvious we're in a forest.

– **Yeah, but where?**

– And why?

– **It's cold.**

– So we're still in Britain then.

– **LOL.**

– **OM gosh. What if it's Russia? What if we've been drugged and we're going to be sold to, like, Russian oily garks.**

– Oligarchs.

– I feel like I was drugged.

– **Me too.**

– Me too.

– **This is cray-cray.**

– Cray-cray?

– What? Is it 2016?

– It's cold.

– **The sun's up there.**

– So?

– **So that tells us something. Doesn't it?**

– Does it?

– **Why don't we Google Map it.**

– Coz we don't have our phones!

– **Yeah. I forgot.**

– **Can't you tell by the stars?**

– So we wait till dark?

– **Fuck that.**

– Could you not swear.

– Sorry, snowflake.

– What's with the colours?

– It's like we're in teams.

– For what?

– If this is like *Hunger Games* I'm fucking dead.

– I can't fight.

– I'm a pacifist.

– Not if your family was dying you wouldn't be.

– WTF?

– Like if you saw your mum being raped you wouldn't be a pacifist.

– What you talking about my mum like that for?

– It was just an example.

– Does anyone remember anything? Anything at all?

– I barely even remember who I am.

– Yeah. Same here.

– Same.

– Same.

– Does anyone know anyone else here?

They all look around. Shake their heads.

– This is fucked.

– OM gosh.

– Why'd you not just say OMG?

– I'm Christian. It's blasphemy.

– But you don't actually say God.

– It's what it stands for.

– You could make it stand for gosh.

– No one would know that though.

— **I'm Christian too.**

— Me too.

— **Maybe that's it. We're all reds. So . . .**

— **I'm a red and I'm an atheist.**

— What else do we all have in common?

— Why?

— If we work out why we've been separated into these colours then maybe we can work out why we're here.

— And where here is.

— **Why don't we all stand in our groups to make it easier?**

— Yeah.

— Okay.

— **Reds over here.**

— Greens over here.

— **So you're like the leaders then?**

— No.

— We don't need leaders.

They all stand in their groups and look across the divide at each other.

— Maybe it's politics. Like, Labour and the Greens or something.

— **Does anyone remember if they like, like, the environment and shit?**

Some of the reds and some of the greens put their hands up.

— So it's not politics.

— **It's not race.**

— It's not gender.

— Eh, gender doesn't exist actually. FFS.

— Maybe it's random.

— **Is anyone else, like, really scared?**

Lots of them put their hands up.

– Nothing to be scared about.

– **Yeah, we just woke up in the middle of nowhere wearing clothes that we didn't put on. Everything's amazing.**

– Sarcasm's so cancelled.

– Yeah, it's not funny.

– It's all g. We'll work it out. As long as we stick together.

– **I'm getting the fuck out of here.**

– What?

– **I'm going.**

– **Me too.**

– Where?

– **To find a road.**

– We don't know if there is one.

– **There's always roads.**

– We don't know what direction to walk in.

– **Come on, reds. We're going.**

– I want to go too!

– **Fine. I don't care.**

– No. We're not going.

– You mean the greens?

– No. I just mean . . . None of us should go until we've made a plan.

– **The plan is . . . we go.**

– That's not a plan.

– **It totes is a plan.**

– **Okay, real talk, yeah? We are fucked. This situation is fucked. We need to move and we need to move now. Before it gets dark and we're stuck here for the night.**

– We need to stay and think about this logically.

– Red, green, I don't care. Come with me if you want to live.

The red exits. Most of the other reds follow. And a couple of greens. There are only two reds left on stage now. They look across at the greens. Then leave too.

Only greens remain.

– So. What's the plan?

– I don't know.

– You said . . .

– I said we need to make one. Not that I had one.

– We need to stick together.

– Yes. Agreed.

– Totes.

– I can get on that.

– Maybe if we wait here someone will come and get us.

– Yeah, I was thinking, it might be a practical joke.

– If the reds get out then they'll send help. Won't they?

– Yeah. Staying here is probably wise. If they make it out they'll send help.

– And if they don't . . . then at least we'll be alive.

– We'll wait for night-time and work out where north is.

– How?

– The North Star.

– Does anyone know where the North Star is?

– In the north.

– Not funny.

– So what if we know what north is? We don't know where we are! North could be the fucking North Pole.

– I've got it. We wait two days.

– Two days?

– No way.

– That's how long it should take for help to come. If it doesn't then we know we have to try ourselves. Early in the morning. To get the most sunlight.

– Two days.

– It's logical.

– I suppose.

– Are we together on this?

One by one, they all nod.

A red re-enters. Then another. And another. Soon they are all back.

– What's wrong?

– **We're on a fucking island.**

– OM gosh.

Scene Four: OTP

A green and a red sit side by side as the rest sleep.

– Hey.

– **Hey.**

– This is . . .

– **Yeah. I know.**

– Do you think we'll be okay?

– **We'll be fine.**

– Yeah. Totes.

– **So. You got a boyfriend or girlfriend or whatever?**

– Don't think so. You?

– **Don't think so.**

– So do you like boys or girls or . . .

– Who's your favourite celebrity couple?

– **The Obamas.**

– Me too.

– **I'm so shipping for that relationship.**

– Me too.

– **They are defs an OTP.**

– OTP?

– **One true pair.**

– Oh. Cool.

– **I was totally draking when they had to leave the White House.**

– Draking?

– **Emotional.**

– Oh.

– **If I had my phone I might send you a picture of an aubergine/ peach right now.**

– I might send you a peach/aubergine back.

(Author's note: in each case, delete aubergine or peach as appropriate for the chosen gender/sexuality balance.)

Another red wakes up and sees them talking.

– **What?**

– Nothing. Just maybe don't talk to the greens, yeah? Until we know what's going on.

– It's all g.

The red goes back to sleep.

– You've got nothing to worry about from me.

– **Yeah. Me too.**

– I think you're hot.

– **Yeah. Me too.**

– Good enough to eat.

– **Same.**

Scene Five: JK

Morning. The reds and the greens have kind of gravitated to either side of the clearing.

– How far do you think it is?

– I don't know. A mile.

– It's way longer than that. You can hardly see the mainland.

– What mainland?

– Scotland?

– We might be in a lake. The island's tiny.

– I walked round it in thirty minutes so it's like . . . two miles in diameter.

– Knowledge!

– What? I'm smart.

– Yeah, and you're thirsty too.

– What does that mean?

– You're looking for attention.

– I'm smart too. Maybe that's how we're split.

– What the fuck does that mean?

– Who got As in their exams?

– I don't even remember.

– Everyone just shut the fuck up!

– Ten miles?

– No. Maybe five. At the most.

– Can anyone swim five miles?

– Without drowning.

– JK.

– That's not funny.

– Sarcasm is cancelled.

– **I'm a good swimmer. I think.**

– You think?

– **Can't really remember. Feels like I could do it.**

– **Savage!**

– **Hashtag impressed.**

– Yeah. I can do it. I know I can.

– **Maybe we're the talented ones and you're the stuck-up arseholes.**

– **Oh! Shots fired!**

– Is anyone else hungry?

– **Starving.**

– Thirsty.

– What, like, looking for attention?

– **No. Actually thirsty.**

– That's why we're all being so mean girls to each other.

– Mean girls. That's a film, right?

– **I think so.**

– **We need to find food and water.**

– One thing at a time.

– **How long can humans last? Without food and water?**

– **Maybe one of the clever-arse greens knows?**

– Chill, yeah? If you get to shore we won't need to worry about that, amirite?

– It's like three weeks without food and like five days without water.

– **You see. It's all g.**

– Yeah but it wouldn't be very pleasant for most of that time.

– **So we need water more than food then.**

– Yeah.

– **There's water all around us.**

– Are you serious?

– How have you made it this far not knowing you can't drink sea water?

– Maybe we are the clever ones. LOL.

– **It might be fucking lake water, remember?**

– Oh yeah.

– **I'll go check.**

A red exits.

– Do you think you can make it?

– **If it's less than five miles. Yeah.**

– Savage.

– **You're, like, my actual hero right now.**

– **When I grow up I want to be like you.**

– **You are so adulting right now.**

– **I can't even swim like a single length.**

– So. Are you ready?

– **Yeah. I'll send help when I get there.**

– Wherever there is.

– **What if there is like . . . North Korea.**

– **That's a bad place, right?**

– Yeah, like we're any better.

– **I think we are.**

– We're from the UK, right? I remember that at least.

– Feels like it.

– Sounds like it.

– **I still say we're in Russia.**

– Scotland.

– You noticed the days seem to last longer here?

– Antarctica then.

– Alaska.

– **How come we can remember countries but not who we are?**

– Short-term.

– **What?**

– Short-term memory loss. Or something.

– This is some sort of . . . experiment. Or something. A joke. A gameshow. We'll be fine. It's all g. Yeah? Greens. Are you with me? It's all g.

– It's all g.

The red runs back in.

– **It's not salty at all.**

– So we're in a lake.

– **Never mind that. We have fucking water.**

– **Which gives us at least three weeks.**

– We won't be here three weeks.

– **I'm just saying.**

– We won't.

– **And I found these on the shore.**

The red holds up empty containers.

– I told you. It's a game show. Someone left them there for us.

– **Did anyone sign up for a game show?**

– **Maybe it's Derren Brown. And he made us all forget we signed up.**

– Yeah.

– Maybe.

– **Derren Brown. He's that magician, right?**

– I remember him.

– **I saw him make a woman try to kill herself once. He's hilarious.**

– **Well. See you all on the mainland then I guess.**

The red exits towards the water.

– **There was something else.**

– What?

– **A name.**

– A name?

– **Like, on a bit of wood.**

– What name?

– **Eilean.**

– Eilean?

– **Yeah. Eilean.**

– Who the fuck is Eilean?

The red shrugs.

Scene Six: YOLO

They all sit, passing around water from the containers. Satiated for the time being. Swatting away at midges.

Two reds and two greens sit either side of the clearing.

– **How long does it take to swim five miles?**

– I don't know. I'm not clever.

– **Do you really think we're the dumb ones?**

– Maybe.

– **What do you want to do? For a living?**

– It's coming back to me. I didn't want to go to university. I think.

– **What do you want to do?**

– Promise not to laugh?

– **Totes.**

– I think I want to be, like, a YouTube celebrity.

– **Oh. Yeah. YouTube. That's lit.**

– Yeah.

– That's so on fleek. I'd like that too. But I don't have any, like . . . talents.

– You don't really need any TBH. There's one channel on YouTube that's just, like, this girl doing shopping and being, like, really salty to sales assistants. And she's got three million subscribers. It's called Salty Shop Bitch.

– This really is the best time to be alive isn't it?

– Savage.

– Yeah. I think you should go for it. When we get home. YOLO.

– YOLO.

– So. Do you really think we're the clever ones?

– I don't know. What did you get in your exams? Do you remember?

– As. I think. Well, a C in maths but that's just like . . . so what? I won't be able to work out what a triangle's like . . . doing or something. Oh no!

– Lulz.

– Maybe we are the clever ones.

– Probs.

– We should probably, like, not listen to them too much then. Like, for what to do to get out of here and shit.

– Defs.

– So, what you going to do after school?

– Something with the environment. Or veganism. Or . . . moustaches.

– Savage.

– Like . . . invent a bar that also does beard-trimming. Like, while you drink.

– What would you call it?

– Like . . . Beerdy Boys. But spelled like beer. Not beard.

– That's, like, genuinely the cleverest thing I've ever heard.

– We are the clever ones, amirite?

– Totes.

– Totes.

Suddenly someone starts shouting from offstage.

**– Hello! Hello! Is anyone there? Hello! We need help! We're
stuck! We're trapped on an island in the middle of the lake
and . . .**

*The swimmer re-enters. They see that they have arrived back where they
left.*

– What the fuck?

They collapse to the ground from exhaustion.

Scene Seven: FOMO

The teens break the fourth wall once more.

– FOMO.

– Fear of missing out.

**– This refers to the feeling of abject, gut-wrenching sadness and loss
one feels from missing out on a night out . . .**

– A party . . .

– A hang . . .

– Messing with your squad . . .

– Chilling with your woes . . .

– The feeling that stops you staying in even when you know you should
because tonight . . .

– Might just be . . .

– *The* night . . .

– And you can't risk missing it.

– You just fucking can't.

– And if you do miss it . . .

– There's no hiding.

– **Because you'll see the evidence of it.**

– Published.

– **Indelibly imprinted on the internet.**

– Forever.

– **You'll see the pictures.**

– The instas.

– **The status updates.**

– The tweets.

– **And you'll know for sure.**

– You.

– **Missed.**

– Out.

– **Whereas POMO . . .**

– The pleasure of missing out.

– **Is what you get when someone outside your squad . . .**

– Your fam . . .

– **Your woes . . .**

– Invites you to an event . . .

– **And you can't make it.**

– One time . . .

– **A bunch of . . .**

– Scientists?

– **Separated a group of non-familial mice into two tribes.**

– And isolated them in a cage.

– **They painted one lot red . . .**

– And the other lot green.

– **And they found something remarkable started to happen.**

– Despite the fact that they knew they were really all the same . . .

– **The red mice and the green mice separated themselves into groups . . .**

– And started to fight with each other over food . . .

– **Water . . .**

– Sex.

– **And then the scientists took a red mouse out the cage and put him in another cage so all the other mice could see him.**

– And a fucking cray-cray thing happened.

– **The other red mice started clamouring at the bars of the cage to try and get out. To try and join him.**

– And all the green mice just sat there, like . . .

– Yawn.

– Boring.

– Whatever.

– **The red mice all got FOMO.**

– And the green mice all got POMO.

– **It's instinct, amirite?**

– Tribes keep us safe.

– **At least they used to.**

– They used to be useful.

– **The instinct, built into our DNA, it used to serve a purpose.**

– But now the instinct still remains.

– **A remnant.**

– A misfiring sequence.

– **While the purpose it serves . . .**

– Has long but gone.

– **And now . . . tribes are going to fucking kill us.**

– Amirite?

Scene Eight: GOAT

*What feels like three days later. Two tribes clearly delineated. Everyone
cold. Shivering. Starving. Swatting at midges again.*

– **These fucking things.**

– Midges.

– You shouldn't swat them.

– **Why not?**

– They deserve to live too you know.

– **Fuck them.**

– **How long can you last without food again?**

– Three weeks.

– **How long have we been here?**

– Three days.

– **Four.**

– Five.

– **Four.**

– **A week.**

– Don't be stupid.

– Why don't you try swimming again?

– **You fucking try.**

– Maybe you doubled back?

– **We've been over this.**

– I just think . . .

– **I swam straight.**

– One more try won't . . .

– **Shut the fuck up**

– How come we can't keep track of the days?

– **It's getting colder.**

– **We need to start a fire.**

– **And find some food.**

– We still don't know what's going on.

– **Yeah, let's work out what's going on while we freeze to death. I'll be so much happier dying if I know why I'm fucking dying.**

– Something's going on.

– **Something weird.**

– **Maybe . . . maybe we're dead.**

– That's cray-cray.

– **I don't feel dead.**

– There's no afterlife so . . .

– **How do you know?**

– Because I'm smart.

– **Fuck you.**

– **Maybe the island's haunted.**

– Maybe it's like quantum physics or some shit.

– A rent in the space–time continuum.

– **Maybe we're in Hurley's dream.**

– What?

– *Lost*. Duh.

– Eh. SPOILER ALERT!

– **You've not seen *Lost* yet?**

– Oh yeah. I remember that show!

– **That show is the GOAT.**

– The what?

– **Greatest of all time.**

– You kidding? Hurley was dreaming it the whole time! It's such a cop-out.

– SPOILER ALERT!

– There's no spoiler alerts for programmes that old.

– I still say it's Derren Brown.

– Well, we've got to eat sometime soon. Is that something both sides can agree on?

– Sides? Why does there have to be sides?

– There doesn't have to be, it's just ... clearer ... okay?

– It's healthy. Keeps both sides honest.

– Checks and balances you mean?

– What's that?

– Like ... we say something stupid, you call us on it.

– Although to be fair, they're more likely to say something stupid.

– Fuck you.

– It's meaningless.

– Well, why don't you take off your T-shirt then?

– I'd rather be in a group than dead, that's why.

– Exactly!

– Never mind what group you're in. We can all agree that we need to eat? Yes?

Everyone says 'yes'.

– Great. So. We need to hunt.

– Hunt?

– Savage.

– I'm vegetarian. I think.

– Well, hunt for cabbages then. Fuck's sake.

– We'll forage.

– I'm not eating moss and fucking poisonous berries.

– Are there animals here?

– There's always animals where there's trees.

– Those Fisher Price books really paying off there aren't they?

– **Salty bitch.**

– What do we use? To hunt?

– **Branches? From trees?**

– How do we make them . . . pointy?

– **I don't know.**

– **Doesn't need to be pointy. Just jab it right into them.**

– **Or beat them to death with it.**

– You're sick.

– **Oh go eat a bush.**

– I'm not killing anything.

– Me neither.

– **Then go make a fucking fire.**

– How?

– **I don't know, do I? But what I do know is that if we don't find something to eat soon . . . we might have to do something drastic.**

– What does that mean?

– **Just don't die first is all I'm saying.**

The speaker exits. Most of them follow. A few remain.

Scene Nine: V

Some greens and reds remain. They try to make fire using sticks. They are not doing well.

– This is v hard.

– Why are we even doing this? It's just so people can eat the things they kill.

– It's v stupid.

– It's v bad.

– It's not just for food. We need to keep warm.

– I'd rather die of cold than starvation.

– I'd rather die of both than eat an animal.

– When did you become a vegan?

– Can't really remember. Ages ago.

– **I'm not a vegan. I'm a veggie.**

– Oh. Me too.

– That's almost worse you know.

– I know.

– **Worse than what?**

– Dairy is the worst of all. I'd rather eat meat than dairy.

– **I do eat meat sometimes.**

– So you're not a veggie then.

– **I'm trying. I know it's bad. Like how can it not be bad? Making animals fuck and fuck so they have kids that we can eat and making them pregnant so they make milk then taking the baby away and keeping them in big sheds and . . . it's not even close to not being bad but . . . I'm just . . .**

– Addicted.

– **Addicted?**

– You know it's bad but you can't stop, yeah? What else would you call it?

– **I suppose.**

– I'm actually a fruitarian now.

– **Fruitarian?**

– I only eat fruit that has naturally fallen from trees.

– **Oh.**

– I mean, vegans are cool.

– I'm trying so hard to be one. I am.

– But I got to thinking . . . how come a plant's worth less than a pig?

– **Because it can't think.**

– How do you know?

– **Seems obvious.**

– Animals, humans, plants. Why is there a hierarchy at all?

– **I think if the thing doesn't even know it's a thing then it's probably alright to eat it.**

– But how do you know what does and what doesn't know it's a thing?

– I don't think plants know they exist to be fair.

– So we can just eat my cousin then. He has the mental age of like a one-year-old so . . .

– I don't think we should eat the disabled.

– Exactly!

– Your cousin's disabled?

– Yeah. So?

– I don't know. Just rings a bell.

– Maybe we know each other.

– Maybe.

– **Isn't it like natural and shit. For us to eat meat. Like carnivores or whatever.**

– It's also natural for us to kill people from other tribes. Should we do that now?

– **I'd prefer you didn't.**

– I do miss bacon though.

– Yeah, me too.

– **It's nice.**

– Nom nom.

– **Nom nom.**

– You're both disgusting.

Scene Ten: Tea

*What seems like one week later. The tribes sit eating leaves and berries.
Some of them are being sick. Some of them are missing from the scene.*

– I don't know why they're bothering. Continuing to hunt.

– Makes them feel good.

– I think these berries are poisonous.

– Yeah, well, no one's died yet.

– Give it time. We've only been here two weeks.

– One week.

– Two.

– Twelve days I reckon.

– Did no one keep track?

– My calendar's on my phone.

– Fuck.

– How can there be no animals?

– It's like someone made this place.

– And kept animals off.

– They'll find something. Eventually.

– I'm going to make another swim for it.

– Are you kidding?

– You're half-dead.

– I'm fucking not.

– You'll drown.

– We're going to die, aren't we?

– No.

– No one's coming, are they?

– Someone will come.

– **No one is coming. And if we don't eat more than poisonous berries and plants we will die. That's just a fact.**

– **Real talk.**

– **I'm going for it.**

– No. Don't.

– **I'd rather drown than starve.**

– Please don't.

– **I'll send help.**

– You won't make it.

– **Well, then, my body will wash up on the shore and they'll send help anyway.**

Silence. The red leaves. No one has the energy to stop them. They all just sit there.

– Maybe they'll make it.

– Maybe we'll be saved.

– **It's a waste. Is what it is.**

– A waste of what?

– **Flesh.**

Silence. Then suddenly, a bloodcurdling scream from the trees startles everyone. A group of reds enter carrying a fallen green.

They dump them in the centre of the clearing.

– Are they . . . dead?

– **I don't think so.**

– There's a pulse.

– What happened?

– Spill the fucking tea!

– Spill the tea.

– **We were out hunting.**

– Hunting nothing.

– **And then I saw this by the foot of a tree.**

They pull out a knife.

– **And we looked up the tree and we saw . . .**

– **A green flag.**

– A green flag?

– **Yeah. I swear.**

– **So this one climbs up the tree. To get it. And two minutes later.**

– **Falls out the fucking tree.**

– **Lands hard.**

– **Broken back maybe.**

– Fuck.

They all look at the injured green.

– Why were they with you?

– **Maybe because they were hungry and realised we were their only hope.**

– **Is no one listening? I found a knife. There's someone else here! We need to find them. They might have food.**

– You probably had that knife on you the entire time.

– **Fucking greens, you guys never believe a word we say.**

– Coz you're fucking stupid. And here's the proof.

– **Don't say that while they can still hear you.**

– Not going to survive.

– **How do you know?**

– Shallow breathing.

– **Look, I'm going to have to say this because I know I'm not the only one thinking it. We're hungry, yeah? Starving. And there's no animals on the island.**

– We got some moss.

– And I think these berries might be alright.

– **Moss and possibly poisonous berries. Really?**

– What are you saying?

– **You know what I'm saying.**

He looks at the injured green.

– WTF.

– Seriously. WTF, man.

– That is seriously no chill, man.

– **I'm just saying. We're hungry. Why not?**

– You're saying we kill them?

– **No. I'm not. I'm saying we wait. And when they die . . .**

– **We have a knife now. We can cut . . .**

– Stop. Please. Just stop talking.

– **Why not? Can someone give me a good reason?**

– How about cannibalism is wrong!

– It's sick!

– **Yeah, maybe it's sick if we killed him but . . . it was an accident.**

– Was it?

– **What?**

– It just seems a little convenient that it's a green.

– Yeah. It does.

– **Convenient?**

– Yeah. You don't want to eat one of your own so . . .

– **It was an accident.**

– **It just happened.**

– How do we know that?

– **We're not animals.**

– Cannibalism is wrong.

– **Why? Don't just keep saying it. Tell me why.**

– Because . . .

– If you don't respect a corpse you can't respect a person.

– We're not eating one of our own.

– **Are you saying you'd do it if they were a red?**

– No. I'm just saying. We know them. We can't just . . . eat someone we know.

– *You* **don't have to.**

– **These are extreme circumstances.**

– **And extreme circumstances call for extreme measures.**

– **It's not our fault the branch snapped.**

– What?

– **It's not our fault.**

– You said they fell.

– **Yeah. Coz the branch snapped.**

– Why didn't you say that the first time?

– **Is it important?**

– You did do this, didn't you?

– **No. We didn't.**

– **You need to stop saying that.**

– Or what? You'll kill us too?

The two sides have squared up.

– **We didn't kill anyone!**

– **And so what if we did?**

– So what?

– **I'm saying, we didn't, but if we did . . . what difference does it make now?**

– What difference does it make? Killing someone?

– **We didn't.**

– I think you did.

– **This is stupid. We'll die if we don't.**

The red takes a step towards the fallen green. Another green gets in their way.

– No.

– This is not happening.

– **We're hungry.**

– **It makes sense.**

– It's not happening.

– **Yes it is.**

– Well you'll have to kill us too then.

– **Fine by me.**

The red tries to get to the fallen green. Another green grabs their arm. A small fight ensues, which ends with the red with the knife brandishing it at a green's neck.

At this point, from the trees stumbles a slightly older person wearing a tatty yellow T-shirt. They look close to death. They wander into the camp and stand in front of the startled teens, who instinctively surround them. At the same time the injured green regains consciousness.

– Were you guys talking about eating me? Because that's so no chill.

Scene Eleven: Finstagram

Some reds are interrogating the yellow. Some greens have gathered down front.

– **What's your name?**

– **Are you Eilean?**

– **Why are you here?**

– **Why are you wearing yellow?**

– **Is there another team?**

The yellow says nothing, just holds their head. They give up for now.

– I couldn't have done it. Could you?

– I don't know.

– I mean, it's just . . . wrong.

– I am hungry.

– Starving.

– Yeah.

– I want to live.

– Me too.

– And I really think these berries are poisonous. So . . .

– We need to get that yellow talking.

– We'll be fine. It's all g.

– It's not all g. I wish people would stop saying that. Nothing is all g. We're born against our will, we struggle, then we die against our will. What part of that is all fucking g?

– Wish I could insta this.

– Insta?

– Instagram.

– Oh yeah. Insta. I don't think I'm on it.

– For reals?

– For reals.

– This is cray-cray, I'd get so many likes. Stranded on an island. Hashtag unique.

– What do you do, like, take pictures and people, like, like them?

– Chuh.

– And that's it?

– Chuh. But I also have a finstagram.

– Finstagram? What's that?

– It's like a fake instagram where you can be your real self and not worry about likes or whatever.

– A fake instagram. Where you can be real?

– Chuh.

Above them, the noise of a plane.

– **What's that?**

– It's a fucking plane!

– **It is. It's a plane.**

– **Hey!**

– Hey!

– Down here!

They all come forward and start to yell and shout and wave their arms about. But the plane flies over and disappears.

– **That looked like . . .**

– <u>Military.</u>

The yellow has finally spoken. They all turn to look at them.

– **What do you know about it?**

– <u>I don't . . . My memory is . . .</u>

– **How old are you?**

– <u>Like, twenty-two?</u>

– **No way. Older.**

– **Lying.**

– **Definitely lying.**

– <u>I'm not lying.</u>

– **Why are you here?**

– <u>I don't know.</u>

– **What did you do to us?**

– **Why can't we remember anything?**

– **Is this your knife?**

– <u>I don't know!</u>

– **You're older than us. You have a knife. You know what's going on here. I know you do.**

– **We should tie them up.**

– What? We can't do that.

– For our safety.

– For the safety of the group.

– What group?

– The reds and the greens.

– Exactly.

– We need to come together.

– We do.

– Yeah.

– Real talk.

– I can get on that.

– <u>Look. I woke up three months ago with no memory of how I got here. I don't know anything about this place.</u>

– Wait. What did you say? Three months ago?

– <u>Yes. Why? How long have you been here?</u>

One of the greens has found a piece of paper on the ground.

– What's this?

– <u>What?</u>

– It must have fallen out your pocket.

– <u>I don't know what that is.</u>

The green opens it and reads.

– WTF.

– What is it?

– It's a list. Of names.

– A list of our names?

– Probably. Yes. There's mine there I think.

– That's mine.

– And mine.

– That's your name?

– I think so. Why?

– Nothing. I just . . . Do we know each other?

– I don't think so.

– Look. They're separated into green and red.

– They're one of them.

– Who?

– I don't know. But they're certainly not one of us.

Scene Twelve: Savage

The group addresses the audience.

– <u>Did you know that when you meet someone new your brain asks three questions?</u>

– On its own.

– <u>Without you even knowing about it.</u>

– Real talk.

– <u>It asks . . .</u>

– Can I kill it?

– (Is there a threat?)

– Can I smash it?

– (Is there a chance to procreate?)

– Can I munch it?

– (Is there a chance to sustain myself?)

– Nom, nom, nom.

– Kill.

– Smash.

– Munch.

– <u>The creatures whose brains did not ask these three instinctive questions.</u>

– **Were not around long enough to pass on their DNA.**

– Savage.

– **What we did. We did to survive.**

– How were we to know what the real cause of our situation was?

– **I mean, we had no idea.**

– **The whole thing was cray-cray.**

Scene Thirteen: Fail

The person in yellow is now tied up. A lot of the group are lying around the space, too weak to move. Some reds and greens are having a conference.

One green is down front, still frantically trying to make fire.

– **Here are the facts. One. They were here before us.**

– **So they know more than we do about this.**

– Probs.

– **Two. They had a list of our names.**

– So they knew we were coming here.

– **Totes.**

– **Three. The list was separated into green and red.**

– So they know why we're here.

– Defs.

– **We need to act.**

– Act how?

– We've already tied them up.

– What more can we do?

– **Do you know the reason we put people in prison?**

– Why?

– **Because we can.**

– What do you mean?

– **We used to just . . . you know in the caveman days . . . if someone threatened a community they would . . . we would just . . .**

– But now we have the money to be ethical.

– **Exactly. But we don't.**

– I'm starting to think these groups aren't split on intelligence.

– **Well, duh.**

– It's random.

– Some experiment.

– **Some cruel experiment to see how we react.**

– Probably satellites recording us from space.

– **For some TV show.**

– On the dark web.

– **For billionaires.**

– **Oily garks!**

– So what are you saying we do?

– **It's simple as far as I see it. We're about to starve to death. Some of them are already practically dead. This yellow one is a danger to us, probably one of the ones who did it to us in the first place. We don't have a prison . . . So . . .**

– Two birds.

– **One stone.**

– **We need to be together on this.**

– How can we be?

– **We vote.**

– On killing . . .

– **And eating . . .**

– **Or we can just die.**

– I'm just glad it's not me anymore.

– This is not right.

– Hey. At least we don't know them.

– So. Put up your hand if you think we should . . . under these very extreme circumstances . . . bearing in mind it's no one's first choice . . . in order to stay alive . . . to survive . . . we should . . . kill and . . . eat this . . . body.

– Person.

– We can't vote with our hands.

– Why not?

– It has to be blind.

– Coz you're ashamed to do it in the open.

– It should be blind. That's how they do general elections. And shit.

– Real talk.

– We should put lots into a hat and draw them so no one feels . . .

– Compelled.

– One way or the other.

– Anyone got a hat?

– Anyone got paper?

– We can use long and short twigs. Long ones mean we do it. Short ones mean we don't. We'll put them in the middle there.

– Fine. Let's get it over with.

– Are we really doing this?

– It's democracy. What harm can it do?

– And what if we don't get rescued? What happens when we've . . . finished him? What do we do then? Who do we kill next?

– We'll deal with that when we get there. Today . . . we live.

The green down front suddenly lets out a yell.

– Hey! Yes! I did it! I fucking did it! I made fire!

The greens and reds look at each other. Look at the yellow.

– Okay. Let's vote.

Scene Fourteen: Goals

The group face the audience.

– **There is a secret military base . . .**

– Well, not so secret now . . .

– **Near Loch Maree, in Wester Ross.**

– Scotland.

– **And on this base . . .**

– So the story goes . . .

– **Military scientists develop compounds.**

– Which obviously will never be used.

– **Unless in an emergency.**

– Unless they really need to.

– **Unless they have no option.**

– The goal . . .

– **Hashtag life goals.**

– Is to develop a weapon that debilitates the enemy without killing them.

– **Because, despite what people might say, the West has morals.**

– Yeah, right.

– **Ethics.**

– Totes.

– Yeah. Right.

– **And we don't want to kill people if we don't have to.**

– **Real talk.**

– Fake news!

– We're the worst.

– **We don't deliberately target civilians.**

– Is that true though?

– **Yes. It fucking is.**

– **We don't drop nerve gas on civilians.**

– **We don't.**

– **We are better than some other nations.**

– No, we're not. We're the worst.

– Yeah. We're the worst.

– Just as bad as any of them.

– **As bad as Saudi Arabia?**

– Well . . .

– **As bad as ISIS?**

– Well . . . No. I guess not.

– **So don't exaggerate then.**

– **We're not perfect.**

– **But we're not the worst.**

– **And it's okay to say that out loud.**

– **Despite what people might tell you.**

– But the problem is . . .

– **These weapons still need to be tested.**

– Otherwise . . .

– **How will they know they don't kill people?**

– And rats are not people.

– **So they have to be tested on people.**

– To make sure they don't do anything too bad.

– **And so . . .**

– Rumour has it . . .

– **That this military base sent a plane to drop this particular compound on an area of Wester Ross.**

– Which is famous for its midges.

– You know, like, the little bloodsucking insects.

– **Whose instinct drives them to bite us.**

– They don't know they're being total dicks.

– They don't know they're ruining our picnics.

– So go easy on them.

– FFS.

– For fuck's sake.

– The compound was designed to do one simple thing.

– Genius really.

– Considering human instinct.

– Animal instinct.

– Same difference.

– It was designed to make people unable to keep track of time.

– To make them think it was passing faster than it was.

– Which would make them understandably anxious.

– Panicky.

– Because human beings need to know what time it is.

– And how long they have left.

– Before they die.

– So they can fix things quick.

– The military released the gas over the area and then monitored the few inhabitants.

– And everyone was safe.

– Confused.

– But safe.

– However, as an unexpected side effect, the military found that the inhabitants' short-term memories were severely compromised.

– Most of them didn't even recognise their immediate family.

– But in a few days the effects wore off and no one was any the wiser.

– And the test was declared a success.

– A secret success.

– But what the military did not know was that a school group from [INSERT].

(Author's note: it is up to you to decide where your group is from.)

– Were on a little island called . . .

– Eilean Sùbhainn.

– Which is, like, Scottish for . . .

– Island of berries.

– **Their teacher . . .**

– <u>Mr/Mrs Johnstone.</u>

– Was a wilderness nut. And he wanted to show the kids they could survive without their phones for a few days.

– **This school group . . .**

– <u>And their teacher . . .</u>

– **Exposed to the effects of the compound . . .**

– Went a little mad.

– **Totes.**

– Savage.

– **Their teacher had separated them into teams.**

– <u>They were going to play capture the flag.</u>

– And had gone to scope out the island.

– **When the cloud of gas was released.**

– The school group were on the island for . . .

– **Three days . . .**

– Total.

– **And when the dead body of one of their number.**

– Was caught in a fisherman's net.

– **The alarm was raised . . .**

– Help arrived.

– **And the school kids were found . . .**

– <u>Eating their leader.</u>

– **None of us choose to be born.**

– We just woke up and we were here.

– **None of us choose to die.**

– One day we'll just go to sleep and disappear.

– **None of us choose to survive.**

– It's just . . .

– **There.**

– It's inside us.

– **It's animal.**

– Tribal.

– **Savage.**

– But the good thing about us . . .

– **About humans . . .**

– Is that we can try to be better.

– **Totes.**

– Life goals.

– **Win.**

– We can try to ignore that instinct.

– **That desire to fix things now.**

– To think only of today.

– **Because we're not going to fix this planet.**

– Ever.

– **Ever.**

– Until we admit.

– **It's not the planet we're trying to save.**

– It's us.

– **The planet just happens to be where we live.**

– It can't be saved now.

– We can't be saved now.

– We have to stop thinking about now.

– Impossible

– No. We can do it.

– If we work together.

– Listen to each other.

– I mean, really listen.

– And think about things in a different way.

– We can do it.

– We're different.

– We're better than animals.

– We're special.

– Right?

They all look at each other. And then at the audience.

Flesh

BY ROB DRUMMOND

*Notes on rehearsal and staging, drawn from two workshops with the
writer, held at the National Theatre, October 2018*

How Rob came to write the play

'As a writer you ask a question of yourself and your audience, and for
Flesh, that question was: "What's wrong with cannibalism?"

I'm interested in how we often accept things, behaviours, codes of
conduct, without necessarily really interrogating them. I'm aware that this
is a controversial and crazy question, and in my first draft this idea was
illustrated to quite an extreme point, but in the drafting process I realised
that it's not for me, it's for you and your companies. In the re-drafting
process I've tried to write something that the performers will love and that
you as directors will make your own.

The play is about an extreme situation and trying to find the humanity
within it. The genre of horror (particularly given where the first draft was!)
still echoes through this draft. In a previous draft the characters got closer
to investigating cannibalism. I just thought that actually if you had no
other choice, there was something interesting in how you'd broach the
subject. Like, ear lobes. A perfect starter. Snip it off and fry it with a bit of
butter! We are addicted to eating meat and I say that in the full knowledge
of the ethical dilemma within that. Those tribal identities of what food we
choose to eat or eliminate also become a battleground – and we can
become very defensive over it.

When writing this, there are certainly some apparent references – *Lord
of the Flies* and the TV show *Lost* for example. The medical research is
based on truth, but slightly altered to make the medical research fit the plot
of the play – in essence, as a writer I'm lying to tell a bigger truth. For
example, the research referred to about the mice on pages 205–6 – the
mice weren't in fact painted different colours, but they were separated and
subsequently split into two different tribes.

In a world where bad people are in charge, somehow chemical gas and
chemical warfare, as slightly more abstract concepts, feel less of a direct
threat. There are experiments that are like this, therefore it's plausible that
it could have happened.'

Rob Drummond, 2018

Approaching the play

LANGUAGE AND SWEARING

The language is deliberately modern, with strong contemporary references, over the top and deliberate, and Rob wrote it knowing that – it is a pastiche.

However, each character needs to take it seriously – if the character thinks it's a funny line it dies, so the text should be spoken entirely in earnest.

With regard to questions around lines like 'don't throw shade at me' – young people don't speak like this, but these characters do speak like this, and that's an exciting acting challenge. The characters have a distinct language of their own, and this language is consistent through the play.

Rob hasn't included pauses or beats or silences intentionally. There is a rhythm and pace to the language, which you will need to pay attention to in your rehearsals.

Regarding the swearing, Rob doesn't mind this being cut if your context stops you from using the swear words. However, there's a resonance and rhythm in the lines, so it's about finding the desire behind it, and the way to deliver the intention of the line without swearing.

PHONES

The group's phones are definitely missing – they've been taken by the teacher.

COLOURS

Rob chose the colours (red, green, and later on yellow) because for him they felt apolitical (though some members of the workshop group questioned this) – as well as being colours at the opposite end of the colour spectrum. Unless these choices of colours offer local problematic challenges, then they feel like the appropriate choices.

LOCATION

The island is a real place in Wester Ross, Scotland, called Eilean Sùbhainn. When Rob was writing the play, he saw a clearing with trees. It feels a little like a no man's land/nowhere island. It is a place that exists now. It's an allegorical and metaphorical island, but it feels current – the references are to now and recent events.

STYLE

They all have residual memory – they haven't forgotten how to speak – and Rob has written from a perspective of what he describes as intrinsic science. What happens at the end of the play is reported to us – we (the audience) are hearing about it more than seeing it, and it feels like that's a powerful way to deliver the final moments.

Everything is significant in the text – the question for directors making the play is to explore 'Is it significant?' and 'How is it significant?' We separate ourselves into tribes all the time – whether that's through religion and politics, or other matters.

With regards to the alternating ways that the characters speak to us, or to each other, which swap from fourth wall to direct address, there are a series of choices that you can make around how you treat this. Can characters change, or is it consistently the teenagers? They could become more like scientists or narrators with knowledge when they speak directly to the audience. It's intriguing for you to explore *when* they are, and to play around to see what sits best. See what happens when you carry these moments into the next scene – and what's the effect emotionally?

Scene Four, 'OTP' (pp. 196–7), offers us a different rhythm and tone – it's like a series of cutaways or mini-stories, and hopefully offers a mixture of what the groups would enjoy doing. Rob has written that scene with this in mind, so it's not just purely an artistic choice.

CASTING

The play is written gender neutral to make it easier to cast. Rob is happy for you to change pronouns from they/them to she/he if it makes sense to the group. This play can be made with any number of cast – and that is flexible. Part of the gift of the creative process and rehearsals is to enjoy finding the characters within this.

With regards to the age of the characters, Rob has written it so that so that the age groups of the performers can be varied, but the characters are all the same age with the exception of the adult.

Exercises

Lead directors Orla O'Loughlin and Tessa Walker invited the group to carry out the following exercises. *(The italics show the lead directors' responses to the group's discussions.)*

LANGUAGE AND CHARACTER

In different-sized groups – a mixture of three, fives and sevens – the group looked at Scene Ten, from p. 213 to p. 218. They were invited to read the text and decide how they would allocate lines.

The group then came together to hear it read it read aloud, and discussed the findings, which included:

- They noted that when dividing the lines up there's a clear leader of reds, and a clear leader of greens, the swimmer and the yellow, so there are already some anchors to work off.
- You could make some characters important and follow their journey through the play.

Letting the audience get to know the characters and building sympathy with them is helpful. For example, if you return to the story of the green and red in their duologue scene, how do you tell the story of those characters and hold onto them a few scenes down the line? When you start to carve the textual journeys of characters, don't let them establish and not change – that's not an interesting choice. It's when the characters behave or say something that we never expected them to. If there's very little chance then there's very little drama. It can be exciting for your actors too in finding the shifts from being a leader to a follower, and I'd encourage you to be bold with these choices. Sometimes you can be radical and then make that work.

- If a character hadn't spoken in the scene and then ended being the highest status then that's interesting.
- It feels dynamic, dramatic – for someone not to speak and then say something, it can be revelatory.
- Hold onto the internal journey.
- In a big ensemble piece, hold onto the revelation that actors don't have to be speaking to be acting.

There should be a number of people on stage doing stuff, that doesn't mean that they should be always saying stuff. In this particular extract, we actually start to know more, and the characters reveal more in this scene to play with than the first establishing scenes. You're wanting to discover and illuminate the turning point in every scene, to ensure that something changes. The risk is that people just say lines, and it's our job as directors to lead the company through discovering where the turning points are. It's the same questions as for a naturalistic play – ultimately it's down to identifying where change happens and to whom.

EXERCISE: SCENE ELEVEN

In the same groups – a mixture of three, fives and sevens – they looked at Scene Eleven.

Again, they read the text and decided how to allocate lines.

The group then came together to hear it read it aloud, and discussed the findings, which included:

- One approach was to have four greens and three reds, to just start and see what happens.
- One group discovered panicky/definitive opposites within the text to inform characters.
- The three-hander version worked well and offered a different dynamic.
- It was interesting having people being in opposition and slightly jittery – with a smaller cast you can really tell the story of individuals.
- The choices that were unexpected were good, because humans are random, so it felt truthful to the situation.

EXERCISE: SCENE ELEVEN – CHARACTERISING THE LINES

Groups read the scene again and kept the line allocations that they had chosen.

They were invited to really characterise those lines – to think about who the person is, what they are feeling, what their name is.

The group then came together to hear it read out loud, and discussed the findings, which included:

- Some people had difficulty naming the characters, which opened a wider conversation about class and stereotypes and how to avoid this.

You could take a name book into rehearsals with you. Naming characters should free people up rather than restrict them.

- It was surprising how long you could let the lines run on for without swapping between multiple characters.
- It read naturally and sounded really genuine.
- Discoveries included finding the role of a peacemaker, and exploring characteristics that are in contradiction with each other.
- One group settled on three clear things that they all wanted: to do something, to eat something, to keep the peace.

Think about objectives: What is it that people want from the scene? What is it that people want from the play? An objective is a thing you want to get, or to do. Objectives are a particularly helpful way to approach the text and the characters if you get stuck.

EXERCISE: UNITS AND OBJECTIVES

With the same scene, the groups were asked to read through the text and put it into beats, or units, of action. A unit is sustained action that keeps going until something changes. It can be a group of lines doing the same thing. They were asked to be specific.

When approaching rehearsals, this can be a good preparation exercise in order to maximise your time in the rehearsal room. Thinking about each moment is a way of making it bite-sized and more manageable. This detailed preparation can also mean that you're not simply rushing through the play scene by scene without the appropriate level of detail within each scene.

When the action changes or the subject changes, then the unit changes. How many different combinations of conversations are there? Keep a tight hold with your actors on who they're directing the line to – these choices will present new things in the room. This process will give you clear indications of links, bonds and ultimately relationships between the characters.

Units can be dictated by a change of objective. In my process I would unit before I do line allocation, but you might have a different approach. The way you choose to work through the text will have a different impact on the way you define your production and the way the story is told. It's all just choices, but this work is what helps the choices to be detailed.

EXERCISE: ASSIGNING INTENTIONS

The groups were asked to take ten lines of the same extract of text and give each line an intention, then write the word/intention they have chosen before the line.

An intention is what you are doing in that moment – or what you're doing with that line. It is not about what you're feeling or what you want to do. It's about what you're doing – use active verbs, e.g. protesting, comforting, sympathising. By working through the lines like this it helps to make the work front-footed. Intentions are all about what people are doing to other people.

If you get to a place in rehearsals where you want an actor to do something, and perhaps you're not explaining yourself very clearly, using intentions can help to move the rehearsal along. If the actors don't know, the audience won't know. If your actors have no idea what you're saying, then we won't, so ensure that every line is doing something active. Remember that you start by making a choice, but you can always change your mind and try something else.

EXERCISE: INTENTIONS ON THEIR FEET

Groups read this text out loud, first reading out the intention, then reading the line directly to the audience. Second, they read the line itself, directly to the character they were saying it to.

They then repeated the exercise, but took away the first instruction (i.e. don't read the intention, just play the intention).

It is interesting to take lines that look like they have an intention to help – 'these berries look poisonous' – and subvert them. In rehearsals it's always a balance of whose choice is what – director or actor? I'd say that it's a bit of both – play around and enjoy finding the discoveries. Whatever your method for assigning text, whether that's on your own, as a whole company or letting the actors do it completely for themselves, be bold with your methodology and stick to it.

EXERCISE: LANGUAGE AND PEACOCKING

Groups were invited to take pp. 187–189 and read through them, and to pay particular attention to the style of the text, to what Rob refers to as the 'youth speak'!

The group then came together to discuss the findings, which included:

- Language – with phrases like 'WTF' say the language exactly as written (rather than 'what the fuck').
- A group commented that it's harder to do this exercise if you haven't assigned the lines first.
- One group spent a lot of time decoding the 'youth speak', and then they found it quite clear.
- When speaking directly to the audience there was a fundamental change.
- Using modern language/slang/abbreviations doesn't limit a person's intelligence – they're not mutually exclusive.
- The style of language can be compared to the rhythms and poetic nature of Shakespeare – people don't talk like that but it's our job to make it sound normal.
- The text is stylised, it's not realism.

If actors are finding it hard to make 'sense' of the line and using it, then it could be helpful to consider the subtext. For example, what is it a character thinks they want to say and what do they actually say? It's really about expression rather than the line.

EXERCISE: TWO TRIBES

Part A

All the company stood in the space with their eyes closed. Orla and Tessa put either a green or a red sticker on each member of the company.

This exercise explores the meeting of two groups – focusing on the two groups just seeing each other for the first time. Everyone opened their eyes and, using no words, established and settled on an image that reflected the two groups really seeing each other.

The group observed that within each tribe there are character dynamics and hierarchies. That's what you have to work out as a company and how to identify individual roles in each tribe.

Someone spoke about how it felt like being a football fan and attending a football match in your team colours. You tend to orientate towards people wearing the same colour without speaking or knowing each other.

The group was then split so half observed and half participated in exploring the space in their tribes. One yellow sticker was given to an observer and they were asked to enter the space to see how the tribes responded to them.

The group then discussed the exercise and how the entrance of a yellow changed the dynamic of the groups and space. This raised questions about ethics and if we are hard wired to remain in our own tribes. Personal space also felt significant.

Part B: Collaborator/suspicious

This time half of the green group and half of the red group sat and watched.

The rest of the company played the game again – this time with a new task. In the other group, find your opposite: who is your collaborator, and who are you suspicious of?

Discoveries:

- It was not as binary as being friends and enemies.
- There was a different focus, working out what others were thinking, echoing other people in their group.

- With memory loss high in their thinking, one person's intention was to find others and work out how to communicate, but it was received as aggressive and confrontational.

You can make substantial discoveries in the power of watching people truthfully watching the other people, but this isn't just about group dynamics and navigating the space. If you are working with large ensembles, you'll have a number of young people to navigate around the space, and this exercise might throw up some ways in which you can do that.

Part C: Strongest and weakest

The groups swapped over so that the reds and greens who were previously watching played the game, and were observed by the other half of the group.

The rest of the company played the game again – this time with another new task:

- Who are the survivors?
- Who are the strongest and weakest in the other group and how are you going to work that out?

Discoveries:

- Instinct took over. There was status in just sitting down and lying down – thwarting the rest, it was very powerful. However, the person who decided to sit was actually trying to say, 'Come sit with me, it's peaceful and safe here'.

You could choose to stage the scene from the culmination of this picture. You could also use this exercise as an audition exercise. From simple discoveries come complex pictures and relationships.

EXERCISE: FIVE PICTURES

The company split into two groups of seven, and two groups of eight with a mixture of green and red within them. The task was to collectively build five conceptual images that showed the change in the group dynamic of the play. Within the images they also took into consideration:

- How hungry they were
- How thirsty they were
- How sleep deprived they were

EXERCISE: TRANSITIONS

The whole company split into three groups, and were given three different sections of text to investigate:

Pages 187–189

Pages 191–192

Pages 230–232

Each group was then designated a director and given twenty minutes to work out the allocation of text, and the transition between one scene to the other.

Here are three key observations, one from each group:

- Starting on the floor, the scene seemed to arise from each performer through a seamless movement fluid from one scene to another, almost an overlap and no join.

- Starting in the audience and talking directly to them was a strong way to start. The actors then made their way to the performance area with a long slow hum – it was primal, minimal and effective.

- The actor playing the yellow in Scene Thirteen, tied up and on the floor, stood up whilst everyone else remained and walked towards the audience, using the first line of Scene Fourteen. This was a surprising and neat way to move from one to the other and to give an emotional punch.

Closing thoughts

A conversation took place about location, which offers companies the chance to enjoy the exercise of mapping out the location and to ask questions:

- When actors are not on stage, where are they?
- When is the play happening?

The key thing to hold on to is that, as directors, you're doing your version of this play and you've made a choice to do this text, so where possible the opportunity is to find your production within the parameters of the text. When rehearsing the play, even within short and challenging timescales, you should aim to rehearse chronologically as this is how the audience receives the play and it can help your company to hold onto the narrative a little better. It's harder to navigate if you do it out of order. In chronological order you can build the narrative – it lends itself to be rehearsed in this way so that the time and impact of events follow the narrative through line.

Enjoy the journey of putting this play together and have fun seeing the play through the variety of lenses that the text offers you, from the psychology of groups, to survival, and the impact of lack of sleep and lack of food on the choices we make. We're supposedly only two meals away from anarchy, so enjoy investigating the impact of these given circumstances.

Suggested references, reading or viewing

Lord of the Flies by William Golding

Lost TV series

Sapiens by Yuval Noah Harari

Why We Sleep by Matthew Walker

The Circadian Rhythm by Dr Satchin Panda

The Island by Bear Grylls

From workshops led by Tessa Walker and Orla O'Loughlin
with notes by Louie Ingham and Laura Keefe

Variations

by Katie Hims

Thirteen-year-old Alice wishes her life was completely different. Then one morning she wakes up and it is. Alice is taken through a series of parallel universes, reliving the same ten minutes over and over again. Maybe different isn't all it's cracked up to be, but once you've started on a path can you go back to normality? A play about family, string theory and breakfast.

Cast size
13

At the time of publication Katie Hims is on attachment to the National Theatre Studio. Previous stage work includes *Billy the Girl* for Clean Break at Soho Theatre. Since 2014 she has worked on the radio series *Home Front*, including three seasons as lead writer. Other radio work includes: *Poetry in Motion*, *Black Dog*, *King David*, *Lost Property* (winner of the BBC Audio Drama Award for Best Original Drama), *The Gunshot Wedding* (winner of the Writers' Guild Best Original Radio Drama) and *The Earthquake Girl* (winner of the Richard Imison Award). Her recent radio adaptations were *The Hot Kid* by Elmore Leonard and *The Martin Beck Killings* by Maj Sjowall and Per Wahloo. She has also written for the long-running television series *Casualty*.

Characters

Alice, *thirteen*
Dan, *sixteen (Alice's brother)*
Lucas, *fourteen (Alice's brother)*
Cinnamon, *thirteen (Alice's friend)*
Chloe, *thirteen (Alice's frenemy)*
Postman, *sixteen*
Jasmine, *seventeen (Alice's sister)*
Pearl, *fifteen (Alice's sister)*
Pablo, *thirteen (Alice/Joe's friend)*
Shelly, *thirteen (Alice as her mother)*
Dean, *fifteen (Shelly's brother)*
Bex, *seventeen (Shelly's sister)*
Joe, *thirteen (Alice as a boy)*

Scene One

2018. The kitchen is stacked high with dirty cups, plates and saucepans.
Dan *is eating cereal.* **Lucas** *is holding a laminated piece of A4 card.*
Alice *comes into the kitchen, doesn't speak to her brothers and starts looking for some breakfast. All three of them are in school uniform.*

Lucas   Do you know what colour you are?

Dan   No.

Lucas   You're the colour blue.

Dan *doesn't respond.*

Lucas   You're the colour blue.

Dan   Okay.

Lucas   And look what colour it is.

Dan   I can't believe you've actually laminated that thing.

Lucas   It's blue.

Dan   Stop waving it in my face.

Lucas   That's you.

Dan   Alright!

Alice *switches on the radio. It's an eighties song. Take your pick from 1980/81/82/83.*

Dan   Alice.

Alice   What?

Dan   Can you turn that shit off.

Alice   I like this shit.

Dan   Well, I don't.

Alice   Well, I do.

Dan *gets up and switches it off.*

Dan   It makes me feel like killing myself.

Alice   All the more reason to keep it on.

She switches it back on. **Dan** *switches it off again.*

Alice   Dan!

She switches it on.

Dan *switches it off.*

Alice   Mum! Mum! (*Calling for their mum to adjudicate.*)

Lucas   She's not here.

Alice   Where's she gone?

Lucas   Work.

Alice   Already?

Lucas   Yes.

Alice   Well, where's my phone?

Dan   How should I know?

Alice   Did she take it with her?

Lucas   How should we know?

Alice   She wouldn't. She wouldn't take it with her. Would she?

Lucas *shrugs.*

Alice   Did she say anything before she left?

Lucas   She wrote us a note.

He reads the note.

'If you don't sort the kitchen out before I come home I will kick you all out and you can go and live with your feckless – (*hesitates*)

Dan   – bastard –

Alice   Does it actually say bastard?

Lucas   – yeh – feckless –

Dan   – bastard –

Lucas   – of a father – I think she's given up trying not to criticise him –

Dan   Do you reckon?

Lucas   – and his twenty-seven-year-old Aussie witch of a girlfriend – and their new baby. I mean it. (*More emphasis.*) I MEAN IT.'

Alice   Wow.

Lucas   Yeh.

Dan   She doesn't. She doesn't mean it.

Lucas   Second time is in capitals.

Alice   They've got their scan today.

Lucas   What?

Alice   Dad and Lilia.

Lucas   Oh.

Alice   So they'll find out. What they're having.

Dan   Great.

Alice   I dreamed last night that they had a girl.

Dan   Was it ugly?

Alice   No she was lovely. She'd just been born and I held her in my arms.

Lucas   Was she covered in blood?

Alice   No.

Lucas   That's not very realistic.

Dan   That's cos it was a dream.

Alice   I held her in my arms and she smiled at me.

Lucas   Babies don't smile till they're six weeks.

Dan   It was a dream, you doughnut.

Alice   Do you think they're having a boy or a girl?

Dan   I literally couldn't give a shit.

Alice *looks in the breadbin/cupboard.*

Alice   Have you two eaten all the chocolate croissants?

Lucas   Otherwise known as pains au chocolat.

Alice   Have you?

Dan   Probably.

Lucas   I only had one.

Alice (*to* **Dan**)   How many did you have?

Dan   Dunno. Three?

Alice   Three? Three chocolate croissants?

Lucas   I prefer pains au chocolat.

Alice   You're so selfish –

Lucas   – although they look at you a bit weird when you say it with a French accent.

Dan   That's because you say the whole sentence in French.

Lucas   *Je voudrais un pain au chocolat.*

Alice *looks in the fridge, takes out an empty bottle.*

Alice   There's no milk. (*To* **Dan**.) Did you use all the milk too?

Dan   Yep.

Alice   You don't care about anyone do you.

Lucas   Your friend is quite a mercenary. I wonder if he cares about anything or anyone.

Dan   What are you babbling about?

Alice   It's from *Star Wars*.

Dan   I know it's from *Star Wars*.

Alice   There is nothing to eat. There is literally nothing to eat.

Lucas   Actually that's not true.

He goes to the cupboards.

There's pasta and flour and golden syrup and glacé cherries and lentils and –

Alice   But I don't want to eat pasta and golden syrup for breakfast do I?

Lucas   No – course not – that's not the point – the point is that you should have said figuratively not literally. People get it wrong all the time. And it's not a modern phenomenon. I expect you think it is – most people do – but it isn't. It's actually been going on for about five hundred years.

Dan   Lucas, can you shut up.

Lucas   But people need to know.

Dan   I don't need to know. I mean I – literally – couldn't give a shit.

Lucas   Why do you have to swear?

Dan   The whole world swears – except you –

Lucas   Nuns don't.

Dan   I'm sure some of them do.

Lucas   Priests don't.

Dan   I'm sure they do. I would. If I was a priest.

Lucas   Then you wouldn't be a very good priest.

Dan   No. I wouldn't.

Alice   Auntie Bex swears. Auntie Bex swears like a trooper.

Dan   What's that got to do with anything?

Alice   Well, she was a nun wasn't she?

Dan   No she wasn't.

Alice   She was. She was.

Dan   How long for?

Alice   I dunno. But like years.

Dan (*to* **Lucas**)   Well, there you go.

Lucas   What?

Dan   Nuns do swear.

Alice   That was my point.

Lucas   But she's an ex-nun. Ex-nuns don't count.

He picks up the note and looks at it again.

Is no one else worried she's going to kick us out?

Dan   No. Because she's not.

Alice   What's that?

Lucas   What's what?

Alice   On the other side!

Lucas   Oh oh . . .

He turns the note over, nods slowly, frustratingly . . .

Alice   What does it say?

Lucas   'PS Alice, I have taken your phone.'

Alice   Shit!

Lucas   You can have it back when you apologise.

Dan   Apologise for what?

Lucas   What did you do?

Alice   Nothing.

Dan   Ha.

Alice   I didn't. I didn't do anything.

Lucas   You must have done something.

Alice   I can't believe she's taken my phone.

Dan   You must have pissed her right off.

Alice   It's like. It's like taking someone's life. It's like she's taken my life.

Dan   Drama queen.

Lucas   People used to live without phones you know.

Alice *rolls her eyes at* **Lucas**.

Lucas   People used to use phone boxes.

Dan   Phone boxes smell of piss.

The landline phone rings.

Dan   That's weird.

Alice   Yeh.

Lucas   I sort of forget it exists.

Dan   Me too.

Lucas *goes to answer it.*

Alice   Don't answer it!

Lucas   Why?

Alice   It might be Cinnamon.

The answer machine kicks in.

Mum's Voice   You're through to Shelly, Dan, Lucas and Alice. We can't take your call right now but please leave us a message and we'll get back to you.

Cinnamon *on the answering machine.*

Cinnamon   Alice, it's Cinnamon.

Alice   See.

Cinnamon   Are you there? Alice are you there?

Lucas   Aren't you going to pick up the phone?

Cinnamon   I tried ringing your mobile but you didn't answer. I tried you a couple of times. Cos you said we might walk to school together but I don't know if . . . I'll just try you again. I'll try you one more time. Okay. Okay. Hope you're okay. Bye.

She hangs up.

Lucas   Why don't you want to speak to her?

Alice *shrugs.*

Alice   Cos we're not really friends anymore.

Lucas   So why's she ringing you?

Alice *shrugs.*

Alice   I mean we are friends sort of. Her and Chloe don't really – get on.

Dan   That's cos Chloe is a bitch.

Alice   She's not a bitch.

Dan   She looks like a bitch.

Alice   That's a very misogynistic thing to say.

Lucas   How do you spell misogynistic?

Alice   I don't know.

Lucas   You should know that. As a feminist.

The doorbell rings.

Alice   That'll be her.

Lucas   Who?

Alice   Chloe.

Alice *answers the door.*

Chloe   What have you done to your eyebrows?

Alice   Nothing.

Chloe   They look funny.

Alice   Do they?

Chloe   Like you've over-plucked them.

Alice   I haven't touched them.

Chloe   Well, maybe you've under-plucked them then. You ready?

Alice   Erm. No, sorry. Erm.

Chloe   Can I come in then?

Alice   Er yeh sorry yeh come in.

Chloe *follows* **Alice** *into the kitchen.*

Chloe   Hi, Dan.

Dan *does not look up.*

Dan   Hi, Chloe.

Chloe *looks round.*

Chloe   This kitchen is disgusting. Did you ask her?

Alice   Ask who what?

Chloe   Did you ask your mum?

Alice   Er no cos erm she had to leave really early this morning so.

Chloe   Ring her. Ring her now.

Alice   I really don't think she's going to say yes.

Chloe   Don't tell her that you're going to a party! Just say you're staying at mine.

Alice   But she can't answer her phone while she's on a shift.

Chloe   Leave her a message. She can text you in her break.

Alice   Erm. She can't text me cos she's taken my phone.

Chloe   She took your phone?

Alice   Yeh.

Chloe   She took your phone?

Alice   Yeh.

She starts packing her school bag, looking for something.

Chloe   I would never ever let my mum take my phone.

Alice   Well I didn't *let* her.

Chloe   I mean that's like that's like taking someone's *life*.

Alice   I *know*.

*She picks up her pencil case to pack it. The pencil case is open and all the pencils fall out. At the same time she knocks a mug of cold tea over and it splashes on **Chloe**'s shoes.*

Chloe   Alice!

Alice   Oh my God. I'm so sorry.

Chloe   You're so clumsy.

Alice   I'm sorry.

Chloe   You're always spilling things or knocking things over or dropping things or whatever. You're like a – you're like a – boy.

Alice   I'm sorry.

Chloe   It's all over my bag.

Alice   Do you want me to. I could clean it.

Chloe   I'll do it.

She goes to the sink.

The sink is full of crap.

Alice   You could clean it in the bathroom.

Chloe *goes offstage to the bathroom.*

Alice (*calling after her*)   I'm sorry. I'm really sorry.

Lucas   Why are you friends with her?

Alice   Shush.

Lucas   But why are you?

Dan   Whose party is it?

Alice   What?

Dan   This party that Chloe's trying to get you to go to?

Alice   It's this boy – called Pablo. His mum and dad are away. So.

Dan   Sounds dodgy.

Alice   What do you care?

Dan *picks up his bag.*

Lucas   Where you going?

Dan   School.

Lucas   You can't leave it like this. (*Gestures to kitchen.*)

Dan   I can. I will. I am.

Lucas   I'm not letting you leave.

Dan   Don't be ridiculous.

Two text messages arrive on two separate phones. Both **Lucas** *and* **Dan** *look at their phones.*

Lucas   It's a boy.

Alice   What?

Lucas   Lilia and Dad.

Dan   They're having a boy.

Alice   I really wanted them to have a girl.

Dan   Get out of my way.

Lucas   No.

Dan   I will hit you. You know I will.

Alice   I really wanted a sister.

Dan *goes to hit* **Lucas** *and* **Lucas** *grabs* **Dan**'s *arm.* **Dan** *starts trying to hit* **Lucas** *with his other arm.* **Lucas** *dodges him but doesn't let* **Dan** *go. It descends into a pathetic fight/wrestle as the conversation goes on.*

Dan   Let go of my arm!

Lucas   I'm not getting kicked out of the house – because of you –

Dan   She's not going to kick us out!

Alice   I wish Jasmine hadn't died.

Lucas   Who's Jasmine?

Alice   Who's Jasmine?

Lucas   Yeh.

Alice   Mum and Dad's stillborn baby.

Lucas (*not very interested*)   Oh yeh yeh yeh.

Alice   Lucas.

Lucas   What? She died before any of us were born. So I forget she existed. She's a bit like the landline.

Alice   She is not like the landline.

Lucas   I mean I never think about her.

Alice   I think about her all the time.

Dan   Let go of my arm!

Lucas   Say you'll do the washing-up!

Dan   No!

They keep fighting.

Alice   Dan.

Dan   What?

Alice   If Jasmine hadn't died then you would never have been born. Do you ever think about that?

Dan   No.

Alice   And I'd have a sister.

Lucas   But you wouldn't have been born either.

Alice   I might. I might have.

Lucas   No none of us would.

Alice   It could have gone, like, Jasmine and then another girl and then me.

Lucas   No because you change one thing and all of it changes.

Alice   Unless you subscribe to string theory.

Lucas   String theory isn't science.

Alice   Some people think it is.

Lucas   It's science fiction.

Alice   Some people think it's possible. Cosmic microwaves. Left over from the Big Bang. Unless there was no Big Bang and it's just bubbles. Just bubbles. One bubble leading to another.

Lucas   The universe is not an Aero.

Dan (*to* **Lucas**)   Let. Go. Of. My. Arm.

Lucas *lets go of* **Dan** *and they collapse onto the floor.*

Dan   Twat.

Lucas   Dickhead.

Dan   Wanker.

The doorbell rings.

Alice   I'll go.

She goes to the door. It's the **Postman** *with a massive box wrapped in brown paper.*

Alice   I hate my brothers.

Postman   Are you Alice?

Alice *nods.*

Alice   I hate my mum. I hate my dad. I hate my best friend. I hate my whole life.

Postman   This is for you.

Alice   What is it?

Postman   How would I know?

Alice   Good point.

Postman   Can you sign here please?

Alice   Aren't you a bit young for a postman?

Postman   I'm sixteen.

Alice   That's young though isn't it.

Postman   Are you going to sign it or not?

Alice   Yes. Sorry. Yes.

She signs.

Scene Two

2018. The kitchen is stacked high with dirty cups, plates and saucepans.
Jasmine *is eating cereal.* **Pearl** *is holding a piece of paper. They are*
both in school uniform.

Pearl   Do you know what colour you are?

Jasmine   No.

Pearl   You're the colour blue.

Jasmine *doesn't respond.*

Pearl   You're the colour blue.

Jasmine   Okay.

Pearl   And look what colour it is.

Jasmine   Don't shove it in my face.

Alice *walks into the kitchen and stares at them both. She is entirely*
freaked out but sort of frozen too.

Pearl   It's blue.

Jasmine   Alright!

Alice   Who are you?

Pearl   What?

Alice   Who are you and what are you doing in my kitchen?

Jasmine   You're not funny, Alice.

Pearl   Mum's gone to work and she's left us –

Jasmine   – a really shitty note.

Pearl   It says.

She reads the note.

'If you don't sort the kitchen out before I come home I will kick you all
out and you can go and live with your feckless –

Jasmine   – shithead –

Pearl   – yeh – father and the neurotic Ukrainian and their new baby. I am not joking. (*With emphasis.*) I AM NOT JOKING.' Second time in capitals.

Alice   Oh my God.

Pearl   Are you okay?

Alice *shakes her head.*

Jasmine   You don't need to freak out and get all dramatic and emotional. She won't do it. She won't actually kick us out.

Alice   Oh my God. Oh my God.

Pearl   Have a pain au chocolat.

Alice   There's none left.

Pearl   Yeh there is.

She gives **Alice** *a pain au chocolat on a plate.*

Alice   Thanks.

Pearl   Do you want a cup of tea?

Alice *nods.* **Pearl** *gets a bottle of milk out of the fridge and pours* **Alice** *a cup of tea.*

Alice   Can I see it? Can I see the note?

Jasmine *passes her the note then switches the radio on. It's the same eighties song from Scene One.*

Jasmine   Oh I bloody love this song.

Pearl   So do I.

Jasmine *starts dancing.* **Pearl** *sees* **Alice** *reading the back of the note.*

Pearl   What's that?

Alice   'Alice, I have taken your phone.'

Pearl   She's taken your phone?

Alice *nods.*

Jasmine   Why's she taken your phone?

Pearl (*taking the note and reading*)   'You can have it back when you apologise.'

Jasmine   Wow.

Pearl   What did you do?

Alice   I didn't do anything.

Pearl   Mmm, not likely.

The chorus of the song begins. **Jasmine** *turns it up louder and* **Jasmine** *and* **Pearl** *begin to sing along. Then* **Pearl** *joins* **Jasmine** *dancing.* **Pearl** *and* **Jasmine** *dance together while* **Alice** *watches. The dance goes slightly wrong and they both laugh.* **Alice** *joins in with them despite being freaked out. This may be the only chance she ever gets to dance with her two sisters. The dancing can be as impromptu or coordinated as you wish.*

Alice   This is so nice.

She dances a few moments longer.

This is amazing.

The song ends. The dancing ends. **Alice** *looks incredibly happy. She switches the radio off.*

Alice   Is this real?

Pearl   Is what real?

Alice   I mean it feels real. But it can't be. How can it be?

Jasmine   What are you talking about?

Alice   This.

Jasmine *picks up her bag.*

Pearl   Where you going?

Jasmine   School.

She is about to leave.

Pearl   You're not allowed.

Jasmine   Ha.

Pearl   I mean it. Jasmine!

Alice   You're Jasmine. Are you Jasmine?

Jasmine   Are you trying to be funny again?

Alice   No no no, I'm not. See my whole life I've wondered what you'd look like.

She goes up close to **Jasmine** *and touches her face.*

Jasmine   What are you doing?

Pearl   Are you crying?

Jasmine   Can you stop touching my face?

Alice   But you're so lovely.

Jasmine *backs away.*

Jasmine   Stop it!

Pearl   Why are you crying?

Alice   Because she's the baby who died.

Pearl/Jasmine   What?

Alice   You died when you were a baby. You were stillborn. Because Mum had pre-eclampsia but no symptoms. And so they didn't know. And Dad felt bad. Because he was medical. Like he should have done something that he didn't do.

Jasmine   Is this a drama project?

Alice   In real life I don't have sisters, I have two brothers.

Jasmine   Is this like some kind of weird school project?

Alice   No. It's real.

Jasmine   It's twisted.

Alice   I'm sorry.

Jasmine   You are completely freaking me out.

Pearl   I don't think she's doing it on purpose.

Alice   I'm not.

Jasmine   Why are you always on her side?

Alice   Are you?

Pearl   No. Yes. Sometimes.

Alice (*to* **Jasmine**)   When's your birthday?

Jasmine   Stop it, just stop it.

Pearl   It's 19 September.

Alice (*to* **Jasmine**)   That's the day you died.

Jasmine   That's the day I was born.

Alice   I used to imagine you all the time. I imagined that we'd really get on.

Jasmine/Pearl   Ha.

Alice   Do we not, do we not get on?

Pearl   No.

Jasmine   She knows we don't! You know we don't!

Alice   But I don't!

Pearl   She could be having a psychic fugue. You could be having a psychic fugue.

Alice   Could I?

Pearl   I watched a documentary on it. And you just kind of forget everything. And you disappear.

Jasmine   Well, Alice hasn't disappeared. She's right here.

Pearl   But she might disappear. She might disappear later. Especially if we don't handle the situation carefully.

Jasmine   For God's sake.

Pearl   You're very cold, Jasmine.

Alice   Dan's very cold.

Pearl   Who's Dan?

Alice   My eldest brother.

Jasmine   Jesus Christ.

Alice   And I always thought that Dan was cold because he came after you. And that Mum was in such a state when he was born that she wasn't quite there or something. Not that it was her fault. Although I think she did blame Dad – for your death. Or he thought she blamed him. But if you didn't die . . .

Jasmine   Can you STOP talking about me dying?

Alice   Sorry. I'm sorry but you did die. But you're not dead now.

Jasmine   No I'm not!

Pearl (*to* **Jasmine**)   Why are you so angry?

Jasmine   Why are you not angry?

Pearl (*to* **Alice**)   She gets angry a lot.

Alice   So does Dan.

Jasmine   Will you shut up about Dan? Dan doesn't exist. He doesn't exist. I exist alright?

Pearl   The other thing it could be is a brain tumour.

Jasmine   It's not a brain tumour.

Pearl   How do you know?

Jasmine   Because they're extremely rare!

Pearl   But a rare occurrence still happens doesn't it. A rare occurrence does still occur.

Alice   I don't want to have a brain tumour.

Pearl   No one *wants* to have a brain tumour.

Jasmine (*to* **Alice**)   You haven't got a brain tumour.

Pearl   You don't know that.

Jasmine   I do because she's obviously making the whole thing up!

Alice   But why would I make this up?

Pearl   Why would she make this up?

Jasmine   Why are you always on her side?

Pearl   I'm not!

The doorbell rings.

Alice   I'll get it.

She answers the door. It's **Pablo**.

Alice   Pablo.

Pablo   What have you done to your eyebrows?

Alice   Nothing.

Pablo   They look funny.

Alice   Do they?

Pablo   Like you've over-plucked them.

Alice   I haven't touched them.

Pablo   Well, maybe you've under-plucked them. Are we walking to school or not?

Alice   Me and you. Walking to school?

Pablo   Unless you're walking with Chloe.

Alice   Erm I'm not walking with Chloe no.

Pablo   I can't cope with Chloe today. Things are bad enough.

Alice   What things?

Pablo   Oh I'm just really stressed about the party.

Alice   Oh right.

Pablo   You ready?

Alice   Er sorry no um can you come in for a minute?

Pablo   Certainly.

He follows **Alice** *into the kitchen.*

Jasmine   Hi, Pablo.

Pearl   Hi, Pablo.

Pablo *ignores them and looks round.*

Pablo   This kitchen is disgusting. Did you ask your mum?

Alice   Ask her what?

Pablo   About the party?

Jasmine   What party?

Pablo   I'm having a party at my house.

Jasmine   Really?

Pablo   It's very nerve-wracking. Did you ask her?

Alice   Erm no cos she didn't come home till late last night. And then she had to leave really early this morning so.

Pablo   Ring her. Ring her now.

Alice   She's got my phone.

Pablo   Why's she got your phone?

Alice   It's a – punishment.

Pablo   Wow. What did you do?

During the following dialogue **Alice** *starts packing her school bag, looking for something, a pencil case. The pencil case is open and all the pencils fall out.* **Pablo** *helps her pick them up.*

Alice   Nothing. Honestly she's been a bit crazy since my dad left.

Pablo   But taking your phone I mean that's like taking your life.

Alice   Yeh. I know.

Pablo   So you must have done *something.*

Then **Pablo** *knocks a mug of cold tea over.*

Oh my God. I'm so sorry.

Alice   It's alright.

Pablo   It's just nerves.

Alice   What are you so nervous about?

Pablo   The party.

Alice   Oh yeh. Sorry.

Pablo   No I'm sorry. About the tea.

Alice   It's fine.

Pablo   Shit.

Alice   What?

Pablo   It's all over my bag.

Alice   Do you want me to. I could clean it.

Pablo   I'll do it.

He goes to the sink.

The sink is full of crap.

Alice   You could clean it in the bathroom.

Pablo *heads offstage to the bathroom.*

Alice   You didn't tell me I was friends with Pablo.

Jasmine   Why would we tell you something that you already know?

Alice   In my other life. In my real life I'm not friends with Pablo. He's just a boy. Who's in my geography class.

Jasmine   This *is* your real life, you freak.

She picks up her bag.

Pearl   You can't leave now.

Jasmine   Yes I can.

Pearl   What about Alice?

Jasmine   She's fine. She's faking it.

Alice   I'm not faking it.

Jasmine   You are. You are faking it. And you're being a complete bitch.

Alice   That's internalised misogyny.

Jasmine   What?

Alice   Calling another woman a bitch.

Jasmine   I don't care about things like that.

Alice   But you should. You should care.

Pearl   I care.

Alice   That's a line from *Star Wars*.

Pearl   Your friend is quite a mercenary.

Alice   I wonder if he cares about anything or anyone. And then Luke says.

Pearl   I care.

Alice *and* **Pearl** *smile at each other, inexplicably pleased.*

Jasmine   I've got to go. Alice, you're not a woman. You're only thirteen. And you are being a bitch. If you're not faking it go to the doctor's.

Pearl *stands in* **Jasmine***'s way.*

Jasmine   What are you doing?

Pearl   I'm not letting you leave.

Jasmine   Don't be ridiculous.

Pearl   I'm not.

She grabs **Jasmine***'s arm.*

Jasmine   Get off my arm!

Pearl   You have to do the washing-up!

Jasmine   You're mad, you're madder than her. (*Indicates* **Alice**.)

Jasmine *and* **Pearl** *get messages on their phones at the same time . . .*

Pearl   Dad and Lilia are having a girl.

Jasmine   Great. Another girl.

Pearl   I really wanted a brother.

The doorbell rings.

Alice   I'll get it.

She opens the door. It's the **Postman** *with the same parcel.*

Alice   It's you.

Postman   Yes it's me.

Alice   You're the same postman.

Postman   Yeh.

Alice   I thought you might be different.

Postman   Different from what?

Alice   From the other one.

Postman   What other one?

Alice   Erm. It doesn't matter. Sorry.

Postman   Can you sign this?

Alice   Er – yeh.

She signs.

Scene Three

2018. The kitchen is stacked high with dirty cups, plates and saucepans. **Dan** *is eating cereal.* **Lucas** *is holding a laminated piece of A4 card.*

Lucas   Do you know what colour you are?

Dan   No.

Lucas   You're the colour blue.

Dan *doesn't respond.*

Lucas   You're the colour blue.

Dan   Okay.

Lucas   And look what colour it is.

Dan   I can't believe you've actually laminated that thing.

Lucas   It's blue.

Joe *comes into the kitchen.* **Joe** *is actually* **Alice** *in the body of a boy. All three of them are in school uniform.*

Dan   Don't shove it in my face.

Lucas   That's you.

Dan   Alright!

Joe   I'm back. I'm back. Ha! I'm back.

Lucas   We didn't know you'd gone anywhere.

Joe   Didn't you?

Dan   Where did you go?

Joe   Er nowhere.

He picks up the note.

'If you don't sort the kitchen out before I come home I will kick you all out and you can go and live with your feckless dickhead of a father and his Swedish skank.' Blimey. Bit harsh.

Lucas (*to* **Dan**)   This is why you've got to wash up.

Dan   She's not going to kick us out.

Joe   I meant calling Lilia a skank.

He turns the note over and reads the postscript. Stops dead.

'PS Joe, I have taken your phone' . . . Is my name Joe?

Dan   She's taken your phone?

Joe *slowly realises that he's a boy. Looks at himself.*

Joe   I'm a boy.

Dan   Well sort of.

Joe   What?

Lucas   Why's she taken your phone?

Joe   Erm I dunno.

Lucas *looks at the note.*

Lucas   She said she's not going to give it back till you apologise.

Dan   What did you do?

Joe   Er – nothing.

Dan   Yeh right.

Joe   Do I look different to you?

Lucas   No.

Dan   You look as shit as usual.

Lucas   Why have you got to swear?

Dan   The whole world swears, Lucas – except you.

Joe   So I don't? I don't look at all different?

Lucas   No you don't.

Lucas and **Dan** *get a text message. They look at their phones.*

Lucas   It's a boy.

Joe   Dad and Lilia are having a boy?

Lucas   Yes.

Joe   So it's gone back to a boy but now I'm a boy.

Dan   What?

Joe   Nothing. Nothing at all. Ignore me.

Dan I do.

Joe I thought some things might have changed. Some things have changed – significantly – but not the things I was expecting. Or hoping for.

The doorbell rings.

Joe I'll get that.

He goes to the door.

Pablo.

Pablo Yeh.

Joe What are you doing here?

Pablo I thought we were walking to school.

Joe Right. Right. Yes.

Pablo Are you ready?

Joe No. No erm.

Pablo What's wrong?

Joe I'm having a really weird day.

Pablo It's only just started.

Joe No no no that's the thing.

Pablo What? What's the thing?

Joe You won't believe me if I tell you. Or you'll think I've got a brain tumour. Or I'm having a psychic fugue.

Pablo What's a psychic fugue?

Joe I don't really know.

Pablo Okay . . .

Joe I'm not. I'm not a boy. I'm a girl. My name's Alice.

Pablo Are you saying you want sex reassignment surgery?

Joe No.

Pablo It's okay. It's okay. You can talk to me. Because I've been wondering lately if I might be non-binary.

Joe Oh.

Pablo   So this is brilliant. This is amazing. Because I had no idea about you. And you clearly had no idea about me.

Joe   Erm. Okay, well, anyway –

Pablo   Can I just tell you one other thing?

Joe   What's that?

Pablo   I've got a paralysing crush on your brother Dan.

Joe   But he's a dick.

Pablo   But he's a gorgeous dick. That sounded weird – I didn't mean it like *that*.

Joe   I know, it's fine. Don't worry.

Pablo   Sorry, sorry, we were talking about you. Erm. Where were we?

Joe   I'm not thinking about what did you call it. Sex reassignment –

Pablo   Surgery.

Joe   Yeh yeh I mean I am a girl. I am actually a girl. I was born a girl.

Pablo   I know I know and that's how a lot of people feel. But you mustn't rush into anything.

Joe   I'm not going to rush into anything.

Pablo   Good. I think that's good. You could just start wearing women's clothes couldn't you. And see how that went. Because that's like reversible. Because clothes are just clothes aren't they. But cutting your – (*gestures to his crotch*) off. Well that's like getting a tattoo. But worse. Because actually now with laser treatment and everything you can get a tattoo lasered off and it's not that bad. I mean there's scarring but you know. You can live with that can't you. Whereas no – you know. The regret if you feel regret. I mean you might not of course. I don't want to discourage you. I want to be supportive. You're my best friend. And I'll stand by you. Only don't tell anyone at school because of how we'll both get the shit beaten out of us.

The **Postman** *arrives with the parcel.*

Postman   Can you sign this?

Joe   It's you.

Postman   It's me.

Joe   Is it you?

Postman   What?

Joe   Is it you that's making this happen?

Pablo   Making what happen?

Joe   This.

Postman   I don't know what you're talking about.

Joe   Why am I a boy?

Postman   How should I know?

Pablo   He's just a postman.

Joe   No I don't think he is.

Postman   Actually I really am.

Joe   If I sign it will we go back to the beginning?

Pablo   The beginning of what?

Postman   I haven't got time for this.

Pablo   I can sign it. If you want.

Joe   No erm no I think it has to be me.

Postman   Well, are you going to sign it or not?

Joe   Yes.

He signs.

Scene Four

2018. The kitchen is stacked high with washing-up. **Dan** *is eating cereal.*
Jasmine *is holding up a piece of paper. Both of them are in school
uniform.* **Alice**, **Pearl**, **Lucas** *and* **Joe** *do not exist.*

Jasmine   Do you know what colour you are?

Dan   No.

Jasmine   You're yellow.

Dan *doesn't respond.*

Jasmine   You're yellow.

Dan   Okay.

Jasmine   And look what colour it is.

She doesn't stop.

It's yellow.

Dan *grabs it and tears it up. And scatters the bits.*

Jasmine   Great. That's great.

Dan   It is actually.

Jasmine   I should have got it laminated.

Dan   Yeh. You should.

Jasmine *switches the radio on. It's the same song again.*

Dan   Can you turn that shit off?

Jasmine   I like this shit.

She dances on her own.

Dan   Well, I don't.

Jasmine   Well, I do.

Dan *switches it off.*

Dan   It makes me feel like killing myself.

Jasmine   All the more reason to keep it on.

She switches the radio back on. **Dan** *switches it off.*

Jasmine   Dan!

Then they both get a text on their phones. They both look at the phones.

Jasmine   Jesus.

Dan   Christ.

Jasmine   Twins.

Dan   Ha.

Jasmine   Poor cow.

Dan   She brought it on herself.

Jasmine   Yeh, Dad had nothing to do with it.

Dan *picks up his bag.* **Jasmine** *stands in* **Dan***'s way.*

Dan   What are you doing?

Jasmine   I'm not letting you leave.

Dan   Don't be ridiculous.

Jasmine *grabs* **Dan***'s arm.*

Dan   Are you insane?

Jasmine   I'm not letting go.

They start to actually fight or wrestle, **Dan** *trying to get away and* **Jasmine** *not letting him.*

Dan   Bitch.

Jasmine   Wanker.

Dan   Dickhead.

Jasmine   You can't call a girl a dickhead, you prick.

Dan   Yeh, you can. I just did.

The fight ends with both of them slumped on the floor and **Jasmine** *holding onto* **Dan***'s leg. They stop for a moment.*

Jasmine   Does it feel like?

Dan   What?

Jasmine   Like someone's missing?

Scene Five

2018. The kitchen is stacked high with dirty cups, plates and saucepans. There is no one there. **Dan**, **Lucas**, **Jasmine** *and* **Pearl** *do not exist.* **Alice** *comes into the room. Looks around. Goes to the note on the kitchen table, reads it. Then turns it over and reads the message on the back. Looks in the cupboard. Takes out a packet of four pains au chocolat. Looks in the fridge. There's plenty of milk.*

The phone rings.

Alice *waits.*

The answer machine kicks in.

Mum's Voice   You're through to Shelly and Alice. We can't take your call right now but please leave us a message and we'll get back to you.

Chloe *is on the answering machine.*

Chloe   Alice, it's Chloe. Are you there? Alice are you there? Why aren't you answering your phone? Are we walking to school or not? Call me or I'm just going to go without you.

She hangs up.

Alice *switches the radio on. It's the same eighties song.*

The doorbell rings.

Alice *switches the radio off. Goes to the door. It's* **Cinnamon***.*

Alice   Cinnamon.

Cinnamon   You said we might walk to school together but then you didn't answer your phone so then I thought she's probably walking to school with Chloe. But then I thought what if she's not alright. So then I thought I better come round and see. But you're alright. You're fine. So I can just go.

Alice   My mum took my phone. That's why I couldn't answer.

Cinnamon   Why did she take your phone?

Alice   Because she's crazy at the moment.

Cinnamon   So it was nothing to do with you?

Alice   Well, we had a sort of argument. Quite a big argument.

Cinnamon   What about?

Alice   She won't let me do anything. She's like over-the-top protective. Do you want to come in?

Cinnamon   Is Chloe there?

Alice   No.

Cinnamon   But is she coming round?

Alice   I don't think so. And I've got four uneaten, unopened pains au chocolat. So we can have two each.

Cinnamon   Okay.

She follows **Alice** *into the house.* **Alice** *opens the pains au chocolat and finds them both a plate. Maybe makes them both a cup of tea too.*

Alice   I'm having a really weird day.

Cinnamon   It's only just started.

Alice   No no that's the thing. The day keeps starting again. But each time it's different so this morning I've woken up with two sisters instead of two brothers. And then I woke up as a boy. Like with a boy's body. Which was insane. Then a minute ago. It all went blank.

Cinnamon   What did?

Alice   The world. It was white. And I was nothing.

Cinnamon *nods*

Alice   Do you believe me?

Cinnamon   Yeh.

Alice   Do you?

Cinnamon   Yeh.

Alice   Why?

Cinnamon   Well why would you make something like this up?

Alice   That's what Pearl said.

Cinnamon   Who's Pearl?

Alice   My sister.

Cinnamon   But you haven't got a sister.

Alice   Have I got any brothers?

Cinnamon   You're an only child.

Alice   Right.

Cinnamon   Sometimes I'm a bit jealous.

Alice   Of what?

Cinnamon   Of the fact that you're an only child. I know I shouldn't say that cos you did have a sister who died.

Alice   But she died before I was born. I mean I don't know if that counts. As having a sister. If I wasn't alive at the time.

Cinnamon   Oh my God.

Alice   What what?

Cinnamon   Is this a trick?

Alice   No!

Cinnamon   Is Chloe here? Is Chloe here all along? Is she like? Is she, like, hiding? Listening to this?

Alice   No no course not.

Cinnamon *starts looking for her.*

Alice   Cinnamon, she's honestly not here. I wouldn't do that. I wouldn't do that.

Cinnamon *stops looking.*

Cinnamon   Do you think I should change my name?

Alice   No. No I don't.

Cinnamon   Chloe thinks I should change my name.

Alice   Well – she's wrong.

Cinnamon   It's really lonely since you started hanging out with her.

Alice   I'm sorry.

Cinnamon   She's not even nice.

Alice   She's not. She's not really. She's just sort of – powerful.

Cinnamon   Sometimes I wish we were still at primary school.

Alice   So do I.

Cinnamon   It was easier.

Alice   What do you think of my eyebrows?

Cinnamon   What?

Alice   Do they look alright to you?

Cinnamon   They look fine.

Alice   Not over-plucked or under-plucked or wrong somehow?

Cinnamon   No.

Alice   How am I going to get back to normality?

Cinnamon   Do you want to get back to normality?

Alice   Yes.

Cinnamon   Why?

The doorbell rings.

Alice That'll be the postman.

She goes to the door.

Postman Can you sign this?

Alice Have I got a brain tumour?

Postman Sorry?

Alice Would you know anything about that?

Postman About what?

Alice If I had a brain tumour or not.

Postman I'm a postman, love.

Alice *signs.*

Scene Six

1983. Kitchen. The kitchen is stacked high with dirty cups, plates and saucepans. **Bex** *is looking in cupboards.* **Dean** *is doing a Rubik's cube.* **Shelly** *comes into the kitchen.* **Shelly** *is actually* **Alice** *in her mother's body. They are all in school uniform. They all have eighties hair and* **Shelly** *wears leg-warmers.* **Shelly** *wears a headband just for added eighties value.*

Bex There's nothing to eat. I can find literally nothing to eat.

Dean (*to* **Shelly**) What are you staring at?

Shelly This is a very eighties kitchen.

Dean That's because this is the eighties.

Shelly The eighties. I wasn't expecting that.

Dean What?

Shelly Nothing.

Bex I could make custard I suppose.

Dean Custard?

Bex There's custard powder.

Dean   But we haven't got any milk.

Bex   We've got powdered milk.

Dean   Can you make custard with powdered custard and powdered milk?

Bex   Shall I try it?

Dean   Why not?

Bex *switches the radio on. It's the same eighties song we heard in the first two scenes.*

Bex   I *love* this song.

Shelly   Me too.

Bex *sets about making the custard. Dancing now and again.* **Shelly** *watches her. Watches* **Dean**. *He has nearly finished the Rubik's cube.*

Bex   Shelly.

Shelly *doesn't respond.*

Bex   Shelly.

Shelly   Er – yeh?

Bex   Are you alright?

Shelly   Have we got a mirror?

Bex (*confused*)   Er – there's one on the wall.

Shelly   Oh yeh.

She goes to the mirror and sees herself. Looks at her face and sees her mother at thirteen.

Shelly   Oh my God.

Bex   What?

Shelly   I'm her.

Bex   You're who?

Shelly   I'm my mother.

Bex   What do you mean?

Shelly *is saved from having to explain further by the phone ringing.* **Bex** *and* **Dean** *look at each other in a slight panic about the phone.* **Bex** *switches off the radio.*

Bex   What shall we do?

Dean   Can we just ignore it?

Bex   Yeh.

Dean   Okay.

Shelly   Do you want me to answer it?

Bex   It's alright.

Dean   It'll stop ringing in a minute.

The phone is still ringing.

The three of them wait.

Wait another three rings.

Shelly   I don't mind. I don't mind answering it.

Bex   Okay. Okay. Answer it but if it's any of the utilities –

Shelly   Utilities?

Dean   British Gas. British Telecom. Or the Electric.

Bex   If it's any of them.

Dean   Just hang up.

Shelly   Okay.

She picks up the phone.

Shelly   Hello? . . . Erm hello – Mick.

Bex *rolls her eyes at* **Dean**. **Dean** *puts his head in his hands.*

Bex   Great.

Shelly (*whispers to them*)   It's Mick.

Dean   Mick the dick.

Shelly (*to* **Mick**)   No no I was just saying to (*Looks at them, hesitates because she's not 100 per cent sure.*) Bex and and Dean (*This is clearly correct.*) – that it was you – on the phone . . . (*To* **Bex** *and* **Dean**.) Erm he wants to know where Mum is. Where where is she?

Bex   We thought she was with him.

Shelly   Oh. (*To* **Mick**.) Erm erm . . . she's not here. We thought she was with you. No no we really did . . . But she isn't here . . . (*Whispers to* **Bex** *and* **Dean**.) He says he's coming round.

Bex   Great. That's great.

Shelly   But she isn't here, Mick. She really isn't . . . Honestly I swear. (*Whispers to* **Bex** *and* **Dean**.) He doesn't believe me.

Bex *rolls her eyes.* **Shelly** *holds the phone away from her ear.*

Shelly (*whispers*)   Now he's just yelling.

Bex (*whispers*)   Hang up.

Shelly *hesitates.*

Dean (*whispers*)   Just hang up.

Shelly (*whispers*)   Won't that piss him off even more?

Bex   Yeh but. (*She shrugs.*)

Shelly (*holding the phone back to her ear*)   Erm, Mick, Mick. Listen. Erm, I'll tell her you called, alright? I'll tell her you called. I promise. I'll tell her to call you right back. Yeh. Cross my heart hope to die . . . okay, okay, okay, Mick. Yeh, okay. Bye, Mick.

She hangs up.

He's insane.

Dean   Yeh.

The doorbell rings.

Shelly   Is that him?

Dean   It can't be.

Bex   It can't be.

Shelly   Why can't it be?

Bex   Well, how's he going to get from his house – all the way here – that quick?

Dean   He can't. He couldn't.

Bex   Unless he was calling from a phone box. Did it sound like a phone box?

Shelly   What does a phone box sound like?

Dean   Echoey.

Bex   With beeps.

Shelly   Erm there weren't any beeps. I don't think.

The doorbell rings.

Bex   If it's him. I just won't open the door.

Dean   Okay.

Bex   Okay.

She goes to the door.

Shelly   You must be really clever.

Dean   Why?

Shelly   I can never do them. Rubik's cubes. I mean I can do one side but that's pathetic isn't it. Anyone can do one side. Most people can do one side. But I think even if I had forever I wouldn't be able to do all of them. All of the sides. I think it's got something to do with being bad at physics.

Bex *returns to the kitchen.*

Bex   It's a man. Wants to see our TV licence.

Shelly   Have we got one?

Dean   No.

Shelly   Oh.

Dean   What shall we do?

Bex   Hide the telly.

Dean   Okay.

Bex   It's only little. Carry it upstairs and put it in the airing cupboard.

Dean   Okay. Okay yeh.

He leaves the kitchen.

Shelly   Bex.

Bex   Yeh?

Shelly   I'm not Shelly.

Bex   You're not Shelly?

Shelly   I look like her but I'm not her.

Bex   Who are you then?

Shelly   I'm Alice. I'm Shelly's daughter. I'm from the year 2018 and you're my Auntie Bex.

Bex   If this is a joke I don't get it.

Shelly   It's not a joke. Erm it's not a joke – but I don't know how I can convince you and I don't know how much time I've got before it ends.

Bex   Before what ends?

Shelly   This.

Bex   Do you mean like a nuclear holocaust?

Shelly   Er no I mean this. This. It's like it's like I'm in um *Back to the Future*.

Bex   What's *Back to the Future*?

Shelly   The film. You must know that film.

Bex   I've never heard of it.

Shelly   Maybe it's not out yet. What year is this?

Bex   1983.

Shelly   *Back to the Future*. Oh I think it was later than that. I could Google it if the internet exists?

Bex   What's the internet?

Shelly   Okay so it doesn't. Forget it. The internet I mean. But you should go and see *Back to the Future*. When it comes out.

Bex   Okay.

Shelly   Michael J. Fox goes back in time to when his mum and dad are kids – teenagers – although he doesn't actually end up in his dad's body. That's more like *Freaky Friday*.

Bex   Oh I've seen that. I've seen that. With Jodie Foster.

Shelly   I haven't seen that one. But they did a remake with Lindsay Lohan.

Bex   Right.

Shelly   So I'm in a kind of mash-up of *Back to the Future* and *Freaky Friday* and something else. *Groundhog Day*! *Groundhog Day* is brilliant. You should see that too. But oh God oh God. I shouldn't be telling you stuff about the future. In case it changes the past.

Bex   Well, you've only told me to go and see two films.

Shelly   Three. If you include the *Freaky Friday* remake. Which I would definitely recommend.

Bex   Three films. So I mean. That could completely change my future but it's not like –

Dean *returns to the kitchen.*

Dean   I put the TV in the attic. In case he goes in the bathroom.

Bex   Perfect.

Dean *grins, pleased.* **Bex** *smiles. She goes back to the front door.*

Shelly   I wish I had a brother like you.

Dean   You have. You have got a brother like me.

Shelly (*realising her mistake*)   Yes yes I do and I'm really glad.

Dean   By the way.

Shelly   What?

Dean   You don't look anything like Mum.

Shelly   Why did you say that?

Dean   When you looked in the mirror you said oh my God I'm my mother or something. But you look nothing like her.

Shelly   I think I do – I think I do a bit.

Bex *returns*

Bex   TV man's gone.

Dean   What happened?

Bex   He wasn't authorised to come in the house.

Dean   Oh. Shall I bring it back down?

The doorbell rings.

Dean   Do you think it's him again? Trying to trick us?

Shelly   Or Mick. What if it's Mick?

Dean   I'll go and look. Out the bedroom window.

Bex   Okay. Okay yeh.

Dean *leaves the stage.*

Shelly   I shouldn't say this cos it's about the future but don't become a nun, alright?

Bex   A nun?

Shelly   You become a nun and you're in a convent for five years. One of those ones that doesn't talk or go out or anything.

Bex   Blimey.

Shelly   But then you give it up and become a lesbian.

Bex   Oh.

Shelly   And you always said that you should have become a lesbian sooner and not bothered with the nun bit.

Bex   Okay. Okay thanks.

The doorbell rings again.

Shelly   I had no idea. No idea at all that my mum's life was like this. She never said anything.

Dean *returns.*

Dean   It's alright. It's alright. It's just the postman.

Bex   I'll get it.

Shelly   Can I get it?

Bex   If you want.

Shelly *goes to the front door. Opens it.*

Shelly   It's you.

Postman   What's me?

Shelly   Is it you?

Postman   What?

Shelly   You look really similar to our postman.

Postman   That's because I am your postman.

Shelly   No I mean our postman from 2018.

Postman   Are you having a laugh?

Shelly   Not really. This is quite stressful.

Postman   Sign here.

Shelly   If I don't sign it will I be like stuck in 1983 forever?

Postman   I honestly don't know what you're talking about.

Shelly   Me neither.

Postman   Are you going to sign it or not?

Shelly   I think I should. I think I better. Okay.

She signs.

Scene Seven

2018. The kitchen is stacked high with dirty cups, plates and saucepans.
Dan, **Jasmine** *and* **Pearl** *are all eating breakfast.* **Lucas** *has the same laminated rota as usual.*

A note for this scene: the asterisks in the dialogue during the dancing are intended to denote gaps in which the characters are just dancing. These gaps can be as long or as short as you like.

Lucas   Do you know what colour you are?

Dan   I'm blue.

Lucas   No you're pink.

Dan   Pink.

Lucas   Yes.

Dan   Why did you make me pink?

Pearl   Why shouldn't he make you pink?

Dan   Because it's a girl's colour.

Pearl   For God's sake.

Jasmine   He's got a point.

Pearl   No he hasn't.

Lucas   You are pink.

Dan   Don't shove it in my face.

Lucas   Pink

Dan   Lucas, stop shoving it in my face or I'm going to hit you. I swear.

Lucas   He's got to do the washing-up.

Jasmine   He does. You do.

Dan   I do not.

Lucas   But you're pink.

Dan   Can you stop saying that?

Alice *comes into the kitchen.*

Alice   This isn't normal.

Jasmine   Yeh it is.

Alice   I mean it's not normality.

Jasmine   Who ate all the chocolate croissants?

Dan   Me.

Lucas   I prefer to say pains au chocolat.

Alice   I was hoping for normality.

Lucas   Why?

Alice   I don't know.

Jasmine   You're so bloody selfish.

Alice   Me?

Jasmine   I was talking to Dan.

Alice   Oh.

Jasmine   But you're not much better.

Pearl *picks up the note on the kitchen table.*

Pearl   Mum's going to kick us out if we don't do the washing-up.

Alice   I know.

Pearl   And she's got your phone.

Alice   I know.

Lucas   Why did she take your phone?

Dan   What did you do?

Jasmine   Yeh, what did you do?

Lucas   What did you do?

Alice   I said things. That I shouldn't have said.

Pearl   What things?

Alice   I don't want to talk about it.

A text message arrives on everyone's phones and they all read the message. Except of course **Alice***.*

Alice   Is it a boy or a girl?

Pearl   One girl. One boy. And the other one they couldn't tell.

Alice   They're having triplets?

Pearl   Poor Lilia.

Dan   She brought it all on herself.

Pearl   Yeh, women just get themselves pregnant all the time. They're very irresponsible like that.

Dan   They are! That's how they trap men.

Pearl   Jesus, Dan.

The doorbell rings.

Alice   I'll get it.

It's **Cinnamon***,* **Pablo** *and* **Chloe***.*

Chloe   Who are you walking to school with?

Alice   I don't know.

Pablo   We could all walk together.

Chloe *pulls a face.*

Cinnamon   Or not.

Alice   Will you come in? Just for a minute?

Cinnamon, **Pablo** *and* **Chloe** *go into the house.*

Chloe   Hi, Dan.

Dan *doesn't look up.*

Dan   Hi, Chloe.

Alice *switches the radio on. It's the same song we've heard all along.*

Dan   I hate this shit.

Jasmine   Oh shut up, Dan.

Alice *starts dancing.*

Chloe   Why are you dancing?

Alice   Because this may be the only chance we get.

Pablo *starts dancing.*

Cinnamon *starts dancing.*

Chloe *rolls her eyes and starts dancing.*

The following conversations take place amid the ramshackle dancing. At some point in time **Pearl** *and* **Jasmine** *and possibly even* **Lucas** *join in. And everyone except* **Dan** *sings along to the chorus.*

Chloe   Your brother is gorgeous.

Alice   My brother is a meathead.

Chloe   I don't really mind that.

Alice   What is wrong with you?

Chloe   What do you mean?

*

Alice   You can do better than my brother Dan.

Pablo   What?

Alice   You've got a paralysing crush on him but you can do better.

Pablo   How do you know about that?

Alice   I. Guessed.

Pablo   Is it that obvious? Is it like written on me?

Alice   No. No. Not at all. Honestly

*

Cinnamon   Your brother is gorgeous.

Alice   My brother is a dick.

Cinnamon   I didn't mean Dan I meant Lucas.

Alice   Lucas?

Cinnamon   Yeh.

Alice   Really?

Cinnamon   Don't tell him I said that.

Alice   I won't.

*

Alice   Pablo's having a party.

Cinnamon   I know.

Alice   Do you want to come?

Cinnamon   I'm not invited.

Alice   Well, I'm inviting you. I mean if I'm going. If I'm allowed to go.
Which I'm not sure I am or will be. But if I am.

*

Alice   I'm going to walk to school with Cinnamon from now on. And
maybe Pablo too. Sometimes we'll walk with Pablo.

Chloe   And what am I supposed to do?

Alice   I don't know. Be nicer to people.

*

Alice *takes the landline phone and moves away from the dancing. The
song ends and everyone else leaves the stage.*

Alice   Mum? It's Alice. I'm sorry for what I said. About how I wished
I'd never been born. And that you were ruining my life. And also calling
you a bitch. You're not. A bitch. I mean.

She is crying.

Erm but this party is not what you think. I mean it's at Pablo's house
and Pablo's my friend. And Cinnamon's going to come with me.

To the party. If I'm allowed to go. And we'll all look after each other. So nothing bad is going to happen. I mean I can't promise that nothing bad is going to happen ever ever. Cos it's like Yoda says – the future is always in motion. But erm erm erm just because you had one daughter who died. It doesn't mean that I'm going to die too. Okay? Okay. Okay. I love you. Bye.

The doorbell rings. She goes to the door.

Alice   Hi.

Postman   Can you sign this please?

Alice *signs.*

Scene Eight

2018. The kitchen is stacked high with dirty cups and plates and saucepans. **Dan** *is eating cereal.* **Lucas** *is holding a laminated piece of A4 card.* **Alice** *comes into the kitchen. All three of them are in school uniform.*

Lucas   Do you know what colour you are?

Dan   No.

Lucas   You're the colour blue.

Dan *doesn't respond.*

Dan   Stop waving it in my face.

Lucas   It's blue.

Alice *goes to the note.*

Alice   It says twenty-seven-year-old Aussie witch of a girlfriend . . .

Dan   We know.

Lucas   We've read it.

Alice   Ha! It says twenty-seven-year-old witch of a girlfriend! (*To* **Dan**.) And you're the colour blue. You're the colour blue aren't you?

Lucas   Yeh he is.

Alice   Ha! That means I'm back.

Dan   What?

Alice   Nothing.

Lucas   You have got to do the washing-up.

Dan *takes the rota from* **Lucas**. *Looks at it.*

Dan   Why have I got to do the washing-up – when – whoever's yellow didn't do their washing-up from the morning –

Lucas   I did do my washing-up from the morning but Alice who by the way is pink – she left all that stuff on the side from the night before.

Alice   Because half of it was Dan's from the morning!

Dan   Why can't Mum just get the dishwasher fixed?

Alice   Because she's broke.

Dan *gets his bag.*

Alice   Dan.

Dan   What?

Alice   We have to clean this kitchen up right now. All of us. Because erm because erm Mum had a really shit childhood.

Dan   What?

Lucas   I don't think she did.

Alice   No she did. She definitely did. I know she did.

Lucas   She's never said that.

Alice   Because she was protecting us.

The doorbell rings.

Alice   I'll get it.

She goes to the door. It's the **Postman**.

Postman   Can you sign here?

Alice   No.

Postman   Sorry?

Alice   I'm not signing it. I refuse.

Postman   Why?

Alice   Whatever it is. I don't want it.

Postman   Okay.

Alice   I want what I've got.

Postman   Okay.

Alice   Okay.

Postman   Okay.

Alice   So so that's it?

Postman   Yeh, that's it.

Alice   Great.

Postman   Okay. Okay.

Alice   It's about playing the cards you're dealt with isn't it. That's what it's about. Isn't it?

Postman   I have no idea what you're talking about.

Alice   I mean instead of wishing that your life was different from what it is you have to play the cards you're dealt with. That's it isn't it?

Postman   I still no have no idea what you're talking about.

Alice   Okay.

Postman   Okay.

Alice   Be like that.

Postman   I will.

Alice   Bye then.

Postman   Bye.

Alice *goes back to the kitchen.*

Lucas   Who was that?

Alice   The postman.

Dan   So where is it?

Alice   What?

Dan   The post.

Alice   Oh. He had the wrong house.

She switches the radio on. It's the same eighties song. She starts washing up. **Dan** *and* **Lucas** *don't move for a while. Eventually they join her.* **Lucas** *first and then* **Dan**.

Variations

BY KATIE HIMS

Notes on rehearsal and staging, drawn from a workshop with the writer, held at the National Theatre October 2018

How Katie came to write the play

'I wanted to write about that feeling we can all have, that we wish our lives were different, particularly when it comes to our families. I also love stories about parallel universes and plays that repeat themselves. I wondered: what if a young girl wakes up repeatedly to all the various families she might have had?'

Katie Hims, 2018

Introduction

EXERCISE: WARMING UP AND CREATING VISUAL STORIES

This exercise was used to start the workshop: it gets everybody active and thinking about stagecraft, space and movement. Initially it just needs one 'leader' to call out simple instructions. It's best to add the instructions gradually one by one as the exercise evolves rather than explaining them all at once.

1   GO: All the participants walk around the room: everyone should be making an attempt to fill the floor, find the space and not move in shoals. Everyone should be moving with purpose, not wandering, acknowledging other people in the space but keeping moving until the next instruction.

2   STOP: Everyone stops where they are and checks around to see if the space is evenly filled, that there aren't groupings or large empty areas, and everyone adjusts accordingly. Keep trying out the STOP and GO instructions until everyone is happy and filling the space efficiently, then add the next instruction.

3   CENTRE: On hearing this direction everyone should rush (safely and without making contact with anyone else) into the centre of the room 'like iron filings drawn to a magnet'.
    Now try adding other directions:

4   AUDIENCE: Everyone turns and looks directly at the audience.

5   SKY: Everyone looks straight upwards.

6   CLEAR THE SPACE: Everyone goes to the edges of the space and makes contact with a wall.

7   REWIND: Take three steps backwards (first checking that it's safe to do so) as if reversing a film. You could do this in slow motion, 'normal speed' or speed it up.

8   VICTIM: Without discussion, *one* person assumes the role of victim and they duck/kneel/fall flat, everyone else remains upright.

9   The instruction SURVIVOR is the opposite of VICTIM and this time *everyone* ducks/kneels/falls flat except one person, who is the SURVIVOR.
     Experiment with ways of going down to the floor and returning to standing using the instructions.

10 and 11   WITHER and BLOOM. WITHER means safely 'corkscrewing' down to the floor over a set count (the group tried it over counts of six and eight), and BLOOM means to 'un-corkscrew' back to standing but with a stronger sense of growth and power.
     The group was then divided into actors and an audience. The actors in the space were given these same instructions in various combinations but this time with the additions of changes of speed, urgency and mood. When trying out this exercise you may want to see how music can affect tempo, rhythm and emotions.

12 The final instruction was for each actor to create a simple, repeatable physical action that represented a kitchen (this location was chosen as it's where the action of the play takes place). On hearing the word KITCHEN the actors stopped moving in the space and began their activity: chopping, eating, stirring, mixing, etc. Encourage your actors to be really precise with these 'mimes' and urge them to be particular and detailed.

To further the narrative possibilities of the exercise, one actor was then chosen to be a 'protagonist', Alice, and the group looked at ways of making her stand out from the crowd and pull focus. In one version everyone was deliriously happy, except Alice. In another, everyone was walking speedily, except Alice, and then vice versa; then everyone still except Alice; then everyone looking at Alice wherever she went in the space whilst still following different combinations of the twelve instructions.

When trying the exercise in this format, discuss with the participants who are acting as the audience to give feedback about what they saw that was interesting, what was unexpected and, importantly, what stories and narratives were growing out of the imagery. This is a good way of reminding your actors that there may, one day, be an audience and they shouldn't forget them completely – get them used to being watched.

The group then added another character into the exercise, the Postman, who entered and exited at various moments. The group then tried this exercise without anyone calling out instructions but taking the movement and actions of Alice and the arrival and departure of the Postman as their cues for variation, either changing to a new activity, moving at a different speed, tempo and various shifts in the levels of tension (calmness, excitement, fear, relaxation, urgency). In these exercises, the arrival of the Postman very much became the clear agent of change and chaos for everyone involved – what's in the package?

Approaching the play

INTERROGATING THE PLAY: FACTS AND QUESTIONS

This is a play containing alternative realities, and with the multiverse it's going to be helpful to establish what the 'real' world is, the control universe, so you can then be clear about the differences and divergences from this standard of comparison.

The lead director, Justin Audibert, suggested you can begin by drawing up two lists: a list of FACTS and a list of QUESTIONS. These will help you on your way to establishing the precise given circumstances of the scene. The FACTS are not opinions or hypotheses but things you know to be true.

Parts were cast for a read-though of Scene One and then the participants started to compile the lists, with everyone making suggestions and the conclusions being written down on a master list that could be continually added to as work on the play progressed.

The first set of FACTS are in the dramatis personae:

Alice is thirteen

Dan is sixteen

Dan is Alice's brother

Lucas is fourteen

Lucas is Dan and Alice's brother, etc.

And then more FACTS in the stage directions:

It is 2018

The scene takes place in a kitchen where there are lots of dirty cups, plates and saucepans

Dan is eating cereal

All three of them are in school uniform, etc.

Then the group began to interrogate the FACTS and came up with QUESTIONS based on the information. For example:

FACT
Alice comes into the kitchen, doesn't speak to her brothers . . .

QUESTION
Why doesn't Alice speak to her brothers?

And then this QUESTION led to more QUESTIONS:

Is this normal?
Has something happened, is she intentionally ignoring them?

Below is a list of FACTS from the text and QUESTIONS the workshop participants came up with that they thought would help to add detail and clarity to rehearsal. Many of these QUESTIONS do not have definitive answers in the text and will be interpretive choices for you and your companies to discuss.

FACTS	QUESTIONS
The kitchen is stacked high with dirty cups, plates and saucepans.	Is this normal? Who usually does the washing-up?
	Why is the kitchen in this state? How long has it been like this?
Lucas is holding a laminated piece of A4 card.	What is this piece of card?
	(Katie explained that the A4 card is the washing-up rota that Lucas drawn up and has colour-coded.)
	Why has Lucas laminated it?
	(This opened a discussion about Lucas and his attention to detail and fastidiousness, also about how he may not be fully aware of how pedantic he can be. Katie suggested that it was important that every character should not know something about themselves.)

FACTS	QUESTIONS
There is a radio in the kitchen	Why is it not playing at the beginning?
	Is it modern and fancy?
Mum is not at home	Where does Mum work?
	Why has she gone early?
	Is it normal that she's not at home when they get up?
	Would she usually not let the children know exactly what's going on?
	If this is unusual then what has happened?
Mum has written them a note	Has Mum threatened to kick the children out before?
	Is it usual for Mum to use strong language?
	(Katie explained that Mum has simply had enough and needed some time; she doesn't want to talk and has therefore left the note.)
Mum and Dad have split up	Why did Mum and Dad split up?
	When did Mum and Dad split up?
	Is Dad still in the UK or elsewhere?
	How long ago did Dad get a new partner?
	Has Dan now taken on the Dad role now Mum's not there?
	Was the divorce hard on Mum and the kids?
Alice's mum has taken her phone	Why has Mum taken Alice's phone?
	What does Alice have to apologise to her mum for?
	What did they argue about?
	Where did Mum take Alice's phone from?
Dad has a new partner from Australia who is younger than him	How does Mum feel about this?
The children are soon to have a new half-sibling	How do they feel about this news?
	Do they all feel the same way?

FACTS	QUESTIONS
Dad's partner is going for a scan today	How much does Mum know about Dad's new baby?
	Did Mum know about Dad becoming a father again?
	Which scan is this? How many weeks into the pregnancy?
Dad's new partner is called Lilia	
They listen to a song on the radio	What is the song?
	Why does Alice like this song?
	Why doesn't Dan like it, going as far as saying it makes him 'feel like killing myself'?
	What is Alice's connection with the song?
There's no milk	Is it normal for there to be so little to eat in the house?
There is nothing to eat	
Dan swears	Why does Dan swear? Does he always swear?
	Why does Lucas dislike swearing?
The kids have an auntie called Bex	
They have a landline phone	Why does Cinnamon have their landline number?
Cinnamon calls Alice on the landline	Why doesn't Alice want to talk to Cinnamon?
	Why are Cinnamon and Alice no longer friends?
	(Katie: 'Cinnamon is solid, she's sound')
Lucas quotes *Star Wars*	Is Dan genuinely familiar with the *Star Wars* quote? If not, why would he lie?
	How much of a *Star Wars* fan is Lucas, and why?
	Are/were Lucas's parents big *Star Wars* fans?
	Was Lucas named after George Lucas?

FACTS	QUESTIONS
Mum does shift work	What's her job? (Katie saw her as a nurse.)
	Does she have much time with her children?
	Does she have to work long hours?
Chloe arrives	Why doesn't Dan like Chloe?
	How long have Alice and Chloe been 'friends'?
	Has Alice done anything to her eyebrows?
	Why doesn't Chloe acknowledge Lucas?
	Has Chloe asked her mum about the party?
	Why is Chloe eager for Alice to go to the party?
	Why don't the boys speak to Chloe?
	Why does Dan say that Chloe is a bitch?
Alice knocks tea over Chloe's shoes	Is Alice naturally clumsy? (The workshop group decided that she's not naturally clumsy but is nervous around Chloe and behaving uncharacteristically. Although in the *dramatis personae* Chloe is described as 'Alice's frenemy', Katie suggested that Alice shouldn't know this and we shouldn't see Chloe as an archetype, or as the baddie.)
Pablo is having a party	Who is Pablo?
	Why does Dan say the party sounds 'dodgy'?
Dan and Lucas get a message telling them they have a brother	Did their dad also send a message to Alice's phone which their mum may have now intercepted?
Dan goes to hit Lucas, and Dan and Lucas fight and wrestle	How often is Dan aggressive towards his brother?
	Does it always get confrontational between them?

FACTS	QUESTIONS
Their parents had a stillborn baby	How difficult is it for them to discuss the baby?
	What happened to the baby?
	How did this affect Mum and Dad's relationship?
Jasmine was the name of the first child	
The Postman is sixteen	
Alice is given a parcel	What's in the parcel?

Interrogating the text: FACTS and changes

This next exercise again needs a close reading of the text. This time the group looked for FACTS in Scene Two that were alterations or completely different from the FACTS in Scene One, and then acknowledged the similarities and listed the divergences.

From the stage directions it is still 2018 and the kitchen is still stacked high with dirty cups, plates and saucepans but things are very different. After a read-through of Scene Two the participants discussed the changes and how and why these differences may have occurred. Below are some of the discoveries:

FACTS	QUESTIONS
There are now two sisters and no brothers	How has this happened? Who are they?
Pearl's washing-up rota is on paper not card and it's not laminated	What might this tell us about the different characters of Lucas and Pearl and their levels of scrupulousness?
Now there is milk and food in the kitchen	Are they better organised than the boys, or less greedy?
They *all* love the song on the radio	How does this change the atmosphere in the kitchen?
They all sing and dance together	
Alice switches off the radio, not Dan	
Alice invites Pablo inside; he doesn't push to be asked in as Chloe does	

The girls greet Pablo

Pablo ignores the girls' greetings

Alice admits having her phone taken was a punishment for something she's done wrong	Why does Alice feel more willing to discuss her the seriousness of the argument with her mum?
Pablo knocks over the tea cup, not Alice	Is Alice more at ease around Pablo than around Chloe?

Alice quotes *Star Wars*

Dad and Lilia are having a baby girl, not a boy

The boys' fighting and wrestling of Scene One is reduced to 'Pearl grabs Jasmine's arm'

Other FACTS came up in Scene Two that help to shed light on or answer some of the QUESTIONS from Scene One, meaning that they could then add to their FACTS list. To answer the 'Who is Pablo?' QUESTION, we learn that Pablo is a boy in Alice's geography class. And significantly we discover that baby Jasmine died as Mum had pre-eclampsia and that their father was 'medical' and felt some sense of responsibility or guilt about the death. If Dad was 'medical' and Mum is a nurse did they meet at work, or even work together?

How does Alice deal with the changes and this strand of the multiverse?

A stage area was designated, the beginning of the play was set up and, with participants cast in role, the group rehearsed the start of the opening scene. The scene was run again and the precise opening images, actions and movements were noted.

The next exercise involved setting up Scene Two as closely as possible to Scene One: same house, same kitchen, same blocking, same onstage starting positions for the actors, but this time they were two sisters, not two brothers. The actor playing Alice had exactly the same previous circumstances but now she would be meeting two strangers when she entered the kitchen.

The group discussed how Alice might react to this shock: would she run away? Justin suggested that the actors need to make the choices of being compelled to stay, being impelled to move forward, or repelled. In this situation, the actors need to understand what it is that compels Alice to stay – does she just find the sister opportunity too irresistible and can't bring herself to leave despite the confusion? The group discussed how Scenes One and Two differ tonally from one another, the second being much lighter and brighter – is that what makes Alice stay?

Interrogating the text: FACTS, QUESTIONS and research ideas

The group then read Scene Six looking for FACTS and QUESTIONS that may also involve some research tasks for a company.

FACTS	QUESTIONS for discussion and research
It is 1983	How different might things look compared to the 2018 scenes?
They all have eighties hair	What is eighties hair? (You might want to check out pop group Bananarama. Katie said she hoped that the play will be fun but should be played 'straight'; this scene shouldn't be a comic exaggeration or parody of the eighties.)
Shelly says, 'This is a very eighties kitchen'	What is an eighties kitchen? What does it look like? (The group discussed fashionable designs and schemes of the day – lots of white, red, grey and flecks of colour. What are the iconic kitchen gadgets of the eighties? Soda Stream, gigantic microwave ovens, deep fat fryers – how might the phone be different?)
Bex dances	What is eighties dancing? (With this in mind, Katie again stressed that this shouldn't be played for laughs – there are no comedy characters and the characters shouldn't know that they are in a *funny* situation.)
Their mum is not there	Why is their mum not there? If she's not with Mick as they thought, then where is she?
Mick telephones	Who is Mick? Why do they call him 'Mick the Dick'? (Katie said that the girls are afraid of Mick 'because he is a frightening and violent man, pretty horrible; he may not necessarily be hitting them but the kids know what he's capable of.')

They hide the telly	What is an eighties TV like? How big is it? Would it be easy to carry up to the attic?
Shelly says, 'There weren't any beeps'	What are the telephone beeps? Many young people may never have used a payphone so the pips might need some explaining
Shelly refers to films she's seen	What are *Back to the Future*, *Freaky Friday* and *Groundhog Day*, and why does Alice reference these films in particular?
Bex says, 'Do you mean like a nuclear holocaust?'	Why might Bex use this reference? (The workshop group discussed the political climate in the early 1980s and the very real fear of nuclear threat.)

Transitions

The workshop group looked at possible ways of moving from one scene into the next. As most of the scenes end with Alice and the Postman, the moment of Alice signing for the delivery was used as the trigger for the transitions.

The group played around with a variety of ways of building new scenes without stopping the impetus; the characters moved into the space at different speeds, tempos and directions, some walking forward, some backward, some being led on/off or carried on/off by Alice or the Postman. The participants tried a variety of points of entrance and exit, different attitudes and routes to get to their opening positions, as well as trying out some of the instructions from the opening exercise such as REWIND and CENTRE.

As well as planning the movement of the actors during these transitions you will also need to plan the journey of the props and where they come from: Are there different props from scene to scene or do they remain the same? Are you going to use the same cereal bowl all the way through the play and if so how does it get from one actor to another? Is it always the same school uniform?

The challenge is to make the transitions creative and varied without holding up the momentum of the play.

Music

The music playing on the radio really should be, as the script requires, from 1980 to 1983. There are lots of music genres to choose from and this might be a useful research project for the companies to find a suitable song that can run through the play. It was suggested that you may want to find out if there have been re-recordings or more recent versions of the song you choose, so it is the same song but in a slightly altered state. The music is a strong through-line so choose your tracks carefully – they need to have a sense of nostalgia when listened to in the 2018 scenes.

In the workshop, the group went for 'Karma Chameleon' by Culture Club from 1983.

Casting

A number of the directors were trying to work out how they might be able to cast their production if they had a small number of boys in their company. In the discussion the Postman seemed the male role that could most easily become a female character. For all the other roles it is not so simple and Katie urged the directors to consider the implications and possible confusions that might arise from changing the gender of the characters. Ultimately it might be less problematic to have girls *playing* boys rather than changing the characters' genders.

For larger casts, the character of Alice could be played by a different actor in each scene. In order to help the audience follow her character through the play, some kind of 'label' would be helpful so the audience knows it's Alice – maybe a consistent identifying piece of costume? Larger casts could also be involved in the creation of the environments and involved in the transitions. Katie suggested that Mum and Dad shouldn't be represented on stage in any kind of prologue or during transitions as they really should be absent – the fact that they are not there, especially Mum, is significant.

From a workshop led by Justin Audibert
with notes by Phil Sheppard

Salt

by Dawn King

Life is never plain sailing, but when a new government initiative comes into place offering young people the opportunity to train and learn skills overseas, droves of teens jump at the chance to secure their future. Once on board the transport ship, the promises of the glossy advert seem a far cry from what lies ahead. A play about generations, choices and hope.

Class size
12–20

Dawn King is an award-winning writer working in theatre, film, TV, VR and radio. At the time of publication she is adapting her play *Foxfinder* for the screen with Elation Pictures and the BFI. She also has a VR film project in development with DMC Films and Felix and Paul Studios. Her previous work for the stage includes: *Foxfinder*, originally produced by Papatango Theatre Company at the Finborough Theatre in 2011 and revived in a new West End production at the Ambassadors Theatre by Bill Kenwright in 2018; an adaptation of Aldous Huxley's novel *Brave New World*, a co-production between the Royal & Derngate, Northampton and the Touring Consortium which toured the UK in 2015; and *Ciphers*, a co-production between Out of Joint, Exeter's Nothcott Theatre and the Bush Theatre which toured the UK in 2013/2014. For *Foxfinder*, she won the Royal National Theatre Foundation Playwright Award 2013, the Papatango New Writing Competition 2011 and Most Promising Playwright, Off West End Awards 2012. She was also shortlisted for the Susan Smith Blackburn Prize and the James Tait Black Prize for Drama. Her short film *The Karman Line* won seventeen awards including the BIFA for Best Short and was BAFTA nominated in 2014.

Characters

Team 2B: **Adé, Rowan, Sal, Kassim, Claudia, Morgan**
Team 1A: **Talya, Elmer, Jo, Nick, Star, Lee**

Author's note

The play requires a main cast of twelve but could also include a number of other performers to feature in the adverts. Please change genders/ethnicities/names of the main cast as best suits the requirements of your actors.

An advert.

Sentimental, sad music. Young people (from team 1A or perhaps others) looking dejected and miserable, some with 'hungry and homeless please help' signs. They talk directly to the 'camera', i.e. the audience. Distribute lines as you see fit among your performers.

– When I finished school, I was broke.

– I couldn't find a job.

– I was hungry.

– I was living on the street.

– I just wanted to work!

– I just wanted a chance.

– Things were bad.

– I was sad.

– I was desperate.

– I was angry!

– I thought about ending it all.

– I felt like I had no future.

The sad music changes to something stirring and vaguely patriotic. Smiling young people – from team 1A – appear, wearing 'FAS' T-shirts.

– Hey, haven't you heard about the FOREIGN APPRENTICESHIP SCHEME?

– No?

– What's that?

– It's a new opportunity for young people aged sixteen to nineteen!

– To get specialised workplace training!

– In electronics and manufacturing!

– Wow!

– How does it work?

– We'll travel by boat to China

– Asia

– Or the United Arab Emirates!

– And live there for two years as apprentices!

– Travel, training, food and accommodation are all included!

– It's free?

– Yeah! We don't have to pay!

– Nice!

– We get valuable experience . . .

– In a real workplace.

– Learn new skills!

– See the world.

– Have a laugh.

– Make friends!

– When we come home . . .

– We'll be able to use our experience to get the jobs we want.

– We're helping ourselves . . .

– And we're doing our bit to help make Britain great again!

– Cool!

– It sounds AMAZING!

– Why don't you JOIN US on the FOREIGN APPRENTICESHIP SCHEME AND TAKE CONTROL OF YOUR FUTURE!

They smile, laugh, hug and high five each other. Music fades.

Below decks on a large ship, in a stark, basic cabin with bunks. Faint engine noise from below.

Claudia *stands in the cabin. She's wearing a FAS T-shirt (everyone on the ship wears the same thing). She is reading to herself from a tablet computer.*

Claudia   'Welcome your team members and check them in. Show them their allocated bunks and remind them to be tidy . . . when they are all present, play the arrival briefing video. Remember to use your leadership skills from the start by Setting a Good Example and Using Clear Communication.' OK. OK. I can do this.

Rowan *comes into the cabin, carrying a rucksack.*

Claudia   Hi, I'm team leader for team 2B. Claudia. Welcome!

Rowan   Hi, I'm Rowan.

Claudia   Rowan . . .

She checks her tablet.

Yes, you're on my list!

Rowan   Whoop! This is really exciting!

Claudia   You're the first. The rest of our team hasn't arrived yet.

Rowan   Nobody knows where they're supposed to go, it's pure chaos up there.

Claudia   All they have to do is find the cabin allocated to their team. It's not that hard. Is it?

Rowan   I found it.

Claudia   You did. Well done! And you're supposed to sleep . . .

She checks her tablet.

Here. Please keep your space tidy for the sake of your teammates.

Rowan   Sure, no problem!

Claudia   I'll wait for the others before I play the arrival briefing. Uh. Do you have any questions you want to ask me?

Rowan *glances around.*

Rowan   Uh . . . do we all, the whole team, sleep in here?

Claudia   Shared accommodation, that's right.

Rowan   The pictures on the website showed two people sharing?

Claudia   That's a different ship.

Rowan   Oh!

Claudia   That's *Sunshine Days* and this is *Bright Future*.

Rowan   I thought it looked . . . different.

Claudia   I was surprised too but it's a good thing for us because . . .

She looks for some info on her tablet. Reads from it.

'Sharing sleeping quarters on the journey helps teams to bond, increases learning opportunities and makes teams more effective.' And that's what matters. Right?

Rowan   Sure!

Claudia   The bathroom's down the corridor. We share it. With three other teams.

Rowan   Sharing isn't a problem for me, at all. I'm just happy to be here. This is our chance to take control –

Claudia   Take control of our future.

Rowan   – take control of our future!

Claudia   Right! I'm glad to have you on my team, Rowan. Can I get a high five?

They high five each other.

Adé *comes down the stairs behind them. He has bruising on his face.*

Adé   Has anyone else noticed this boat is a shithole?

Pause.

Claudia   Hello, I'm Claudia, I'm team leader for team 2B.

Rowan   It's a different boat to the one on the website.

Adé   Uh-huh. I noticed.

Claudia   Can I have your name, please? I have to check you in on the system.

Adé   Adé.

Claudia *checks him in on her tablet.*

Adé   This is it? This is where we have to sleep?

Claudia   Yes . . .?

Ade   It's like a prison cell.

Claudia   It's perfectly fine, and has everything we need.

Rowan   'Pleasant, shared accommodation'. Just like it said on the website.

Adé   'Pleasant'?

Claudia   There's no money for luxuries, Adé.

Rowan   We're lucky to be here at all.

Adé   Lucky. Uh-huh.

Claudia *looks at him.*

Claudia   What happened to your face?

Adé   Nothing.

Claudia   Is that . . . blood . . . on your shirt?

Adé   I tripped getting on the boat.

Claudia   Why didn't you say? I'll take you to be looked at by the registered first aider.

Adé   I don't need to be looked at –

Claudia   But /

Adé   – thanks. It smells down here. Stale feet, tinned sweat.

Rowan   I can't smell anything.

Adé   Uh-huh.

Claudia   You'll get used to it. That's where you have to sleep, Adé. Please keep your /

Adé   It's this bad now, what's it going to be like in a week? Or two weeks, or twenty-three days? That's a looong time . . .

Claudia   Adé, it *is* disappointing that we weren't assigned to the other ship but this isn't a pleasure cruise. It's an amazing opportunity and we need to stay positive and make the most of it. Could you possibly try to be a bit less negative, please?

Adé   I can try.

Sal *comes down the stairs.*

Claudia   Hi, welcome to team 2B! I'm Claudia and I'm your team leader. This is Rowan and Adé. You are?

Sal   I'm Sal.

Claudia   Sal.

She ticks **Sal** *off on her list.*

Claudia   This is your bunk, please keep your space tidy. We're still waiting for two members of the team to arrive. Yes, this is a different ship to the one on the website. Do you have any questions?

Sal   Uh . . . no.

Adé   I've got a question for you, Sal. Why are you here? Why did you sign up for this amazing opportunity?

Sal   Uh. I was trying for a scholarship. To uni . . . to study engineering.

Claudia   You're a scholarship student? That's fantastic!

Sal   No, I uh, I failed my exams.

Claudia   We're still glad to have you on our team, you could be a real asset!

Sal   If I can handle it. I don't know if I can . . . I don't know if this was a good idea . . .

Rowan   You're probably nervous. I've never been on a boat before, that's making me nervous.

Sal   It's a ship. Uhm. Ships have boats on them and this ship has a lifeboat so it's, uh, a ship.

Adé   Lifeboats are good. This rust bucket could sink any minute.

Rowan   You really think we could sink?

Claudia   No, the boat, ship, is absolutely not going to sink. And there's no need for anyone to be nervous. A team is only as strong as the weakest member. We'll work together to support each other! Can I get a high five, Sal?

Sal   Uh . . .

Awkwardly, she returns **Claudia***'s high five.*

Morgan *and* **Kassim** *come down the stairs.* **Morgan** *is noticeably smaller/younger-looking than the others.*

Morgan   Told you it was this way.

Kassim   2B?

Claudia   Yes, we're 2B, welcome!

Kassim   You the team leader?

Claudia (*nodding*)   I'm Claudia.

Kassim   I'm Kassim.

Morgan   Morgan.

Claudia *checks them off.*

Claudia   This is Adé, Rowan and Sal and now we're all here I want to officially welcome you to /

Kassim   Can I ask you something?

Claudia   Yes . . .?

Kassim *points to* **Morgan.**

Kassim   Is there any way we can, like, swap him for someone else?

Claudia   That's not very welcoming.

Kassim   It's not personal. He looks about twelve –

Morgan   I'm sixteen.

Kassim   – he's not going to get high scores.

Morgan   Seriously?!

Kassim   I've got nothing against you but I can't have anyone dragging me down!

Morgan   Fuck. Off.

Claudia   This is our team. We can't change members.

Kassim   Brilliant.

Claudia   We all want high scores. I'm sure Morgan is going to work hard, right?

Morgan   Harder than him.

Claudia   Friendly competition, great! Which one of you can get the best numbers?

Kassim *and* **Morgan**   Me.

Kassim *and* **Morgan** *scowl at each other.* **Claudia***'s tablet beeps.*

Claudia   OK, can you all pay attention please, I have to play the arrival briefing video.

Kassim   What did you do?

Claudia   What?

Kassim   To get to be a team leader?

Claudia   I applied.

Kassim   I applied too. Filled in all the extra boxes, did the online test. Didn't get it.

Claudia   That must be disappointing for you.

Kassim   Disappointing? It's bullshit. I've got three little sisters and four young cousins, I know how to be in charge.

Claudia   Team-leader selection isn't only based on experience. A number of factors are /

Kassim   It's gonna say 'team leader' in your placement report so you get a better job at the end of all this. It's not fair.

Claudia   I'm your team leader, Kassim, and I'm going to do everything I can to help you, to help us, achieve our best.

Rowan   Claudia's a good team leader.

Claudia   Thank you.

Kassim   We'll see.

Claudia *'s tablet beeps again.*

Claudia   We're behind schedule so if you can all pay /

Rowan   Can I ask a question?

Claudia   I have to play the arrival briefing video now.

Rowan   We're going to be really, really far away from land . . . what if something goes wrong with the ship?

Claudia   This is a smart ship, it's programmed with our route and it's practically unsinkable.

Rowan   Yeah, but . . . if something does go wrong, there's no crew, right? No lifeguards or . . . Nobody to help us . . .

Claudia   If there's a problem, the team leaders can access the ship's computer to launch the lifeboats or divert the ship to the nearest port, but nothing will go wrong.

Adé   I hope you all know how to swim.

Rowan   I can't. I can't swim.

Claudia   We're not going to sink.

Adé   Good luck, everyone!

Rowan   Oh, God . . .

Claudia   Adé, do you remember what I said about being positive?

Adé   I said I'd try.

Claudia   Try harder. We have to do the arrival briefing now or we'll be behind schedule.

She props up her tablet and presses a button. The video plays. It's team 1A, smiling and happy. Distribute lines as you see fit.

– Hello and welcome to the FOREIGN APPRENTICESHIP SCHEME!

– You have begun your journey . . .

– A journey that will take two years . . .

– But will benefit you for a lifetime!

– Take a moment to congratulate yourselves and each other . . .

– Well done for getting this far!

They all clap. **Claudia** *encourages 2B to clap too.*

– Please, do not interfere with any equipment on board the ship.

– This could be very dangerous!

– Pay attention to all instructions given to you by your team leader.

– They have received high-level training . . .

– They know what's best for you!

– Enjoy getting to know your teammates on board the *Sunshine Days*.

Claudia   *Bright Future*, our ship is the *Bright Future*.

– Relax . . .

– Have fun!

– But remember . . .

– You will be continually assessed for your placement reports . . .

– And that process starts today!

All   SO WORK HARD, FOR YOURSELF, FOR YOUR TEAM, FOR YOUR FUTURE!

Smiles, hugs, high fives. The video ends.

Claudia   Guys, I know that we can be one of the highest-scoring teams this year if we try.

Kassim   Not one of. The highest. The best.

Claudia   Yes, the best! So we need to start strong and really get our numbers up during training, OK?

Kassim   We got to concentrate. All of us.

Sal   I don't know if I can . . . get high scores, I mean . . . what if I mess up?

Kassim   No room for mistakes. No excuses. I've got a lot riding on this.

Morgan   We all do.

Claudia   Someone as smart as you, a scholarship student /

Sal   I'm not a scholarship student . . . I failed . . . I failed my exams . . .

Claudia   You won't have any problems with training. You'll find it easy!

Sal   I . . . I can't . . .

She is gasping.

I. Can't. Breathe . . .

Claudia   Sal? What's wrong?

Sal *gasps some more.*

Morgan   She's going blue.

Rowan   Claudia?

Claudia   Uh . . .

Rowan   What do we do?

Kassim   Hey, team leader! Do something!

Claudia *begins flicking through her tablet screen.*

Claudia   'Emergency protocols . . . medical emergency . . .'

Sal   I'm. Dying. Help.

Rowan   Oh God.

Claudia *is frantically paging through her tablet.*

Claudia   Where is it?

Adé   Easy, Sal. Wait for it to pass. You're not going to die. Not right now, anyway. Do like I do. Breathe . . . slow . . . calm . . . that's it . . .

Sal *and* **Adé** *breathe together.* **Sal**'s *breath is slowing down.*

Adé   Better?

Sal *nods.*

Claudia   Here it is. 'In the event of a medical emergency . . .'

Kassim   Too late.

Claudia   I was about to call the registered first aider. I can still do that if you want?

Sal   No. Sorry. Embarrassing.

Claudia   We uh . . . we just handled our first crisis. As a team.

Kassim   You didn't do anything.

Claudia   Well done, Adé!

Sal   Yes. Thanks.

Adé *nods. Pause.*

Claudia   If you're really OK, Sal . . .?

Sal   Uh, yeah, really.

Claudia   I have copies of our timetable showing our cooking and cleaning shifts . . .

Adé   We have to cook?

Rowan   It said on the website that we have to cook.

Adé   Didn't read most of it.

Rowan   Oh.

Claudia   Cooking and cleaning duties are split between the teams on board. Tonight, for our first night, it's pizza!

Morgan   Pizza. Cool.

Claudia   Dinner is at seven and afterwards we can go up on deck for recreation and to meet the other teams if we like. Then we should get an early night so we're well rested for our first training session. Guys, I'm really proud to have all of you on my team. Can I get a high five?

Rowan   Go team!

Morgan   Go 2B!

She high fives them all, but **Adé** *frowns.*

Claudia   Adé . . .

Adé   Yeah, yeah. Positive.

He high fives her, reluctantly.

Claudia   See? Not so hard, if you try.

Adé   Uh-huh.

Shaking his head, he goes to his bunk. They all begin to unpack their things, shaking out sleeping bags, etc.

Rowan *notices that* **Sal** *has a small radio in a plastic bag.*

Rowan   Were we all supposed to bring a radio? I don't remember that being on the list.

Sal   They're useful to have at sea.

Rowan   Why's it in a plastic bag?

Sal   We're at sea.

Rowan   We're not going to get wet. Are we?

Sal   We're *at sea*.

Rowan *looks worried.*

Beep. **Claudia** *gets a message on her tablet.*

Claudia   Oh. Guys, they say that we're going to have some rough weather tonight so we're not allowed on deck for recreation. We come straight back here after dinner.

Rowan   Rough weather? How rough?

Claudia   Just a little storm. Nothing crazy.

Later.

A storm rages. The ship is lurching up and down. Through the noise of the storm comes the sound of the shipping forecast from **Sal***'s small radio.* **Morgan** *is groaning and gripping a bucket.*

Forecast   And now the Shipping Forecast, issued by the Met Office on behalf of the Maritime and Coastguard Agency at 00.48 today. There are warnings of gales in Rockall, Malin, Hebrides, Bailey, Fair Isle and Biscay. Humber, Thames –

Rowan   Oh . . . God . . . I really feel . . .

Morgan   I will not puke again.

Adé   I puked up my soul. I'm empty.

Claudia   It would help if you would all stop talking about /

Morgan *pukes into the bucket.*

Claudia   OK, that's all right, we'll be all right, the storm will be over soon.

Forecast   – Southeast veering southwest 4 or 5, occasionally 6 later –

Kassim   You understand all this?

Sal   We used to live near the sea. My granddad taught me to sail.

Forecast   – Thundery showers. Tyne, Dogger. Northeast 3 or 4. Occasional rain. Moderate or poor. Rockall, Malin, Hebrides. Southwest gale 8 to storm 10, veering west, severe gale 9. Biscay. North 7 to severe gale 9. Heavy showers. Moderate icing. Trafalgar /

Sal *switches the radio off.*

Kassim   So what's it mean?

Sal   Uh. We're sailing through a severe gale. A . . . a very bad storm.

Claudia   Sailing through. We'll be out the other side soon.

Sal   Maybe. In a couple of hours . . .

Rowan   Hours? I can't!

Adé   Why did they send us straight into a massive storm?

Sal   Conditions at sea can change quickly.

Adé   And they can't look at a weather forecast?

Claudia   Obviously headquarters haven't done this on purpose.

Adé   It's all right for them, sitting in some office . . .

Claudia   The storm will be over soon. Hang in there, team!

Morgan   I am never. Eating microwave pizza. Again.

The storm rages and they suffer. **Kassim** *is looking at* **Morgan.** *He talks to him quietly.*

Kassim   What school did you go to?

Morgan   What?

Kassim   What school?

Morgan   Cheshunt Secondary.

Kassim   Two of my cousins go there. Called Nisha and Issa. You know them?

Morgan   Lots of people called lots of things at my school.

Kassim   What's your date of birth?

Morgan   Ninth of May, twenty . . .

Pause.

Kassim   You don't know your own date of birth?

Morgan   I know it.

Kassim   What is it then?

Morgan   Ninth of May, twenty oh nine.

Kassim   Bullshit. You didn't know it.

Morgan   I'm sick! I couldn't remember, so what?

Kassim   You're not sixteen.

Morgan   Leave me alone. I feel sick. I might puke on you.

Kassim   Maybe I should tell Claudia to message headquarters and check your background. When you were born, shit like that – what do you think?

Morgan   No. Don't.

Kassim   So tell me.

Pause. **Morgan** *wary.*

Kassim   I won't tell the rest of them. OK?

Morgan   I'm fourteen.

Kassim   Fourteen? You can't be!

Morgan   I added two years on my birthday on my application. It went through fine.

Kassim   Brilliant. It's probably illegal for you to be here!

Morgan   Don't tell anyone, then!

Kassim   What the fuck are you doing here? You should be in school.

Morgan   School is a waste of time! I do this now, I get ahead of everyone my age.

Kassim   You're just a kid, you won't be able to handle it.

Morgan   I can work as hard as the rest of you. Harder. I've got more energy. Are you gonna tell them?

Kassim *thinks for a moment.*

Kassim   If you hit the high numbers, I won't have to, will I?

Morgan   Worry about your own performance, old man.

The ship lurches again and they struggle to stay upright and not puke.

Rowan   The storm's getting worse.

Sal   We uh, we shouldn't be at sea at all, in conditions like this.

Rowan   It feels like the ship's going to tip right over. We'll be trapped in here. We'll drown!

Claudia   Think about something else, everyone! Think about . . . going home in two years, think about the job you'll get. Think about your first pay day . . . taking money home to your family . . . how happy they'll be.

Kassim   I'm gonna buy them a feast. Loads of delicious food. Healthy. With vegetables.

Morgan   Stop talking about food.

Claudia   I'm going to repay my mum. Help her pay off . . . some debts.

Kassim   Get new shoes for my little sisters. New school uniform.

Claudia   And buy her something. A present, to say thank you.

Rowan   I'm going to make my family proud of me.

Morgan   Yeah show them all what I can do.

Sal   Show them . . . I'm not a failure.

Claudia   We'll tell stories about tonight, about this storm and how sick we all got, and laugh!

Pause. They look happier.

Adé   When we get there . . . to China . . . what's it going to be like?

Rowan   'Hard Work . . . a Real Challenge . . . But Fun.' It says that on the website.

Adé   Uh-huh.

Pause.

Did any of you see that video?

Claudia   No.

Adé   There was a video of people on placement in a factory, making trainers . . .

Claudia   It was a fake.

Adé   You said you didn't watch it.

Claudia   I didn't, I read about it in my leadership skills training online module. But it was a fake, that's why they took it down.

Adé   Didn't look like they were having fun.

Claudia   It wasn't real. It was a fake, a joke. People trying to cause trouble.

Rowan   There are lots of official videos showing what the FAS is really like, you should have watched some of those.

Pause.

Adé   Why did they take our phones when we got on the ship?

Claudia   For safekeeping. We get them back when we arrive.

Adé   Do we?

Claudia   Yes.

Pause.

Adé   Maybe they took our phones away to stop us from taking photos or video when we get there?

Claudia   No, why would they want to do that?

Adé   You're the team leader, you're supposed to know everything . . .

Claudia   We get our phones back when we arrive.

Pause.

Adé   Claudia . . .

Claudia   Yes.

Adé   These jobs we're supposed to get when we get back home. Where do they come from?

Claudia   What?

Adé   There are no jobs for us in Britain now. Why will there be jobs for us when we get home?

Claudia   No, you've misunderstood. You really didn't read the website, did you! There won't be *more jobs* but we will be *more qualified.*

Rowan   We'll be 'qualified apprentices eligible for a greater selection of employment opportunities'.

Adé   Uh-huh.

Pause. More lurching. The wind howls outside.

Adé   You know what they call it when you work but don't get paid?

Kassim   Oh, man, you need to shut up. I am sick of listening to you.

Adé   Slavery.

Kassim   Bullshit.

Claudia   We're apprentices, it's a work placement, for experience, that's why we don't get paid . . . it's not that hard to understand, is it?

Sal   Slavery is . . . working without choice and we all, we all had a choice.

Adé   You chose something you saw on a website. This isn't even the same ship!

Claudia   Obviously there's more than one ship on a scheme this /

Adé   Don't be surprised when we get there and it's not like you think it's going to be. And don't be surprised when we get home, and you still can't get a job.

Claudia   If that's really how you feel about the scheme, why did you sign up?

Kassim   Yeah, why are you here making the rest of us miserable with your irritating questions?

Adé   Had to get away.

Kassim   What did you do?

Adé   Nothing.

Kassim *grabs* **Adé**'s *chin, looks at his face.*

Kassim   Someone gave you that smack. Is that why you're here?

Adé *pulls away.*

Kassim   Poor little Adé . . . running away from home . . .

Claudia   Kassim!

Kassim   Joke, I'm joking.

Claudia   Everyone's tired and not feeling great, let's just go to sleep, OK?

Rowan   I won't be able to sleep with the ship moving like this.

Claudia   Try.

Rowan   We could sink while we're sleeping. The water would come in, in the dark . . .

Sal   Probably better not to think like that.

Rowan   We wouldn't even wake up we'd just . . . drown.

Claudia   We're not going to sink! Just lie down. Please. And close your eyes.

They lie with their eyes open, sleepless.

The cabin. Daytime.

Claudia *gives out tablet computers to everyone in the team.*

Claudia   OK, can we get ready please? Training begins in . . . thirty seconds!

They take positions on their bunks or the floor. **Claudia** *watches her tablet as it counts down the time, perhaps playing 'countdown' music.*

Kassim   We've got to concentrate, yeah?

Sal   I feel sick.

Claudia   Fifteen seconds.

Kassim   If you gotta puke just do it on the floor –

Morgan   Grim.

Kassim   – and carry on. Don't waste time!

Claudia   Five . . . four . . . three . . . two . . . one . . .

Her tablet beeps and possibly begins to play 'motivational music'.

Go!

Everyone bends to their tablet and begins 'training', completing various online tests. There's something robotic, rhythmic, about the intensity with which they tap and swipe at their screens.

*Everyone is trying hard. Except for **Adé**. Although he joins in at first, he grows more bemused as training continues. He frowns. Looks up.*

Adé   What's the point of this?

Claudia   Training sessions are timed, Adé.

Kassim   No time for chat.

Adé   What kind of 'training' is this supposed to be?

Claudia   'On-board training sessions will teach you important skills for your upcoming work placements and improve hand–eye coordination.'

Adé   Uh-huh. A monkey could do it if they had enough practice.

Claudia   We can discuss this later! Continue with your work, please.

*More intense tapping away at the tablets. **Adé** carries on for a bit, then stops. He watches the others. Shakes his head. Puts his tablet down.*

Kassim   Woah, pick that up!

Adé   I'm not doing it. It's pointless.

Claudia   You have to, Adé!

Adé *turns, walks out.*

Rowan   Where's he going?

Claudia   Ignore him, carry on everyone please, we're nearly out of –

Her tablet beeps and they all stop.

– time.

Kassim   Brilliant. Fucking brilliant!

Morgan   What's his problem?

Claudia   I uh . . . I'm not sure.

Rowan   He said, 'I'm not doing it'.

Pause, they all look at each other.

Sal   Uh . . . how did we score?

Claudia *looks down at her tablet.*

Claudia   It's still processing.

She waits for results of the team's scores and ranking of which team did best on the ship. This appears with a beep.

Considering that we had one team member who wasn't participating properly, we did very well.

Kassim   Just tell us.

Claudia   There are two teams on the ship who did worse than we did.

Groans all round.

Morgan   It's his fault. Adé.

Kassim   He's totally blown our first set of scores!

Sal   I uh . . . I made mistakes too. I tried not to but . . .

Rowan   He didn't even try. He left!

Kassim   What are you gonna do about him? Team leader?

Claudia *flicks through her tablet. Reads.*

Claudia   I tried 'Leading by Example' and 'Clear Communication . . .' uh . . . 'Motivate Your Team'. That's the next leadership skill. I'll talk to him. Explain why this is so important.

Kassim   Talk to him?

Claudia   Yes! I know what I'm doing, Kassim.

On deck. Wave sounds. Engine noise.

Adé *is alone, reading and sipping a can of drink.*

The others come up from below decks and approach him.

Claudia It's nice up here, isn't it?

Adé Uh-huh. Fresh air. Peace and quiet.

Claudia Could we have a talk?

Adé I'm reading.

Claudia *sits down next to him. He sighs.*

Claudia Did you find the training exercises confusing, or . . . too hard?

Adé *turns a page of his book. Sips his drink. Doesn't answer.*

Claudia Perhaps you didn't realise, as you've not read the website properly . . . but placements are allocated according to how highly we score during training. Don't you want to get better, more interesting work? Learn more valuable and employable skills?

Adé *shrugs.*

Kassim You got a bad attitude.

Claudia Adé, our individual scores are linked to our group score. Your performance affects all of us. So we need you to join in and /

Adé You can do as much 'training' as you want. I'm not playing.

Morgan Dickhead.

Adé This scheme is a joke.

Claudia That's your opinion and we respect it.

Kassim I don't.

Claudia But we're your teammates. We care about you and we want you to do well.

Adé You want me to do what you want.

Claudia It's your responsibility to us to be the best that you can be!

Adé Did your computer tell you to say that?

Claudia You're in my team and you have to listen to what I'm /

He gets up, walks off.

Kassim Talk to him. That worked. Well done.

Claudia He won't listen.

Kassim   I got people counting on me back home, yeah? My little sisters are hungry. My dad can't pay the bills. We can't turn the heating on in the winter, do you know what that's like? Do you?

Claudia   Yes, I do.

Kassim   I got to get a good score, so I can get a good job and help my family. I'm not gonna fail them, because of him!

Rowan   I really don't want my placement report to say I was part of a team that wouldn't participate properly.

Morgan   Nobody employs a troublemaker.

Sal   If he won't even complete training . . . he'll drag down our group average . . . we won't be able to get our numbers back up. It'll be impossible for us to get good report scores. We . . . we'll fail.

Claudia   I'm not going to let that happen. I'll think of something.

Kassim   What?

Claudia   I obviously need to talk to him –

Morgan   Tried that.

Claudia   – again and . . . find the right way to motivate him.

Rowan   He really doesn't seem like he cares, Claudia.

Claudia   Don't worry. I . . . I'll think of something.

Pause. All looking at her, uncertain.

Kassim   What happens if someone on the team gets sick, or . . . can't go on? What happens to our numbers?

Claudia   Uh.

Claudia *flicks through information on her tablet. Reads.*

Claudia   'In case of sickness or sudden incapacity, group average is recalibrated without the missing team member.'

Kassim   I know how to 'motivate' him. Tell him to get his shit together or we throw him over the side.

Pause. They're all shocked. Looking at **Kassim**.

Kassim   If he's not here, he can't drag our numbers down.

Claudia   I'm going to assume that you're joking.

Sal   No, I'm not doing that.

Kassim   We don't actually do it!

Morgan   I see . . .!

Kassim   Just make him think we will.

Morgan   Scare him?

Kassim   Until he does what we say.

Claudia   Adé is on my team, I'm responsible for his safety, I'm not going to let you threaten him.

Kassim   If you have a better idea how to stop him messing up our scores and ruining our entire fucking lives, speak now! I'd like to hear it!

They all look at **Claudia** *but she's got nothing.*

On deck.

Night. Darkness. Wave sounds, engine noise.

There's a sense of hushed movement happening in the darkness.

Muffled yelling.

Torches light up the scene. They are held by **Sal** *and* **Morgan**. **Rowan** *and* **Claudia** *are holding* **Adé**. *They have put a pillowcase over his head so he can't see.*

Kassim   We got together and we had a talk, Adé. We agreed . . . we don't need your bad attitude and your bad numbers on our team.

Adé *is yelling, but it's muffled by the pillowcase.*

Adé   Get off, let me go!

Kassim   We could throw you over the side. Into the sea. Say it was an accident. No one would know.

Adé *goes still, stops struggling.*

Kassim *pulls the pillowcase off.* **Adé** *looks at them.*

Adé   Let go.

Kassim   Are you going to behave? Do what we tell you like a good boy?

Adé   Fuck all of you.

Kassim   Right. Throw him over.

He grabs **Adé** *around the waist.*

Kassim   Help me lift him.

Rowan *and* **Claudia** *help* **Kassim.** **Adé** *is fighting them.* **Kassim**
punches him in the stomach, winding him so he can't struggle.

Sal   Don't!

Rowan   Oh, God . . .

Kassim   Grab his legs. Lift him up.

Sal   No.

Kassim   One of you take his fucking legs! Sal! Morgan!

Sal *drops her torch and steps back.*

Sal   Stop it.

Kassim   Morgan, help us!

Morgan *hesitates.*

Kassim   What's wrong? Can't handle it? Grow up!

Morgan *grabs* **Adé***'s legs.* **Morgan, Kassim, Rowan** *and* **Claudia** *heft*
Adé *up until he's hanging over the water.*

Adé   No, no no please . . .

Kassim   Are you gonna behave?

Adé   Yes!

Kassim   Are you going to get high scores?

Adé   Yes, yes!

Claudia   All right, let's put him down.

Kassim   We're better off without him. He could still fuck this up for us.

Claudia   Kassim!

Pause.

Kassim   Joke. I was joking.

They let **Adé** *go. He struggles to get his breath back and calm down. A
long pause as they all look at him, a bit shocked at what they've just
done.*

Claudia   Are you . . . all right?

Kassim   He's fine.

Adé   Did . . . did you read about that in your leadership skills training module, Claudia?

Claudia   I . . . I hope that tomorrow we can put this behind us and move on, together, as a team. We can achieve great things!

Adé   Uh-huh.

Kassim, **Morgan**, **Claudia** *and* **Rowan** *go below deck. As they go –*

Kassim   You did well, kid.

Morgan   Yeah?

Kassim   Knew I could count on you.

Sal *stays on deck. She picks up her dropped torch.*

Sal   Uh . . . are you really . . . all right?

Adé   Oh yeah. Never been better.

Sal   I didn't want to . . . to do that.

Adé   Uh-huh.

Sal   I'm sorry.

Adé *nods. For a little while* **Sal** *and* **Adé** *look out at the dark ocean.*

Adé   Would they have done it? Dropped me over?

Sal   No. I don't know. Maybe.

Pause. **Adé** *thinking about this.*

Adé   It wouldn't be so bad, drowning. Going down into all that black. There are worse ways to die.

Sal   I think . . . when you realise there's no air . . . you panic. It's terrible. Torture.

Adé   Don't drown. Noted.

They look at the ocean some more.

Sal   We . . . we have to work together now. For two years.

Adé   'Put this behind us and move on, together, as a team'.

Sal   How do we do that?

Adé   Don't ask me.

Sal Adé, why *did* you come?

Pause.

Adé I didn't want to be like him.

Sal Like . . .?

Adé My dad. He loves telling me what to do. Yelling at me. Pushing me around. And the rest.

He indicates his bruised face.

Sal Oh . . .

Adé I usually just breathe. Wait for it to be over. Don't react, don't get angry. But . . . I couldn't do that anymore.

Pause. She waits for him to speak.

I fought back. He's laying into me and I'm laying into him and I thought . . . like father like son. So I ran out of there. I was walking around town with the feeling of his fingers around my throat and I saw an advert for sailing away on a boat . . . Didn't read the website. Didn't really know what I was signing up for.

Sal You're not, not like that, not at all.

He shrugs. They look out at the water for a while.

Sal I uh. I used to go out fishing. With my granddad.

Adé Oh yeah?

Sal When I was little. Before things went wrong. Before I . . . fucked everything up.

Adé It's not too late. You've still got plenty of years left to fuck up.

Sal I should have been at university right now doing my scholarship. If I'd held it together through my exams I would have been. I didn't just fail, I lost it. Completely. I thought being out here might make me feel different.

Adé Does it?

Pause. Sal thinking about this.

Sal I'm really sorry. That we hurt you.

The cabin.

It's late. Team 2B are in their bunks, asleep. **Claudia** *is awake. She gets out of bed, sneaks to* **Kassim**'s *bunk. Shakes him awake.*

Kassim   Huh?

Claudia   They hate me now.

Kassim   What?

Claudia   Sal and Adé. They hate me.

Kassim   Sal doesn't hate you.

Claudia   He didn't give me a choice. Adé, I had to do something . . .

Kassim   He'll fall in line, don't worry.

Claudia   Maybe he doesn't realise it now, but if I'd let him go on like that, the way he was, I would have been neglecting my duty as his team leader, to help him achieve his best. Wouldn't I?

Kassim   You ask me, Adé should be thanking you. You did what you had to do.

Claudia   Yes, for the good of the entire team, I'm glad you see it that way.

Kassim   Good night.

Claudia   Good night.

Pause.

Claudia   Kassim?

Kassim   What?

Claudia   You said you weren't going to hurt him.

Kassim   It's late. I want to go to sleep now.

Claudia   But you did, you hurt him.

Pause.

Kassim   Like you said. He didn't give me a choice.

He lies down, turns away to the wall.

Claudia *goes back to her bunk. Sits for a moment, troubled. Then lies down.*

An advert.

Jaunty music plays. Team 1A are working, doing something interesting and fun. They talk direct to camera.

– Signing up for the Foreign Apprenticeship Scheme was the best thing I ever did!

– I've already learnt so much . . .

– We work hard, but we have a good laugh!

– I've made the kinds of friendships that will last forever!

– And my team leader is my best friend!

– I feel good knowing I've helped myself, and helped my country!

– Why don't you JOIN US on the FOREIGN APPRENTICESHIP SCHEME and TAKE CONTROL OF YOUR FUTURE!

The advert repeats, but it's broken up, jumpy.

– Signing up for the Foreign Apprenticeship Scheme was the best thing I ever did!

– I've already learnt so much . . .

– We work hard, but we have a good laugh!

– Signing up for the Foreign Apprenticeship Scheme was the best thing I ever did!

– I've already learnt so much . . .

– We work hard, but we have a good laugh!

– I've made the kinds of friendships that will last forever!

– And my team leader is my best friend!

– I feel good knowing I've helped myself, and helped my country!

– And my team leader is my best friend!

– Why don't you JOIN US on the FOREIGN APPRENTICESHIP SCHEME?

– And my team leader is my best friend!

– Why don't you JOIN US

– TAKE CONTROL OF YOUR FUTURE!

– JOIN US

– YOUR FUTURE

– JOIN US

– JOIN US

– JOIN US

The cabin.

Many days have passed. The team are huddled around **Claudia***.*

Claudia   OK, guys, before we begin our last training session I want to thank you for your hard work over the past couple of weeks! We're team number two in the ship ranking of training scores, which is really good /

Kassim   Not good enough.

Claudia   Tonight is our last chance to hit the number one spot. Rowan, your numbers are right up there but you're letting us down in pattern recognition testing.

Rowan   I can get it, I know I can.

Claudia   Morgan, what can I say?

Morgan   I'm this team's secret weapon. Nobody expects me to be this good.

Claudia   Keep it up. Sal, you're still letting some basic mistakes slip past.

Sal   Sorry, I . . . I panic and then I . . .

Kassim   Concentrate!

Claudia   You can do it. Adé . . . you're doing so well, can I show you your scores? Here's the huge improvement you made after uh . . . after . . . But you've hit a plateau, you haven't improved for a couple of days.

Adé   I'm tired.

Kassim   We're all tired. Push through it.

Rowan   I couldn't sleep last night. I'm so . . . excited.

Claudia   Me too. Tomorrow's the big day!

Rowan   I went up on deck. There was a boat in the water. A small one. It was really close to us.

Claudia   It was probably a fishing boat.

Kassim   Doesn't matter now. Focus your mind, yeah?

Rowan   Sorry.

Claudia   Can everyone take a tablet and sign in to your personal training portal please . . .

She starts giving out the tablet computers. **Adé** *and* **Sal** *talk quietly.*

Sal   I keep making stupid mistakes.

Adé   Relax. Getting stressed makes bad things worse.

Sal   I can't relax with those two putting pressure on me!

Adé   Don't let them get to you. It doesn't matter, whatever they say.

Sal   No. I guess not.

Kassim   What are you two muttering about?

Sal and Adé   Nothing.

Claudia   Is everyone ready? Training begins in twenty seconds!

Morgan   Yes!

Rowan   I'm ready.

Kassim   No mistakes. No excuses. I want that top spot.

Claudia   Go, 2B!

Kassim   Go, team!

Morgan   Go, team!

Rowan   Go, team!

Sal   Go, team.

Pause.

Adé   Go, team.

Claudia   Five, four, three, two, one.

Claudia's *tablet beeps and plays 'motivational music'. They all tap away furiously. This time* **Adé** *is trying hard. When he stops and looks up for a moment,* **Kassim** *glares at him.* **Adé** *bends his head back to his tablet.*

They work with furious intensity until . . .

Beep. The music cuts out. They collapse back onto their bunks.

Sal   I think . . . I did OK that time.

Morgan   I think I was sheer brilliance.

2B huddle around **Claudia**, *who's looking at her tablet.*

Kassim   What's it say, Claudia?

Rowan   What's our score?

Claudia   It's processing.

Morgan   Come on!

Claudia   Wait, wait . . . processing . . . wait . . .

She yelps with delight.

We hit number one!

Rowan   Whoop!

Kassim   Yes!

Morgan   2B! 2B! 2B!

Sal   We did it?

Claudia   Yes, we did, all of us, together! We're the best team on the ship! Well done, everyone!

Hugs, celebratory high fives, etc. **Adé** *is not joining in and* **Claudia** *notices this.*

Claudia   Adé?

Adé   Uh-huh?

Claudia   I know this hasn't always been easy for you but you really came through for us today. Thanks.

Adé   I'm happy you're happy.

Claudia   High five?

She stands there ready, looking hopeful. Eventually he high fives her.

A ship's horn sounds from outside.

Claudia   Oh, that's the transport ship to pick up the first set of teams. It's early.

Morgan   We're team number one, why don't we get to go first?

Rowan   It doesn't work like that . . .

Claudia   Our factory isn't near this port. We have to sail around the coast for another few hours.

Morgan   Don't want to wait. I'm ready now!

Claudia   Our transport ship will arrive to take us to our port at 04.00 hours tomorrow morning.

Groans.

I know, yes, it's early, but tomorrow we start our placements. For real.

Rowan   I hope we're going to do OK.

Kassim   Course. Crack team like us, we're gonna smash it!

Claudia   That's right! Come on, let's go up to say goodbye to the other teams . . .

They go out.

The cabin is empty. Maybe we can hear the far-off cheers of the departing teams being waved off and calls of 'Goodbye!' and 'Good luck!'

Then, in rush team 1A. **Talya**, **Elmer**, **Star**, **Nick**, **Jo** *and* **Lee**. *They look tired and pale. Their FAS T-shirts are faded and old.* **Nick** *takes up a position just by the door and looks out to keep watch. The others begin searching the cabin.*

Talya   Quick, quick, quick.

Elmer *finds the team training tablets.*

Elmer   I found some!

Jo   Training tablets won't work.

Lee   We have to be logged in as a team leader, I said that.

Talya   Keep looking, their team leader might have left their tablet in here . . .

Star   It's not likely. They cling onto those things like babies with dummies.

Talya   Try under the bunks . . .

Nick   Hurry up, they could be coming after us already!

Elmer   If they catch us . . .

Star   I am not going back there.

Talya   Keep looking.

Star   There's nowhere left to look!

Pause. They stop looking.

Lee   I knew this was a stupid idea. We're going to be in so much trouble now, it's going to be even worse!

Talya   Stay calm. We need a team-leader tablet, so we take one, just like we planned.

Pause.

Elmer   Whoever they are . . . the team in this cabin . . . they're just like us. Like we used to be, anyway . . . They could help if we explain what /

Talya   We already discussed this.

Nick   It's too risky. What if they don't believe us?

Star   Yeah or someone reports us to headquarters?

Talya   Everything will be fine, if we all stay calm and stick to the plan. Alright?

Nick   Ssh! Someone's coming.

Star   Get in position.

Talya   As soon as I have it in my hands, block the door.

*Some of 1A arrange themselves in 'casual' postures. **Star** sits with her head bowed, looking upset. Others are loitering near the door.*

*2B are coming down the corridor towards the cabin, led by **Claudia.***

Claudia   We need to pack tonight before bed, we won't have time to do it when we wake up . . .

As she enters she sees 1A.

Uh . . . hello?

Talya   Hi, I'm Talya . . . this is my team!

Claudia   Uh, hi, I don't remember meeting you. I thought I'd learnt all the team leaders' names.

Talya   I can't remember your name either. Funny!

Rowan   I recognise you. And all of you, actually.

Nick   From recreation. Or the canteen.

Rowan   Yeah . . .

Sal   Why are you in our cabin?

Talya *beckons* **Claudia**.

Talya   Can I talk to you, in confidence? Team leader to team leader?

Claudia   Sure.

Talya   I'm sorry for crashing in on you like this, one of my team –

She indicates **Star**.

Talya   – is having a bit of a crisis and I need to send a message back to shore.

Claudia   What kind of crisis?

Talya   It's personal. I can't really say. Can I borrow your tablet?

Claudia   Where's yours?

Talya   I dropped it over the side.

Claudia   You dropped it? You're going to lose so many points for that!

Talya   Tell me about it. So can I borrow yours? I'd really appreciate it.

Claudia   Uh . . . sure . . .

As she takes out her tablet . . .

Rowan   The videos! 'Join us and take control of your future', that was you! That's how I know you!

Sal   You're not from this ship.

Talya *grabs at* **Claudia**'s *tablet, snatches it from her hands.*

Claudia   Hey!

Talya *gives the tablet to* **Lee** *and* **Jo**.

Kassim   What the fuck?

Claudia   That's mine. Give it back.

Talya   We need it. Sorry. Is it working?

Jo   No! It's locked.

Lee   She has to unlock it or we can't turn the ship.

Kassim   Did you say 'turn the ship'?

Talya *turns back to* **Claudia**.

Talya   I need your password.

Claudia   Rowan, Kassim, can you go and get some more team leaders in here, please?

But **Nick** *and* **Star** *are in front of the door.*

Kassim   Move away from the door or you'll regret it.

Nick   No, you move away.

Team 1A pull out improvised weapons. A shocked silence.

Claudia   Don't, don't hurt us.

Nick   We don't want to hurt you but we can't let you leave.

Talya   What's your name?

Claudia   Claudia.

Talya   Claudia, I need you to tell me your password.

Claudia   I can't do that.

Adé   Why don't we calm down and have a conversation. Discuss this.

Claudia   Good idea, Adé! I'm sure I can help you, whatever the problem is! I'm a team leader, I /

Star   What, so we can trust you? Ha! I don't think so!

Elmer   Talya, let's try, let's explain it to them . . .

Nick   Make her give us the password!

Pause, **Talya** *thinking.*

Talya   We're team 1A –

Nick   We really don't have time for this . . .

Talya   – we were on the first ship out last year when the scheme started.

Claudia   You still have a year left of your placement?

Talya   We knew one of the FAS ships would be coming back to port, to bring more apprentices . . .

Elmer   Fresh meat.

Talya   So we escaped. Stole a boat in the harbour and snuck on board.

Rowan   It was you that I saw. Not a fishing boat.

Kassim   I don't get it. Escaped from what?

Elmer   From our factory.

Talya   From the scheme, the FAS!

Pause.

Kassim   What?!

Claudia   Do you know how many people applied for every space on the scheme, how many people would love to have this opportunity and you're throwing it away?

Kassim   You're fucking crazy.

Star   You don't know what it's like!

Talya   For the first couple of weeks it was fine.

Elmer   Almost fun.

Talya   That's when they asked us to do the videos.

Star   'Travel, have a laugh, make friends.' Ha. Ha. Ha.

Talya   Then . . . the people from FAS headquarters left and everything changed. The factory supervisors put us on a shift assembling mobile phones.

Elmer   The pieces are tiny. It kills your back bending over all day . . . .

Nick   The lights are so bright. After a shift you can't see properly.

Lee   I still can't see properly.

Nick   That's all we did. Tiny bits of phones in the bright room. The same thing for a whole year!

Rowan   But . . . we're supposed to do workplace training and learn different skills. That's what it said on the website.

Talya   There was no training, it was just work.

Elmer   Our shifts were six hours long . . . then eight.

Star   Twelve.

Lee   Fourteen hours.

Kassim You had to work hard. So what? What were you expecting, it's not a holiday!

Talya It was dangerous. The equipment wasn't safe!

Jo I hurt my back.

Star I burnt my hand.

Jo They said I had to go back to work.

Claudia Every factory has had a thorough health and safety check, I mean . . . the standards are very high. They wouldn't send us somewhere dangerous.

Star Keep telling yourself that.

Elmer We slept in a room with mattresses on the floor.

Talya Not the team leaders. We slept in beds. Proper beds.

Elmer When you get up, someone lies down in your place.

Lee The food . . .

Groans.

You got anything to eat? Anything at all?

Sal *gives* **Lee** *a snack bar from her bag.* **Lee** *devours it. It's disturbing to watch.*

Elmer We talked to the other teams. It wasn't just us. It was the same for everyone.

Sal It sounds . . . horrible.

Elmer It was hell.

Lee That's the best thing I've eaten for a year.

Pause.

Claudia OK, so . . . the experience itself wasn't all that you'd hoped and you had a few accommodation and health and safety issues –

Star A few?!

Claudia – but you're going home as qualified apprentices. No matter how hard it was . . . the benefits are invaluable.

Kassim Yeah, stop pissing and moaning about a bit of hard work, it's pathetic.

Nick　They treated us like robots!

Elmer　No, the robots were treated better. They treated us like /

Adé　Slaves.

Kassim　Not this again.

Claudia　Did you talk to the supervisors and explain you weren't happy – that's what you should have done.

Talya　Of course, I tried – they weren't interested!

Nick　We were lucky we got Talya as our team leader. Some of the others . . . all they cared about was getting high scores in their placement reports.

Talya　Once you've paid out all that money to be a team leader you don't want to admit that the FAS is a bunch of crap.

Kassim　What money?

Talya　The money that team leaders pay.

Kassim　What's she talking about?

Rowan　Claudia?

Pause.

Claudia　It's an administration fee . . . that team leaders have to pay so they can complete the online training course and get their positions. It's completely legitimate.

Kassim　So this skill set . . . that means you get to be team leader and I don't, that's what – money? The rich kid pays to get ahead!

Claudia　I'm not rich.

Kassim　Richer than me.

Claudia　You don't know how hard it was for my family to get that money, you have no idea!

Kassim　You're not better than me. I should have been team leader, not you.

Talya　Being a team leader means being responsible for pushing your team to work harder, faster, all the time!

Elmer　Some of the teams . . . their leaders got physical with them if they messed up.

Pause.

Claudia   I'm sorry I just don't believe any of this.

Rowan   Do you have any proof?

Star   I'll show you the scar where I burnt my hand. See?

Rowan   God . . .

Kassim   That doesn't prove anything. You could have done that before.

Morgan   You've got no proof!

Adé   Let me ask you something. Did they give you your phones back when you arrived at the factory?

Jo   No. 'Security protocols.'

Adé   I knew it. I told you it wasn't going to be like you thought and you ignored me.

Kassim   This is bullshit. Total bullshit.

Talya   Why would we lie?

Kassim   Maybe you're looking for excuses. Maybe you got a crappy placement because you were lazy during training and now you can't hack it. But we're not lazy.

Morgan   Yeah, we're the best on the boat! Team number one!

Kassim   They'll send us somewhere good.

Talya   That's funny. We were team number one on the ship too.

Pause.

Claudia   Guys, don't let them upset you.

Kassim   They're lying. They have to be.

Sal   If they are . . . lying . . . why do they look so . . . broken?

Pause. Everyone considering this. No explanation coming.

Sal   I believe them.

Claudia   Even if what they're saying is true . . . we're not going to their factory. Our placement won't be like theirs.

Rowan   How do you know?

Claudia   It's a different place, so obviously it's going to be different. The best thing would be if I contact headquarters and tell them that you're here –

Elmer   No, you can't . . .

Claudia   – they can help you resolve the issues you've been having with your factory and you can enjoy the second year of your placement.

Star   We're not leaving this room, nobody's leaving this room until you give us your password.

Claudia   Well, I'm not going to do that.

Rowan   Claudia, this is really not what I signed up for.

Kassim   They're exaggerating.

Claudia   It's going to be fine.

Rowan   I changed my mind. I don't want to do the placement.

Kassim   We start tomorrow!

Rowan   You can tell headquarters that I don't want to do it anymore.

Claudia   I'm sorry, but . . . it's not possible for you to pull out of the scheme at this point.

Rowan   What do you mean?

Claudia   Uh. It costs a lot to get someone out on this ship and it's paid for by the work we do. Technically we owe them money. We have to do the placement to pay for our trip out and our trip back.

Rowan   They can't force me to do it if I don't want to.

Sal   The contract. Did you sign the contract?

Rowan   Yeah . . .

Sal   I think . . . legally, we have to do it.

Rowan   Oh my God . . .

Adé   We don't have a choice. So we are slaves.

Claudia   It's a work placement!

Rowan   I wish I'd never signed up. I believed those stupid videos. I thought this was going to be so great, that it was going to change my life . . .

Claudia   It will! We have to stay positive.

Rowan *is upset.*

Claudia   Positive morale is really important for team performance. When we get there and get started, you'll see, it will be fine!

Adé   I don't want to go. Rowan doesn't want to. What about you, Sal? Do you still want to go on?

Sal   No. But it's too late . . .

Adé   It's not.

Morgan   I don't care what they say. I want to do my placement.

Kassim   Nobody's going home. You lot might be weak. Scared to work, but I'm not. You think I care if it's hard and the food's bad? I'll work round the clock to help my family, I'll work till my fingers bleed.

Star   They will. They'll bleed, don't worry.

Sal   We're being used, Kassim. It's not a training scheme, it's unpaid labour.

Kassim   Work experience. That's why we fucking came, isn't it?

Claudia   Even if it is going to be . . . hard, we can still make something positive out of it. You can always make something positive out of a negative if you try.

Kassim   Yeah, we can't just give up.

Talya   Signing up to be a team leader on this scheme was the worst mistake I've ever made.

Adé   Give me your password, Claudia.

Claudia   No . . .

Morgan   Don't tell them.

Pause. **Claudia**, **Kassim** *and* **Morgan** *surrounded by the others. An implied threat.*

Kassim   You want it you have to go through me.

Star   Won't be a problem.

Star *and* **Nick** *grab* **Kassim**. *He struggles.*

Kassim   Claudia . . . don't . . . think about going home when all this is over. And taking money to your family, and how proud they'll be . . .

Adé   I'm asking you calmly. Give us the password. Please, team leader.

Claudia   What are you going to do if I won't? Hurt me?

Pause.

Adé   I don't know.

Claudia *and* **Adé** *look at each other. It's intense. Finally,* **Claudia** *holds out her hand for the tablet. He gives it to her and she enters the code. He watches her so he learns it.*

Kassim   Fuck.

Star   Yes!

Claudia *gives the tablet back to* **Jo** *and* **Lee** *and they immediately start punching in instructions.*

Lee   We're in!

Jo   I don't understand the system . . .

Lee   It's so complicated.

Elmer   What does that mean?

Jo   I can't do it, I don't know how.

Star   They'll catch us. They'll send us back . . .

Sal   Let me look at it.

She takes the tablet.

Adé   Can you do it?

Rowan   Can you take us home?

Sal   Uh. Maybe.

Star   Maybe yes or maybe no?

Sal   Maybe!

Adé   She's the smartest person on this ship. If she can't do it, no one can.

Talya   Do it.

Star   Get us the fuck out of here!

Slowly, **Sal** *nods. She hits 'enter'.*

Sal   Done.

Salt   353

Claudia   You're making a horrible mistake.

Adé   Our mistake. Our choice.

Pause.

Rowan   The ship . . . it's turning. I can feel it!

Later.

On deck.

A party atmosphere rules. Team 1A are drinking and dancing to music.
Rowan is with them. Morgan is on the edge of the party. Claudia sits
with Kassim, isolated. Sal is not on deck. Adé sits, watching the party.

Kassim   How am I going to explain this? Going back with nothing.

Claudia   The money my family paid. It's gone. Wasted.

Kassim   We were doing great. We were team number one! Why did you
tell them your password?

Claudia   I had no choice.

Kassim   Bullshit. Adé wasn't going to do anything to you.

Claudia   Wasn't he?

Kassim   You should have held out.

Claudia   I was scared, OK?

Kassim   A good leader takes the pain, sucks it up for the rest of the
team.

Claudia   I wish I was a good leader, Kassim.

She gets up, and walks off. Kassim shakes his head.

Sal comes on deck carrying Claudia's tablet. Walks up to Adé and sits
down next to him.

Sal   Hey.

Adé   Hey.

He offers her a can of drink. She takes it.

Sal   When we told the other teams . . . that we'd turned the ship around
I thought . . . it could be a mutiny.

Adé   They understood. Most of them. We told them the truth.

Sal   We still might have trouble. From the people who wanted to go on to the factory so . . . I threw all the other team-leader tablets into the sea.

Adé   Smart.

Sal   I've been checking out the navigation system. When I turned the ship around . . .

Adé   Which was brilliant, by the way.

Sal   I don't know exactly how to get us home.

Adé   Uh-huh.

Sal   We might be . . . lost.

Adé   Uh-huh.

Sal   In fact I think we are. Lost.

Adé   So we're lost. We'll get somewhere. Eventually.

They sip their cans.

The End.

Salt

BY DAWN KING

Notes on rehearsal and staging, drawn from a workshop with the writer, held at the National Theatre, October 2018

EXERCISE: STOP/GO

To break the ice, lead director Amy Leach led a game of Stop/Go (everyone moves around the room on Go, freezes on Stop). She added an instruction to smile and nod as they pass others; then to add a wink; then a wink and a shimmy. Then they played a version of the game where everyone high fived as they passed each other.

EXERCISE: LINE-UPS

Amy asked everyone to line up in order of the distance travelled to get to the workshop. She then asked the group to line up in order of the best to worst jobs everyone had as teenagers. The final line was to line up in order of cast size.

How Dawn came to write the play

When approached by the National Theatre about writing for Connections, Dawn had already had the idea of a story about young people on a ship. Originally, she had thought of it as a radio play, but it proved challenging to make a radio drama involving such large numbers of young people.

The impetus behind the play was the idea of youth that had been sold. The first idea for the FAS was as a forced work scheme for imprisoned young people. In developing the play, she became more interested in the idea that the scheme had been sold to them. Earlier drafts of the play were more dreamlike: there was a version of the play with sea shanties and another with a whale. A big part of rewriting the play was grounding the play clearly in the reality of a near-future world.

Dawn also wanted to write something that would give young people the opportunity to play detailed characters who feel like real people and have clear character arcs throughout the piece. She was influenced by talking to one of last year's Connections performers who said, 'You should make it emotional and make it different'.

The original idea of young people being sold remains really important in the play. The young people are told by the older generation that things will be okay for them if they follow the scheme. Like much of Dawn's work, the play is partly about not believing authority. But it also asks: What is it to be part of a team, or to be a good team player? What does a good leader do? How do you deal with it if people won't do what you want?

Q&A with Dawn

Q: Can we change gender and ethnicity?

A: You should feel free to change genders, ethnicities, etc. I've tried to make the names gender fluid though this isn't always the case. Names can be changed, and it's fine to adapt the language in the play to reflect casting (e.g. there's a reference to 'old man' which you'd need to change if Kassim is played by a female actor).

Q: Is the play politically motivated?

A: All my plays are politically motivated, but the story is the priority. There's a lot of political ambiguity in this play. For example, it's possible to ask who the better leader is: Claudia, who is trying to lead team 2B by the book, or Talya, who is trying to get team 1A out of their situation. There's also ambiguity about the work that the young people will be doing – work that's being done by young people in other countries in the real world right now. And by turning the boat around, the characters are heading back to a Britain which doesn't present them with any opportunities. It's up to you to determine the focus of your production; it's also a play that can provoke debate within each company.

Q: What will happen when team 2B gets to their destination? Will they end up in a sweatshop?

A: The script is deliberately not 100 per cent clear; we only see one team tell us about their experiences in a sweatshop. The leaked video has been taken down and there's a lot of official video out there telling a more positive story. And it's only the second year of the scheme. You can decide in your group whether there are some other FAS groups that are having a really great time. Maybe team A1 give up too early.

Q: What age are the young people in the play?

A: In the reality of the play, the young people are sixteen and up, but Morgan is younger. It's up to you how to cast the play. It'd really help if you have one kid who's really young-looking who could play Morgan. But I personally can't tell by looking the difference between one person who's fourteen and one who's sixteen.

Q: How important is the swearing?

A: I wanted them to feel like kids, and real kids swear, so the play contains real swearing. The swearing is a key part of the characters.

Q: There seem to be many similarities between the characters in Team 1A and Team 2B. How deliberate is this?

A: It's not intended to be an exact, character-for-character match. In some ways 1A are a closer team; they love Talya and listen to her, which is very different from Claudia's relationship with her team. There's a possible back-story where Talya starts out like Claudia and is changed by her and the team's experiences.

Q: Do the characters have different economic backgrounds?

A: Yes. For example, Claudia is slightly better off than the others – but she still has a need to be on the boat.

Q: Why is it set on a ship and not, for example, a plane?

A: I was thinking about slave ships, but also the idea of going to sea as a way of making your fortune, and refugees being forced to cross the sea. Are Team 2B intrepid adventurers off to seek their fortune, or are they slaves who've been sold?

Q: Why is it called *Salt?*

A: Salt in a wound – the feeling of the older generation screwing over the younger. And, of course, the title connects to the sea.

Directors added other thoughts: the young people as the salt of the earth; humans are mostly water; sweat (as in the sweatshops they may end up in) is salty; we need salt to survive but too much salt can kill you.

Staging: location

Amy invited the directors to divide a page in a notebook into six columns:

- Scene/title
- Location
- Time – time of day, time of year, time that's passed through the play
- Weather and atmosphere

- Which team is present
- Any key props/costume

She asked everyone to spend six minutes going through each scene and fill out this table. Amy suggested that directors could come up with scene titles in collaboration with their cast. This could help the company take ownership of their production. You could also invite actors to give their own, personal name for each scene.

Amy divided everyone into six groups of about six people, exploring the *below* and *above decks* worlds of the play. The groups began by noting down what it feels like to be above and below decks: what happens in the space, how characters describe it and how it feels. They then began creating a below- and an above-decks world using just their bodies and voices; finding a transition from below to above decks and back again.

Some of the techniques and reflections that came out of this were:

- Body percussion and humming as engine sound
- Slow motion, gliding arm movement and breath for above decks – the freshness of the air
- Working on the floor when below decks; standing up when above decks
- People clinging to one another – because they need to, or because they want to
- Rocking motion – echoing the storm
- Team 1A becoming the ship if you don't have a budget for the set
- Leaning over the rails of the ship – the feeling of looking out to sea as opposed to being cramped below decks
- You don't necessarily need to create the ship naturalistically – one group explored a long diagonal line for above decks
- The effect of being below decks, with no natural light, constant engine noise and vibration, on the bodies and minds of the characters
- The power of crushing actors into a small space onstage
- Clambering over one another's bodies when below decks, and only one person being able to move at a time; compared with the ability to stretch when above decks
- Even up on deck, there may not be that much space, as the ship is full of people
- When one person turns over in their sleep, everyone else has to move; coughs and snoring in people's sleep

- If someone gets sick on the ship, everyone else is going to get ill
- If the people playing the boat move, this creates movement in the characters

Characters

EXERCISE: CHARACTERS IN SPACE

In their groups, Amy invited everyone to think about each of the characters in Team 2B, jotting down as much information as possible about them (she suggested leaving out gender as the gender of the characters might change according to who is in each company). Then to think what animal they might be. Ideas included:

Claudia   meerkat, parrot, hamster, Labrador, snake, cat

Rowan   meerkat, Boxer the horse from *Animal Farm*, squirrel, anxious giraffe (*Madagascar*), puppy

Adé   disaffected Collie, escaped circus bear, fox, lone wolf, a young wolf, porcupine

Sal   tortoise, scared but clever hedgehog, greyhound, a rescued dog, a prey animal

Kassim   stereotypical Staffie, young bull, gorilla, a kestrel that wants to be an eagle

Morgan   robin, working ant, young buck, Yorkshire terrier, Chihuahua.

- Each group was assigned one character. Working individually, they were asked to choose one of the animals they'd come up with. Everyone closed their eyes. They were asked to think about the animal that they'd chosen. Amy counted down from five. When she got to one, everyone created a pose of that particular animal. In that animal, they then started to move around the space. As they moved around, Amy asked them to find a greeting noise for their animal as it passed others.
- Then they were asked to think about a scale at which ten is most animal; one is a human version, which retains some of the qualities of the animal. Working down from ten to one, they went from absolute animal to human.
- They explored each character entering a small, 'cabin' space, inhabiting that space, then leaving (at level one).

- Then they explored characters entering the space, and staying in there while others joined: Claudia, then Rowan, then Adé, then Sal, then Kassim, then Morgan (starting at one, working through to ten, then back down to one).
- Then Claudia and Rowan, level one, adding the first couple of lines of text.
- Then they created the animals in the cabin; then everyone closed in from the circle and the rest of the room reacted to the 'threat'.

Reflections on the animal work included:

- Creating the confined space was very effective.
- It was really fun to see all the characters in the space together.
- Identifying characters as *predators* and *prey* was exciting.
- The variation in tempo was engaging. Energy could also be a really good way of exploring age.
- The tension between the characters in confined space is really exciting, and it's possible to play that in a way that's very heightened. In the story, the characters have spent weeks confined together and this often leads to people becoming heightened versions of themselves.
- Animal work is an exciting way to avoid 'head and shoulder acting'. We understand animals from a really early age, and they can be a very effective shortcut to helping young people develop physicality.
- It was great to allow time to pass on stage without feeling the need to rush into dialogue.

Cast size

The room was split into groups for a discussion about the challenges and opportunities of cast size. What do you do if you have fewer than twelve actors, or if you have twenty-nine?

With a cast of eleven actors, Star's lines could be redistributed to one of the Team 2B actors. This is the only circumstance in which lines can be redistributed.

If you have a cast of exactly twelve, the challenge may be how to keep Team 1A involved throughout the performance. They could appear in transitions; they could also be used as 'Team Leader' ushers to bring the audience into their seats at the beginning of the show. There might be images of Team 1A in the factory.

There was a discussion about splitting the audience into teams of six and isolating them from family members, etc., using Team 1A to create that space. Finding more immersive forms of seating might be interesting if your venue is flexible. Otherwise this could be challenging.

With a larger cast, it would be possible to have the ensemble as additional teams. Dawn said that there are many teams on the ship with whom Team 2B are in competition; they see them when they go on deck, or for meals. We might see other teams during the training sequence, as if we can see through the walls. The advert sequences could be performed in multiple versions simultaneously – as if there are many teams watching the adverts at the same time on many screens. We might also see images of FAS headquarters, the nerve centre back in the UK which controls the ships.

Another option might be for roles to be shared – so that Claudia is played by a different actor between the first scene and the second scene. This would involve detailed work on the actors' performances for consistency, as well as thinking about transitions and design.

There was discussion of whether dialogue could be re-allocated to performers who weren't in Team 2B. This would not be acceptable in the scenes; but dialogue in the adverts is unassigned. Team 1A need to be seen in the adverts, but other actors could also appear in these scenes.

Amy talked about audio description and captioning; she had recently worked on a production where actors who weren't onstage became audio describers. It might be possible for the 'war room' at FAS headquarters to be represented in captioning or audio description; or for actors in FAS uniforms to be used to create the ship. Even if actors aren't speaking, they can still feel a sense of ownership as collaborating as directors and theatre-makers – creating a back-story for speaking characters, working on response pieces, etc.

Having a bigger cast might be an opportunity to explore the political world of the play; with a smaller cast there's a chance to focus on the intimate relationships between the characters.

Staging: adverts

Back in groups, Amy gave each group ten minutes to stage the first eight lines of the advert scene on p. 338, playing Team 1A.

Then a further five minutes to explore the next part of the scene, when the advert breaks down.

Then combining two groups together; one group playing Team 1A and one Team 2B, with 2B watching 1A.

Reflections on the exercise and images that were striking:

- Repeated physical action when the text starts skipping
- Each of Team 1A working at different tempi in the repeat section
- Stuttering as if the video was buffering; or inserting a very long pause between words both worked well
- It was exciting to see the comparison between putting 2B in the background and focusing on Team 1A, versus putting Team 2B in the foreground and focusing on their reactions
- Claudia mouthing along with the advert as if she'd watched it many times
- Seeing the tablets onstage (represented by folders or papers) clearly told the story of Team 2B's situation
- It was interesting to see Team 1A crammed together in physical space
- Laughing together after 'we had a good laugh' worked well
- Team 2B sharing a tablet created interesting interactions when the ad started breaking down
- We don't necessarily need to see Team 2B at all in this particular advert scene; but we do need to see them in the briefing video scene starting on p. 319
- Team 1A singing a 'jingle' – then repeating it at different speeds
- Having members of Team 2B step into the moving tableau was intriguing
- Deconstructing the high five
- Ad-libbed lines aren't necessary – we can read Team 2B's reactions on their faces
- An over-high energy to Team 1A makes the audience tense
- Each of Team 2B responds to the video in a different way

Final reflections

- Dawn talked about the ending of the play and the ambiguity about whether turning the ship around is right. Claudia, Kassim and Morgan don't get the future they want; the majority have taken charge of their destiny, but they may never get home. Margaret Atwood's *The Heart Goes Last* was an influence on Dawn writing the play.

- The tests are about getting ready to do the work in the factories: pattern recognition, spotting mistakes. They're not intellectually demanding, it's about speed of response. But also, the tests are busywork – things to get the teams competing during the journey and pass the time. It's up to you to determine the balance between these in your production.

- It is interesting to look at the way tablets can be represented through simple things like paper and clipboard. Attaching a small set of LED lights – or magician's thumb lights – to a piece of paper or folder could be really strong ways of creating the tablets without spending thousands of pounds. Remember we're slightly in the future and the next iPad could be made of clear plastic!

- It's important that Claudia has a tablet (however staged) to communicate with base.

- Adé says the ship looks like it could sink any minute. Maybe it's a repurposed cruise liner or container ship. Team 2B could be sleeping on the floor in a storage area.

From a workshop led by Amy Leach
with notes by Tom Mansfield

Ageless

by Benjamin Kuffuor

In a not-too-distant future, the Temples pharmaceutical corporation has quite literally changed the face of aging. Their miracle drug keeps its users looking perpetually young. With an ever-youthful population, how can society support those who are genuinely young? A play that questions what it means to be young and what happens when generations collide.

Cast size
14

Benjamin Kuffuor graduated from the National Film and Television School in 2011, and his first project following graduation, *Youngers*, was developed by Big Talk Productions for E4. Prior to his time at the NFTS, his first short play, *Bobby James*, was produced at Theatre Royal Stratford East in 2007, and he participated in the Young Writers' Programme at the Royal Court Theatre in 2008. At the time of publication he is currently developing projects for theatre, television and film.

Characters

Cast age between fourteen and nineteen
Cast size 14

Elliot Temples, *eighties; appears in his late teens*
Jacob Aduba, *sixties; appears in his teens*
Helen, *sixties; appears in her teens*
James, *sixties; appears in his teens*
Siana, *sixteen*
Cassie, *sixteen*
Dylan, *forties; appears in his teens*
Emmy, *forties; appears in her teens*

Reactive group members, mid-to-late teens:
Mustafa
Cleo
Antonia
Paul
Jonathan
Bilal

Scene One

Pharmaceutical exhibition.

Temples *glides across the stage with the poise of a clergyman. There is a TED Talk quality to the nature of the evening. He doesn't attempt to sell or convince, but merely spread his gospel to the visiting congregation.*

Temples   Historians debate between who, what and when in terms of which civilisation devised the fountain of youth. You can find writings by Herodotus, the great Greek historian, where he fantasises about a well from which a sip or drop on your skin would preserve youth for eternity. There are stories of kings and queens sending fleets of soldiers in search of this well, in the belief that if death was indeed a promise, then there must also be the promise of eternal life.

It wasn't hard to think that I was being as naïve as those ancient kings and queens when I set off to design T1. Sure, the changes were small and cosmetic, but it was the first time a formula had been created to tamper with DNA to make the human skin appear younger than it is. Later, there was T2. I always felt that both drugs could only ever succeed in turning our consumers into expensive cars with tin parts under the hood. We were modifying DNA to make things appear one way. With T3, we managed to alter DNA so things actually are . . .

Like any life work, you recognise what you've stumbled on as soon as you see it. Here was a formula that could slow down the rate of human deterioration. Naturally, my mind soon turned to the idea of a drug that could not just slow down the process of ageing but stop it altogether, and then . . . Then we can look to a future where the promise of eternal youth is fulfilled. The impending doom of later years banished into extinction; an idea that once was, but is no longer. At the Temples Institute I don't allow my colleagues to use the words biology or gerontology. Why? It's because they don't accurately describe what it is that we do. No, we are architects building a gateway to hope and happiness in a younger, brighter and freer world. I stand before you, an eighty-year-old man without a tear in my skin or a wrinkle in my heart. (*Gestures to himself.*) Still, I know that this is not success. This is the beginning.

Scene Two

An abandoned warehouse.

Mustafa *and* **Siana** *stare each other down in a Western stand-off. In between them,* **Cleo**, **Emmy**, **Antonia**, **Paul**, **Jonathan** *and* **Bilal** *are seated on the floor in a half circle. They pass around a vape pen.*

Antonia   Moostie, sit down . . .

Siana (*to* **Mustafa**)   You've hidden my tablet.

Emmy   If you have, Moostie . . . Can you just . . .

Mustafa   Paul, you working?

Paul   Moostie . . .

Mustafa   Jon, what you saying?

Jonathan   What's the point? You know I haven't . . . None of us.

Siana   Give it back.

Mustafa   I told you already that I don't have it . . . Bilal?

Bilal   Hmmm?

Mustafa   Any prospects?

Bilal   Y'know me, Moostie. I'm an entrepreneur, brother. My company's just gone up on the Masdaq.

Emmy   It's the Nasdaq, lovely.   **Antonia**   Nasdaq, you fool.

Mustafa   Antonia?

Antonia   I'm not playing, Mustafa.

Siana   None of us are. Where's my tablet?

Mustafa   Cleo?

Cleo   You're bringing the whole vibe down.

Mustafa   There you go. None of us have got nothing. We'll call it the under-forty curse. It goes like this, if you're TY, truly young like everyone here, then life is shit. If you're one of the AY, artificial young popping T3 every night, you're probably winning. We don't need your tablet to figure that out.

Siana   Mustafa, give it back.

Mustafa   I don't have it.

Siana   I know you do. Bilal, did you see him put it anywhere?

Mustafa   You calling me a liar?

Bilal (*to* **Siana**)   I would've said. You know me, I keeps it real.

Emmy   We can start without it. There's no reason we can't start without it.

Cleo   Can we have peace? All this is making my head hurt.

Antonia   Cleo, sssh.

Siana   Everything was bullet-pointed and annotated and . . .

Paul *stands.*

Paul   Moostie, if you've got it.

Mustafa   I said I didn't.

Siana *snatches the vape pen from* **Cleo**.

Cleo (*slow reaction*)   Hey . . .

Siana   This is going right over that wall if no one tells me where the tablet is.

Cleo   That seems extreme.

Bilal (*to* **Mustafa**)   Allow it, bruv. It's long.

Everyone   Give it back, Mustafa, come on. What's the point? Can't you just . . . You're longing it.

They all shout at **Mustafa** *until it reaches a crescendo.*

Siana *arches her arm to release.*

Mustafa   Alright.

He walks to a cupboard. He returns with the tablet.

Here's your fucking tablet.

He drops the tablet violently on the floor. He heads off to the corner to sit with his back to the room.

Siana   This isn't easy for any of us, y'know. We're all sacrificing to be here . . .

Cleo   Let's just start now. It might be better if we just . . .

Siana   If you're going to act like a little boy.

Mustafa   Keep talking, Siana. I swear. You keep talking.

Jonathan   Whoa, you can't threaten her like that . . .

Emmy   He doesn't mean it. He doesn't mean any of it. He's aggravated, that's all. We can all get like that.

Antonia   Cleo's right.

Cleo   Am I?

Antonia   We should just start.

Siana *tries to regain composure. She spreads the tablet case open.*
Mustafa *smokes alone in the corner.*

Siana   We might as well start with unemployment figures for the truly young. How many names have we managed to get on the online petition, Tonia?

Antonia   We're pushing close to two thousand now.

Paul   Jon and I have been on the ground, just chatting to any TY we can spot.

Jonathan (*to* **Siana**)   We get 'em to show their ID cards now like you said. Make sure they're properly under twenty-one just in case we get talking to any artificials in their forties or whatever. We're close to getting bigger numbers than last time.

Antonia   They know who we are?

Mustafa *lets out a sarcastic cackle.*

Jonathan   Some do . . .

Paul   If they don't, we just tell 'em we're from a group called Reactive, run for and by under twenties . . . Blah. Yah. All that.

Emmy   Soon as we get the numbers up I'll get on to drawing up a proposal for a permit. Shut down city centre.

Mustafa (*laughs*)   Permission. Permission from the older lot, most of them artificial young anyway . . .

Siana *slams the tablet down.*

Siana   So what do we then, Mustafa? Go on, you must know. You're shitting on everything all the time, so what's your answer?

Mustafa *continues to smoke.*

Siana   Yeah, exactly.

Jonathan   You can leave here and be like everyone else our age. Still at home with their families accepting things as they are.

Mustafa   Maybe they've all got it right. There's always gonna be T3, so there's never gonna be a way for any of us truly young to have a place in their world. They don't need us. All of this talking about stuff, demonstrations and petitions, it don't mean a thing.

Cassie *and* **Dylan** *enter, holding hands.* **Dylan** *clutches a duffle bag. An eerie silence takes over the room.*

Cassie   You alright, everyone?

Siana   Cass.

She rushes to **Cassie***. They share a long hug. No one else walks over to acknowledge* **Cassie***.*

Antonia   Where you been?

Cassie   I did tell Siana . . .

Antonia   This is not the kinda thing you can walk in and out of.

Cassie   I know that.

Siana   Guys, it's Cassie.

Jonathan   She still hasn't said where she's been . . .

Emmy   Let's lay off. She's here now, isn't that the important thing?

Mustafa   Nah, it ain't.

He takes steps towards **Cassie***.*

Dylan   You wanna be careful . . .

This is the first time that the group is made to acknowledge **Dylan***.*

Cassie   Everyone, this is Dylan. I've been telling him all about Reactive and what we do here. He thinks the same as us.

Paul (*adversarial*)   Oh yeah, like what?

Antonia (*to* **Cassie**)   So what, are you here to stay now?

Cassie   I got my bags with me.

Bilal (*to* **Dylan**)   What are your views?

Paul (*don't entertain it*)   Bilal . . .

374   Benjamin Kuffuor

Bilal   What? All us lot do is scuff these days . . . He might show us something.

Pause.

(*To* **Dylan**.) Don't worry, we're all friends here.

Dylan   What one of you does the meetings? Maybe I can talk to him first.

Cleo   Oh . . . . Why would it have to be a him?

Dylan   Sorry.

Siana   It doesn't work like that.

Cassie   I explained it to him. (*To* **Dylan**.) I told you already . . .

Siana   There are no leaders here . . .

Antonia   It's s'posed to work as a democracy in the truest sense of the word. Leaders, all of that is how older people and artificials do things. Us truly young need to establish a new order.

Dylan   I couldn't agree more, (*Holds for a name.*) . . .

Antonia   Antonia.

Dylan   Right on, Antonia. Right on.

He and **Antonia** *shake hands.*

Dylan   Cassie told me you lot left your families to start this. That's the kinda commitment we need.

Cleo   Yah, it started to feel like there weren't any choices if you're a TY.

Antonia   It feels like there's nothing out there for us.

Mustafa   Yeah, but you still got loads of us who are blessed with living in a system that oppresses them. It's like they can't even see it.

Dylan   They see it. Trust me, they see it. They just don't know how to stop it, so they live. It's hard to go against tradition – your parents, all the AY, the older people.

Cassie   I think Dylan can help us. We need to think bigger, recruit wider and take this to the next level for our impact to be felt.

Antonia (*dismissive*)   Oh yeah. Is that what we need to do?

Siana (*stop*) Toni . . .

Cassie He has ideas and . . . And, show 'em what you got.

Dylan Nah, we should probably leave it. They don't seem like they . . .

Cassie We might as well. We come all this way. Show 'em.

Dylan *holds, undecided.*

Mustafa What is it?

Dylan *glances at* **Cassie**. *He thinks.*

Dylan Yeah, alright.

He reluctantly pulls out a machine from his bag that looks a lot like a barcode scanner.

Mustafa (*excited laughter*) Oh my . . .

Jonathan Fucking hell.

Bilal *steps forward with his hand out.*

Bilal Can I . . .

Dylan *forces him back.*

Dylan That's an A1 piece of machinery there, brother. Nah, we can't have anyone stroking that.

Mustafa How'd you get it?

Siana I thought they only kept them in police stations and airports.

Antonia Legally, yeah.

Cassie Should I tell 'em how you got it?

Pause.

Dylan I took it.

Bilal From an airport?

Paul From the feds?

Dylan These lot ask a lot of questions.

Siana Why'd you bring it here?

Emmy Yeah, I don't know if we would need that.

Cassie It's for self-protection. In case any AY try to infiltrate us.

Dylan   How'd you know everyone here is who they say they are? The kind of stuff you're trying to put together is the kind've thing they'd wanna stop if they knew about it.

Siana   Cassie, we're not scanning people here. We've all seen each other's ID cards anyway.

Dylan   Do you know how many artificial young taking T3 cycles to look like us are out there walking around with fake ID cards saying they're truly young when they're in their sixties or whatever?

Mustafa   That's what I been saying. The only way to know who anyone is for sure is to scan 'em.

Cassie   You're always saying things aren't going anywhere. We're here for change, right. That's what we all want.

Mustafa   That's exactly what we want. So far all we've done is get a few petitions signed and hold hands on a couple of marches.

Dylan   The stuff I wanna talk about, I won't be comfortable saying unless I know we're all . . . (*to* **Bilal**) friends.

Cassie   It's for the good of the group.

Antonia   Where was the good of the group when you fucked off without telling anyone?

Emmy   Antonia does have a point.

Dylan   That's no problem. Forget it ever come up. We can go.

Cassie   Siana . . .

Dylan   If they don't want it, babe, we'll leave it.

Cassie   Siana . . .

Antonia   It's not Siana's choice alone.

Long pause.

Siana   We should do it.

Emmy (*what do you mean?*)   Siana.

Siana   I think we should do it. We can't keep going on like we've been doing.

Emmy   Don't let today cloud your judgement.

Siana   It's not just today though is it. It's every week.

Dylan   Are we on it? If we are, I need everyone to line up.

Antonia   I won't do it.

Emmy   Neither will I.

Paul   We're all doing it.

Bilal   It's a minor. We might as well just hear what he's saying.

Jonathan (*to* **Emmy** *and* **Antonia**)   Don't be like that.

Dylan   If they're not doing it, they'll have to go and if yous take on board anything I say then they can't come back.

Antonia   He's telling us what to do now?

Cleo   Toni, Emmy . . . Don't go, please.

Cassie (*to* **Antonia**)   It's only fair.

Emmy   I'm going.

Siana   No, No. None of you should go

Mustafa   We all know we're legit anyway, what's it gonna matter?

Siana   We need you. We need all of us. Everyone in this room. Everyone has to stay. Moostie's right. We know who we are. We don't have to take on anything Dylan says after, but we'll listen and decide as a team.

Antonia *and* **Emmy** *turn to each other.* **Antonia** *reluctantly takes her place in the line-up.* **Emmy** *follows soon after.*

Dylan   I'm gonna need you all to show me the palm of your hand.

This can be indicated by sound or visually. **Dylan** *moves down the line, scanning the hands. Each person should have their age flash up on the back of the stage for the audience or their passing of the age test should be indicated by a 'ding' sound. Failing the test should sound like getting the wrong answer on a game show.* **Dylan** *scans* **Emmy** *last. The sound indicates a problem.*

Siana   That can't be right.

Bilal (*laughs in disbelief*)   It says you're forty-three.

Cleo   Emmy, why would it say that?

Antonia   It's wrong. Do it again.

Dylan *scans* **Emmy's** *palm. The sound is negative.* **Emmy** *is now visibly shaken, close to tears.*

Mustafa (*to* **Emmy**)   You liar.

Siana (*hurt and disbelief*)   Emmy.

Emmy   It's not true.

Siana   Do it again. She's saying it's not true.

Dylan   Of course it's true.

Siana   Do it again.   **Antonia**   Do it again.

Dylan   It was right for all of you weren't it . . .

Cleo   One last time. Please.

Dylan *scans* **Emmy's** *hand. The result is the same.*

Mustafa   She's an informant.

Emmy   No. No. I'm a sympathiser.

Paul   She's lying.

Jonathan   You're an artificial. I feel sick.

Emmy   I'm telling the truth. You have to believe me. I'm telling the truth.

Dylan   There's one of two ways this can go . . .

Siana   We don't want you here.

Jonathan   Piss off.

Emmy *takes a long look around. She doesn't have a friend in the room. She exits.*

Dylan   Letting her go is a mistake. You could have feds swarming this place in less than an hour.

Siana   We're gonna find a new site.

Dylan   I said there would be one though didn't I.

Mustafa   Yeah, you did.

Cassie   I told you. We should listen to his ideas.

Siana   Let's get out, then we'll talk.

Scene Three

Helen *and* **James, House i20**. *Front room. The stage is dimly lit.*

Helen *enters, slips out of her heels and peels off her blazer. She delivers a set of commands while performing the rituals of returning home from work.*

Helen   Lights.

The lights go up. She squeezes her finger to bring them down ever so slightly.

Do we have any white in the fridge?

House i20   There is no wine in the fridge. There is also no wine in the cellar.

Helen   Right, call James. . .   **House i20**   Would you like me to
                                                                      call James?

Helen   Yes, could you please.

She pulls a tablet from her briefcase.

House i20   I keep getting through to his voicemail.

Helen (*to voicemail*)   James, can you grab two bottles on the way home?

She sits on the sofa.

Typing.

House i20   Typing.

Helen (*scrolling through tablet*)   1 March. The defendants are Kim Cole and Michael Warne. Ages, fourteen and fifteen. Both are first-time offenders, charged with domestic burglary with intent to inflict grievous bodily harm. Category one . . . (*In response to an image on the tablet.*) Jesus Christ.

Pause.

Sorry, delete Jesus Christ.

House i20   Delete.

Helen   Um . . . (*Tries to find herself again.*)   Category one. Greater harm and higher culpability . . .

House i20   Unidentified guest.

Helen   Tell them to reveal to the camera.

Pause.

House i20   Unidentified guest.

Helen   Are they refusing to be identified?

Pause.

House i20   Unidentified guest.

Helen   Can you make sure all windows and doors are locked please.

The sound of several locks and shutters closing at once. She walks to the door.

Hello . . . Hello, can you reveal yourself to the camera.

Long pause.

Tell me who you are or I'm calling the police.

Jacob (*off*)   Helen, it's me.

Pause.

Helen   Who's . . .? (*Realising.*) Jacob?

Jacob   Yeah, it's me.

Helen   Right, hold on. (*To* **House i20**.) Unlock all windows and doors please.

Jacob *enters. He appears dishevelled, like he hasn't been sleeping too well or even sleeping at all.*

Helen   You didn't put your card up for the camera.

Jacob   I forgot my ID at home.

Helen   It would be a silly thing to go to jail for . . .

Jacob   I know. I'm forgetful at the minute.

Helen   The only drawback of all of us taking T3 to stay young, even in our sixties – we still have to prove how old we are to buy a drink.

Jacob   Or just to walk the street.

Helen   Indeed . . . You gave me a scare.

Jacob (*mocking*)   Really? That's nothing like the Helen I remember. You must be getting delicate.

Helen   I must be . . .

Jacob   How are you? It's good to see you.

He leans in for a hug. She embraces him.

Jacob   You look well.

Helen   Thank you . . . You're not holding up too bad yourself.

Jacob   Very generous of you to lie like that.

Helen   Oh, James isn't back yet.

Jacob   I know.

Helen   You didn't come to see him?

Jacob   Of course, yeah . . . But I knew he wouldn't be back just now.

Helen   Okay, well. Sit down. Sit down. Would you like anything to drink? There's no wine. I don't know about beer.

She leads him to the sofa.

Jacob   Just a tea, please.

Helen (*mock surprise*)   We must be getting delicate. Okay, tea. (*To* **House i20**.) Tea, please.

She stands by **Jacob**.

Helen   It takes a while. This house . . .

He rubs his hand against the floor. She looks on, confused.

Helen   To what do we owe the pleasure? It's not like you to turn up anywhere out of the blue.

Jacob   I was around.

Helen   Here? You were just around here?

Jacob   What's the model?

Helen   House i.20   **Jacob**   Feels like the i.20

Jacob   Why such an old model?

Helen   We thought about an upgrade but we might be moving out of the city.

Jacob   Yeah?

Helen   Change of pace from the hustle and bustle. Feeling our age a bit.

He laughs.

Helen   What?

Jacob   It's funny to me how expressions like that still find their way into conversation.

House i20   Tea's ready.

Helen   You see how long it takes.

She heads to the kitchen.

Jacob   It still might be worth the upgrade, even if you're only here for another couple of years.

She exits.

He feels across the walls and the floor. He's searching.

The i25 has a feature that brings your food and drink over to you.

Helen (*off*)   So I've heard.

Jacob   The security is better too. There's no such thing as an unidentified guest.

Helen (*off*)   Milk?

Jacob   No. No. Black.

*He finds a panel at the side of the wall. He forces it open to find a red and yellow wire. He carefully snaps both wires. The sound of a computer shutting down rings around the room. On hearing **Helen**'s footsteps, **Jacob** closes the panel and rushes back to the sofa.*

Helen *enters.*

Helen   Did you hear that?

He stares blankly. She hands him the tea.

Jacob (*noticing the tablet*)   That looks nasty.

Helen   And guess who's been given the job of defending it . . . The kids who done that, allegedly . . . They're fourteen and fifteen years old. They were this close to killing that man. I'm not sure why these things never stop surprising me.

Jacob   They shouldn't though, should they. We're taught that part of getting older is to accept things for the way they are. I think maturity is to never stop being affected by things that we know to be wrong.

Pause.

Helen   Jacob, why are you really here?

House i20   James is home.

James (*off*)   Got your message. Could only get a crate so that should hold you till . . . Tomorrow afternoon at least.

James *enters. He stands shocked on seeing* **Jacob**.

James   How long has this been going on?

Helen   James.

Jacob *smiles.*

Helen   It's never been funny. Jacob was just in the area . . .

James   I bet he was. Behind my back. The whole time.

Jacob *holds his hands up in jest.* **James** *rushes to* **Jacob** *excitedly. They hug.*

James   Why?

Jacob   What?

James   Why were you in the area?

Jacob   Wandering around.

James   You shouldn't be ashamed to say you were missing me.

Jacob   You got me.

James   What we doing? We should all head out.

Helen   I can't.

James   Grab something to eat.

Helen   I have a brief to get ready for the morning.

James   Okay, then we'll stay in. I'll order something. You can at least sit with us.

Helen   I've got a lot to do.

James   How often is Jacob here? It'll be like old times. (*To himself.*) Old times. It creeps up on you doesn't it.

Jacob   You start to sound like that. (*To* **Helen**.) What was your one?

Helen   Hmmm?

Jacob   From before?

Helen   Oh . . . I said we were starting to feel our age.

James smiles.

James   Thanks to the work you do over at Temples, I haven't felt my age yet.

He taps **Jacob** *on the back.*

Helen   Unfortunately, I'll have to leave you boys to it . . . Don't think I'm being rude, Jacob.

Jacob   No. No.

Helen   Let me know when you're leaving.

She exits.

James   You'll drink with me.

Jacob *nods.*

James   Good man. (*To* **House i20**.) Two draught beers?

House i20   Two draught beers.

James   I'll have to go and grab it. We've only got the i20.

He exits.

Jacob *sits again.*

James (*off*)   We're thinking of moving.

Jacob   Helen mentioned it.

James (*off*)   Potential early retirement.

Jacob   Oh really? Where are you thinking of heading?

James (*off*)   I don't get to make decisions, I'm married you see. That's kind of how it works. She wants somewhere with water . . . Retirement in our sixties, it's insane, but I guess when you don't have kids and . . . You know.

He enters, holding two pints of beer. He hands one to **Jacob**.

Jacob   Cheers.

James I'm not sure what life is for if not to work. I mean how long can you stare out into an ocean before you've worked out how many different ways it can move.

Helen (*off*) James. The cameras aren't working.

James Are you sure?

Helen (*off*) Of course, I'm . . . It's the kind of thing it's easy to be sure about.

James Okay. Okay. I'll have a look . . .

*He opens the panel that **Jacob** invaded earlier. He handles the frayed wires.*

Jacob I did that.

James You did?

Jacob Don't worry, I'll pay for it to be replaced.

James Why did you do it?

Helen (*off*) Have you checked the panel?

Jacob *stares at* **James** *calmly. It's clear what he's saying – don't let on.*

James Yeah, one of the wires is frayed. I'll have to get on to them.

Helen (*off*) Should I do it now?

James Don't worry, I'm already on to it. (*To* **Jacob**.) Why did you do that?

Jacob I didn't want the house to record what I'm here to tell you . . .

James What's going on?

Jacob There's a lot of stuff at work. I'm thinking of leaving.

James So you damage my house?

Jacob There can't be a record of any of this . . . I don't want Helen to have to worry either.

James I don't understand what you're telling me here.

Pause.

Jacob When we were ready to distribute T3 to the public, a contract was drawn up with the state and us at Temples. They made us all sign a confidentiality agreement . . . One of the clauses allowed them to modify

T3 away from my original design. I should've questioned it more at the time but I was . . . I was young. I didn't know what I was agreeing to.

James   What was it?

Jacob   He was so great at wheeling out these brilliant speeches that would make people look the other way. Temples. What was it, a brighter, younger, freer world? It was never about anyone else but him. Fuck the world . . . With artificial youth, we were creating an ageing population that didn't age. There's only so much of everything, right . . . Only so much air, only so much water, only so much cattle, only so much space and that's why we're given only so much time or we were given only so much. The state were becoming concerned about the economic implications. Too many workers and not enough industry. If over-resourcing was the problem, he would need to find a solution in the drug that would limit the possibility of human surplus . . . It seems so obvious now. He was determined to do anything.

Pause.

James   What are you saying?

Jacob   All of these files were kept classified. If I had known . . .

Helen *enters.*

Helen   What did they say?

James   Hmm?

Helen   I knew you wouldn't . . .

James   Oh, the cameras . . .

Helen   If I leave it in your capable hands we'll be waiting months. Sorry about this, Jacob.

Jacob   No. No. No need.

Helen (*to the* **House i20**)   Can you call the maintenance team about the cameras?

House i20   Calling.

Helen   If you want something done.

Scene Four

Abandoned warehouse.

Members of Reactive are scattered across the room. **Dylan** *is holding court in the centre.*

Dylan   Across the world . . . Temples has factories from here to Brazil producing T3 on the clock, around the clock and we're . . . We're organising peaceful demonstrations about affordable housing and what happens after you leave uni. It's like we're missing the point somehow, don't you think?

Mustafa   That's what I been saying.

Antonia   Mustafa, sit down.

Cassie   There's a reason we got Dylan here to help us.

Antonia   You.

Cassie   What?

Antonia   You got Dylan here.

Siana   How many TY do you think are willing to risk as much as you're saying?

Dylan   That's what we should be doing here . . . That's the point. We're s'posed to be showing 'em that they ain't got nothing to risk at all. The risk is in shutting up and letting it all happen without a fight. Then you're in your forties and still living at home cos the AY are still running the show.

Cassie   When we first started this . . . The plan was to build a better future for the truly young.

Dylan   None of us matter. Not a single one. We haven't mattered since T1 happened. That's why we left our families right? Petitions, protests and a bunch of vlogs aren't gonna stop what they've got . . . They probably don't even know who we are.

Bilal   Temples . . . They got money, weapons, tank guns . . .

Paul   Why would they have tank guns?

Bilal   I read it. Yeah, they do.

Jonathan   You made that up.

Bilal   No actually . . .

Cleo   Boys . . . Not today.

Dylan   It doesn't matter what they got. We've got us . . . That's what we got. We've got us. All of the truly young. We can go against the artificial lot if we want to.

Cassie   Dylan's right.

Antonia (*sarcastic*)   Oh is he?

Cassie (*ignoring*)   We have to start pulling in more resources. We can't build a movement that we control on our own.

Dylan   We're barely shifting the dial at the minute.

Cassie   It should be like we're mobilising an army.

Mustafa   Separate units across the city. Like divisions.

Dylan   No. The world. Everywhere. They'll all take their orders from us but they will act under the banner of Reactive. Millions of the truly young coming together to show our force, to let them know we won't stand for being kept at the bottom of everything.

Siana   And how we gonna control that? Say someone wants to do something crazy; hurt people and say they're doing it for Reactive. No, I don't like it.

Dylan   That's par for the course, innit. If it happens, we come out and say what it is. That it's not us. But we still have to be prepared to take that kinda action if need be.

Mustafa   At this point, I'm willing to do anything . . .

Antonia   Mustafa, I've seen you run down the street cos you heard a barking dog.

Mustafa   That's a slander and you know it.

Antonia   It was behind a fence.

Bilal   That happened. I was there.

Mustafa   Bullshit.

Siana (*to* **Dylan**)   We don't go after anyone, we told you that when you came. If that's not for you then . . .

Dylan   Yeah, Emmy said that . . . If it weren't for me she'd be here right now. You had an AY on your grounds and you ain't even know it.

Siana   We're not going to lead TYs into thinking they can violently go against a company like Temples . . . It's not how it works and we know it.

Dylan I'm not saying it has to be physical.

Siana The repercussions will be. If we do what you're suggesting, somewhere down the line people will get hurt or go to jail.

Mustafa That's what this feels like anyway. Jail. Just in the open but it's jail, right. That's what it is.

Cassie It's not like we have choices do we. It's not like we've got opportunities either.

Dylan That's exactly what it is. It's a prison. They never made these drugs just so they could live longer. They made 'em so old ideas could live longer too. The artificial young will forever be telling us what to do if we don't take a stance on this now. What are we saying?

He stares around the room for support. **Siana** *steps towards him before his idea can take flight.*

Siana Dylan, when we went about building this, we were all clear about what we were building it for and how we were going to move forward. You've only just got here. You don't get to tell us about how we're going to do it.

Dylan *takes another look around the room.*

Dylan When I first got here yous told me there was no leaders.

Siana There aren't.

Dylan You said that was how the AY do it. So if any of you think we need to start building divisions across the country to build a bigger following. We'll start small first . . . What are we saying?

Cassie's *hand shoots up straight away. Then* **Mustafa's.** *There is a long pause.* **Jonathan** *raises his hand. He taps* **Paul,** *who then raises his hand.* **Bilal** *raises his hand. Lastly,* **Cleo** *raises her hand.*

Siana *and* **Antonia's** *hands stay by their side.*

Scene Five

Temples' Institute. Laboratory.

Temples *and* **Jacob** *stand side by side, overlooking a chain of screens.* **Temples** *cuts a distant figure from the man we saw in the opening scene. He is tense and overbearing.*

Temples   The day that you and I discovered how well T3 was working
. . . We stood in this very room and you asked me about the broader
social implications.

Jacob *shows little to no reaction.*

Temples   You mean to tell me you don't recall? It's not your way to
lose sight of detail. It's why you're such an asset here.

Jacob   You're asking me to remember a moment over thirty years ago.
It's a long time.

Temples   Memory . . . It's the main reason I came to be obsessed with
ageing.

I didn't ever want there to be a time in which I couldn't remember
details. Do you recall your earliest memory?

Jacob   I don't know. My father and I. He's pushing me on a swing. It's
summertime. Probably three or four years old. No, it would've been four.
I know it was four because my mother had bought me a red Harry Potter
coat for that birthday.

Temples   A coat?

Jacob   Yes. It had all of the characters dotted around on the sleeve and
the hood.

Temples   You said the memory was of you in the summer.

Jacob   Ahhh, there was a wind. My father was very cautious. It could
be eighty-eight degrees but if there was a wind . . .

Temples (*validated*)   Detail . . . Mine is with my mother. She was
pregnant with my younger sister. I was so excited as she grew fatter and
fatter over the coming months. By the time she was ready, I was clued up
on near enough everything to do with the process. When my sister was
born I was hardly allowed near her.

My mother cared for her like she would melt in the rain. Fiercely
protective . . . I never understood that feeling as an adult until you and
I created T3. I'm not even ashamed to admit that . . . There's this political
group. They call themselves Reactive. They tried a cyber attack the other
night.

Jacob   Did they come away with anything?

Temples   Other than learning that our system is built like a fortress? It's
nothing to worry about. Just a bunch of kids yet to understand that when

you build something from the ground up, when it comes from inside of you, you will do anything to make sure it's safe.

Pause.

Jacob   Or maybe it's that they do understand. Maybe they want the chance to be fiercely protective of something of their own.

Temples   Is that what you think?

Jacob   I wouldn't know. It's been a long long time since I was a young man, sir.

Temples   Did you think it would go unnoticed that you've come off your cycle?

Jacob   Honestly, someone mentioned it the other day . . . I think we've been working so hard on the stems for T4, I just haven't had the time to . . .

Temples   No. That's not it. I keep thinking it's a protest.

Jacob   Are you trying to catch me out, Elliot? If there's something you want to ask me . . .

Temples   Broader social implications.

Jacob   You're holding me to a comment I made over thirty years ago that I can't even remember. We've worked as closely as partners for years. If there's something that you would like to ask me, I always thought you could just come out and say it. It's the same courtesy I would pay you.

Temples   Be sure to start back up on your cycle. The size of the chef often indicates his level of skill if you know what I mean.

Jacob   I always know what you mean, Elliot.

Scene Six

Abandoned warehouse.

Mustafa, Cleo, Bilal, Paul *and* **Jonathan** *enter the stage in single file; they each hold a small table or chair. They set about organising the room.*

Mustafa   It is kinda like what I was saying though?

Cleo   I don't remember you saying . . .

Mustafa   Yeah, it was.

Bilal   Bruv, it sounds like you trying to credit . . .

Mustafa   Nah, I did.

Jonathan   Always trying to take credit.

Paul   What's he taking credit for now?

Mustafa   At the end of the day, it's all about control. It's always been about control. That's what Dylan was saying. That's what I always said. T3 never come out cos they wanted people to live longer. It was only ever made so old ideas could live longer.

Cleo   Didn't Dylan say that last part?

Mustafa   I know he did, I was paraphrasing, innit.

Cleo   That's not paraphrasing. That's quoting.

Mustafa   Whatever.

Bilal   Would you though?

Paul   Would I?

Jonathan   He's saying would you take T3?

Mustafa   What? Never!

Paul   Course, we wouldn't, that's what this whole thing's about.

Bilal   That's what it's about right now because us men and Cleo are young. I mean truly young. But have you ever asked yourself?

Mustafa   If I'd make myself artificial young in a few years? Never.

Jonathan   Wouldn't even think about it.

Paul   Nah, not me.

Cleo   I've thought about it . . . When we get older, we'll want different things.

Jonathan   But I would still care enough for the people coming up behind us.

Cleo (*mockingly*)   That's the same way we care for them ahead of us.

Mustafa   We would care if they'd treated us better. Thought about things before they made decisions that are gonna affect us for years to come. They started all this. We would've taken care of them if they'd done right by us but they didn't. End of. That's all there is to it.

Antonia *enters.*

Antonia   What are you lot doing?

Long pause.

Cleo?

Cleo   We're having a meeting.

Antonia   A meeting? Siana's on a protest.

Pause.

This is Dylan. He organised this. Cleo, you're so easily led.

Cleo   I'm sick of you thinking that I can't make decisions for myself. Dylan has been right about a lot of things. Siana didn't want us to start building divisions but now we have and people are listening. Look how many of us there are online. The world over. We've got them scared of us. They actually know who we are.

Siana (*off*)   Dylan!

Paul   Oh, for God's sake.

Bilal   How's she back?

Mustafa   Calm it.

Antonia   It's just like all of you to cock this up.

Mustafa   Shut up, Toni.

Antonia   You can't even stage a coup properly. What chance have we got in taking down Temples?

Siana (*off*)   Dylan.

Mustafa, Cleo, Bilal, Paul and **Jonathan** *form a barricade in the centre of the stage.* **Antonia** *stands with her arms folded. She takes a step away from them so it's clear that she is in opposition to the group.*

Siana *enters. She's taken aback on seeing the formation.*

Siana   Where's Dylan?

Paul   Now might not be the best time.   **Jonathan**   He's not here.

Mustafa   He's busy.

Long pause.

Paul   He wouldn't want to talk to you right now, Siana.

Siana   I want to talk to him.

Jonathan   It's not a good idea.

Siana *notices the layout of the room.*

Siana   What's all this?

Antonia   I didn't know anything about it. I swear I didn't.

Dylan *and* **Cassie** *enter.*

Dylan   I heard you screaming.

Siana   Do you think I don't know what's going on?

Dylan   What you accusing me of now?

Siana   Why'd you send me away today?

Cassie   Send you away?

Siana   You keep telling everyone to keep things away from me.

Cassie   Siana, stop.

Dylan   Everyone's here, you can ask 'em.

Pause.

But you won't.

Siana   Cos I know what they'll say. You've got them all under your thumb.

Dylan   That's what this is about, really. You've been pissed ever since you lost the vote.

Siana   I told you what would happen if we started divisions that we couldn't control. Some of the people we had at the protest today want blood. They're too angry.

Dylan   You're not angry?

Siana   Some of them can't be controlled.

Cassie   Did anything actually happen?

Siana   No, but . . .

Jonathan   Then what's your point, if nothing actually happened?

Siana   They're the type to start making plans on their own.

Dylan   Nah, they won't.

Siana   You weren't there. You didn't see them. They wouldn't listen to me or anyone else.

Cassie   We need more people. That's the only way our message is going to get out any further.

Siana   Do they know why we all got together in the first place? It can't just be anyone joining can it?

Dylan   What is it, you wanna do it again? You want us to vote on this again.

Siana   It's beyond that now.

Dylan (*not listening*)   Anyone who wants us to stop recruiting . . .

Siana   That's not what I'm saying.

Dylan (*ignoring*)   Put your hands up.

Hands stay down.

That's that, then.

Long pause.

Siana   Cassie, can I talk to you a minute?

Mustafa   We all decided.

Siana   I want to talk to Cassie.

Cassie   It's fine.

Dylan   You've got fifteen minutes, then we need the room.

Antonia   Siana, I didn't know anything about this.

Siana   I know you, Antonia. I know you didn't.

Dylan *exits, followed by* **Mustafa**, **Cleo**, **Bilal**, **Paul**, **Jonathan** *and* **Antonia**.

Cassie   The more people we have, the more chance we have of getting them to hear us. Then we have a chance of making things fairer for all TY everywhere.

Siana   Who does he think he is?

Cassie   We're all here for the same thing, it doesn't make sense to fight each other. It's a waste of time.

Siana   What does he want?

Cassie   The same thing as us. Why would I bring him here in the first place if he didn't?

Siana   He doesn't want the same thing as me. That's why he never wants me around.

Cassie   That's not true. We were all supposed to tell you about today. It's our fault. It isn't his.

Siana   He's planning something. I know it. You're with him all the time. What does he want?

Cassie   What is your problem? Don't you want progress?

Siana   Four months ago, we didn't even know who he was. Now he makes decisions for all of us, all of the time. I need to know where he plans to take us. What does he want?

Cassie   This is why he never wants you around. This is why no one ever wants you around.

Siana   Because I ask questions.

Cassie   You think you're always right about everything.

Siana   No one should be in control. We said we weren't going to be like them. No hierarchies. No leaders because it leads to corruption. That's exactly what we outlined in our manifesto.

Cassie   It's like he said . . . We're going after Temples. We're going to stop them manufacturing T3. Whatever it takes. There's no secret. It's like he said.

Siana   He's going to get a lot of us arrested or worse than that . . .

Cassie   It's better than this though, innit.

Siana   Good luck.

She exits.

Cassie   Siana, don't. Come back. Siana!

She chases after her.

Scene Seven

Helen *and* **James, House i20**. *Front room.*

Helen *talks animatedly as she sells her ideas across to* **James**, *who appears unenthused.*

Helen   Somewhere on the coast would be nice, wouldn't it?

James   Ummm.

Helen   Don't you think, somewhere on the coast? Like Devon, Torquay is really lovely or even closer like Cornwall. We could get an i25 around there.

James   Yeah.

Pause.

Helen (*playful*)   It doesn't even have to be England. It could be anywhere, California even?

James   No, there would be Americans there.

Helen   I knew I could wake you up.

James   I'm trying to unwind a little.

Helen   You look anxious.

James   Because you won't let me get on with it. With the unwinding.

Helen   There's nothing else?

James   You want the move. Just say where and I'll pack a case, as well as everything else.

Helen   That's just silly. I need for you to be happy too. Otherwise you'll have that face on for the next forty-something years.

James   I'm happy now, here.

Helen   I'm not.

James   Okay, then wherever you want. Not America.

Helen   Have you ever thought about why?

James (*trying to understand the question*)   Why?

Helen   Why I would like to move so much? Why it's so important to me.

James All the time.

Pause.

It's because there are no children here.

Helen I remember the first day we moved in, every single detail, the dents in the wall, the chipped floorboards, the smell. Oh my God, the smell. The hopes of what we were going to be. The parties we would have, the friends we would invite over. You were the first man I had ever lived with and that made me nervous but I was sure we were . . . Sure that I had made the right decision . . . When it was clear that part of what we hoped for wasn't going to happen, this place started to mean something very different for me.

Pause.

James I always quite liked Weymouth. I would go with my family as a boy. Chesil Beach was fun and they've got the harbour. I could take up fishing.

Scene Eight

Abandoned warehouse.

Jacob *wanders onto the stage alone, wearing a rucksack. He takes a set of timid steps to the centre of the room. He notices something in the distance that causes him to freeze.*

Mustafa, **Cleo**, **Bilal** and **Antonia** *enter, stage left.* **Paul**, **Jonathan**, **Cassie** and **Dylan** *enter, stage right.* **Jacob** *is surrounded.*

Cleo Who are you?

Dylan How'd you find us?

Mustafa *snatches* **Jacob***'s hand. He scans him.*

Jacob I'm sixty-one.

Cleo He still hasn't said how he found us.

Mustafa (*to* **Dylan**) He's sixty-one.

Dylan Check outside.

Jacob I'm on my own.

Dylan Go check.

Jonathan and **Paul** *follow the command. They exit.*

Dylan   Search him.

Jacob   I'm not here to hurt anyone.

Bilal *searches* **Jacob** *thoroughly. He reaches for the rucksack.*

Jacob   Leave the bag.

Bilal *obeys.*

Dylan (*to* **Bilal**)   What are you . . .

Bilal *attempts to grab the rucksack, but* **Jacob** *snatches it closer.*

Cassie   Give us the bag.

Jacob   No. No. My name's Jacob Aduba. I'm here to help you.

Dylan (*to* **Antonia**)   Check that.

Jacob   I have my ID here.

Antonia *rushes to a laptop or tablet.*

Antonia   He works for Temples.

Jacob   No. No. I used to work for Temples.

Cleo   He's listed here as an employee.

Jacob   I'm probably still on their . . . I only left last night. I'm going to need for you to trust me. I'm holding classified files. Files that could help you.

Bilal   It feels like a trap to me.

Jacob   There's no trap. They will come back and tell you that I'm on my own. Why would I walk in here on my own if I came to do you harm?

Dylan   How. Did. You. Find. Us.

Jacob   I found one of your divisions. They were sloppy and didn't encrypt their IP address. When I got there, they didn't ask enough questions and led me to you . . .

Mustafa   These rats. Name names. Name names and we'll go there now . . .

Cassie (*calm down*)   Moostie.

Antonia   They could've got us all arrested.

Dylan   Or worse.

Cassie   If it was so easy for him to find us then there could be more on the way.

Jacob   I'm sure of it. Temples promised to shut you down with every tool in his arsenal. We don't have time.

Cassie   What do you have to show us?

Jacob   I want . . .

Jonathan *and* **Paul** *enter.*

Jonathan   We couldn't find anyone.

Cassie (*to* **Jacob**)   What do you have?

Jacob   I have classified files that may keep them away. They'll know that I leaked them. That'll make me a marked man.

Dylan   You're here for protection.

Jacob   Yes. If I give you the files, you'll leak them. It's a big win for Reactive and everything you've been doing.

Dylan   Or you've led them to us, and they will just kill us all.

Jacob   That's possible. I won't lie to you. But this is what you've been fighting for?

Cassie   Yes, it is. What do you have?

Dylan   Wait. It still feels like something's wrong here . . .

Cassie   He's on his own.

Bilal   That's how they would make it seem though . . .

Cassie   No. No. He's on his own. This could help us. This is what all the speeches, marches and protests were about. This is why we've been going against Temples in the first place.

Jacob   They modified the drug . . . They modified T3. They knew there would have to be a trade-off. If we could live longer then some of us were going to have to be sterilised.

Mustafa   Bullshit.

Jacob   They banked on people not asking enough questions. They wouldn't ask because they had the opportunity to live so much longer. Who wouldn't want that? But they don't know that their choice is being taken away.

Antonia (*to* **Mustafa**)   Why wouldn't you believe that?

Mustafa   Half of the country can afford a cycle . . . They would be sterilising half of the country.

Jacob   The world.

Paul   It's a trap.

Jacob   The promise of T3 was that women could bear children into their sixties. How many have we seen?

Antonia   We've never trusted anyone at Temples. What he's saying makes complete sense.

Dylan   You're right. We've never trusted anyone at Temples . . .

Jacob   I don't work there anymore, I swear.

Pause.

I have everything here on the chip. All the correspondence between the state and Temples.

Cassie (*to* **Dylan**)   We should give him a chance.

Jacob   I'm going to have to go into my bag.

He rifles through his bag. He takes out a tube of toothpaste. He pulls it apart to reveal a microchip.

Jacob   Upload the chip. It's all on here. Everything.

Mustafa *takes the chip and signals to the sky. Perhaps a projection of the file hits the back of the stage. A multimedia collage of letters and words that the audience can't make sense of. The group reads with stunned looks as what they're learning reveals itself on their faces.*

Antonia   They were. They've been . . .

Paul   This is legal?

Jonathan   Of course it ain't.

Dylan   They're murderers. It's a silent genocide.

Jacob   When we leak it, the world will know that. They will join us on our mission.

Cassie   We've got it!

Mustafa   This is what we've been waiting for . . . This is.

Cleo   This is it. It's over.

Jacob   We need to leak this now.

Jonathan   Things are about to change.

Paul   Forever. Once the world sees.

Cleo   They'll realise that we're on their side.

Antonia   They've been lying to them at the same time . . .

Cassie   They've been lying to us.

Bilal   There'll be marches.

Mustafa   Head of state torn limb from limb.

Cassie   They'll want Temples' head on a spike when they find out about this.

Bilal   It's just step one though.

Cleo   Yeah, they'll listen to us now.

Antonia   Being young won't mean that you don't know anything anymore.

Jonathan   The same way being old won't mean that you know everything.

Paul   Cos if we were right about this.

Antonia   Then we're probably right about everything else.

Cassie   That will be a scary realisation for them when they wake up . . . When they wake up to find out that we've been right the whole time. It's going to be scary for them when they wake up to read their messages and their feeds. When they wake up in Africa . . .

Bilal   Asia.

Mustafa   The whole of Europe.

Bilal   Mozambique.

Antonia   That's in Africa, you . . .

Bilal   I ain't know that's what we were doing.

Cassie   I can't wait till they wake up.

Dylan *snatches the microchip from* **Mustafa**. *The multimedia installation or projector image should dissolve at that moment.*

Dylan   You didn't find this out last night though did you?

Pause.

Jacob   No.

Dylan   He worked on T3. You got someone here who knew about this all along and what did he do . . .?

Jacob   I only found out a few weeks ago.

Dylan (*to* **Mustafa**)   Are you buying that, Moostie?

Jacob   I signed a confidentiality agreement. That's all.

Antonia   Does it matter? This is going to help our cause.

Dylan (*to* **Jacob**)   Nah, that's not it. Your story's too neat. We're alright with protecting someone who stood by knowing that people were being sterilised.

Jacob   I didn't know.

Cassie   Why can't we believe him?

Dylan (*to* **Jacob**)   If you don't stop lying to me.

Mustafa   What did the agreement say?

Dylan   Great question.

Jacob   Only that they could modify the drug at any time. It's a fairly standard . . .

Dylan   How'd you find out?

Jacob   I gained access to a classified file . . . The population figures were wrong. I followed it through because I had long suspected.

Dylan   Didn't I say? He'd long suspected . . .

Cassie   That doesn't mean he knew anything.

Dylan   Mustafa? Cleo? Antonia? This is our hero now. We forgive easily don't we? (*To* **Jacob**.) Thank you for your service. (*To everyone*.) He'll have to leave now . . .

Jacob   He doesn't want you to know that he's using T3.

Mustafa   What?

Jacob   The tell is around his eyes and his wrists.

Dylan   He's lying. Can't you see that? Can't you see? That's why they sent him here.

Cleo   He's lying.

Jacob   They said you scanned one and another . . .

Jonathan   We . . .

Paul   We've never scanned him.

Dylan   Are you that stupid? You don't think the man from Temples wants to see this happen to us?

Cleo (*to* **Cassie**)   What should we do?

Mustafa *descends onto* **Dylan** *with the scanner.*

Antonia (*to* **Jacob**)   If you're lying I swear . . .

Dylan   If you bring that machine anywhere near me, they would've won. That's all it is. They want us to fight amongst ourselves. Not to trust each other. They want this for us. Don't you see what this is? Are you all this stupid?

Mustafa *takes* **Dylan**'s *palm. He scans. Either a projection or the negative sound should tell the audience that* **Dylan** *has failed the test.*

Mustafa   You're forty-five.

Cassie   You . . .

She charges at **Dylan**. *The group fight to hold her back.*

Cassie   He's a liar. Let me kill him. Please. Let me kill him.

Dylan   Didn't I organise you, Cass? Wasn't it me that took you lot further than you'd ever been? Do you not think I stand for what you stand for, huh? We were the first generation this happened to. Look at us. Things aren't great if you're forty either.

Cassie   Take him downstairs . . .

Dylan   I needed you. I needed you all. My generation . . . They've accepted things as they are.

Cassie   Take him out of here.

Mustafa *forces the microchip out of* **Dylan**'s *hand.*

Bilal, **Paul** *and* **Jonathan** *arrest* **Dylan**. *They drag him to the exit.*

Dylan   I knew you would fight. I knew you would fight. I knew you would fight.

Bilal, **Paul** *and* **Jonathan** *exit with* **Dylan**. *We hear his screams fade into the distance –* '*I knew you would fight*', '*I knew you would fight*', '*I knew you would fight*'.

Cassie   Upload the chip.

Scene Nine

Same night.

Helen *and* **James' House i20**. *Front Room*. **Helen** *is on the sofa, reading from a tablet.* **James** *stands by her side.*

Helen   They're talking about marching from the Temples building to Parliament Square.

James   Yeah.

Helen   Truly young and artificials coming together . . .

James   It's getting late . . .

Helen   That may be the only good thing that comes out of this. We'll all be on the same side.

James   Don't you have a brief in the morning?

Helen   I couldn't care less . . . Have you not heard about what's just happened?

James   We're not going to sort it out tonight are we.

Helen   A march seems too polite. Too British. We should be setting them alight.

James   Helen.

Helen   You haven't raised your voice once tonight. Not once . . . I pray they're brought to justice. Not by the courts. Not by us, no. There's no such thing as justice for rich men.

James   I really think it's important for you to take some time to rest tonight. You haven't put that thing down in almost four hours.

Helen   It was never like him to just arrive somewhere was it? I'm talking about Jacob. Even at uni, he would mark everything in a calendar. I should've known when he came here, that day when he came here. He wanted to say something. He kept that to himself all those years.

James   We don't know that.

Helen   He worked there. Practically invented the thing.

James   Still, we don't know.

Helen   He watched us struggle – doctors' appointments, all kinds of treatments, I thought there was something wrong with me. All these years, I thought there was something wrong with me.

House i20   Siana's home.

James   We can talk upstairs.

Siana *enters.*

Siana   You alright?

Helen   We would prefer it if you didn't go out so late.

James (*to* **Siana**)   We had a chat about this before.

Siana   There's nothing out there scarier than what I've already seen. Promise.

James   Seriously. Not anymore.

Siana   Tea?

James   We were just heading up.

Helen   How was it out there?

Siana   Quiet. I think people are gonna need the night before they react . . . Or maybe they'll just take all their anger out online.

Helen   Not this time.

James   Night.

He holds for **Helen** *to follow him upstairs.*

Siana *exits once they leave.*

House i20   Unidentified guest.

Pause.

Unidentified guest.

Siana *returns with a travel case. She hides it in the corner of the room, before heading to the door.*

Siana   Hello. Hi. Please put your ID up.

Cassie (*off*)   Siana, it's me, Cass.

Cassie *enters.*

Helen (*off*)   Who is it?

Siana   No one . . . Don't worry. They've gone.

Cassie   You alright?

Siana   I said not to come.

Cassie   Don't always do what I'm told though, do I?

Pause.

(*Looks around the house.*) This is nice.

Siana   I'm leaving soon.

Cassie   What's happened?

Siana   Nothing.

Cassie   Where you going?

Siana   It must've taken you ages to get here.

Cassie   You're still angry with me.

Siana   No, I'm not.

Cassie (*bollocks*)   Alright, you're not.

Pause.

Did you see what happened?

Siana   Course.

Cassie   It bothered me that you weren't there. You should've been. It was your vision all of this.

Siana   I can't take credit for that.

Cassie   You said there would be a way to get them to listen to us. To have things be fair for us. You said we should put a group like Reactive together.

Siana   How is everyone?

Cassie   The same. They're a little more . . . Excited, I guess. Everything's looking up.

Siana   Is that how you're seeing it?

Cassie   They're talking about Temples closing down. People are furious, as they should be.

Siana   Then you're right. That's it. The revolution is here. Well done!

Cassie   Do you want me to beg you? If you want me to beg you, I will.

Pause.

Siana   I don't want you to . . .

Cassie   You know what I want. I'm sorry but I never wanted you to leave in the first place. I want you . . . We all want you to come back. We need you. This . . . This doesn't even suit you. Living here like a domestic animal. We have plans. Big plans. Dylan isn't there anymore.

Siana   I don't care about that.

Cassie   It's important to me. It should've been bros before hoes, right. Sisters before misters. I broke code. I get it if you don't want to forgive me but I would love . . . We'd all love if you come back. I promised everyone that I would bring you home.

Pause.

Siana   Living here's reminded me about adults and how they think. It was good to get away from everyone and their opinions about older people in Reactive . . . When the leak happened I was so happy. My uncle looked distraught. His wife was so angry. She never got over not being able to have children of her own. It's why she likes having me around so much . . . The time for their second pill of the day was ten. They both didn't take it and I thought that's it. We've done it. It's done. An hour and a half later they remembered. I watched them take their daily cycle. That's when I went for my walk. I forgot that about adults. That's how their minds work.

Cassie   They're just two people. You just have to go online to see the real impact. People are talking about bringing Temples to trial. The state too.

Siana   It's a nice idea isn't it? On my walk I realised that tomorrow won't give us the answers but three weeks from now, this will probably all just be a story.

Cassie   Bullshit.

Siana   The worse thing . . . The worse worse thing about it is that with every birthday I start to think more and more like them. All the things I want to change but learn to accept because that's what getting older is at the end of the day.

Cassie   This is why it's not good for you to stay here. It will turn you into this.

Siana   Cassie, I can't come back with you.

Cassie   I promised them you would come back. Don't do this.

Siana   Take care, Cassie.

Cassie *searches for something to say but can't find it. She stomps out.*

Siana *sits with her head in her hands.*

Helen *enters, sheepishly.*

Helen   (*like she's unaware*)   I thought I heard two voices.

Siana *doesn't respond.*

Helen   Where are you going?

Siana   I don't know. Lahore. Johannesburg. Phuket. I'm gonna spin a globe and close my eyes. Wherever my finger lands.

Helen   You should hope it's not Antarctica.

Siana *grabs the travel case from the corner of the room.*

Helen   Were you planning on not saying goodbye to your uncle? To me?

Siana   I thought it'd be easier if I just . . . Uncle James asks a lot of questions. He's protective and that.

Helen   You're that ungrateful. You were in tears when you showed up here. Your uncle didn't even think twice about bringing you in.

Siana   I haven't forgotten any of that. It's more so . . . I thought about a lot of stuff on my walk . . . (*Decides against talking.*) I should go.

Helen   Whatever you want to say will stay with me.

Siana   You're his wife.

Helen   I promise . . .

Pause.

You were right . . . It was hypocritical of James and I to take our cycle. It's a habit, I guess.

Siana   It's not just that . . .

Helen   So it is a part of it?

Siana   You said Jacob Aduba was here, before the leak.

Helen   Yes.

Siana   I don't know for sure but I feel that maybe Uncle James . . .
Maybe he knew more than what he's letting on.

Helen   James never worked for Temples.

Siana   I know, but they were so close. You might just think I'm making
assumptions but I'd rather leave now than know for sure. You will tell
him I said bye?

Helen   I have some money here. You'll need money.

She rushes to a small chest on the table. She walks to **Siana** *with a fistful
of notes.*

Siana   Thank you.

Helen   Let me know where your finger lands . . .

Siana *exits.*

Scene Ten

Pharmaceutical exhibition.

Temples *alone on stage, addresses the audience.*

Temples   I would like for you all to close your eyes . . . (*He goes to
the audience to make sure.*) All of you, go ahead, close your eyes . . .
Picture, if you can, a modest bicycle repair shop along a cobbled
street in Mannheim, Germany, eighteen eighty-six. A busy community
where pedestrians rush with hurried feet past horse-led carriages and
motorised stagecoaches. From here Karl Benz patented the
Motorwagen, the first automobile designed to generate its own power.
In only three years, Benz went on to unveil the Motorwagen Three.
For the Wright Brothers, Wilbur and Orville, land and roads were not
enough, they wanted the sky. Only nineteen years after the Motorwagen,
the first practical fixed-winged aircraft took flight in Kitty Hawk, North
Carolina . . . Now when we fly, our main concern is when will they be
serving the food. It's no bad thing. You, the consumer, shouldn't have
any use for understanding how a plane takes flight or how a car takes
you from A to B.

I had always thought about how our creations had managed to accelerate past the progress of man. Our story has stayed the same from the very beginning. We're born, we grow old and we die. This was true for Karl Benz as it was true for the Wright Brothers as it will be true for you and me. That middle part of the story is where I would like to fix your attention . . . We grow old. Well, says who?

He opens his hand to reveal a small pill. He holds it aloft.

If you haven't already, can I ask that you open your eyes? . . . This is our first step towards hope and happiness in a younger, brighter and freer world. Ladies and gentlemen, we are here to present T1 . . . Generations to come will view this as the moment that the curse of ageing was removed, and the world was able to look to tomorrow without the fear of a failing body or mind. But more than likely, in years to come we will take our pill with no more thought than we give the toaster in our kitchen.

The End.

Ageless

BY BENJAMIN KUFFUOR

Notes on rehearsal and staging, drawn from a workshop with the writer, held at the National Theatre, October 2018

How Benjamin came to write the play

'When approaching the play I asked myself, "If I were fifteen, sixteen, seventeen, what would I want to see at the theatre?" Writing for a young cast forced me to think about a premise that interrogated the idea of youth. This led me to think about how ageing is viewed in the West as something to fear: many industries owe their existence to our quest to avoid ageing in a cosmetic sense and increasingly in a more cerebral sense too.'

Benjamin Kuffuor, 2018

The accessibility of theatre – who gets to see plays and who doesn't – is really important to Benjamin and he wanted this play to work for someone who hasn't seen a play before. The writing style is closer to cinema than it is to theatre.

When he began writing, he thought about what's pertinent now and it struck him that there are currently a lot of conversations going on about a 'generation war'. Being young is harder than it's ever been, people are staying younger for a lot longer than previous generations; like being thirty-five and living with your mum, for example. Both economically and professionally what you can aspire to be is different now.

Benjamin is interested in the question: what are older generations holding on to and what effect is that having on younger people?

Discussion about the play

Lead director Laurie Sansom ('LS') initiated an open discussion between Benjamin ('BK'), himself and the group of directors to further investigate the play.

LS How difficult is it to be young now?

Group Young people can struggle to see their place in the world; it's so quickly changing in terms of what jobs are available, for example.

School doesn't set young people up for the modern world. They are starting to find that there's a disconnect between what they do at school and jumping into the world.

There's a pressure in education for everything to be job driven; university is no longer affordable, they feel that too much debt will take away future prospects. There are no facilities for younger people in some areas.

It is difficult for young people to go home and shut off because of phones and social media; there's no end to the day. Young people are spending less time with their family because of social media and the pressure and strain that puts them under. They seem to be desensitised to things they are exposed to that would shock adults.

LS   There seems to be a lack of opportunities for young people to find a purpose or a function because older people are hanging onto the jobs.

Young people can see it all happening, through social media, through the news, but if they're not old enough to vote then people don't think they should have a say yet. They need to do something bigger to make themselves noticed.

There's something about feeling passionate but powerless in teenage groups.

There's a prevalent feeling today amongst our generation that, when we were young, we were allowed to learn from making mistakes. For today's young people though, with the audit trail that is left on social media, the opportunity to fail isn't there anymore; you have to be perfect all the time.

The artificial young in this play are the 'baddies' – there's a link to being allowed to make mistakes: they were allowed to be young, the truly young aren't.

LS   Thinking about the artificial young in the play. What's the difference in the AY characters we meet [from the truly young] and what's their attitude to the scenario they find themselves in?

BK   You have characters like Helen or Jacob who recognise that getting what you want and being young forever is not the natural order – you should move on and there's a reason that cycle exists. This is true of Emmy also; she's an AY but is on the side of the TY.

LS   Helen is in a place where she's thinking, 'I want to retire, I want to move to Devon.' She also feels betrayed when her biological need (to have a baby) is halted by Temples and T3.

BK   James has a different attitude, which is a satellite of what happens as a whole in the play; when the world becomes aware of what it means to take the drug, they choose to carry on, to the detriment of new life. You can compare this to climate change: it doesn't stop us from living the lives we're living. If T3 actually existed, people would probably choose the drug over the idea of new life entering the world.

Group   Young people can be idealistic – they struggle to understand how people can see problems but do nothing about them, like the refugee crisis. They are aware of the situation but feel powerless due to their age.

LS   That's fertile land to explore – in this play everybody has a different way in which they respond to the situation. You can compare this to America's five stages of climate-change denial – just for short-term economic advantage.

LS   How do characters respond to the scenario, which is seemingly impossible to change?

BK   There's a scene where Siana knows that getting older is accepting there are things you can't change and she's conceding to the world as it is. James received information from Jacob about the mass sterilisation, but he chooses to withhold it.

Group   Siana is accepting that there are things you can't change. We've all been teens and felt that feeling of powerlessness, but then becoming an adult and conceding – where does the feeling of passion go?

LS   Where does that desire to change the world go?

BK   It leaves because your concerns become about what your immediate day-to-day is – that becomes the extent of your thinking. If you wanted to write a Brexit play, you would write about a family; that would tell you everything you needed to know.

Group   This is why it's so hard to be a young person with social media – theoretically they have the ability to have massive concerns, but it also makes their world smaller, because they are thinking of their image and how they present themselves.

LS   The play is set in a dystopian future that reveals what happens when people's priorities become about what they look like. It's a metaphor about selfishly holding on to something and not letting go and not letting younger people take over.

Group   How much is taking the T3 pill about older people feeling rejected by younger people? There are some cultures that reject older people and some that embrace them.

BK   This is very much a Western story in terms of what being old means – other cultures see being old as something else, not past your prime like the West.

LS Does passive resistance or peaceful protest actually do anything? Or if we expand the network – satellite organisations, for example – will violence work then?

LS The question at the centre of the Reactive group is: how should we protest?

The battle that goes on in Reactive and the battle in House i20 is about how you protest or respond to this scenario. Jacob is a classic whistleblower whilst Helen is trying to convince James to retire.

LS Is it helpful to talk about systems of organisation and group dynamic?

LS Systems of organisation are interesting – how does power organise itself? The group can appear to have a philosophy to work in one way, but that doesn't mean it actually works like that. Dylan comes in and becomes a 'strong leader' – what does that do to a group dynamic? Does it open conversations about potential other organisations of power? The play offers up an interesting question around intergenerational groups – how does that dynamic work?

LS What other things will young people feel passionate about that can be a useful touchstone?

Group The world is becoming smaller, people are holding on to what resources they have – why do some people hang on to what they've got and not let others in, what's their reasoning? We could try and connect the thinking.

BK Social media shows how younger people retreat from active things. Siana and Reactive know their position, but don't necessarily know how they want to move forward – they don't know how to get what they want. If it weren't for the older characters they wouldn't act. Dylan is about direct action – he is the driving force because he understands how adults think. It's the adults that move them forward and release the information to them. Adult thinkers are needed for the younger people to move forward.

LS Where does Dylan fit? The younger people are rejecting the adults but they perhaps need to accept help . . .

BK Reactive is a group that doesn't trust older people, because they are the cause of their current scenario. Dylan is different to Emmy because what he's promoting is quite self-serving. He's helping them as a way to feel powerful.

LS Dylan shifts the dynamic of the group and brings in a hierarchy which serves perhaps as a metaphor – we are living in current outdated and patriarchal structures that are at breaking point.

LS   Is there anything to consider when casting in terms of gender and ethnicity?

BK   In terms of gender – I guess we're playing with perception because we're playing with age so there are some things you can't move around. It's tricky. When you write something in your mind it's very specific, the characters are vivid when they come from you – there are things that characters do that are very 'male', like James knowing that women are being sterilised and not doing anything about it. Same with Dylan – he has quite a male energy.

LS   You need to direct the play as written, but there are circumstances where a group will throw up different casting challenges. In this case it's about identifying what's a writer's intention and what's a directorial decision. So a girl can play a boy and vice versa, but you cannot re-gender the roles.

The play can be performed with any ethnicities. With names like Mustafa and Bilal, you can imagine in a post-apocalyptic world that names have become less culturally specific.

BK   Even if the names can't be attributed to people of those cultures, please keep them – we don't get names like that in plays that often.

LS   What about if you're trying to stage the play with a larger cast?

LS   For a larger company, a good solution is the House i20; it could be created using people.

LS   Can any of the parts be shared? Are you happy with the odd line being split between characters?

BK   You would need to justify a large cast. It's important to very quickly establish what the world of the play is. There's a lot that can be confusing.

LS   There's definitely a theatrical convention you can play with in terms of the multimedia offerings in the play. Or the riots. One of your jobs as director is to work out how to make the play make sense to the company, as long as you're being sensitive to what the play is doing and the writer's intentions.

EXERCISE: 'QUADS', FROM FRANTIC ASSEMBLY, A WARM-UP EXERCISE

This is a physical exercise that warms up the body but also aids ensemble building.

The instructions for the exercise are as follows:

Depending on your group size set up lines of four people per line.

Get some music playing – something upbeat – the workshop had Kylie!

Everyone has to jump on the count of eight.

First line starts and on the eighth jump turn 180 degrees. Each line does this for the next eight, and the next eight and so on.

The last line turn 180 degrees on the eight and then continue to jump for the next count and then turn on the seven; one by one each line jumps and turns on the seventh count, then the sixth and so on until you're down to one.

(Always turn to your left.)

Addition: on the sixth count you could add a 'Beyoncé' arm action.

(No counting allowed!)

Addition: say a 'Barry White' 'Yeah!' on the second jump.

LS As your group get better you can make it harder – you can introduce 90-degree turns so that the lines changes, etc.

Approaching the play

The workshop focused on the following areas:

- Characterisation
- Scene work

CHARACTERISATION

Laurie split the group into four smaller groups to look at the different characters in the play. He assigned each group three characters and asked them, in their group, to apply the following questions to each of their characters:

1 **What information do you know about them?** What's said about them? What do they say about themselves?

2 **What's their dramatic function?** What's their attitude to T3 and protest/resistance?

3 **Imagined back-story?** Some have very little back-story present in the play, so what can you create yourselves?

The groups worked together for twenty minutes and then fed back the following suggestions for character profiles.

418   Benjamin Kuffuor

Elliot Temples

1 He is the oldest character, in his eighties. He is intellectual, arrogant, obsessed with ageing. He likes to be in the public eye. The group likened him to Elon Musk. He has a lot of money – what's he going to do with it? He compares himself to Greek mythology, the Wright brothers, Karl Benz. He has changed the world.

2 He is the architect of the whole play. Interesting question: does he believe what he has done is good?

3 Why youth? Perhaps he had an issue with people dying around him? He has created a world in his own image. He has a God complex. Legacy is so important to him, he believes this is his world.

Jacob

1 When we first meet him he doesn't have his ID, he looks dishevelled, he's quite technically sound, he speaks nostalgically about his childhood.

2 He is a whistleblower.

3 He's friends with Helen and James from university; it is hinted that he and Helen have a romantic history.

Helen

1 She lives in a House i20, but she would like to move and retire to Devon – perhaps she wants to be old? She wants children but it's not been possible. She is friends with Jacob with a possible romantic history. She has a high-powered job as a lawyer.

2 She is playing the older responsible role, and embodying the consequences of taking T3.

3 She is married to James whom she met at university.

James

1 He is married to Helen, in his sixties, selfish, not stupid, a lawyer.

2 He represents choice, keeps information to himself.

3 He wasn't very mature, young spirited, and that's stayed with him.

Siana

1 James and Helen's niece, she is opposed to Dylan, she brought Reactive together and refers to the manifesto. She is an idealist and a theorist, and more frightened of action than the others.

2 She has a pragmatic and peaceful function in the play; she has a moment of realisation at the end of the play, starts thinking like the AYs and leaves. She is a bridge between TY and AY. She is active.

3 Why is she staying with her aunt and uncle? Where are her parents? (BK: her parents didn't have access to the pill so they died.)

Cassie

1 She is pro the expansion of Reactive.
Question: did Cassie and Siana have a romantic relationship?
BK They're best friends, so the betrayal is really significant – her friend picked a boy over her. Cassie's love of Dylan is very immature – it's a young new love. Dylan is in his forties and there's the question of whether their relationship is meliorative on his part?

2 She introduces the group to Dylan.

Dylan

1 He's older, first-generation T1; his motives are different for taking it, he's been taking it for a long time. He comes into Reactive and tries to infiltrate and has a scanner; perhaps he's trying to divide the group, or at least get them to do what he wants. He likes the idea of a fight; he's coming in to make it less of a democracy, which is in opposition to Antonia. He wants to make his own life better, perhaps be a part of something. There is an age gap between him and Cassie. Does he actually love her? Or is he attracted to her? Or is she just a pawn in his game? He's an anarchist but from a decent background, now lives as a nomad.

2 He understands that the group can help him stop Temples.

3 He is disillusioned with his generation and the pill.

Emmy

1 She is in her forties and an AY but posing as a TY. She gets scanned by Dylan and kicked out. She allows herself to get scanned. She's trusting but not trustworthy, wants to help the young, change the order, but she's hypocritical – she wants change but takes the pill.

(**BK** Emmy and Dylan are the same but different; she really wants to help them, she sees the injustice. She knows she needs to be like them to help them.)

(**LS**   Dylan uses the Emmy situation as a smokescreen and it buys him immediate leverage and power.)

2 Emmy bolsters Dylan's credibility.

3 Perhaps she worked with young people?

Mustafa

1 Known as 'Moostie' to his friends. He is enthusiastic, not very bright, bored of the hiatus they're in, likes to stir action. He becomes resolute at the end of the play; his frustration allies him to Dylan.

(**BK**   Reactive as a whole shows the audience what being disenfranchised does to people – it makes people angry, makes people fight, makes people quiet, makes people despondent, makes people get high.)

2 Mustafa supports Dylan when he arrives.

Cleo

1 She has a vape – what's in the vape? She's high.

2 She backs Dylan and stands up to Antonia. Dylan takes advantage of the fact that they're divided.

Antonia

1 She's smart, in the know, she calls Dylan out and questions his motives. She's got a backbone, doesn't agree with some of Dylan's actions; she's not afraid to call people out and wants an identity for the young. She is peaceful in her manner.

(**BK**   They talk of no hierarchy, but there is: Antonia is Siana's lieutenant.)

2 She is Siana's ally, an outspoken voice of the group, the voice of reason, the voice of true Reactive. The philosopher.

Paul

1 He's a sheep; he demonstrates that some of them are too young. Comparable to *Lord of the Flies*.

2 He is an enforcer, not a thinker. He's a doer, a foot soldier, a recruiter.

3 Perhaps he had a bad childhood and therefore needs looking after?

(**BK**   Casting wise, if necessary, Paul and Jonathan could be condensed into one role.)

Jonathan

1 He is very similar to Paul, suspicious of Cassie when she returns, has a fear of infiltration. He is logical, aware, considered in his approach. He stands up to Moostie, serves the group and is proud of the group.

2 He is an enforcer, not a thinker. He's a doer, a foot soldier, a recruiter.

3 He is similar to Paul and, again, in smaller casts they could be condensed into one role if this is helpful.

Bilal

1 He has a company, has other priorities, a boastful nature, feels pressure to achieve, asks a lot of questions (sometimes arbitrary); he is a wheeler dealer, a cheeky chappie, daft!

2 He provides some comic relief in the play.

EXERCISE: CHARACTER IMAGINATION AND PHYSICALISATION

Part One

Laurie took the group through a two-part character exercise that could be useful to use with your companies.

Laurie asked the group to each pick a character and then answer the following questions on a piece of paper. It is imperative that they write the first thing that comes into their head and to be spontaneous. The answers should start to fill in some gaps about each character. Laurie stated that this exercise is as much about where the gaps in knowledge are as it is about what we know.

Questions:

Write the full name of your character.

Actual age.

The age they appear to be.

Family background – where they're from in terms of family, are their parents alive? Siblings? Children?

Where do they live? Be specific about location – describe it.

What clothes do they wear on an ordinary day, going about their business?

Education – what level, were they good at school, did they go to university, etc.?

Are they on any medication? If so, what?

Who is their best friend?

Who is their antagonist?

What do they like to eat for lunch?

What music do they listen to?

What do they like to do in their spare time (if they have any spare time!)?

Have they got any pets?

What is something they say a lot? Something they live by? It might be something they say a lot in the play. Laurie calls this a 'watch cry'.

Is there anything unusual about them physically? Maybe they're not unusual.

What is their super-objective – i.e. what is it that drives everything they do?

What's their secret?

Laurie then asked the directors to look over what they'd written for a couple of minutes and to use what they had written to start to visualise their character.

Part Two

Laurie delivered the following instructions which the directors individually followed:

Get into a neutral position – feet are parallel under your hips, nice and relaxed, keep the knees soft, shoulders open, chin parallel to the floor and find focus.

Close your eyes.

(Laurie played some atmospheric music here.)

Imagine you're walking down the street and in the distance is your character.

Imagine you slowly walk towards them, and as you get closer they're coming into focus.

What are they wearing? What is their facial expression? Is it comfortable walking towards this person or is it anxiety inducing? How are they holding themselves? What have they got on their feet? You're getting close enough to see their eyes, what colour are their eyes? What emotion is in them? You're directly standing in front of them – how does that feel?

On the count of three step forward and step into their body. Let your body see how it fits inside their skin, and scan now from the top of their head to the bottom of their feet. Try things out until something feels right. Think about each separate part of your body, the knees, the feet, etc.

Walk around the room.

Find the character's natural tempo – is it fast, slow? Smooth, staccato?

Try one part of the body leading, see what fits. If one thing doesn't work, try something else.

Move fast.

You have two tempos now – relaxed and fast, chop and change.

Now see how they sit, might be on the floor, might be on a chair.

Find their voice – start saying their 'watch cry' – use those words to find their voice. Be bold!

So now you can move fast, move slow, keep saying their 'watch cry'.

Find an object in the room, relate to the object, use the object.

Have their inner monologue going through your head and say it out loud.

Find an activity they do on a regular basis. Find it and do it, keeping the interior monologue going.

Keep moving between activity, walking, interacting with an object, and always keeping their inner monologue going.

Find something that they would be surprised about.

Show them at their happiest – is it possible for them to be happy or not?

We're coming to the end of the day, so they're going to make their way to wherever they sleep – where do they sleep? Find your way there.

Always keep the inner monologue going.

In thirty seconds they're going to be asleep.

Countdown, twenty seconds

Ten seconds

End.

Reflections

LS This is a good exercise for switching off the brain and 'doing' instead, getting actors to think about the conflicting sides that exist in one human being. This exercise is a way of embodying a character before you intellectualise them.

Actors often get locked into choices a character has made in a play, but be sure to ask why they don't change it – it's good to discover why they aren't taking a different path. There's a whole world for you to make choices about – in particular, where do they live? What are the details of their environment? It's a blank canvas! There's so many different ways to approach those questions that specify your world.

There's something to add to the exercise when you do it – get the actors to find three instinctive physical tics they do – they can often be quite age specific. It allows them to make some choices about the characters' physicality, rather than their own. Maybe the AYs have some that are about them being older that they try to hide, for example.

EXERCISE: SCENE WORK

Laurie split the group into four, with the instructions that one member of each sub-group would need to nominate themselves as director.

He asked the groups to each read their given scene together and talk about it, with the director leading the discussion. He suggested that the discussion should last around five minutes and then the group should work for thirty minutes on staging the scene.

The scenes were divided up as follows:

Group A: Reactive, pp. 374–376

Group B: Jacob and Helen, pp. 379–382

Group C: Temples and Jacob, pp. 389–391

Group D: Cassie, Helen, Siana, pp. 407–409

After the allotted time, Laurie gathered the group back together to share their scene work. Each scene was performed to the rest of the group and a discussion was held after each showing, led by Laurie, who gave the 'actors' notes and the scene was performed again.

Group A: Reactive, pp. 374–376

LS My question for the director of this group is: what were the challenges in staging this scene?

Director Trying to make the characters feel natural and comfortable, particularly in terms of how you differentiate them as characters, and playing against the difference of Dylan.

LS With more time you'd look more at their environment. What can you do to make that world a little more lived in before you start staging it?

LS There are exercises to do to specify the space – have you got areas that the members make their 'home'. Questions to ask your actors: Where do they sleep? What facilities does the space have?

LS It struck me how dysfunctional the group is when Dylan arrives – he acts as a catalyst for the conflict that already exists, and he exploits how they are not very unified right now. However suspicious they are, the injection of someone new is needed right now because the dynamic is not productive.

LS Some useful language: *Intention* – what a character wants. *Tactics* – how they are going to achieve the thing they want.

I tend to create a scene by exploring: what does a character want? How are they trying to get it? Then using that to let the actors explore the scene and the characters and find their journeys – the more you can create the world and let the actors inhabit it themselves, the more organic it's going to feel. You're handing over control to the young people and then you edit it. It's okay for them to make a mess whilst they explore and then moment to moment you're asking what the drama is between characters.

For example, what does Dylan want when he appears in the room? He wants to be a leader. All his tactics are about how to get to that point.

The group performed the scene again with Dylan trying to be the leader by charming them all. And Reactive being suspicious of him, but also being charmed by him.

Feedback from the group: it changed the genre – from serious to lighter.

LS It's always a good idea to try the opposite of your instinct; for example, alpha people often underplay themselves to get what they want, e.g. Dylan pretending to leave.

LS Allow your actors to be bold with reactions – actors often worry that they will upstage the actor speaking if they react too much – look after that with your actors. They can make sounds, etc. Keep it live and in the moment. The drama lies in what happens between two people, not just the person speaking.

Some thoughts on staging: End on can be tricky because you can finish up with everyone facing downstage – don't be afraid to face actors upstage if the person reacting is visible.

Group B: Jacob and Helen (and House i20), pp. 379–382

House i20 was made up of eight cast members who gave House i20 lines and delivered furniture, etc.

After the scene was presented the group discussed how far you could take the personification of House i20; someone compared it to a car factory, another to Hogwarts. It was suggested that different performers could have different roles; i.e. one makes tea, one types her report, etc. You could extend the jobs that the house does; a door could be a person, etc.

BK   This is the scene that took the longest to write, it's really important – it's a rhythm shift, and we learn a lot of information regarding the sterilisation and what the tablets do. Remember, Jacob's intention is to tell James rather than Helen. It's a secret; he wants to hide that he is there to tell secrets.

LS   In terms of the language we spoke about earlier, Jacob's *intention* is to come and give this secret information to James and, when he arrives, what are his *tactics*? How does he want to appear? Normal! He doesn't want to give the game away but he's early!

LS   There is something interesting in him trying to find out what the model of the house is so that he can disengage the camera – but all without Helen realising what he's doing. All the while their romantic history is fizzing under the surface, there's unresolved sexual tension.

The group tried the scene again with Jacob working harder to cover up that he is there to do something secret.

Check in with the given circumstances of the scene – for Helen, an unidentified guest turns up, which is scary, and then her friend has shown up without his ID card (illegally) and isn't really saying why he's there . . .

Group C: Temples and Jacob, pp. 389–391

Director   The power dynamic between Temples and Jacob was very interesting, quite extreme, which felt surprising.

Group   At the top of the scene Temples knows that Jacob has come off his cycle – and he thinks he is doing this in protest. It's a suspicious society because lots of people aren't what they appear to be.

LS   Why does Temples bring up memory? Perhaps because he knows Jacob has come off his cycle so his memory is going; having memory is a value of being young so he uses it as a threat. Temples is warning Jacob: don't mess with this because I will fiercely protect it.

LS   What does Temples want? To get Jacob back on board?

BK   Both of them are really scared – Jacob is Temples' lieutenant; if he left he would lose everything, and Jacob is scared too because he wants to *do* something but Temples is this father figure.

Laurie asked the group to try the scene again and spend more time trying to read the other character for clues as to what they are thinking, because there is so much not being said. They both want something from the other person but they can't go directly for it.

Jacob's intention could be to give the impression that everything is fine.

Temples wants Jacob to stay on his side.

What changes when Temples reveals he knows Jacob has stopped his cycle?

Group D: Cassie, Helen, Siana, pp. 407–409

LS   Where is Siana at this point? Is this the moment when her youth dies perhaps? You get a sense that she is understanding what being an adult feels like – and this is from watching them take their tablets despite knowing the truth. She doesn't feel like she can win. She's at a turning point and she's scared of feeling like that too – she sees being an adult as not caring and letting it all go. They achieved what they set out to achieve but it hasn't changed anything and Siana is mature enough to see that, whereas Cassie is not. She loses respect for Helen and James, and Helen is aware of that. Her identity is thrown into flux.

LS   Where is Siana off to?

Group   To get lost in the world. She's quitting that struggle and fight. Perhaps going somewhere where the pills aren't available?

BK   She loses twice over; she gets rejected by her peers and them choosing Dylan over her, and then she realises that she's not like the adults either. She's got a jaded old person's world view. Her hope is gone, extinguished.

Q&A with Benjamin

Is there any specific reason you don't have anyone in their twenties and thirties?

BK   Honestly, no. Maybe because I've been in my twenties and I'm in my thirties now – for drama you want the extreme of youth or age.

How involved do you want the multimedia to be?

BK   Everything I've written, I want. But not everybody has access to that stuff, so do what you can, don't do what you can't.

Can you do more multimedia than is written?

BK   If you're going to try more stuff, just don't forget the characters. It's a character-driven play, and they could perhaps get lost if it becomes too elaborate.

Does the pill sterilise the men too?

BK   No.

Does the physical deterioration of age show on the AYs at all?

BK   I'm against that because it's in the language and actually we should see how successful his pill is. What distinguishes the AY from the TY is that they don't move like teenagers.

How many people don't take the drug? How many genuinely old people are there?

BK   Most people take them – because the threat to Reactive has to be big enough. This generation of TY are the first generation where they are about to become unique.

Is it mainly in other parts of the world that people don't take the pills? Because they can't afford it?

BK   Yes. You have to pay for the drug. And the drug can only stall you at the day you started taking it. When some new technology comes out it's the plaything of the wealthy – it began for just the super-rich, whereas now they are available over the counter.

When did Dylan first start taking the pill?

BK   I said that Dylan took T1 because those are the ideals that he holds as a character – of the older generation.

How much might an AY character play some of their real age?

BK   In everything they do you can tell that they are old souls, have old brains – not necessarily physicality, because they've never had an old body. There are hints in the text and you need to work out how much you want to play them. Teenagers have a really particular way of moving; they're fidgety and self-conscious, and things could be more considered with the AYs. That's the distinction you want. James will move like a sixty-year-old in the way that he isn't young anymore. Perhaps you could draw on inner tempo exercises with your company.

Have the houses always existed as they are? Are the houses evolving as the drugs do? Do normal houses exist?

BK These are normal houses but they're electronically run. It's a time thing really – I'm letting you know that we're not in 2018.

Can you talk about how the pills have developed and what each version does?

BK T1 – this meant that you looked young, but your insides still age.

T2 and T3 – your body, inside and out, ages very slowly.

T4 – this pill reverses age.

If you stop taking the pills, you slowly start to age again – you wouldn't accelerate, you'd just start ageing normally.

You can die when you're taking the pill – you can be hit by a bus! But diseases that largely target the elderly are eradicated.

From a workshop led by Laurie Sansom
with notes by Hannah Joss

terra / earth

by Nell Leyshon | choreography by Anthony Missen

A contemporary narrative dance piece. A group of classmates are torn apart by the opportunity to perform their own dance. As they disagree and bicker, two distinct physical groups emerge and separate into opposing teams. When a strange outsider appears – out of step with everyone else – the divide is disrupted. A piece about individuality, community and heritage.

Cast size
10–50

Nell Leyshon is an award-winning playwright and novelist. Her plays include *Comfort Me with Apples*, which won an Evening Standard Award, and *Bedlam*, the first play written by a woman to be performed at Shakespeare's Globe. She also writes for BBC Radio 3 and 4, and her first radio play, *Milk*, won the Richard Imison Award. Her first novel, *Black Dirt*, was long-listed for the Orange Prize and *The Colour of Milk* has been published worldwide. She taught creative writing for many years with marginalised communities, and is a trustee of the Globe.

Anthony Missen is a Clore Fellow and FRSA. He received formal training at the Northern School of Contemporary Dance and went on to dance with companies including Scottish Dance Theatre, Mad Dogs Dance Theatre and Cie. He was Movement Director for Dundee Rep's 2007 production of *Playhouse Creatures*, their 2008 production of *Romeo and Juliet* and the 2015 production of *Oresteia* at HOME, Manchester. He has taught in most major British contemporary dance institutions, to several professional dance companies and in many countries including South Africa, Ethiopia, Israel, Trinidad, Morocco, Sweden, Spain, France, Italy, Germany and Austria. He has led many choreographic and skills-based residencies and he is a founding member of New Movement Collective. He co-founded Company Chameleon in 2007, producing and choreographing critically acclaimed performance works both for the stage and outdoor contexts. He has developed many successful educational programmes in different countries, with a particular focus on young men, disadvantaged children and children at risk. He has made touring works for La Mov (Spain), Norrdans (Sweden) and most recently Ballett-Theater Chemnitz (Germany).

An Introduction to Reading the Story and Text Script

terra/earth is a synthesis of text, movement and character. Equal attention should be paid to each of these aspects of the work: the words will inform the characters, the characters will inform the movement and everything should work together to tell this story.

The play comprises two scripts: a story and text script, which is a more typical play script, outlining the story and dialogue for the piece; and a movement script, which explains how the physical language of the play should be created and built. You should infuse the characters and their movement with your own identity, while keeping true to the story and intentions of the play.

The following story and text script indicates the different points at which movement exercises (from the movement script) should be developed with the text. The movement exercises will help with the creation of the dance, while the stage directions in this script will indicate exactly when the dance moment is performed.

Nell Leyshon and Anthony Missen

Characters

Terra, *a teenager who is neither obviously male or female; s/he is covered in mud from head to toe*

Dancers:

Group F: (at least)
Fran, *leader*
Michael, *dancer*
Primo, *dancer*
Jayde, *dancer*

Group A: (at least)
Alex, *leader*
Bekka, *dancer*
Krystina, *dancer*
Dean, *dancer*

MOVEMENT EXERCISE 1: SOLO TASK – GENERATING MOVEMENT

This exercise is not performed.

Prologue

Dark.

We hear a sound, a steady, growing drumbeat. It is the sound of a mother's heard from inside the womb. It is so loud we feel it in our own chests.

Terra *appears. His/her body and hair are coated in mud. We can't see skin or hair. We can't see clothes. We can't see gender.*

Terra   I am here.

Here.

I am here.

Terra *disappears.*

Thursday

The beginnings of a rehearsal. The dancers arrive and prepare, begin to warm up.

Alex *stops. The others stop.*

Alex   When are they choosing?

Fran   Saturday.

Alex   We only have two days.

Fran   So. We can do it.

I've got ideas. Start with this.

She shows one move. **Alex** *is dismissive.*

Alex   I'm not doing that.

Something like this?

Alex *shows a move.* **Fran** *hates it.*

Fran   I told you before. It's stupid.

438   Nell Leyshon

Alex   Stupid?

Fran   We need new stuff.

Bekka *steps forward.*

Bekka   What about this?

She shows a move.

Alex   That's good.

Fran   No. Too similar to the last time.

Alex   I like it.

Fran   What else is there?

She points at the dancers.

MOVEMENT EXERCISE 2: SHARING SOLO MOVEMENT

The other dancers show their moves.

Alex *sees* **Dean**'*s move.*

Alex   Do it again.

Dean *repeats the move and everyone watches.* **Alex** *loves it.*

Alex   Let's start with this.

Fran   No.

Alex   Yes.

Fran   I've seen it before.

Krystina   We need to work together.

Fran   I can't.

Alex   I'm not working with her.

Fran   Good.

She looks around, talks to them all.

Who wants to work with me?

Alex   Who's with me?

They divide into two groups.

Group A is formed with **Alex**.

The others are now Group F with **Fran**.

Fran (*to her group*)   Meet here later.

Alex   We'll stay all night if we have to.

Fran   They'll pick us.

Alex   It'll be us. We'll dance till it hurts.

Fran (*mocks*)   'Dance till it hurts.'

It'll be us.

The two groups turn their backs on each other and pull out their phones. The light reflects up blue on their faces. They are transfixed, no longer with us.

They set up their two groups, ready for followers.

The music slows. The blue lights die down.

MOVEMENT EXERCISE 3: JOURNEY TO THE CLASSROOM

The school day begins. The school environment is created through movement and suggestion.

Jayde   Quick. She's coming.

Alex *puts his hand up.*

Alex   Here, Miss.

They put their hands up, one by one.

All   Here.

Here.

Here.

MOVEMENT EXERCISE 4: THE LIFE OF THE CLASSROOM

They listen, some bored, some engaged.

The school bell sounds and the day ends.

They stand in the two groups and look at their phones. Their faces are blue, illuminated.

Alex   Eighty-six more followers.

Fran   One hundred and five.

Alex   Another.

Fran   Another.

Alex   Okay, we've only got two days till we have to show them. Ready?

Fran   Yeh, ready?

MOVEMENT EXERCISE 5: GROUP IDENTITY

Both groups begin.

Fran *starts with* **Michael**, *shows a move, teaches him.*

Fran   Like that.

Okay?

The others join in.

Fran *repeats the move again, then the whole group copy.*

Alex *steps forward* and *shows a move for his group, teaches them.*

Alex   Got it?

They all do it.

Okay. Let's run it.

Fran *turns to her group.*

Fran   Let's run it.

Alex   Ready?

Fran   Ready?

Both groups begin. They find their moves which will be in their routines. They stop, start, practise.

We begin to hear the heartbeat. **Terra** *enters, watches unseen.* **Terra** *really watches, absorbed, fascinated.* **Terra** *makes small, tentative copies of their movements.*

The two groups fall away to the two sides.

Terra *stands in the centre. Still, silent.*

Friday

The two groups enter one by one, see **Terra**, *then approach. They circle.*

Fran   What is it?

Dean   What are you?

Jayde   Say something.

Alex   Is it human?

Primo   It stinks.

Krystina   Is it an animal?

Michael   What is it?

Bekka   It doesn't speak.

Terra   I can speak.

They jump back.

Krystina   Is that mud?

She reaches out with a finger.

Alex   It's disgusting.

He reaches out with a finger.

Terra *pulls back from them all.*

Fran   Can't you smell yourself?

You stink. Go and wash.

Bekka   What's wrong with you?

Michael   What are you?

Alex   Shush. The teacher.

REPEAT EXERCISE 4: LIFE OF THE CLASSROOM

They repeat the school choreography, the imaginary desks and books.

They are at school.

Terra *searches for a place to sit, is rejected by all.*

Terra *sits on the floor.*

The school bell and the day ends.

They divide back into their two groups. **Terra** *is on his/her own.*

The **Dancers** *all stop, pay attention, listen to an imaginary instruction.*

They point at **Terra**.

Alex   We have to dance with that?

Fran   No.

Alex   No.

Fran   The stink of it.

Stink.

All   Stink.

Stink.

Stink.

MOVEMENT EXERCISE 6: FLOCKING

They begin a flocking movement.

Every time **Terra** *approaches they reject him/her.*

Bekka *comes out of the mass, circles* **Terra**, *examines him/her. She gets sucked back in.*

Bekka *comes out again. The group retreats.*

She holds her mobile. She turns it on and a blue light appears on her face. She scrolls.

Bekka   I can't find you anywhere. You're not on anything.

Terra   I'm here.

Terra *reaches for* **Bekka**'s *phone, asking to see it.*

Bekka   You're not touching this. Look at your hands. It cost a lot.

Terra *is confused.*

Bekka   Money. It cost money.

Terra *is still confused.*

Bekka   Are you even real?

There's nothing on here. (*On her phone.*) Not one footprint.

Terra *lifts a foot, looks at it.*

Bekka *puts out a finger, touches* **Terra***'s arm.*

She looks at her finger, wipes off the mud.

Bekka   I don't know anything about you.

Are you male or female?

Why are you covered in mud?

(*Gestures with her phone.*) I can't find you.

She goes back into the crowd.

Terra   I'm here.

Right here.

Terra *is alone centre stage.*

They continue to flock and reject **Terra**. **Michael** *breaks out. He approaches* **Terra***, touches the mud, looks at his hand.*

Michael   I can't see your skin.

I don't know anything about you.

You have no money. No phone. No ID.

Everyone has a phone. Everyone has money.

Terra   They're only *things*. What about me?

Michael   You?

Terra   Me, yes.

Me.

Michael *hesitates, gets sucked back into the movement.*

The flocking stops. They start to walk one at a time across the stage.

Fran *walks past* **Terra**.

Terra   Hello.

Fran *doesn't respond.*

Alex *enters from the opposite side.*

Terra   Hello.

Alex *doesn't respond.*

They all walk, all ignoring **Terra**.

Terra   Can I?

Can I?

Can I?

The heartbeat, loud.

Please.

Please listen to me.

No one listens but **Terra** *continues.*

I know I have no pockets. No shoes.

I have no labels on my clothes.

I have nothing.

But I have something else.

Something inside me.

When I was a child I could never sit still. And every time I heard music I would start to move.

My arms, legs, like this.

Terra *moves arms and legs.*

When they told me to stop.

Terra *stops.*

It felt as though my skin would break, and the thing inside would burst out.

All I want to do is dance.

Terra *is swallowed as the two groups move forward.*

Friday Night

It's dark, night-time. There is a cold light from the moon. Everyone is rehearsing their routines.

MOVEMENT EXERCISE 7: DRILLING DUETS

Pairs from each group are drilling their movements and repeating throughout the scene.

They are increasingly exhausted, but **Fran** *and* **Alex** *are still determined.*

Terra *watches unseen throughout this. S/he observes, quietly copies movements, learns.*

Bekka *and* **Alex** *are a pair. They break out to speak. Meanwhile, everyone continues their drilling behind.*

Bekka   I can't see.

Alex   There's a moon.

Bekka   I'm tired.

Alex   It's tomorrow. Come on. Let's do it.

She moves.

Again. Lighter this time. Light as air.

She repeats the move.

You're heavy. You've been eating.

They retreat to the other drilling group pairs behind.

Fran *and* **Michael** *move forward.*

Michael   I can't see.

Fran   I can. Come on. It's tomorrow.

Michael   My ankle's sore. I'm aching.

Fran   You're not fit enough.

She pushes his belly.

You're soft.

She smells her hand. Realises.

It stinks.

It's that thing. It's been here.

Did you tell it to go?

Michael?

You didn't, did you?

They retreat to the other drilling group pairs behind.

Bekka *moves forward with* **Alex.**

Bekka   I was hungry.

Alex   You need discipline.

Bekka   I have discipline.

Alex   You need more.

Bekka   I don't know if I can be like that.

Alex   Maybe you want to be like that mud thing.

Bekka   Thing? Thing?

They retreat to the other drilling group pairs behind.

Fran *moves forward with* **Michael**.

Michael   It's not hurting anyone.

Fran   It's hurting my nose. It's disgusting.

I don't want you talking to it.

Michael   I can do what I want.

Fran   But I can't dance. I feel sick. The smell won't go.

It's ruining everything.

They return to the drilling.

The **Dancers** *in both groups are exhausted and begin to collapse.*

Bekka *steps forward alone. She jumps, sees if she is landing heavily. Checks her body.*

We start to hear the heartbeat.

Terra *approaches.*

Terra   What are you doing?

Bekka   I need to be smaller.

Terra   Dance isn't about being lifted by a man.

It's something else. Something here (*inside*). It's like something's alive inside me. It takes over.

Bekka   Who are you?

Terra   Do I stink?

Bekka   No. No you don't.

Alex *steps forward, sees* **Terra**, *stops. Behind them the drilling ends and the exhausted dancers begin to leave.*

Alex *points at* **Terra**.

Alex   Why's *that* here?

Terra   I want to dance.

Alex   No. Not you.

He tries to start dancing with **Bekka**.

Terra *is watching.*

Alex *stops.*

Alex   Stop watching.

Get out of here. Go.

Terra (*to* **Bekka**)   Bekka. Say something.

Say something.

Bekka *says nothing then leaves.* **Alex** *follows.*

The two groups split and leave.

Terra *remains alone.*

Terra *tries out some of the dance moves from both groups.*

Saturday

Both groups gather on the stage for the presentation to decide which of the two groups will perform.

They are exhausted from last night's drilling.

Terra *is hidden among them.*

Fran *and* **Alex** *address their groups.*

Fran   Okay. It's Saturday. Let's do it.

Alex   You ready?

Fran   It has to be us.

Alex   Us.

They turn to the audience.

MOVEMENT EXERCISE 8: GROUP DANCE EXHAUSTION.

They start their routines but the dancers are clearly too exhausted.

Fran Come on.

Alex Do it.

But they can't. They all back away.

Only **Fran** *and* **Alex** *are left.*

Fran We've got no choice.

MOVEMENT EXERCISE 9: ALEX AND FRAN OPPOSITION DANCE

The music begins. They circle each other, then approach and attempt to dance together but they can't: they are two enemies with two different dance routines.

Underneath the music we start to hear the heartbeat.

Terra *appears.*

Terra Stop.

The music stops.

The dancing stops.

It's ugly.

Alex I told you to go.

Fran Take your stink somewhere else.

Alex You've ruined it.

Fran Look at it. It stinks, doesn't it?

(*To* **Michael**.) Doesn't it?

Michael I can't smell anything.

Fran You can. Say you can.

Michael *is frozen. He lowers his head.*

Fran *turns to* **Terra**.

Fran You've ruined everything.

Fran *is aggressive, pushes* **Terra**.

Fran   Get out.

Terra   Where do I go?

Fran   Where you came from.

Terra   I want to be here. I want to dance.

Fran *pushes* **Terra** *harder.*

Terra   Don't.

You're hurting me.

Michael *steps forward, pulls* **Fran** *away.*

Fran *looks at her hands, horrified that they have mud on them.*

Fran   That's disgusting.

Michael (*to* Terra)   Are you all right?

Fran   I didn't hurt it. I didn't do anything.

She looks around.

I did nothing.

Looks around.

I didn't touch it.

Only **Alex** *believes her.*

Alex *pushes* **Terra**.

Alex   Get out.

Bekka   Stop.

She moves, defends **Terra**. **Michael** *too.*

Alex   What are you doing?

Terra *steps away, protected.*

Fran   Look at it.

Alex   Yeh. Look.

Fran   It can't even speak.

Terra (*loud, strong*)   I can speak.

I can speak.

Terra *stands forward, claims the centre of the stage.*

I have a mouth, and a tongue.

And I have two arms and two legs.

I can move like you can. I can do what all of you can. I have a body that wants to dance.

And maybe I look different but inside I'm the same as you and you and you. (*Points at them.*)

I have veins and arteries long enough to stretch around the whole world.

I have lungs. They breathe in and out as yours do, as does the tide of the sea under the pull of the moon.

Inside my body is my heart. It is no bigger and no smaller than your hearts.

It's the size of a fist.

It sits behind the bones of my chest.

And it beats.

Holds a hand like a fist, as though to punch.

The size of a fist.

But a fist opens.

Opens it into a welcoming hand.

Into a hand.

Terra *takes mud from his/her skin and wipes it on* **Fran**.

(*To* **Fran**.) You stink.

Tell her.

You stink. You stink.

They all copy. Chant.

All   You stink. You stink.

They turn their backs on **Fran**.

Terra *repeats with* **Alex**, *wiping mud on him*.

Terra   Get out. Get out.

They all repeat. Chant.

All Get out. Get out.

They rush forward, jostle, try to force **Fran** *and* **Alex** *out.*

Terra Stop. Leave them.

Terra *addresses* **Fran** *and* **Alex**.

Terra You think your skin is hard but it isn't.

Skin is soft.

It's permeable.

It lets things in.

My name is Terra. It means the earth that we stand on.

Without me there is nothing.

And now it's my turn. You can watch.

Terra *holds out both fists.*

A heart is a fist (*opens his/her fists*) is a palm is an open hand.

The music begins.

Terra *repeats: fists, palms, hands.*

It becomes a dance move.

MOVEMENT EXERCISE 10i: TERRA'S IMITATION SOLO

Terra *then begins to dance, at first replicating and combining some of the dance moves from the two routines the groups have prepared.*

Then it changes.

MOVEMENT EXERCISE 10ii: TERRA'S IDENTITY SOLO

Terra *moves into a new dance, which is one of the fire which has been trapped inside. It is as though* **Terra**'*s skin has burst and the dance has erupted.*

The other dancers watch, amazed at this new thing.

MOVEMENT EXERCISE 11: COMING TOGETHER

They are all slowly drawn into **Terra**'*s world and start to copy until they are all one new group, united.*

As they dance, almost in a trance, **Terra** *wipes mud onto the other dancers, until they are all the same.*

The music dies down and is replaced by a strong heartbeat which then slowly dies down until there is . . .

silence

and

darkness.

An Introduction to Reading the Movement Script

The following movement script is to be used alongside the story and text script. The exercises within it are to be used to create movement material for the play. The story and text script indicates where each movement material should sit within the play.

The movement script is structured chronologically in relation to the play. While it is possible to work through this movement script chronologically, you may decide to approach the exercises in groups, looking at which exercises directly build or follow on from each other. For instance, material generated in Exercise 1 is developed by Exercise 2, which is then further developed in Exercise 5. Therefore, you might choose to structure rehearsals in the order: 1, 2, 5.

If you choose to approach in a non-chronological way, I would recommend the following order:

1, 2, 5 (Group Identities)

3, 4 (School Environment)

6 (Flocking)

7, 8 (Duets and Drilling)

9 (Alex and Fran)

10, 11 (Terra's Solo and Coming Together)

Movement Exercise 1 gives us the 'ingredients' for many of the exercises and therefore the movement that we go on to develop, so it's important that the first movement session begins with this.

In general, I would give at least a 30-minute warm-up and, ideally, a 10–15 minute stretch at the end to cool down.

It is advised to film rehearsals so details are not lost or forgotten in between movement sessions.

Exercise 1: Solo Task – Generating Movement

Everyone

The following is to generate a palette of movement material, elements of which will be used in different ways in the play.

'Sign your name'

Scribe your first name with a finger.

If your name has four or fewer letters then scribe first and surname.

Notice the shape of the letters, any punctuation marks (for example letter i), and any parts that accelerate (for example the top line of a capital T) or have a particular energy in the way you scribe them.

Use different parts of your body to sign each letter of your name. If desired, break each letter into several parts, and use different parts of your body to make that shape – for example left elbow to make the horizontal line of the letter T and the head to make the downward stroke.

As we do this, don't automatically go with the first choice that comes to you – experiment until you find something interesting and satisfying. Think about changing:

SPEED: use the idea of a scale from 0 to 10 as a reference here – 0 being completely still, 10 being the quickest you can possibly move. Make sure you work through as many of the numbers as possible. It may also be simple to say slow, medium, fast – in either case, encourage variation!

PLANE: think about 360 degrees around the body – if a movement happened in front of you, consider making it above/below/behind/sideways/diagonally, etc.

SIZE: sometimes reduce the size of the movement, sometimes enlarge each stroke you make, and allow some to be fixed with your personal space and some to expand so they move through the space (e.g. walking/running/large curve – visualise looking at it from above).

Exercise 2: Sharing Solo Movement

Everyone

Give everyone an opportunity to share their movement from Exercise 1.

Once they have shared their movement, split the cast into groups of two or three. They should now show their own movement to the other members of their small group.

The rest of the cast should observe the move – they could film or take notes.

Using the observations, create a short 20–30-second sequence as characters in the play attempting to share and compete with their own, individual movement.

Use this exercise to separate the cast into two groups. **Group A** must include **Alex** and **Group F** must include **Fran**. These groups will remain the same throughout the play.

Exercise 3:   Journey to the Classroom

Everyone

This is a whole-group task, with the aim of creating a journey for pupils moving towards a classroom. As an aid, it may be useful to begin by marking the floor with a plan of where desks would be set up in the classroom.

All start at one side of the room. Imagine you are entering through a single doorway.

1   Walk from the door to where your seat is – make it an indirect route; i.e. go to other parts of the 'classroom' first.

2   Go back and repeat the pathway, walking first, then running at other moments.

3   There will be a moment where you cross paths with someone else. When your paths meet, spend a few moments walking with the other person.

4   Work with the following words in your encounters with people, or try to figure out how to do this by yourself.
    – Piggyback
    – Annoying someone (push/shove/pull trousers down/skirt up/flick)
    – Wipe an imaginary smell on someone
    – 'Being good'
    – Military-style goose-steps
    – Human climbing frame – imagine each other as pieces of furniture or walls, and navigate yourselves over, under or around them; maybe two people use one other as a swing

Set/create the scene from the above investigations.

Exercise 4: Life of the Classroom

Everyone

After the journey to 'the classroom', everyone organises themselves into a formation that looks like pupils sitting behind desks in a classroom. Think about making a grid formation.

Knees should be bent if possible to appear as if sitting down on a chair.

Music plays, and we identify at least four rhythms that work across the beat.

Notes: make interesting choices with the rhythm so some movements can elongate over several counts, or each count can be punctuated with several movements – work with the beat and off-beat.

Movements should be simple and repetitive and include ideas such as:

– opening and closing the lids of the desk

– yawning, falling asleep and suddenly waking up

– writing something (with an expression of assured pleasure or
   confusion)

– exasperation and looking around at others for answers

– bored and wishing to be elsewhere, daydreaming

All movements should be repeated with each bar – repetition will give us the feeling of being stuck/caught in time/mundanity.

Music suggestion: https://faizalmostrixx.bandcamp.com/track/dreamer-child-kamungolo

Exercise 5: Group Identity Task

5i: *Group A*

Now you have split the company into **Group A** and **Group F**, each group will work on building their own sequence.

Share and take moments from each person's Exercise 1 solo (not all of them!) and combine them so that the group has its own shared 30–50-second sequence.

5ii: *Group A*

Using the sequence that you have developed in 5i, begin to 'colour' the group phrase. Focus on making the movements smooth and flowing. Think of:

HOW WATER FLOWS

HOW SOUND WHISPERS

ALL MOVEMENT BEING ROUNDED AND CONNECTED.

Once created, imagine the ceiling has been lowered to the height of the navel of the tallest person in the group. Redevelop the material so it is all floor-bound – i.e. so that no one 'bumps' their head on the imaginary low ceiling.

5iii: *Group A*

Now use the words below to help the movement expand more into the space:

JUMP

SLIDE

DIVE

PROPEL

SHIFT

Integrate these wherever you feel they will work, and also allow these to change some of the movement (for example taking one movement and sliding with it).

5iv: *Group F*

Share and take moments from each person's Exercise 1 solo (not all of them!) and combine them so that the group has its own shared 30–50 second sequence.

5v: *Group F*

Using the sequence that you have developed in 5iv, begin to 'colour' the group phrase, thinking about:

VARIATION IN RHYTHM

As a guide, use the words:

ROUGH

BOUNCE

PUNCTUATE

JAGGED

5vi: *Group F*

Now use the words below to help the movement expand more into the space:

DIVE

ROLL

SLIDE

SHIFT

PROPEL

Integrate these wherever you feel they will work, and also allow these to change some of the movement (for example taking one movement and sliding with it).

By the end of this exercise, there should be two physically distinct dance sequences of 30–50 seconds. One for **Group A** and one for **Group F.**

Identify the key movements from each sequence for Terra to attempt to imitate in the background of the scene.

Exercise 6: Flocking

Everyone

Use the following as a group exercise in preparation for choreographing the scene.

Walk as a whole group without a leader. When someone stops, we all stop. We all keep an awareness of the group and when the speed increases or decreases we all do the same.

Now introduce **Terra**. The group continue walking as a whole, but when **Terra** moves toward you, you move away from him/her and closer together as a group. As it settles, we occupy the whole space with the walking until **Terra** approaches someone again. Then again move away from him/her and closer together as a group.

Continue to choreograph this scene referring to the text in the script:

Every time **Terra** *approaches they reject him/her.*

Bekka *comes out of the mass, circles* **Terra***, examines him/her. She gets sucked back in.*

Bekka *comes out again. The group retreats.*

She holds her mobile. She turns it on and a blue light appears on her face. She scrolls.

It may be useful to continually go back and replay the action for the purposes of retention.

Exercise 7: Drilling Duets

Groups

Split the groups into pairs. Members of **Group A** should be paired with other members of **Group A**. Members of **Group F** should be paired with other members of **Group F**. **Fran** and **Michael** should be a pair. **Bekka** and **Alex** should be a pair.

Each pair should identify a **Person 1** and **Person 2**.

Exercise 7i: Group A Pairs

With your partner, use the words CONNECT–RECONFIGURE–RELOCATE as a map to create duet material (see below).

After we use the word RELOCATE we loop back to the beginning, i.e. CONNECT–RECONFIGURE–RELOCATE, CONNECT–RECONFIGURE–RELOCATE, CONNECT–RECONFIGURE–RELOCATE, CONNECT–RECONFIGURE–RELOCATE etc.

We **alternate** using the words, so:

Person 1 connects to **Person 2** –

Person 1: Identify a part of your body, and then find a way to connect it to another part of **Person 2**'s body. Be imaginative and think about all parts of your bodies.

The pathway to your partner can be direct or indirect.

Think about varying the:

SPEED

ENERGY

QUALITY OF TOUCH (forceful/tender/aggressive/gentle/tentative etc)

Person 2 then leads both people to RECONFIGURE.

Essentially, keeping the newly found contact point, **Person 2** starts to move and **Person 1** simply follows.

Person 1: Go with this motion, allow your body to respond and between you your bodies will reconfigure.

This could happen in a smooth way, mechanically like a transformer, slowly or quickly.

With this reconfiguration, we will find that we now have other parts of our bodies in contact with each other.

Now **Person 1** leads again, and they initiate the RELOCATE. This is essentially moving somewhere spatially, and should be led by pushing into or pulling one or more parts of the body that are in contact.

We then go back to **Person 2** who loops back to the beginning of the map to use the word CONNECT. You can either come away from **Person 1** and then move back in to find a point of contact, or find another directly and let go of whatever parts were previously in contact.

We then continue with the map to create a short duet of 5–10 seconds. This duet is repeated throughout the scene.

Exercise 7ii: Group F Pairs

We are going to create a duet using the words ASSIST and AVOID.
    With this, we never make contact.

To ASSIST we draw imaginary lines from parts of our body, and move them in relationship to the other person's movement, so it looks like we are steering them, almost like puppet strings.
    To AVOID take some of your movement and direct it straight at the other person. The person will have to get out of the way to avoid being hit.
    Use parts of both people's solo material and work with both words.

We then continue with the map to create a short duet of 5–10 seconds. This duet is then repeated throughout the scene.

Exercise 8: Group Dance Exhaustion

Groups

Separate into **Group A** and **Group F**. In your group, use the duet material and Exercise 5 group sequences to create a short dance.
    Think about spatial patterns. Break up, alter and re-form parts of the sequences as appropriate (e.g. two people do a little of the group sequence whilst two others do a different part of the sequence and two others do a bit of a duet).
    Learn bits of each other's duet material so there's a bigger palette of shared duet material to use.

Quality: This sequence should have a sense of discord and exhaustion. Avoid structuring it so it's all unison, and think bigger and smaller configurations within your group. It should feel incomplete and broken.

Group A and **Group F** sequences should last 10–20 seconds and build to failure or collapse. They are performed at the same time.

Exercise 9: Alex and Fran Opposition Dance

Alex and Fran

Alex uses what he or she has made in Exercise 5.2 and **Fran** uses what he or she has made in Exercise 5.5. Use this material to try to 'discover' each other – imagining for example that you are two different animals that have come across each other for the first time. Think about your different movement qualities:

Alex – SMOOTH, FLOWING, CLOSE TO THE GROUND.

Fran – JAGGED, ROUGH, STRONG.

Use the movement to try to:

FIT TOGETHER or move

OVER

UNDER or

AROUND each other.

Use the words:

TENTATIVE

AWKWARD

DISCONNECTED as intentions.

Exercise 10: Terra's Solo

10i: Terra's Imitation

Terra

Revisit the instructions in Exercise 8, using the material from both **Group A** and **Group F**, and develop the material to EVOLVE it using the following words as a guide:

EXAGGERATE

EXPAND

ENLARGE

ACCELERATE

SLOW MOTION

Everyone should now spend some time picking out some of these key movements for **Terra** to perform. This dance should reflect **Terra**'s observations of the warring groups through the play. It should imitate some of their character and physicality. The phrase should last around 20–30 seconds and clearly have the DNA of the movement we have already seen through the play.

10ii: Terra's Identity

Terra

Terra now devises some solo material that represents her own identity – different from the movements of **Group A** and **Group F**. NB This dance will initially only be performed by **Terra**, but other members of the company may want to help devise movements for **Terra** to perform in the solo.

The focus should be on the opposition of poise and calm, against a release of great force and attack.

For these movements, think of **Terra** as a river, sometimes still, sometimes a torrent. S/he has been largely quiet and suppressed by both the group and her/his inability to express. This solo material will show that even with quiet, there's an incredible amount of force, power and beauty that sits under the surface, which when released is done so with immensity.

The 'poise and calm' movements can use the following words as a guide:

GRACE

PEACE

MEDITATE

POURING

STROKING

Think about Tai Chi, and perhaps find your own interpretation of some of the forms, including:

– Part the wild horse's mane

– The white crane spreads its wings

– Brush knee and twist step on both sides

– Hand strum the lute

– Step back and whirl arms on both sides

– Grasp the bird's tail left

– Grasp the bird's tail right

– High pat on the horse

– Push down and stand on one leg

– Needle at sea bottom

The 'attack' movements can use the words:

ERUPT

ELECTRICITY

SHOCK

BURST OUT

It can perhaps be thought of as the release of the Chi.

Again, think about martial arts, and consider using your own interpretation of the opposing Tai Chi forms, including

– Turn, parry and punch

– Single whip

– Flash the arm

– Turn and kick with left heel

– Strike opponents' ears with both fists

– Kick with right heel

With both the poise and calm movements and the attack movements, focus on the quality words and use these to create your own movement as well as interpreting the Tai Chi forms as described above.

Arrange the movements so they move between a series of calm/poise into a series of the attack movements and then back again. This solo moment should last around 60 seconds.

Visual reference: https://www.youtube.com/watch?v=dBFe54glhTs (but not as rigid – think rounded and work with levels, and variation of length of both attack and release moments).

Exercise 11: Coming Together

Everyone

Choose moments from both of **Terra**'s solo moments – from Exercise 10i and 10ii.

Recombine these so there is a repeatable phrase of approximately 20–30 seconds in duration.

This phrase can then be looped several times.

It should be arranged so that **Terra** begins by himself/herself and draws people in, slowly accumulating more and more dancers (e.g. three join, then four join, then two, etc.).

Terra can come in and out of the looped phrase to smear the mud until the blackout.

[Note: for combining material, it may be useful to create a short phrase that repeats three times so we can gradually accumulate dancers.]

terra/earth

BY NELL LEYSHON, CHOREOGRAPHY BY ANTHONY MISSEN

Notes on rehearsal and staging, drawn from a workshop with the writer, held at the National Theatre, October 2018

Warm-ups – led by choreographer Anthony Missen

1 **Step warm-up 1:** The group marched together keeping a rhythm in their footsteps. On the first beat, they clicked with the right hand, and then on the second clapped their hands together in front of them, on the third they clicked with the left hand, and on the fourth they clapped hands together behind them, on the fifth they hit their thighs with their hands. This got quicker.

2 **Step warm-up 2:** In this version the group faced one direction whilst marching on every two-beat to the four points of the compass (east, north, west, south) – to the left, then forwards, then right, and finally backwards – each time returning to the central point. The beat then increased to moving on every third beat, then fourth, then fifth, etc. with each circumference of the sequence. This sequence then increased in tempo with the company moving in more of a jogging motion and clapping on each beat when they stepped.

3 **Jumping tag:** The person who was 'it' started at the centre with all other company members touching this person – huddled closely to them. The company could only move by jumping, and could only jump when the person who was 'it' jumped. On the first jump the rest of the company's objective was to get as far away from the person who was 'it'. From this point the same rules of tag applied – if the person who is 'it' touches you, you are out.

How Nell came to write the play

'I wanted to write a play that used the language of the body as well as the tongue. The point where text meets movement is a fascinating place to explore, and I thought it important to engage young people who might not be interested in straight performance, but something more dynamic. I also wanted to address how many judgements we make when we meet new people, both conscious and unconscious.'

Nell Leyshon, 2018

Q&A with Nell Leyshon (writer), Anthony Missen (choreographer) and Emily Lim (lead director)

Nell has worked with marginalised groups over a long period of time – and she wanted to make work out of all of these ideas. This story was born out of a trip to Peru with the British Council talking about the racism people experience there. Nell went to Lima and worked with Peruvian teenagers whom she asked to draw a 'typical teenager' – who in their eyes was a blonde wealthy character (very different to how anyone in that room looked). Nell wrote a version of this play for that project, and this narrative then got stripped down and movement brought in for the piece to evolve into *terra/earth*. The worldwide notion of making up our minds about people when we first meet them still sits very much at the heart of it.

This is not a way that Anthony or anyone he knows has worked before. His company (Company Chameleon) is about always adapting the best form that supports the work – hence, 'chameleon'. He loved the story of *terra/earth* – and was thrilled by the challenge of working movement into this format, and then empowering people to create their versions of the work/movement. A thing that came out early on was the idea of contrast of styles/groups in the forms of movement. What might differentiate people in terms of traditional forms/new forms? There were loads of conversations to create the framework for this. What was happening in the action? And what does it need? Were there moments where the movement replaces dialogue? Movement is communication – how do we create a frame where we can allow people to interpret that into this piece?

Nell   We were all the time learning what we could do with this play. There are a couple of things that would potentially not work – Terra must be alone and excluded as a character, for example. Choral speech is definitely an option people could explore. But the isolation and cruelty is integral – Terra should not be included in things until the end.

Emily   The text and the movement text should be honoured with the same discipline. The joy and the invitation of the piece is to honour the problem-solving and experimental journey that the show has gone on up to this point.

Anthony   Even though there are blocks of 'movement' within the script you need to ensure that the text and movement of the piece exist together – not as separate blocks that stop and start and will end up feeling disjointed.

Nell   The text and the movement come from the same impetus and therefore shouldn't be separated.

Emily   Follow and trust the recipe and instructions that Nell and Anthony have created.

Approaching the play

EXERCISE: '*TERRA/EARTH* IS THE STORY OF . . .'

Emily asked the group to define the play in a single line. They came up with the following:

- The cult of me
- Someone who is being themselves but to others they are different
- Excluding, including and bringing a community together.
- Finding your identity in a place you do not know
- Terra changing the predetermined ideas of a group
- Discovery, identity and feeling as though you are not welcome in a place
- Assumptions and unconscious bias being challenged and differences ultimately being celebrated
- A kid that doesn't yet understand who they are, in a society that doesn't yet understand them
- Belonging through not belonging in an unknown place

Emily said that she challenges herself to always be able to answer this question for any production, so that at any point in your making process you can refer back to this as an anchor and reflect on whether you are telling that story. Try not to use huge abstract thoughts/nouns when doing this exercise.

How are you going to ensure your company understands the play? The group discussed practical approaches to be used with their companies or as preparatory work as directors:

- Make a timeline of the play.
- Who are the characters? Create an information bank about the characters.
- Make sure the cast have real agency over the narrative as well as the movement.
- Do the '*terra/earth* is the story of . . .' exercise (see above).

- As director, read the play and make a note of the images and pictures that come to you – create a sort of mood board. Words and language aren't always the best form of framing things – images can help us create frames you can refer to in the rehearsal space.

- Create tableaux/freeze-frames and then layer on thought tracking, choosing specific moments. Or choose the four key milestones in the story and ask the cast to portray these: a rapid-fire retelling of the story. Videoing these exercises can sometimes be helpful, possibly using centralised ways in which people can access these films (e.g. Dropbox).

- Create a 'thought tunnel' – one person (in character) stands at the end of a tunnel created by the other members of the company. As the character at the end processes through the tunnel slowly, those creating the tunnel vocalise to them what their character, or what they personally, think about the character walking through the tunnel. These opinions and thoughts are formed from the group's knowledge of the script.

- Create a social media profile for each character.

- Have two raised platforms – Teams A and B – create a physical/visual map of their journey through the play. This could be with different T-shirts – seeing the visual representation of how the movement of groups looks. This could be helpful for visual thinkers. There are potentially two narratives – the exclusion of Terra and the division of the groups. These stories then map alongside each other. Colour can be a useful way of us exploring this visually.

- A Venn diagram – who is where and when in the play?

- Plot: a character log for each of the roles – what do they say, what is said to them, what is said about them, what happens to them, what are their key events – emotionally/physically – what do they say, what do they do? This can develop alongside the movement developing.

- You could have a full version of the play split up into scenes/movements/numbers which exists like a big scene by scene – across the wall – so the company can chart their progress.

- Encourage questioning in the space – during a first read-through – and think about what the physical impulse is to move (away or towards the person they are speaking to/with).

- Actors create their own inner monologues for their characters when they might not be speaking. What's the spoken conversation that Alex and Fran are having when they are dancing? What's the language they would use that can then be physicalised?

Context: Where? Who? When?

How could you explore the context of the play with your company?

- Create a map of the play. What is happening where? What are the locations in the play?

- Never assume people are all on the same page – check that everyone is clear as to what is happening in each scene/moment/ ground this literal reality to help the company understand what the story is and what is happening at each moment. Focus on the concrete facts.

- Emily asked if Nell had any specifics in her head that directors should know. Nell said she wants people to be specific but to choose this for yourself as a company. Don't let it be generic. Nothing should be an assumption – authentically research and interrogate your decisions.

- You could split the play up into day by day – look at twenty-four hours, go through the hours in the day and get the cast to enjoy that.

Question: What is the simplest version of this play you can tell with your groups?

In terms of how you facilitate the creative process, you could:

(a) Split off and just start making the movement.

(b) Read the script first.

(c) Or your own version of this?

Safe contact: exercises to introduce this to your group

- Games are a great way in – 'Stuck in the mud'/'Grandma's footsteps'/'Creating a human assault course'/'Human playground' – making playground furniture (swing/slide, etc.) using bodies.

- Walk around the space – meet somebody – shoulder to shoulder/ back to back/press against each other and go down to the floor. No hands.

- Counter-balancing – if working with a partner how can individuals use counter-balances to move themselves and distribute weight and understand/explain safe contact?

  Extension: one person is the base (like a lamppost) – first they express where contact is not acceptable, then using that lamppost see how they can make the other person hold their weight. First just with hands – pushing, then pulling – then using different parts of the body – slowly developing this into roles blurring and the two people understanding how to distribute and use weight to create contact movement.

- Lead/follow exercise – follower closes eyes, and leader leads them with contact – first with hand to hand – then leader has contact with different parts of the follower's body – and then the leader using different parts of their body. Finally, using the idea of pressure so they can start using that as an indicator and what the instruction is. The direction of contact could be an extension of this exercise.

- Crossing the floor – ask the company: how do they move across the space on fire, with a space full of water, only moving with hands and feet contacting the floor, using spirals, working with partners? This can then be used for different parts of the body – eyes, or hands, or simple movement, not necessarily feet. Walking through the space and greeting people. Driving and steering people in the space, and then releasing them to do the same to someone else.

- Ask the group in pairs to come wrist to wrist with their hands clasped on arms facing one another. Root themselves, bend their knees.

Exercises led by Anthony

EXERCISE 1: SOLO TASK – GENERATING MOVEMENT
(FROM MOVEMENT SCRIPT)

Anthony asked the group to write their names using their finger, then their signature, then their name fully like a signature but with all the letters fully formed.

Then he asked them to think about their whole body writing it. How do they break that up? For example, 'A' has three strokes and so Anthony used three movements to create that letter. Then examine how they can make that more interesting – think about size, making alterations . . . he encouraged them to have a play!

The group were given a few minutes to create/physicalise the first three letters of their names and turn these into movement sequences. Anthony told people to think about the 360 – what is up, down, below. Anthony added music to this and everyone worked on their individual sequences.

Using this sequence each person had created, the group then looked at Exercise 2 in the movement script.

Emily reminded everyone that this was not about being professional dancers and encouraged them to trust that Anthony's exercises will lead them to create beautiful work and movement.

EXERCISE 2: TEACHING AND SHARING SOLO MOVEMENT
(FROM MOVEMENT SCRIPT)

With your company, give everyone an opportunity to share their individual movements from Exercise 1.

Once they have shared their movement, split the cast into groups of two or three.

They should now try to teach their own movement to the other members of their small group. The rest of the cast should observe the process of teaching the movement – they could film or take notes. Using the observations of teaching movement, create a short 20–30-second sequence as characters in the play attempt to share and compete with their own, individual movement. Use this exercise to separate the cast into two groups. Group A must include Alex and Group F must include Fran. These groups will remain the same throughout the play.

Key ideas Anthony asked the group to think about:

- Teaching is a key concept in the process.
- Competitiveness and ambition are key emotive feelings to bring into the animation and expression of this movement.
- Feel free to interrupt people.
- What happens if you are unsuccessful?

The groups were then tasked with creating pages 437–439 of the text script, working with both movement and text scripts.

Emily encouraged each group to first identify: 'This is the part of the script/story where . . .

Emily reassured the group that it was not about making sure that the movement was perfect – it was about ensuring that they had interrogated if this movement answered the questions about what part of the story they were telling.

The groups then showed their work and after each one, Emily asked:

- What is the story?

- Was the story clear?

Observations from watching each other's work:

- Movement can be distracting from action.

- Know which bits of the story are crucial for an audience to receive and ensure movement doesn't overwhelm key information/ narrative points.

- It is potentially distracting if everyone is moving all the time.

- A movement sequence that symbolised the idea that they should try and work together helped inform the audience who characters were and what their relationships were. The leaders were quickly identified in the use of the space and configuration.

- The establishment of the game and rules of this scene were made very clear through the expressions and reactions of those in the background.

- Anthony said to consider 'foreground and background' almost like a volume button – what do you want to amplify and what do you want to turn down/mute in a moment?

- Think about the stakes – what are these in the moment?

- Nell talked about how stillness can also be a choice of movement. What is the key story moment in the scene – is it when the groups split? Therefore how do you use the movement?

- In the piece Anthony and Nell want these moments to feel stylistically like the groups are practising and creating a 'work in progress', not their final dance.

One group used ghosting of the text layered over the top of the movement – with one person speaking the lines and not moving – whilst the others did the movement. This was suggested as a good rehearsal technique, but maybe could be too radical a choice to layer on top of the text – which has already been extensively interrogated.

One group made a fantastic entrance with a sense of optimism and ambition, which felt exciting.

Using one of the groups, Emily used Nell and Anthony to craft an 'example' version of the scene – thinking about everything the group had discussed. The following thoughts and ideas arose as a result:

1   Stretching and prepping in a semi-circle for the opening dialogue created excitement.
    Question: What is the clearest and simplest way of showing people sharing ideas, copying and doing?

2   The scene was spaced like a dance class, with one 'teacher' at the front, and those behind copying.

3   Does each person have to have their chance at the front? What if each person made an offer and then you add each offer together each time, e.g. $a + b + c + d \ldots$

4   There are many possibilities. Could it be the crafting of a routine? Or a showcase of what each of the group's talents are?

5   Nell highlighted that this was about showcasing the confidence and competitive nature of dance.

6   Was vocalised sound helpful in bringing the scenes to life? Agreements and noises could potentially bring another layer into the storytelling.

7   You could start the scene with a single pair and then add more bodies into the scene to create a larger sense of group.

8   It was quite easy for the group to pre-empt its division, so it feels integral to create a strong sense of team spirit from the start.

9   It is helpful to consider why Fran and Alex's relationship falls apart. How do you find the escalation of frustration with one another? Does one of them knock the other, or threaten the other in some way?

10 How will you tell the story of why the group splits at the end of the scene? Could it happen gradually and drip through into dissent by the end?

11 What is the reason for the competition? It is helpful for everyone to have a shared understanding of the context.

Emily stressed the importance of 'focus' when staging this scene. When a character speaks they should become the focal point of the scene – and everyone onstage should look at this person. Nell said that perhaps it starts as something competitive and the notion of teaching comes in later.

EXERCISE 6: MOVEMENT SCRIPT – FLOCKING VS ANTI-FLOCKING

The group moved around the space, constantly moving closely together whilst rejecting and steering away from the individual representing Terra. Then they reversed this idea of flocking by having the group disperse when Terra approached them and regroup when Terra left. You can then see how this work might fit back into the scene.

Emily talked about how the dynamics in this exercise were really strong – people were brought into a flock at the arrival of Terra – that was the catalyst – for 'safety in numbers'. The group wanted to protect itself. Be careful not to get swamped in abstractions or distractions that deviate from the storytelling of the piece by providing clear intentions for the cast as you go.

Emily asked the room to consider how you can clean the work as you go, making sure it's tight and controlled and always serving the needs of the scene or moment. She cautioned against the work being abstract and encouraging your audience to see too many things – focus on telling the story first!

Terra needs to belong – he/she is desperate for connection and this needs to be made clear in this scene. The question of why Terra was isolated – and who or what kind of character he/she is – is an important question to address. What makes him/her different? Or is it the group that chooses to treat him/her as if he/she is somehow alien?

Using flocking and anti-flocking could be useful to show that Terra is new in the scenario – he/she is confused and disorientated and does not know the rules of the game.

It is important to do the groundwork with your company, to avoid creating scenes or sequences that aren't rooted in an understanding of the context and world of the play, as well as considering the evolving arc of characters in the narrative. Ask your company: Who are their characters? What is their relationship to one another? What is their attitude/relationship to Terra? Without those anchors you will not be asking the questions of the piece and telling your audience the story that this play demands.

The importance of the mud

The spreading of the mud at the end of the piece is about them all becoming united/unified. Terra teaches them a new language that is defined by a new group that dance together. The idea is that Terra teaches people to be as one and there's a new world – and they join Terra's world. It's a new identity. This is possibly a metaphor for growing up and defining a new identity and individuality away from the pressures of peers.

It is important that the mud shouldn't be taken off Terra, as that might suggest that she was somehow 'imperfect' – and though the washing of Terra is a powerful image – this is actually not the message of the piece Nell is trying to convey about acceptance through non-conformity.

The group discussed the practical application of the mud in the play and how they might achieve this. Ideas included:

- Face paint
- UV paint
- Real mud
- Paint and oatmeal
- Brown make-up
- Fullers earth and copydex
- Wearing it on a suit
- Clay spa facemasks

Interrogating what the mud is doing or saying has to come first. Why is it such an important image? Be careful not to create a metaphor of a metaphor. It is actual mud.

Top tips from Anthony and Nell

- Length: your show should not exceed sixty minutes. There is excitement in something short, tight and totally rigorous – think of this as one story, one piece of an ever-evolving poem or dance or piece of music.

- Serve the story – think of your audience. Be tough and be rigorous. Take your pacing from the story. At what point were you bored? At what point were you confused? Get people in and ask for their feedback. The outside eye is a powerful tool!

- Story hound: even if Nell isn't in the room, imagine she is – are you always telling the story?

- Terra is a real person. Nell said she was happy for groups to decide on the pronoun (him/her/them) and that it was deliberately not included in the speech, only the stage directions, to allow for this.

- Trust that Nell and Anthony have explored the process already – and the work is there for you to launch from.

- The exercise where you ask your whole group to tell the story in just sixty seconds (or something similar) is a really great way of ensuring it's *clear* to your company!

- You could try cutting the script up into pieces so young people don't have to carry round a whole script whilst working with their lines and the movement together.

- Show your audience – don't tell them. Be careful and sensitive about your use of music – it should enhance and not whack us over the head with emotion.

- Back-story and character work is important.

- There are clever reallocations of lines you can make if you have a larger cast. Nell said there is a minimum but no maximum number of cast. It's important, however, to carefully follow the narrative arc of the character throughout the piece if reallocating lines to ensure that you don't lose character development further down the line.

- There are lots of opportunities for ensemble work – regardless of having a named part.

- You are *not* permitted to add any lines into the script.

- Background noise/reactions/soundscapes: this is fine – it's about responding and reacting – but don't add new dialogue or foreground new words/lines.

- Honour the words and movement that have been created – abstracted ideas and opportunities are there to be discovered.

- Music wise, Anthony is always trying to find new tracks to use. Look at artists and then explore similar or other artists on the same label. Avoid music with lyrics that tell the wrong story. See below for some music tracks that Anthony uses in his work.

- Potentially creating/composing your own music for the work could be an option.

- The days detailed in the script are important.

- Terra should not be played by multiple actors – just one.

- Actors playing multiple roles: this is for individual companies to apply the logic that best serves the needs of their group.

- The question of dialect was raised – Nell said that the text was stylised and not written for any particular regional dialect. She noted that though the text is not defined as belonging to a particular place, the physical language/movement could portray different regions and cultures (geographically relevant dance forms) as movement *can* be in place and time.

Music

Some suggestions from Anthony for artists whose work might be good for this piece were:

- Ben Chatwin
- Ryuichi Sakamoto
- Max Richter
- Swarms
- Alvo Noto
- Andrew Hill
- Vasillis Tsabropolous
- Autechre
- Boards of Canada
- Faizal Mostrix
- Compa
- Efzeg
- Olafur Arnalds
- Lamplighter
- Murcof

From a workshop led by Emily Lim
with notes by Elvi Piper

Chaos

by Laura Lomas

A girl is locked in a room, a boy brings another boy flowers, a girl has tied herself to a railing; a boy doesn't know who he is; a girl worries about catastrophe; a woman jumps in front of a train; a boy's heart falls out his chest; a butterfly has a broken wing. *Chaos* is a symphony of dislocated and interconnected scenes. A series of characters search for meaning in a complicated and unstable world. Bouncing through physics and the cosmos, love and violence, they find order in the mess of each other.

Class size
8–30

Laura Lomas is from Derby. Her plays include *The Blue Road* (a co-commission for the youth companies at Dundee Rep, Derby Theatre, Royal & Derngate and Theatre Royal Plymouth); *Joanne* (Clean Break/Soho Theatre); *Bird* (Derby Live/Nottingham Playhouse/UK tour); *Blister* (Paines Plough/Royal Welsh College of Music and Drama/Gate Theatre); *Open Heart Surgery* (Theatre Uncut/Southwark Playhouse/Traverse Theatre/Soho Theatre); *The Island* (Nottingham Playhouse/Det Norske Oslo); *Wasteland* (New Perspectives Theatre/Derby Live). Her radio work includes: *Fragments* (Afternoon Drama, BBC Radio 4); *My Boy* (Somethin' Else Productions/BBC Radio 4 – winner of Best Drama Bronze, Sony Radio Academy Awards 2013); *Lucy Island* (The Wire, BBC Radio 3). In 2011 she wrote *Rough Skin* for Coming Up (Channel 4/Touchpaper), which was nominated for Best British Short at the BIFAs and Best UK Short at Raindance Film Festival. She also wrote two episodes of Jack Thorne's series *GLUE* which was broadcast on E4 in 2014. At the time of publication she is currently under commission to the Royal Court Theatre and Nottingham Playhouse. Laura is developing the original drama TV series *Mercy* with Clerkenwell/BBC Worldwide, a new series for Potboiler and an original feature for Film4. She was a Macdowell Colony Fellow 2013 and a Yaddo fellow 2014.

Rules

Where character names are given it is for clarity and to encourage continuity between scenes; this should be adhered to if possible.

Where characters are numbered they need not be played by the same actor each time.

All characters are suggestions, but names, genders and pronouns can be changed if necessary and parts distributed to suit the needs of the company.

The scenes should be symphonic, acting like a piece of music that grows and evolves over the course of the play.

Companies are encouraged to find the connections. It's nice if stories emerge, it's ok if they don't. Not everything needs to make sense.

Objects can vary – different sized balls, flowers different colours, etc.

Stage directions can be spoken also.

/ marks a point of interruption.

[   ] is to give clarity of intention but where words should not be spoken.

Maybe all the cast are on stage throughout.

Maybe there's music.

Maybe there's movement.

Maybe it's chaotic.

Lights up.

A boy is bouncing a ball.

He catches it.

Looks at it.

Lights out.

                             Lights up.

                             A girl is stood with a bunch of flowers.

                             She looks at them.

                             Lights out.

Lights up.

A butterfly. With a broken wing.

It flickers on the ground. Electric.

Lights out.

Part One

Train

So it's Tuesday and I'm stood on this train platform and it's busy, rush hour so everyone is like packed, like jammed in, you know an it's early, like twenty to eight or something, that time in the morning when the sun's not fully up, and the air feels still, almost wet somehow and I wouldn't normally even be on this platform, cus normally, my mum, she gives me a lift but since, she and my dad, since they like . . .

split, I've been getting the train when I stay at my dad's and so I'm standing there on this platform, and I can feel all these bodies . . .

All these bodies, and it's like they're too close, somehow, too much, cus I can feel them, it's like we're one organism, one thing, moving, breathing, we're that tight and I look to my left, and out the corner of my eye, I can see this
boy
my age, maybe, or maybe younger, and he's bouncing this ball

this small, like tiny ball, he's stood at the back of the platform, listening to music on his headphones, not really concentrating, and I look at the clock and it says 7.42, and I know that the train is coming, cus although I can't see it, I get that feeling in my legs like vibrating, and the air is changing, on the platform, it's sort of sucking us, and I look to my right and there's this woman next to me

she's holding these flowers, yellow, and she's moving, like sort of pushing her way, just a little bit, and I don't think anything, and this boy at the back is still bouncing this ball, bouncing and catching, bouncing and catching, and I look at the clock and it's 7.43 and the train is coming, cus I can see the lights now it's sort of pulling, and the feeling in my legs is now in my stomach and the platform is getting ready, we're like, getting ready to like fight cus we're not all getting on, and the boy bounces this ball, and there's suddenly this moment, this *feeling* where I know, where I know exactly what's going to . . . but it's too late, cus the ball is already . . . and the train is already . . . and I feel the ball hit me and it's like there's a rip, like a tear in the universe, cus this isn't, none of this is supposed to . . . I look up and see this
butterfly
this tiny
fragile
thing

sort of hovering, suspended somehow for a moment, and then I feel it . . .
the force, and I'm falling, sort of
spinning through space and I turn my head and there's this flash, this sort
of snap, of something
yellow
and the train it screeches, sort of staggers, and I look to my right, and the
woman
she's not there
the flowers are . . .
and the boy is looking at his hands, he's looking at his empty hands . . .
and the woman she's just . . . she's just . . .

Butterfly

Two people. One is bouncing a ball.

1   So it's this idea about the world, ok?

2   Ok

1   And the world is basically *made from chaos*, ok?

2   Ok

1   And if the world is chaos, then it means there's no order, and if
there's no order, then it basically means that *anything is possible*

2   Right

1   And if *anything is possible* then it means that *anything could happen*,
and if *anything could happen* then it means that *anything might actually
happen*, and if *anything might actually happen* then it means that
anything will probably happen.

Beat.

2   Right

1   At anytime

2   Ok (*Beat.*) So . . .

1   So if a butterfly like . . . *flaps* its wings, in say . . . Brazil.

2   Ok

1   Then that could cause a massive tornado, in like . . . Texas

Beat.

2   I don't understand

1   It's complicated

2   But I don't –

1   It's all about consequence

2   Consequence?

1   The input

2   Ok . . .

1   and the output

2   I don't

1   You can't always predict it

2   So it's

1   Unpredictable

2   Right

1   A change in the initial condition of the system, that disrupts the order

2   disrupts the order / of . . .?

1   One thing that changes everything

2   One thing that / . . .

1   Chaos

Beat.

2   Chaos?

1   Yeah

Beat.

2   So what do we do?

Hands

Dan *alone. His hands are both bandaged. He removes the bandages from his hands. His knuckles are bruised, bloodied. It's painful.*

Emily *enters.* **Dan** *is shocked, embarrassed.*

Emily   Sorry . . .

Dan   . . .

Emily   I didn't know anyone was in here, I'm sorry . . . I'm . . .

A beat. **Dan** *picks up his bag, his bandages.* **Emily** *notices his hands.*

Emily   Wait

Dan   What?

Emily   Your hands?

Dan   It's nothing.

Emily   They're bleeding . . .

Dan   It's nothing.

He leaves.

Betrayal

Imogen, **Sal** *and* **Lauren** *are applying make-up in a mirror. They drink vodka.* **Bee** *hangs back.*

Imogen   So anyway, I was like OMFG, WTF, are you actually kidding me?

Sal   For reals

Imogen   Like to see her there

Sal   I know

Imogen   An, the way she looked

Sal   Seriously

Imogen   Like the way she actually looked at me

Lauren   I know

Imogen   With her face

Lauren   Honestly

Imogen   Just standing there. Looking at me. With her face

Sal   For real

Imogen   Pass me the vodka

Sal *does.* **Imogen** *drinks.*

Imogen   I said, if you've got something to say you can say it to my face

Lauren   Exactly

Imogen   I said you see this face

my face

if you've got something to say you can say it to this face

Sal   Good for you

Imogen   An' do you know what she said?

Beat.

Imogen   Nothing

Sal   Exactly

Imogen   Absolutely nothing

Bee   Do you think she might have been . . .

Lauren   Too scared

Sal   Probably

Imogen   Too scared to say something, to my face

Lauren   Coward

Imogen   An' did you see what she was wearing?

Bee   I . . . /

Lauren   I know

Imogen   What she was actually wearing

Bee   I . . .

Imogen   An' she had the same shoes on as Charlotte, and so Charlotte said she was going to set them on fire when she got in

Lauren   Exactly

Imogen   Said she didn't care if her mum gave her them for her birthday, she'd just tell her she lost them. She said it was a matter of loyalty

Sal   That's friendship

Lauren   Exactly

Imogen   An' did you see her coat?

Sal   Don't

Imogen   I swear, I seen it in a charity shop

Sal   I know, don't

Lauren   It's gross

Lauren   So gross

Imogen   I can't believe she would do this to me

Sal   I know

Imogen   I keep thinking that it's such a betrayal, cus she knew I liked him

Bee   But do you think . . .

Imogen   She knew

Bee   Do you think . . .

Imogen   She a hundred per cent knew because I told her that I like, liked his jumper when we were doing cross-country

Sal   Judas

Imogen   I said that to her

Sal   I know

Imogen   No word of a lie I said that to her

Sal   I know

Imogen   And now they're going out

Bee   Do you think that they might be . . .

Imogen   What?

Bee   Just friends?

They might be just friends?

Beat. A look.

Imogen   Anyway, I don't even care about him anymore

Lauren   Good for you!

Imogen   I think he's gross. I think she's gross. I think they're both gross

Sal   Good.

Imogen   I mean, have you seen the state of his hands? What he's done to them.

Sal   It's disgusting

Imogen   I mean, who would do that

Sal   Exactly /

Bee   Apparently his dad was like *witness* to this thing that happened and he had this like massive / heart attack and so

Imogen   I don't wanna hear about it /

Bee   I know, but I'm just saying, like /

Imogen   I said I don't care, so I don't care, so if I don't care, then I don't care /

Bee   I know but . . .

Imogen   I don't care /

Sal   She said she don't care

Imogen   I don't

Bee   I know / but

Imogen   I don't care

Pause.

Imogen   I keep thinking about them together . . .

Sal   Oh, don't

Imogen   About them kissing . . .

Lauren   It's horrible

Imogen   I can't get it out my head. You know she was supposed to be my friend

Sal   I know

Imogen   My best friend

Sal   I thought I was / your

Imogen   One of my best friends . . .

Sal   Right

Beat.

Imogen Well I hope they're happy together.

Lauren Exactly

Imogen I hope they're really bloody happy together

Lauren Yea

Imogen I hope they're like, totally, ridiculously completely happy together

Lauren Me too!

Beat.

Imogen What?

Lauren What?

Imogen What d'you mean?

Lauren What?

Imogen You want them to be happy together?

Lauren I'm just agreeing with you

Imogen I don't actually want them to be happy together

Lauren Oh

Imogen I want them to be miserable, Lauren

Lauren Oh

Imogen What's wrong with you?

Lauren Nothing . . .

Imogen Pass me the vodka

Lauren *does.* **Imogen** *drinks.*

Apology

A boy alone.

Another boy arrives.

Aleph Hi . . .

Michael　Hi

Aleph　I wasn't sure if you'd . . .

Michael　I know

Aleph　Thought you might've . . . /

Michael　I didn't

Pause.

Aleph　How you been?

Michael　Alright.

Aleph　Yeah?

Michael　Alright . . .

Aleph　Good. That's good.

Michael　Yeah

Aleph　Really good.

Beat.

Aleph　Haven't seen you . . .

Michael　No

Aleph　About, or /

Michael　No

Aleph　Called you

Michael　I know

Aleph　Few times

Michael　Yeah

Aleph　Sent messages / and

Michael　I been busy

Aleph　Yeah /

Michael　Really busy /

Aleph　Keeping a low profile is it?

Michael　. . .

Pause.

Aleph   I wanted to say /

Michael   You don't need /

Aleph   What happened . . . /

Michael   You don't need to /

Aleph   I'm sorry if I /

Michael   It doesn't matter, it's not a big deal

Aleph   I know but . . . with the . . . flowers and . . .

Michael   Doesn't matter /

Aleph   Was weird and

Michael   Was fine

Aleph   Bit weird

Michael   I didn't mind /

Aleph   But I'm glad you came because I wanted to say, I wanted to say

Michael   I have to go /

Aleph   But

Michael   I'm sorry

Aleph   I know but /

Michael   I'm sorry, I have to go, I have to go

Parents

Two girls.

Jane *is bouncing a ball.* **Somalia** *watches her.*

Somalia   Are you ok . . .

Jane *bounces the ball.*

Somalia   Can you hear me . . . ?

Jane *ignores her, continues bouncing the ball.*

Somalia   Can you . . .

Jane   I'm ok

Somalia   You're not.

Jane   I am. I'm fine.

Somalia   Talk to me

Jane   I don't need to, I'm fine

Somalia   Please /

Jane   I'm a bit busy right now, actually, so /

Somalia   You're bouncing a ball

Jane   It takes a lot of concentration, you have to get it right

Somalia   Look at me

Jane *bounces the ball.*

Somalia   What did she say?

Jane   Nothing

Somalia   She must've said something

Jane   She didn't

Somalia   So she said nothing. Nothing at all?

Jane   She said that something happened on the train this morning and it made her think about things

She bounces the ball.

Somalia   So you just got home from school and he was there?

Jane   Yeah

Somalia   Just moved back in?

Jane   Yeah

Somalia   Just bags unpacked, just there?

Jane   I said yeah

Somalia   An she didn't explain

Jane   No

Somalia   She didn't even try to . . .

Jane   She said she loved him

Somalia   But she didn't /

Jane   She said she loved him, it's complicated, she said it's messy, she said it's not straightforward, she said the world doesn't . . . she said when you're older the world doesn't always make . . . She said she was doing what felt right . . . She said to trust her. She said people make mistakes. She said the world is not straight lines. She said it's rough edges. She said it's chaos but we do the best with it. She said she had a feeling in her stomach and it felt like the right one. She said she was doing her best.

Somalia   So . . .

Jane   So.

Somalia   That's . . .

Jane   That's

Somalia   Everything?

Jane   Yeah.

Dance One

A dance routine. It's really boring.

Someone makes a mistake.

Everyone stops. Looks at them.

Protest

Chiarra *has covered herself in flowers and tied herself to a railing.* **Mo** *talks to her.*

Mo   How long will you be there?

Chiarra   As long as it takes

Mo   But it could be forever

Chiarra   Then I'll stay forever

Mo   But really . . . it could be, forever

Chiarra   Then I'll stay forever

Mo   I'm being serious

Chiarra   So am I

Mo   I'm being properly serious

Chiarra   Me too

Mo   But what are you protesting?

Chiarra   Everything

Mo   But that's too much

Chiarra   I know

Mo   Because it won't change

Chiarra   It has to

Mo   But what if it doesn't

Chiarra   We have to try

Mo   But what do you think will . . .

Chiarra   Violence on our streets

Mo   I know but

Chiarra   Rise in sea levels

Mo   I know but . . .

Chiarra   Nations divided and /

Mo   Listen

Chiarra   Wars and wars and wars and

Mo   Yeah, but /

Chiarra   Government corruption, corporate greed /

Mo   Listen

Chiarra   Police brutality, toxic masculinity, racism! Sexism!

Mo   Yeah, I know but

Chiarra   Families torn apart, and /

Mo   Yeah but . . .

Chiarra   Ice caps melting, polar bears dying, *people* dying

Mo   Yeah, I know but . . .

Chiarra   Nuclear weapons

Mo   It's not helpful to . . .

Chiarra   Fear of women, fear of men

Mo   I know, but I don't see /

Chiarra   Apartheid, genocide, temperatures rising, people migrating, the earth revolting, flowers dying, *fish* dying, wars breaking out, the planet pulled apart, and our hearts breaking / into pieces and

Mo   I know but . . .

Chiarra   I saw this thing on a bus, this thing and it changed me. It changed me.

Beat.

We have to try, don't we, we have to try, we have to try

Hope

A boy and girl in a field.

The girl has a butterfly in her hands.

Boy   What is it?

Girl   A butterfly

Boy   Can I see?

They look at it.

Its wing is broken

Girl   I know

Boy   Will it be ok?

Girl   I don't know.

She holds it up. Looks at it.

Maybe

Kiss

Two people. Any gender.
They kiss.

Late

Two sisters waiting at a bus stop.

1   You think he's still coming?

2   Course

1   He's late

2   His bus is late

1   *He's* late

2   Not that late

1   How long do you think you'll wait here before you leave?

2   What?

1   How long do you think you'll wait here, before you leave?

2   What are you talking about?

1   Like an hour?

2   I don't know

1   Like two?

Said he'd be here at five, didn't he?

2   So?

1   So aren't you worried?

2   No

1   Cus it's already, like, half past

2   He'll be here

1   But he's late, he's already, like, pretty fucking late so /

2   Why are you here?

1   What?

2   Why are you still here?

1   Waiting with you

2   Shouldn't you go home?

1   No

2   Won't Mum be worrying where you are?

1   No

2   She will be

1   She won't

2   She will

1   She won't

2   She will

1   She won't cus I told her I was hanging out with you for the evening

Beat.

2   What?

1   She said I could

2   I don't want you to

1   Well I am

2   Well, you're not

1   Well I am

2   Well . . . you're not,

1   Well I am

2   Well . . . I'm going to have to kill you then

Beat.

1   Ok

2   Fuck's sake

1   Shouldn't swear

2   Fuck off

Pause.

1   Why do you care so much?

2   What?

1   Why do you care so much, about seeing him, when he's late?

2   I don't

1   Do you think he'll bring you flowers?

2   What?

1   Do you think he'll turn up and bring you flowers?

2   Have you been reading my messages?

A beat.

The Output

Two people. Bouncing balls.

1   The input equals the output

2   What?

1   The input equals the output, it's easy

2   I don't get it

1   It's like if you bounce a ball here, at like a certain speed, a certain sort of force, you can predict where the ball will go

2   I don't understand

1   Like if I bounce it like this

They bounce it.

1   It lands like that

2   Ok

1   You try

They bounce the ball.

1   You see?

2   Sort of

1   Try again

They bounce the ball again.

1   So the input equals the output. It's easy, you just have to understand it /

2   But . . .

1   What?

2   What if?

1   What?

2   What about wind?

1   What?

2   Wind

1   What about it?

2   What if there's wind?

1   That's not the / experiment

2   Or rain

1   Rain's not really what we're /

2   Or a puddle

1   What?

2   Like if you just bounce it and you bounce it in a massive puddle

1   I don't really know what /

2   Or a storm

1   A storm?

2   Yeah, say there's a storm /

1   A /

2   A hurricane

1   What?

2   Massive hurricane, say there's a massive hurricane, comes tearing through the country

1   I don't think you're quite /

2   Or a tornado?

1   What?

2   A tornado, ripping up . . . / everything in its path

1   That's not the experi-

2   Or a tsunami. Massive. The sea swallows the land /

1   I don't think /

2   Forest fires, Earthquakes

1   Look, you're not really . . .

2   Massive earth quake, split in the earth, the whole world falls apart

1   I don't think that . . .

2   What if it doesn't?

1   I'm confused

2   I'm just saying, what if it doesn't?

1   What?

2   The input?

1   I don't understand?

2   What if doesn't, equal

1   What?

2   The output.

Depression

1 *has locked themselves in their room.*

2 *stands outside.*

2   You have to come out

1   No

2   You have to

1   No

2   You have to or I'll get your mum

1   I don't care

2   You will do

1   I won't

2   You will

1   I won't

2   You will . . .

Nothing.

2   I'll get your dad then

1   I'm not bothered

2   Your dad?

1   I don't care

2   But your dad is like . . . [scary]

1   He's not. And I don't care.

2   What if I just went to get him . . .

Nothing.

2   If you come out I'll buy you an ice cream

1   I'm ok

2   If you come out we can go down the field

1   . . .

2   If you come out, we can ride on our bikes, and we can sit in the grass
and we can look at all the *wild flowers* and we can chat about anything,
anything you want, and we can nick beers from my dad's garage, and I
won't even blame you, I won't even blame you if he finds out, and we
can listen to music, and we can practise dance routines, and I won't even
laugh when you get it wrong, and we can look at the sky, and try and
catch a butterfly and lie on our jumpers, and make daisy chains, and
won't you just come out of your room?

Silence.

2   It's been ages

1   . . .

2   Don't you miss it?

1   What?

2   Living?

1   . . .

2   Don't you miss it?

Life?

Dance Two

*A dance routine. Someone gets it wrong. Everyone looks at them. They
don't care. They carry on.*

Love

A girl talks to others.

Aaisha   He said he can't think about nothing else.

He said they were sat there in this field of wild flowers and he knew, he
just knew.

He said when he goes to sleep he, like, dreams about him, and when he
wakes up, he's the first thing in his head.

He said when he closes his eyes he sees his face on the back of his
eyelids and when he puts his hand to his heart it's *his* heart he can feel
beating. He says he feels like it's glowing.

He says he can't sleep no more.

He says he doesn't eat.

He says when he thinks about him, which is *all the time*, he feels like
there's butterflies in his stomach.

He says when he opens his mouth they fly out.

He says his heart is stretching.

He says his heart is a balloon and it's stretching and when he breathes in,
he thinks it might burst, he thinks it actually might burst, he thinks it
might explode into a thousand million tiny pieces, or *fall out his chest*,
he says his blood is thicker now, he says his soul is stretching, he says he
didn't know what it was to be a person, before, he says he didn't know
what it was to belong to the universe, he says the sky is in his cells, he
says he knows infinity, he says it's chaos in his head, he says it's like he's

spinning round really fast, he's says it's like he's in free fall, whirling but everything makes sense, he says his skin is raw nerves, he says there's no edges to his body, he says his eyes are wide open, he says he's different now, he says it's better, he says it scares him but it's ok, he says his eyes are the petals of flowers, and his mouth is the wings of a butterfly,

He says his heart might fall out his chest,

He says it's better now. It's better now.

Anxiety One

Three people. One of them with a football.

1   He's not coming in

2   Why?

1   He wouldn't say

2   What?

1   I asked him, an' he told me, said he didn't want to talk about it, said he was going home, he didn't want to say

Beat.

2   When?

1   On the way here

2   What?

1   He text me, on the way here

3   So he'd left?

1   Yeah

2   He'd got up, left the house,

1   Yeah

2   Left the house, got the train

3   Trains were cancelled, he would've got the bus

2   Ok but he left the house, got the bus, he was coming

1   I don't know, I guess so, he just said /

3   That he'd gone home?

Beat.

1   Yeah.

Beat.

2   You reckon something's happened?

1   I don't know

2   You reckon something's happened, on the bus

1   I don't know

2   You reckon something bad's happened on the bus and he's not saying

1   I don't know /

3   We should call him

1   I've tried

3   Call him again

1   No.

2   I'll call him

1   He won't pick up

Beat.

2   If I count to ten and walk backwards then it will be ok

1   What?

2   If I count to ten and walk backwards it'll be ok

1   What are you / . . .

2   Or if I touch every flower, in the park then it'll be ok, so . . .

1   I don't understand

3   Or if you catch a butterfly, if you could like . . . catch a butterfly then I think it'd be ok

2   Yeah?

3   I think if you could catch a butterfly then it'd be ok

1   I don't think that would really / . . .

2   I'm not sure I can

3   What?

2   Catch . . . a butterfly . . .

3   Oh

1   I don't think we should worry so / much

2   You reckon we should call him?

Beat.

3   I don't know?

2   You think he's ok?

Shoes

A girl enters. She's not wearing shoes.

–   What happened to your shoes?

Charlotte   I set them on fire.

–   Oh. (*Beat.*) Ok.

Spinning

A single person is spinning in circles.

Another person enters. They watch them. They join in.

Race

Chiarra *speaks to someone else.*

Chiarra   So I'm on the bus, and it's hot, trains all been cancelled, so
the bus is kinda full. It's busy, but I got a seat and I'm sitting there, I'm
just sitting there, not really minding nothing, got my headphones in,
listening to something . . . I can't remember but the sun's coming in
through the window, an' it's like bright, nice, and the bus is calm, you
know, it's got that feeling like when everyone's like

happy

you know, cus it's summer and it's sun, and the windows are open and
there's a breeze, coming in, coming through like cool, and the bus stops
and you can feel it shake, sort of shudder a little, and this white guy gets

on, this guy and you can hear him from down the stairs, cus his voice is
kinda loud, and he sounds maybe . . . I don't wanna presume, but he
sounds maybe like he's been . . . drinking which is weird, cus it's early

and he comes up the stairs, and his face is like

red

you know and he's got this look on it that's like . . . you do not wanna . . .
you do not wanna mess, with him cus the look on his face, is . . .

an everyone is silent, cus we know . . . we can just feel it, the way the air is

and there's this boy, he's sitting, few seats up, and he's just sitting there,
minding his own, and you can see this guy, he's like looking for . . . he's
really looking for a fight and this boy, he's not even thinking . . . he's like
paying him, no attention, like listening to music

he's got these flowers, in his hand, these

yellow

flowers

and this guy walks up to him and is like

'move'

Beat.

Just like that. And you can see this boy is like . . . ['what?'] cus he's not,
he hasn't been anticipating, you know he's just sitting there, he's on his
way, meet a friend, maybe a date I don't know, but whatever it is, this
isn't . . . he hasn't got time and what I haven't told you is that this boy is
black and I don't know if that's why, cus this guy, he looks . . . he sort
of looks like the type, the kind of guy that might and I'm doing all this
maths, in my head . . . and this other guy he just says it, again to the
boy, goes

'Move'

an' he looks at him, his face close to his face

and the boy goes

'No'

Just like that. Calm, but firm, and the guy . . . you can see his face,
contorting, cus he's not the kind of guy who looks like people really say
that to him, that often. And so he says it again

'Move'

But this time he spits it, and he's so close to this boy's face now, and the bus is like charged, all of us, holding our breath, and we know that this is on us, you know, that it's on us, to do something, it's on us. And there's another boy, a different boy sitting next to me, and you can feel his whole body *tighten*, he hasn't seen anything like this, he didn't know the world could look like this, you can feel it, you can tell

and the boy with the flowers just looks at the guy, standing there above him, looks at him, calmly

and he reaches out and touches his face, just gentle, he touches his face

and the guy, the guy he just . . . he just . . .

Rage

Dan *walks into a room. He smashes it up.*

He punches the wall.

He hurts his hands.

Rules

1 *explains to a group.*

1   So I was like 'No', but she was like

'Yeah'

So I was like 'you can't'

An she was like

'Well I am'

And I was like 'you're not allowed' and she was like

'I don't care'

So I was like 'Well what about the rules'

And she was like 'So what?'

So I was like

'if you do it I'm going to call the police' and she was like 'I don't even care', so I was like . . . *getting my phone out* and she was like

'are you fucking serious?'

and I was like 'yeah, cus it's *illegal*', and she was like 'what the fuck is wrong with you?' and I was like 'Nothing' and she was like 'well yeah there is' and I was like 'Well no there isn't' and she was like 'well yeah there is or you wouldn't be being like this, you know' and I was like 'it's just the rules, it's just order, it's just the way things need . . . it's just the way things are supposed to be, and maybe you don't think so, but you don't get to choose so . . . you know, cus you're not like *God* or whatever, you just have to accept . . .' but then she cut across me and she was like . . . *'Have you seen my life, do you even know my life, do you know anything about my life, does my life look like order to you, does my life look like rules, does my life look anything like fucking order to you, do you know my life, do you know anything about my life'*

An' I was like . . . nothing. I just said nothing

She had scratches on her legs

She looked like she was going to . . .

I just said . . . nothing.

I just said. . . .

Scream

Someone screams.

Violence

1   He said since it happened it's changed him, he said it's different. He said before he used to think things were possible, he said he used to have hope. He said he'd see a

butterfly with a broken wing, and he'd think it'd be . . . you know . . . he'd think it would be . . . [ok]

he said he knew things weren't perfect

he knew the input didn't always equal the output but he thought he like . . . felt that people were, fundamentally in their *hearts* he thought people were . . . the world was good, that the universe was . . . even though it was messy, he said he knew that, but he didn't think . . . he said he never felt, before that people could be so . . .

he said it's changed him

he said his body is tighter now

and someone brought him flowers but he couldn't . . . he said he couldn't even . . .

he said everything feels like it's hard, and rough edges

He said his heart is broken

he said it's blasted to pieces

he said he looks at the sky against the trees and nothing seems right

he said it's different

he said he's changed

he said it's changed him, it's changed him

Universe

1   Well we are essentially the same as stars

2   What?

1   Yeah, I know, it's kind of complicated but it's actually true, the inside of our bodies is essentially /

2   Stars?

1   Exactly

2   But I don't /

1   Cus when the Big Bang happened it was basically this explosion, and everything that had been like circling around space for like *billions* of years or *whatever* sort of kind of *clumped together* in this explosion of like *heat and light* and you know *matter*, and all that and then the planet was made and you know stars, the universe, the *Sun, etc.* . . . .

2   Etc. . . .?

1   Yea and like, the carbon from that is like in our bones you know?

2   What?

1   Yeah, it's fucked up

2   From the Big Bang?

1   Exactly

2   Well . . .

Guess that explains a lot

Phone

A girl on the phone. She bounces a ball.

Jane   So I was like 'Babe, you have got to chill out, he is not worth it'

I know

a huh

I know

Insane

I know

Another phone rings.

Hang on.

She answers the other phone.

Hi . . .

Yeah ok

Yeah ok

Yeah we had this conversation

Yeah ok

Yeah so I know

Yeah so I don't care

Because I'm an autonomous, sentient being with my own agency

No I'm not being facetious

Yeah because I already told you

Yeah because you know I did

Yeah when you called me like five minutes ago

Well, I think you're a dick

Yeah, well, I think *you're* a dick

Yeah well I think you're a dick too

Yeah well I don't care if you're my mother

Family is a social construct

No, I'm not coming downstairs

Yeah, because you know why

Yeah because you do

Because you do

Because you do

You do

Because I'm not coming downstairs till he is gone

Beat.

Because we spoke about this

Because I don't wanna speak about it again

Because you know what he said to me

Because it's not OK

Because it's not

No I won't open the door

No, I don't want to upset you

No, because you know that

Because you know that

Because you know I love you, it's not about that

Because I can't deal with this no more

Because it hurts me too

Because I'm sorry

Because I'm sorry

Because I'll talk to you later

Because I have to go

Because I have to

Because

Because

Because I'm sorry, because I have to

Because

She puts the phone down.

She picks the other one up, holds it in her hand.

A butterfly flies across the space. She watches it.

Part Two

Perhaps the pace picks up. Perhaps the scenes start to overlap.

Platform

1   So I'm on this train platform and it's busy, rush hour so everyone is
like packed . . . like jammed in . . . An' it's early,

Eight, maybe eight or nine or something, I can't remember and I wouldn't
normally even be on this . . . but it doesn't . . . [matter] that's another . . .
[story] . . . and I'm standing on this platform, and I can feel these bodies,
moving and I look at the clock and I know the train is coming, cus
although I can't see it, I can feel it and the air is changing, it's sort of
sucking . . . and there's this boy at the back with a ball, a tiny . . . no wait,
a football and he's bouncing, or is he kicking . . .? and I look to my left
and there's this woman . . . She's holding flowers

these

blue

flowers

and she's pushing, like sort of pushing her way, just a little bit. And I
look at the clock, and the train is coming and the air is changing, it's sort
of pulling, and the feeling in my legs is now in my stomach, and the
platform is getting ready, it's getting ready to . . . [fight], you know cus
we're not all getting on, and I look down and there's this butterfly, just
lying on the ground, it's wing looks like it's broken, and I turn my head
and the ball it goes flying, like spinning, through the air and there's this
flash, like just a snap, the smallest like . . . lick of something

Blue

and I see this woman, stumbling and so I

grab her

Just sort of

take her

and I pull her to me

and the train it like screams . . . it's like so fast it sort of . . . screeches
and I look at the woman

and my heart is . . .

and I look at this woman

and the flowers are . . .

and I hold her

I hold her, the woman, I hold her, I just hold her

Safety

Two girls, outside a house.

Jane   I'm sorry.

Somalia   It's ok

Jane   It's late

Somalia   It's ok

Jane   I tried to call

Somalia   Don't worry

Jane   I didn't know what to do

Somalia   You're cold

Jane   He wouldn't stop shouting

Somalia   You're freezing

Jane   I could hear him from upstairs

Somalia   Your clothes are wet, it's raining

Jane   She was crying, my mum, I could hear her crying

Somalia   You're shaking, look at you, you're shaking

Jane   I climbed out the window. I crawled down the garage, I banged my knee on the drop. I landed in the flowers, I scratched my legs on the thorns, I could hear the TV inside the house. He wouldn't stop shouting

Somalia   You're ok.

Jane   I didn't know what to do

Somalia   You're ok, you're here now. You're ok.

Flowers

Two boys. The school corridor. One is carrying flowers.

Aleph   I brought you these

Michael   ...

Aleph   To make sure you were ok . . .

Michael   . . ..

Aleph   I thought you might like . . .

Michael   ...

Aleph   Because . . .

Michael   I can't

Aleph   But I thought

Michael   I can't

Aleph   I thought . . .

Michael   Everything's changed, everything's different

Aleph   But . . .

Michael   I'm sorry

Aleph   Wait . . .

Michael   I can't

He leaves.

Operation

Dan *in a hospital waiting room.*

Emily *is with him.*

Dan   You don't have to be here

Emily   I know

Dan   I'm ok on my own

Emily   I know

Dan   I don't need anyone to . . . I don't need anyone to like be here, or look after [me] . . . or . . .

Emily   I know.

Silence.

How long has he been . . .?

Dan   A while

Emily   How long?

Dan   A few hours

Emily   How many

Dan   Six

Short pause

His heart, they have to take it out. They have to like . . . open up his chest and take out his heart and re-route his blood, so that they can fix . . .

Emily   Are you ok?

Dan   Yeah

It just feels . . .

Emily   I'll stay

Dan   You don't have to /

Emily   I can stay

Short pause.

Emily   How is your hand?

Dan   Ok

Emily   Can I hold it?

Dan   . . .

Emily   Can I hold it?

Beat.

Dan   Ok

Platform

Any number of actors.

–   So I'm on this train platform and it's busy, rush hour so everyone is like

–   packed

–   like

–   jammed

–   An' it's early, eight, maybe

–   nine, ten or

–   and I wouldn't normally even be on this platform, but

–   I'm

–   Here

–   I'm standing

–   Here

–   on this platform, and

–   I can feel these bodies,

–   moving

–   here

–   and I look at the clock and I know the train is coming, cus although I can't see it, I can

–   feel it

–   This butterfly

–   and the air is

–   changing,

–   sort of sucking . . . and

–   there's a boy bouncing

–   Kicking

–   This ball and

–   I look to my right

- left

- and there's this woman . . . She's holding

- flowers

- yellow

- blue

- flowers

- and she's pushing, like sort of

- shoving

- her way, and I look at the clock, and the train is coming and the air is
changing, and the feeling in my legs is now in my stomach, and the
platform is getting ready, it's getting ready and I turn my head, I turn my
head, I turn my head, and . . .

Structures

Zara   Because your structures are not my structures, because your
body is not the same as my body, because my feelings are not the same
as your feelings, because the things I feel, the things I think, the things
I want the things I need . . . Because it doesn't fit me. Because it's too
small. Because I can't grow and I can't be and I can't breathe inside your
structures, because they're not my structures. Because your language
doesn't fit in my mouth, because your words can't define me, because my
body is not your body, and my body is my body. Because the way I feel
is the way I feel, because it's not straight lines and hard edges. Because
there are no corners. Because it's curves, and coils and heat and colour,
because there are things I can't name, because your language doesn't
give me words, because my feelings are my feelings and my body is
my body and my heart is *so full* it's breaking out, out of my chest, it's
spilling over, because your language can't define me. And your structures
they don't . . . they just don't . . .

Input and the Output

- The input equals the output

- So?

– The input equals the output

– I don't care /

– The input equals the output, if I throw this ball with a certain speed and a certain force, then it lands /

The ball is taken and thrown away.

The following scenes start to overlap and fold into each other.

Flowers

Aleph *and* **Aisha**.

Aleph   I thought he'd like them

Aisha   I know

Aleph   I thought he would . . .

Aisha   I know

Aleph   I thought it'd make him *feel* the way I feel, the way I want him to feel, and we were sitting in this *field of wild flowers that day* and I realised that when I'm around him it's like the sky is so much bigger, and the world is turning so much faster, but now he says that something has changed him, it's different, he saw something *on the bus and it's changed him, his body is tighter, he's different and I can't make him feel the way I feel* if he doesn't feel that way / and so

Anxiety Two

Three people.

1   So what she said was that we're all gonna die

2   True

1   Which she knew, she like . . . already knew

2   Ok

1   But the thing is, she said she can't stop thinking about it

2   Oh

1   An' like, since she's been thinking about it, it's sort of become like *an obsession* it's sort of become like *all* she thinks about

2   Oh right

1   It's sort of become like . . . her whole brain

2   Right

3   An' she started reading about it

2   Oh

3   Yeah, she like, found all these articles, online or whatever

2   Ok

1   About like the climate, and like *drought* and how people are dying cus they haven't got enough water, and like over population and the war in Syria, or the *assault on* Palestine, or the war in the Congo, and the refugees, / like all the millions of refugees, and the waters rising and the forests dying, and the hurricanes, or the earthquakes, and she can't stop thinking about it, she just said she can't stop thinking about it, she said she just can't stop.

Someone spins across the space.

Throughout the next, the structure falls away. The piece should be as messy and physical and chaotic as it can be.

SO I'm on the bus and it's hot, the sun's

coming in through the

And it's nice, like, summer, the air is like. . . .

                                                    WINDOWS!

– The output

– What?

– It equals?

– What

– The input
WIND

                              And I feel like my heart might fall out, I
                              feel like my heart, might just fall out my
                              chest or . . .

A girl spins through the space

> *Because I can't stop thinking about it*

        And don't you miss it?
        Don't you miss it?

> You have to come out

NO!

These are for you [flowers]

– What is it?

– A butterfly   Do you think it will be ok?

– Its wing is broken   <u>AN EARTHQUAKE</u>

– Will it be ok?

> *A boy walks into a room, he smashes it up*
>
> *he hurts his hands*
>
> *His heart falls out his chest*

Because I feel like it's glowing

        My heart!

Many balls bouncing

                        I feel like it's glowing

Because the universe, is chaos, and

It rains

        The ruling principle is . . .

SOMEONE SCREAMS!   *A tornado*

The carbon from the Big Bang is in our bones! Did you know that? We're
made of stars

> She said she loved him, it's complicated, she said it's messy, she said
> it's not straightforward, she said the world doesn't . . . when you're
> older the world doesn't. She said she was doing what felt right . . . She
> said to trust her. She said people make mistakes. She said the world is
> not straight lines. She said it's rough edges. She said it's chaos but we
> do the best with it. She said she had a feeling in her stomach and it felt
> like the right one. She said she was doing her best.

Someone opens their mouth – butterflies fly out

– Because we have to try

– I know but /

Someone bounces a ball

– We have to try

The ice caps will melt, the polar bears will die

The rivers will dry up

Two people kiss

A field of wild flowers

The land will crack   The fish will die

The waters will rise

A dance routine. Everyone gets it wrong. No one cares

Someone cries

The crops will die, and the temperature will rise, and the people
will migrate, and the fuel will run out, and the earth will revolt,
and the fish will die, and the flowers will dry out, and the wars
will break out, and the planet will be pulled apart, and our hearts
will break into pieces /

*And do you know my life, do you even know my life, do you know
anything about my life, does my life look like order to you, does my life
look like rules, does my life look anything like order to you, do you know
my life, do you know anything about my life /*

Someone is sick

You have to
come out

And will you hold
my hand?

No

Because I worry

You have to   about the ozone
layer

Will you hold my hand?

No

And I worry about
the sea

I'll call your
mum

And I worry about
the fish

Will you hold my hand?

No

And I worry about
the wars wars wars

I'll call your dad

I don't care

And I worry about
the people, all the
people people

*And it feels like it's just everything
everything everything everything
everything everything everything
everything everything everything
everything everything everything
everything everything everything
everything everything everything
everything everything everything
everything*

EARTHQUAKES
IN CHINA

*Will you hold
my hand?*

**My soul is
stretching**

A BOY
BOUNCES A BALL

Part Three

The space should suddenly feel very calm, still even.

The speaker should be the same as in the very first monologue.

Over the next the space gets slowly lighter.

— So it's Tuesday.

Summer.

I'm in the car with my mum, cus . . . I stayed at hers last night

And we're driving.

She's giving me a lift.

It's early, but . . . not too early. The sun is up.

It's just after rush hour so the traffic is moving, slowly, calmly

And everything is easy

It feels kind of peaceful

And I look out the window and . . . I start to notice the world

a boy with a ball

a woman with some flowers

a little girl spinning in circles, just on her own

and I know it sounds weird but as we're driving I start to imagine all the possibilities, you know? All the different things that can happen, in a day, or a moment, or a life, or a world. And I know this will sound strange, but it's like I start to see it, it's like I start to see this map of everything, everything that we're made of and how everything is connected and what it means and how it fits or doesn't fit, and how this map is chaos, like in my head this map is just total, complete . . . you know?

but it's beautiful

and I have this thought that maybe it's us, like the inside . . . somehow, that maybe it's us

and I know it doesn't make sense, but I know that

it's . . .

right

somehow. It's right.

And we drive past the train station, and I look out the window.

me and my mum

we drive. We just keep driving.

The stage should now be very bright.

In the light we can see everyone. The whole cast.

A field of wild flowers.

Everyone holding bouncing balls.

A butterfly flies past.

The End.

Chaos

BY LAURA LOMAS

Notes on rehearsal and staging, drawn from two workshops with the writer, held at the National Theatre, October 2018

How Laura came to write the play

'I'm interested in chaos. I think most of the time we try to impose order on our lives – we're scared of the mess of being alive; we want to contain it, to put our hands around it. I wanted to write something that embraced chaos, that celebrated it, in all its strange, unpredictable energy, in all its trouble, and its beauty. I didn't want it to always make sense, but I did want it to feel very alive – all the ways I remember feeling as a teenager. The play is strictly non-linear and non-naturalistic.'

Laura Lomas, 2018

Warm-ups

Lead directors Debbie Hannan and Lisa Spirling ran a series of warm-ups and ice-breakers to get the group working together and thinking physically about the themes of the play.

GEEKY PASSION

Stand up and look around the room.

Make eye contact with someone across the space.

Go over to them and take a seat together.

Tell each other your geeky passion, which might be your current passion or one you've had since birth (it can be anything – Harry Potter books, stamp collecting, bird watching, etc.).

After five minutes, introduce your partner back to the group with their geeky passion.

In Lisa's directing work she will often get the actors to do this exercise later in their rehearsal process for their characters to add another layer to their choices and to deepen the work around the world of the play. About halfway through the process can be a good time to use this one.

SHARK ATTACK

Give each company member a piece of A3 paper or newspaper. They place them on the floor randomly. They then move about the space.

When the director calls 'Shark Attack' they have to get to a piece of paper to stay safe . . . with each round, a piece of paper is removed so they have to share to stay safe . . . with each round, it becomes more tricky and, eventually, the whole company might be trying to get onto one piece of paper.

This is brilliant for co-operation and as an ice-breaker exercise.

PHYSICAL WARM-UPS

Debbie gave the following instructions:

Stretch out the body. Then walk around the space individually, filling up space, altering the pace of your walk – perhaps running a little late/very late. Add to movement a nod of acknowledgement when you make eye contact with someone, then maybe a smile. Then maybe shake hands. Now, when indicated, strike a pose – freeze in position. Remember your pose. Next time, when indicated, find another person and strike your poses together, in relationship with one another. Now animate these poses in some way. Now add sound.

Next Debbie asked the participants to create an image of *order*. The shape of the bodies in space immediately changed. Almost everyone was standing up tall, some with military gestures. Over a count of five, Debbie asked the participants to find a new image of order. Some people formed lines, others chose clear gestures – Debbie commented on the appearance of a 'Victorian wife' and also someone sitting in a lotus position looking very zen, and they discussed how this was a representation of 'internal order' and the connection between order and peace.

Next Debbie asked the participants to create a still image of *chaos*. The shapes created by the participants were very different again – one person lifted a chair upside down and high above her head, another collapsed in on themselves. Over a count of five, Debbie asked for a new image of chaos, and to really explore the dynamic angles and shapes. People began using the architecture of the space they were in to help create their images – in particular breaking the rules of the space, such as climbing up pillars. They discussed how this might be useful to consider when staging the piece – what are the rules of your performance space, and how can you disrupt them to create a sense of chaos?

Participants then chose one of their images of chaos and made it into a gesture that could be repeated, then they added sound to this repeating image. Next they were asked to find a very normal domestic action that they could do in roughly the same position they were in for their chaos move. People chose things like putting glasses on, tying shoes, waving, cleaning floor, doing hair, etc. They gave this domestic action a sound as well. Debbie then split the group in half, so that half the group could be observers with their 'director heads' on. The 'onstage' group were asked to bunch together and then perform their chaos moves all at the same time, and then to switch back to their domestic moves, and then back to chaos, etc. Debbie commented that an exercise like this uses the creativity of the whole group to provide a director with a huge palate of options to choose from.

Read-through

The group read the script through, swapping the reader after each character's line(s). This meant that sometimes they only said a word, or even a silent '. . .' but that the same speaker read the whole of any monologue. It was important that one person read the whole monologue because it helped give a sense of the pacing. The only exception to this was during the overlapping scene that starts on p. 524, when Debbie asked one person to read all the words on the pages, but also said that everyone else could read any line whenever – just joining in when they felt like it – to help create a bit of a sense of the chaos the scene needs.

   Debbie also mentioned that, during a first read-through at the start of a rehearsal process, she would be noting the following things:

1 Any interesting imagery
2 Any questions it prompted
3 Things that excite her about the play
4 Any noticeable first audience reactions (e.g. laughter, awkward silence)

She encouraged the directors to do the same during their first read-through with their companies.

Your production: finding your vision

Lisa and Debbie asked the directors to respond to the following provocations:

1 Write down five questions that come to mind after reading the play.

2 What is your reaction to the different parts of the play? (You could just have one word per part.) How are you going to make the three sections as different as possible?

3 What do you think the writer is saying/investigating in this play?

4 What are three images that stand out for you in the play? They don't even have to be ones that are described in play – could be just something that came into your head from reading it.

5 Note down two pieces of music that you think this play is.

6 Choose a third bit of music that you think is the theme song for this play. This can be as personal as you like – don't try and get the 'right' answer.

7 What colour is the play for you? Try and be as specific as possible (i.e. not just yellow, but is it neon yellow or mustard yellow?). Don't think too hard – just write whatever comes into your head first.

8 Write down three sounds in the play. What sounds do you remember? Doesn't have to be described – e.g. train sound isn't described, but you may remember it.

9 What is the most important moment in the play? Just go with your gut instinct.

10 If this play had a speed to it, what would it be? It could be several speeds – e.g. could be fast, slow, squidgy and fast again.

11 If the play was a movement, what kind of movement would it be (jumping, rolling around on floor, flying, running into a wall)?

12 What do you think the play is saying or investigating? Don't try and be correct – try and be personal. You don't have to use full sentences – it can just be single words.

13 Who is the character that you had the clearest picture of / who stood out the most for you? Write a bit about them – just a couple of details.

14 If you could stage this in your dream space what would it be? Imagine your dream production.

15 Imagining the actual space you are going to do it in. Pick out your thoughts from above questions and put them in that space (e.g. the colour in that space, music in that space).

16 What is your personal connection to this play? It might be a very small thing – say one line that felt meaningful to you. Or it could be the overall atmosphere of the play. Try and get a complete sentence.

Approaching the play

Text work: FACTS and QUESTIONS

You could frame this exercise as 'investigating the play in detail'. The group read the first scene and noted down any FACTS and QUESTIONS, like this:

Facts	Questions
There is a train platform of some kind	What kind of train? A tube?
There is a girl	Who is she? How old is she? Where is she going? What has just happened to her? Is she running late? Has she eaten?
	Also, is it the same girl when the event is recalled again in Part Two? (Platform)
She speaks to us	Who is 'us'? The audience? Rest of cast?
It's busy/rush hour/packed/jammed	Who is on the platform with her? School kids? Business people?
It's 'early, like, twenty to eight or something'	Why is she vague here and then later in speech becomes specific? Does she see a clock?
She is not normally on this platform	So why is she here today?
She has a mum and a dad	What is her attitude to her mum? Her dad? What do they look like? How do they behave with her?
Her parents have split up	When did they split up? How long ago (two days, two weeks, two months, a year)? How does she feel about it? Why is there a '. . .' before she says 'split'? Why doesn't she use the word divorce?
She gets the train when she stays at her dad's	Has she been staying at her dad's last night? How far away from each other do her parents now live?
There is a clock which says 7.42	What kind of clock? Analogue, or digital? Do you want to represent the clock realistically on the stage?
The train is coming	Where from? From which direction? Is there a sound?
There is a woman next to her on her left	Who is she? How old is she?

Facts	Questions
The woman is holding yellow flowers	Why does she have flowers? Did she buy them or was she given them? What kind of flowers are they?
The woman is pushing	How is she pushing – politely, or aggressively? Why is she pushing – to get on the train or to get in front of the train?
A minute has passed – the clock says 7.43	
She can see the lights of the train	Why does the train have lights? Is it still dark? What time of year would that make it? Or is it an underground train?
She turns her head and sees a flash/lick of something yellow	What is the quality of this memory? What does she see? How accurate is her memory?
The train screeches, staggers to a halt	Is this the normal way the train stops or is it a sudden emergency stop?
She looks to her left and the woman is not there	Why is she not there? Where is she? Has she fallen? Jumped? Been pushed?
The flowers are . . .	Where are the flowers? Gone? Dropped? How do you finish that sentence?
The woman's 'not/ she's just'	What is the woman not? What is end of this sentence?
There is another person with the girl	Who is this other person that she is telling the story to? Is it a close friend? A stranger? Where are they while she is telling the story? A cafe or school?

Thoughts from the FACTS/QUESTIONS exercise

- Debbie and Lisa commented that as a director you can answer these QUESTIONS as you are going along, because you can always change your answers as you rehearse. For example, you may realise an answer you chose is wrong or that you need to choose a more interesting/high-stakes answer to a QUESTION in order to stop the scene from being low energy.

- They also pointed out that what has shown itself even just from this short exploration of FACTS and QUESTIONS is that you will need to decide on a set of rules for your production. For example, do people always play the same character? Or do people always play a different character? Do you depict the events described onstage alongside the spoken words? Do you depict things realistically or non-realistically (e.g. is the clock a real clock that is part of the set for that scene or does a person play the clock)?

- You could choose to explore the idea of the unreliability (or chaotic) nature of memories by creating dissonance between what is said and what is seen. For example, if you choose to depict the woman at the train station with the yellow flowers, is the actor holding yellow flowers or is she/he perhaps holding a blue balloon? Perhaps this becomes one of the rules of your world, that whenever there is a mention of yellow flowers we see something blue? However, if you are choosing a contradictory image, you must also consider whether you are helping or hindering the audience.

- Quite a lot of characters are recalling events in this play, a fact that may be helpful in influencing any decisions you make about the staging and the rules of your piece.

If you wanted to make the FACTS and QUESTIONS exercise more practical and physical, you could combine it with a staggered read-through as follows:

Create a large space in the centre of the room.

On the outer perimeter are tables and chairs where everyone who isn't in a scene sits.

Working anti-clockwise, assign an actor to a character.

If there are two people in the first scene, they are each assigned a note taker. The note taker's job takes stock of FACTS, QUESTIONS and OPINIONS about their specific character.

The note taker writes the character's name and page number at the top of each sheet.

All stage directions are read out.

When someone comes across a FACT, they can slam the table.

When someone comes across a QUESTION, they get to their feet and *ask* the QUESTION.

When a character gives an OPINION, someone can pump their fist into an open hand.

The actors enter the central space and trust their instincts; they are free to explore spatial relationships and discover options in the scene.

The process can be fast and energetic. The whole company can work through the timeline, logic and begin to make decisions around the world of the play.

Some useful exercises in rehearsal

The following exercises were suggestions from Lisa that directors could try with their companies to further text and character exploration.

NAMING THE SCENES

Lisa said that it could be helpful to come up with a name for each scene with the actors. This title should contain within it the essence of each scene. Laura has named the scenes already, but it could also be helpful for the actors to come up with their own titles that they can relate to.

EXERCISE: PUSH AND PULL WITH TEXT

Lisa explained that this exercise is aimed to help the actors move away from the cerebral and engage their bodies. Looking at one section of the play, each actor is asked to push or pull the other while using the text. It is important to clarify the physical boundaries for the group to ensure the actors remain safe. The actors are encouraged to physicalise the action, to sustain physical contact and to actively change each other with each line.

The world of Laura's play is rooted in interaction. It is concerned with cause and effect. This exercise allows the actor to live through each moment and focus just on either pushing or pulling. This binary choice can free the actor from over-intellectualising the work and make stronger, more instinctive choices.

EXERCISE: LINE FEEDING

Lisa said that this can be a freeing way of rehearsing a play. Each actor is assigned another person. This second person feeds the first their lines. This means they don't have to worry about holding a script or reading and can be totally open to responding to their scene partner. The line reader gives a neutral reading. The actor then plays the line while keeping eye contact with their scene partner.

The actors are encouraged to make bold physical choices and respond to each other's impulses.

Another phase is for them to play the whole scene as if it is interpretative dance, encouraging them to follow their instincts to the extreme.

The next stage involves the actors and director identifying the key events or moments of change in the scene. Finally, the actors improvise the whole scene to truly embody the reality of what they are playing.

Lisa explained that her rehearsal process starts with nobody in the company learning any lines or text. The aim is that the company discovers the work together. She works with line feeding, improvising the scenes, establishing the beats, then prompting if an actor needs a line before finally everyone in the company is confident with the text.

EXERCISE: THOUGHT RUNS

Lisa said that this can be useful to do near the end of a rehearsal process when the actor is confident about the world of the play. The actor verbalises the inner thoughts the character has before they speak their text. This is particularly good in large group scenes where there are characters who may remain silent for long periods of time. It's helpful for ensuring that you are serving all the actors in the scene. The idea is that the character is always doing or having a reaction to what is taking place around them.

Movement work: creating dance routines for companies who don't have movement backgrounds

There are two scenes in the play where a dance routine is called for. These exercises are a way of creating dance routines with/for people who aren't confident dancers. The aim is to create a 'boring' dance routine. You can use different pieces of music as backing tracks throughout these exercises – changing the tune changes the tempo and quality of the dance.

EXERCISE 1

Debbie asked the group to think of a simple move that expressed an experience of chaos in a small everyday way.

1 Debbie suggested, as an example, swiping through millions of emails on your phone and demonstrated this move by swiping the index finger of her right hand across the palm of her left hand. The whole group copied this move until they were doing it in sync with one another. They explored speeding the move up and developing it. Then Debbie asked one member of the group to get it wrong.

They just suddenly stopped doing the move and stood still looking at the rest of the group.

2 The next everyday chaos move suggested was based on a stressed teacher having ten people demanding their attention all at once. This move was created by turning the head sharply to look in lots of different directions. Debbie suggested the participants added in facial expressions of the stressed teacher and then encouraged them to really get into the dance, as if they were really enjoying this groovy dance move – this led to them clicking fingers as they moved. Again, someone was asked to do it wrong. This time the person going wrong kept moving, but just got completely out of time and started doing moves in the wrong direction.

3 The third everyday chaos move was based on sorting through the laundry. Lots of pulling and throwing moves, which were developed and stretched in order to expand the move. Once again the group were asked to turn this move into a dance move and really enjoy doing it all together. Once again, someone was asked to go wrong. This person *really* went to town on going wrong – completely dropped to the ground, lay down and then started rolling across the floor!

Debbie noted that it was interesting that the 'going wrong' built as the exercise went along. (1) just stopped; (2) out of time and wrong direction; (3) rolling on the floor.

The group then explored doing the moves in double time, then in slow motion to see how that changed the dance. It was interesting to see whether they chose to work with the tone of the music or against it. Next they tried doing any one of the three moves at any time but changing the tempo at irregular points.

EXERCISE 2

Debbie split the group into smaller sub-groups and asked each group to find three moves that they could repeat to create a routine. Ideally they should be related to the play in some way – either chaos or an action from the play – such as punching.

The groups used various different moves, such as checking their watch, bouncing a ball, answering the phone and punching, as well as more abstract moves. Then they had to find an interesting way that one person gets it wrong.

Debbie asked one group to do really small, boring moves (such as scratching the head, tapping the foot). Then when one member of this group went 'wrong' by doing some much bigger more 'obvious' dance moves, he looked really cool and creative. The minimalism of the original routine made him appear to be the strongest dancer.

Another group chose some strong moves including banging on a table, drinking and punching, which were all performed totally in sync, and they had the person who went wrong just leave the group and start spinning. Debbie commented how simple but effective it could be to have a whole room full of people and only one person spinning on their own in the middle.

After watching all the groups, the group discussed the various different ways that the routine can go wrong – for those who go wrong, it can be an accidental error or a deliberate decision; for the rest of the group, it can be a slow realisation that there's something wrong, or an immediate clocking.

They discussed what they liked about these routines and what they'd like more of. Things mentioned included:

- The clown-like quality of some of the moments when the routines go wrong
- How strong it is visually when everyone is doing the same thing
- Movement that travels
- It's nice to have an attitude with the gesture
- The different attitudes to the person going wrong
- They liked seeing people who enjoyed being the chaos
- They liked the idea of it being about limitations. The minimalist group was limited by their dance routine, and so the person who goes wrong isn't the worst dancer, but the best dancer who just wants to break free from constraints.
- Chaos is not necessarily negative

Debbie commented that the person who goes wrong could be the anchor for this scene. She suggested that you should always ask yourself: 'Who's my anchor in the scene?'

Movement work: groups

To begin this exercise Debbie asked the participants to name some groups of people. Suggestions included:

- Nuns
- Nurses

- Soldiers
- Business people
- Yummy mummies
- Politicians
- Journalists

Debbie asked a small group of participants to cross the space as nuns. They did so, and the quality of their movement included small steps and hands together in prayer. She then asked them to cross back as soldiers – ordered, upright and regimental. They then crossed back again as journalists – movements were more bent over, looking around, watching, spinning, and much more chaotic than the soldiers or the nuns. One person was asked to stop midway – and suddenly became the focus of the scene. Other groups were tried too, including the yummy mummies. The instruction Debbie gave midway during this crossing was that one yummy mummy was to suddenly decide she hated yummy mummies and to rebel against everything she had previously been – this subverted expectation and created comedy.

They also tried having two people reading the first scene, whilst another group of journalists/soldiers, etc. crossed the space around them.

Debbie explained that using groups crossing the space can be really useful for *transitions*. It is a helpful way to 'swipe scenes' as it allows you to pick up people and absorb them into a larger group moving offstage, as well as allowing you to leave people onstage to begin a new scene.

Atmospheres: Michael Chekhov

As a way of introducing Michael Chekhov's work on atmospheres, the group were asked to spread out and embody a high state of tension and then relax.

Chekhov's atmospheres can be:

- Up or down
- Heavy or light
- Expanding or contracting (and you can expand and contract towards or away from things)

The group were asked to spread out and embody a high state of tension and to consider this body in relation to Chekhov's atmospheres. Are you up/down, heavy/light, expanding/contracting? Debbie gave the instructions:

check what your body's doing, where your hips are, where the tension is in the body, what your neck's doing, what gestures you've got. Then over a count of five shift back to your current body and consider that in relation to the atmospheres work. Check what happened to your jaw, your forehead, legs, arms. What gestures are you making now?

The group was given three different environments and the following instructions:

1 *Library*: What is the atmosphere of a library? The group responded: down, heavy (cerebrally heavy – head heavy), contracting. Debbie asked the group to form a library over a count of three, and become more heavy, more contracted – considering the objects they were contracting into (is it computer screen, phone, book?). The group then animated the library with minimal movement. Someone then shouted 'mouse' – the group reacted to how a mouse running through the library would change the atmosphere and noted what the effect was.

2 *Sunny park*: Think about the atmosphere for this environment? The group responded: light, up, expanded. Debbie asked the group to animate the scene with joggers, swinging, smoking, etc. Then when she gave the instruction that when someone is tapped on the shoulder they will scream, which will change the atmosphere. She told the group to stay in the new atmosphere until it felt okay to go back to the original atmosphere. This might happen at different times for different people.

3 *Church* (private prayer): Again, Debbie asked the group to consider the atmosphere. Then animate the scene – and consider what happens when somebody moved, even slightly. One person was given the instruction to start crying. Debbie asked: What happens to the atmosphere? Do you become heavier? Do you expand or contract in reaction? Do you stay in your own thing? Everyone was instructed to join the crying character in the centre of the space, to feel the pace of this and to go when they felt the instinct to go.

Debbie asked: Who could you ask to start speaking the text? How would you put a scene into this? Some background music was added to the scene and those onstage were asked to choose a move from earlier, and keep it really heavy and down, thinking about what's wrong with the crying lady and if there is any way that they can help her.

Debbie then added some background music to the scene and to slowly change the quality of movement, with the following questions and directions:

- Perhaps begin with a little toe tap.
- When do you catch the rhythm?
- When does a little dance move catch you?
- It's really growing now.
- The finger clicks start to come in.
- Maybe you start dancing with someone else
- Add in flowers.
- Move around the church.

Debbie then counted to three and everyone stopped and looked at the audience. Then one person began the first speech.

Following this exercise the group discussed what was interesting about this scene. Some responses were:

- There were lots of changes of levels.
- No eye contact was made.
- It felt like everyone in the space was an individual with a different story to tell.
- You could pull any of the duologues in the script out of it at any time.

Using atmospheres can offer a quick way to get your group to react to an event, individually and collectively. You can also choose to have an event that an audience doesn't know about. The audience might just see the reaction and change in atmosphere. If the audience don't know what happened, that can create a sense of chaos.

You might want to put the atmospheres of scenes up on the wall, to score it – like a symphony as it says in the text.

Approaching characterisation

The group looked at the scene with Jane ('Phone', pp. 512–14).

First, Debbie asked two different members of the group to read the scene, to show how different voices change the way we interpret the character. She commented that although it is always good to recognise the importance of your instincts and first impressions, and the most natural thing is to go towards this, it is sometimes helpful to consider what is the opposite of your immediate assumptions.

Next Debbie led the group through an exercise that uses imagination to build character. She asked the group to find a comfortable position and close their eyes. Then she led them through a series of questions – starting at the moment when Jane was born, through her early life, family life, teenage years, personal likes and dislikes, right up to the moment we meet Jane in the play. This was a very detailed exploration of this character (including questions such as: What was her infant life like? Did her family have money? What does she look like? Is she black? White? Asian? How does she play? Did she cry on her first day at school? Is she good at anything? Does she have a group of friends? Has she been ill at all? How has her body changed now she's a teenager? What does she think about her body? Is she doing well at school? How often does she use the phone? Has she had a drink yet? How does she imagine her future?). And Debbie regularly encouraged the participants to 'go against your default' to find more interesting choices and that if a detail becomes important you don't have to move on to next question – stay with it. See if anything surprises you as you start to invent things.

Then Debbie asked the group to open their eyes, and immediately stand up, but keeping their version of Jane in their mind. Then she asked them to imagine they had a bit of clay in front of them and to mould their version of Jane out of clay. Working down from hair and face to tips of toes. Keeping it as detailed as possible – fat, thin, scars, tilt of head/body, fingernails. What are the things she thinks are special about herself? Debbie also suggested that you don't have to keep it totally realistic – what does her heart feel like? Spiky? Soft?

The participants were then asked to leave the sculpture be – and look at her. Then to step forwards, step into the sculpture and let it affect your body. Debbie coached: lean into the heart of the character. Now walk around the room as Jane. How does her body move? It should be different from your body. How does she show up in her gestures – is she chewing, embarrassed? What happens when Jane is under stress – how does that body move? Maybe some words will slip out. You know her voice – you can try a few lines that you remember from the script. Now what's Jane like at her best/relaxed/having a good day?

Then half the group watched as the others moved around as Jane.
Participants' comments after the exercise:

- People enjoyed seeing less obvious choices – less over the top (stereotypical) about what people think young people are.

- The high energy some people had as Jane on a good day was a nice contrast.

- Some people liked when people didn't change much externally whether it's a good day or bad day – even when happy, Jane still had a tough face.

- The fact that Jane has two phones. She could be a girl who has many different lives. Debbie commented – why only two phones? You could be more expressionistic – she could have a bag of phones.

- You could have five different Janes in room all at the same time – lots of different versions of the same character. You could make it clear it was the same character through costume, but use different actors (male/female). It could be an interesting way of opening out the piece.

Stage-direction challenges

KISSING

Regardless of the experience of the actors, there can often be anxiety about intimacy. One of the provocations given by the writer at the beginning of the play is that stage directions can be spoken also.

Using three volunteers, Debbie explored different ways of reading out stage directions in 'Kiss' (p. 498).

1 Two people read dialogue, one person read stage directions. Even with no other choices, the reader of the stage directions has the potential to have his/her own personality.
2 Next, Debbie set up two chairs for the characters to sit on and asked the stage-direction reader to stand behind. In this version the stage-direction reader became a kind of character in the scene – egging them on.
3 The group then explored what would happen if the characters could hear and react to the stage directions being spoken. This created quite a bit of comedy.

Lisa suggested that another way of dealing with the kiss physically is to explore what a kiss feels like and express that, rather than being literal about it. So what does it feel like? A star jump? A dance? A shiver through your body? So, in this version, the actor reading the stage directions was set up like a tennis umpire in between the two characters, and when he mentioned the kiss, the actors playing the characters shivered. This developed so that the stage-direction reader was almost giving them 'notes' – 'tentatively at first' – so they had a little shiver, and then after he said 'then they get into it' they went crazy shivering.

They also explored getting rid of the stage-direction reader and having the character speaking their own stage directions at the same time as each other – this created a new dynamic to the scene as each character's attitude to the kiss began to come through.

Lisa and Debbie encouraged the group to suggest other theatrical versions of kissing/dealing with the kiss. Some of the ideas suggested were:

- Perhaps the kiss could be passed on. Perhaps she could give the stage-direction reader a peck on the cheek and he passes it on to the boy.

- Perhaps they could turn their backs to the audience and wrap arms round themselves as if kissing.

- Or face audience – full-blown kiss facing the audience.

- Or maybe go full movie – massive heightened romantic snog.

- Perhaps the stage-direction reader could cover it up/censor it?

- Perhaps we see them pre-kiss, about to kiss and then you use the groups crossing the stage as a transition and when the group has left the stage we see them post-kiss – maybe a bit dishevelled?

Butterflies

The group were asked: What does the image 'Butterflies come out of your mouth' mean to you? Words that came to mind were: butterflies in tummy, nerves, anxiety and release.

The group then explored the feeling of anxiety/having butterflies in your stomach. Participants mentioned bubbles, wings fluttering, trapped wind, sickly.

Debbie then coached: feel this in your stomach, and then increase it: Two butterflies – how does it affect your body? Five butterflies – perhaps it stops you being rooted? Twenty butterflies – maybe you have to move? Thirty butterflies – maybe they are coming up through the body? Maybe it's unpleasant, itchy? Try stretching, and without thinking now just release out of mouth with sound.

That could be one way of dealing with the butterflies imagery. The question for you is what aspect of this image do you want to depict? Other suggestions were:

- Speaking the word butterfly or the phrase 'Butterflies come out of your mouth'. Maybe one person says butterfly, and the others say it back to them like an echo. Or perhaps you could cannon it: one person says butterfly after another, after another, etc. – this option could be directional across the space. Or maybe one person says it, two people say it, three people say it, etc.

- Or perhaps the butterflies are a movement – maybe using a light material like chiffon.

- Butterflies could also be a particular sound – the cast could move as if a sound is about to come out of their mouths and then we hear a non-human sound, perhaps a cello.

Debbie remarked that whatever the creative choice for portraying this, it's about the director having control of their imagery. Score it throughout the play so that it has a meaning. They are like phrases in a symphony.

Scoring a play

There is an instruction at the beginning of the script that says 'Scenes should be symphonic, acting like a piece of music, that grows and evolves over the course of the play'.

In response to this provocation, Debbie shared her way of 'scoring' a play with the group. They read through two scenes: 'Protest' (p. 495) and 'Hope' (p. 497).

Debbie gave the following instructions:

For each scene, get a piece of paper, draw a large square that represents the scene and write the title of the scene at the top. In this square note down your first reactions to the pace, temperature and colour of this scene – is it speedy, slow, flowing, short, sharp, cool, hot, red, pink or blue? If you are musical you can use musical words such as legato or staccato, or you could imagine the type of instrument the scene is – a cello is very different from a trumpet! Leave some space so you can start to draw lines later. You can even do little drawings or doodles to represent how the scene feels to you. It can be completely silly looking – it doesn't matter as long as you understand your own score.

When you've done them all, look at them in order. Perhaps, for example, you might have:

Protest: driving, drums, crescendo, hot, red

Hope: delicate, pizzicato, warm, yellow

Now if you're going to put a join in between these things – what kind of join do you need? Fast, slow? Warm, cold? The aim is to develop a linked set of images and words that reveal the overall shape of the piece. Once you have this you can enjoy exploring the complete contrasts between scenes. Having a mapped-out version also helps you know exactly what to change. You might start out thinking a scene is legato and a cello, but then later discover it needs to be pacier. Or if you've got, say, six blue scenes in a row, you know something's wrong. Thinking in colours can also feed into technical choices in terms of design and lighting.

Debbie encouraged the participants to find their own way of scoring. You may want to engage your cast with the exercise in order to get your students to realise for themselves the right choices.

Tasks on paper

This exercise might be particularly useful for the section towards the end of the play where there is all the overlapping.

The participants were asked to think of a task and write it really clearly on a piece of paper. It could be simple or more complex (e.g. try to fly, jump five times, say any line of Shakespeare you know, try and touch everyone's face). Fold the piece of paper. Come into the centre of the space and put it somewhere on the floor. Whenever you want you can get up, find a piece of paper, open it and start doing the task. The rule is that there must always be three people doing individual tasks from the floor at any one time.

This exercise created a crazy mash-up of actions and images. Reflecting on the exercise, some of the group's comments were:

- It was fun when people left the confines of the space, such as climbing the wall to hug a pillar, when they broke the rules of the space, including invading people's (especially the audience's) space – e.g. when someone sat on someone's knee.

- They liked it when images looked normal – you think you can see a respectable person giving a speech, but then when you listen closely you realise they are speaking complete gibberish.

- Being tied to someone physically – shoelace to shoelace – creates strange movements.

- Everyone having a rule that they completely understand, but the audience don't.

- In amongst all the chaos, people who were doing their tasks/actions at a slow pace drew the attention – they were calmer and drew focus.

You could use this exercise as a way to find interesting and chaotic imagery. You can have two things going on at once. After doing the exercise consider which of those movements, images and text work with one another.

Chaos game

This exercise could help find theatrical possibilities for the staging of Part Two, where scenes overlap and repeat.

The group begins in a circle.

The first person turns to the person on their left and gives them an instruction (you run outside the circle three times, then rest and go again).

The next person gives another instruction (you run and cheer).

The following person gives another instruction (you dance like an old man at a wedding).

The energy should build and build until the whole of the company is engaged in a task. You can then play with the duration and timing of the game.

Talking with Laura

Laura talked through some of the story beats from the headline stories in the piece. Although they aren't in chronological order in the script, she is describing the events in chronological order here:

Hands – the Dan and Emily story: Dan finds out that his dad has to have a serious operation and he smashes up a room. Emily walks in on him. Emily's friends reject her. Emily and Dan become close and she goes to visit him at the hospital and holds his hand.

Flowers – the Aleph and Michael story: Aleph is in love with Michael and there is a connection between them. Michael witnesses a moment of violence on a bus and it changes his perspective on the world. Aleph goes to give Michael some flowers to check he's okay, but Michael rejects the flowers. Aleph calls a meeting with Michael – wanting to check he's okay. In the meantime, Aleph talks to Aisha and says he's in love with Michael – this is what Aisha is talking about in 'Love'.

Parents – the Somalia and Jane story: Jane doesn't like her mum's new
    boyfriend. Somalia asks if she's okay. Then there is the scene with
    Jane on the phone. Then Jane's mum and stepdad have a massive
    argument and she climbs out of the window and gets cuts on her arms
    and legs – from the thorns. Jane goes shoplifting and the other girl
    calls her out ('Rules'). She goes to her friend Somalia's house and
    seeks refuge there.

Laura offered up some other possible links in the stories: Laura imagined
that the boy on the bus (who is carrying flowers and is the victim of a racist
assault) is the same boy who the two sisters are waiting for at the bus stop.
She also imagined that it could be Michael who hasn't turned up to meet
his mates in 'Anxiety One'. However, these are offers – if you'd rather not
connect things up so much you don't need to.

Laura said that the character names are simply offers, and that names,
genders and pronouns can be changed if necessary and parts distributed to
suit the needs of the company.

Laura also added that she would prefer it if the characters of Somalia
and Jane are consistent, and it is made clear that Chiarra is talking about
the same racist attack on the bus that Michael witnesses, and that it is that
event that radicalised her and inspired her protest. *But* if this really doesn't
work for you and you need to find a different way, then you can.

The overlapping scene should be chaotic, but there is an order that
should be observed. Laura wants it to feel like things are smashing
together, but there is a form and it builds, and hopefully the form affects
the sense of chaos in a positive way.

Questions for Laura

**Is there any possibility of changing phrases – for example 'didn't do
nothing' – to fit with local dialect for the performers?**
Laura   I'm happy for you to make phrases like that work for your area,
yes.

Is there scope to change the order of the scenes?
Laura   No. The scenes have been ordered specifically and rhythmically
to correspond to a sense of rising chaos (i.e. the ending) and also so that
different moments answer each other across different story threads – for
example, Dan punching the wall is placed next to the description of the
fight on the bus, etc. This is to create a sense of individual and also
collective chaos.

Is it possible where a scene is written for two characters to invite the ensemble to join in the scenes too? For example, the Protest scene. Perhaps you start with two people but add more people in as the scene goes on?

Laura   I'm happy for others to be present in the scene, but it might complicate story threads across scenes if speakers are changed. For example, it's deliberate that Chiarra witnesses the violence on the bus, and that this then inspires her to protest other injustices. If this is diluted it might not be as clear and therefore as powerful.

Do you intend the words in square brackets to be said?

Laura   No. The words in the square brackets are just to let you and your actor know what the character was going to say, but they should not actually be said. In terms of other punctuation, a slash (/) means an interruption. An ellipsis (. . .) means the character would say something but can't say it or can't find words. It is different to a beat or a pause, which is when someone is not responding.

What would you like the participants to take away with them about the play?

Laura   I hope you will make your productions a celebration and an empowerment of your young people, so that they can own it, in all the complexities, difficulties and joy of it.

From workshops led by Debbie Hannan and Lisa Spirling
with notes by Helen Leblique and Shane Dempsey

The Small Hours

by Katherine Soper

It's the middle of the night, and Peebs and Epi are the only students left at school over half-term. At the end of their night, Red and Jazz are former step-siblings trying to navigate their reunion. With only a couple of hours till morning, Jaffa is trying to help Keesh finish an essay. As day breaks, Wolfie is getting up the courage to confess a secret to VJ at a party. Their choices are small yet momentous. The hours are small but feel very, very long. And when the night finally ends, the future is waiting: all of it.

Cast size
8–12

Katherine Soper's first play, *Wish List*, won the Bruntwood Prize for Playwriting and The Stage Debut Award for Best New Play, and caused her to be nominated as Most Promising Playwright at the Evening Standard Theatre Awards. It was performed at the Manchester Royal Exchange and the Royal Court Theatre, directed by Matthew Xia.

I know this much: that there is objective time, but also subjective time, the time you wear on the inside of your wrist, next to where the pulse lies.

Julian Barnes (2011, aged sixty-five)

Characters

Epi
Peebs
Jazz
Red
Jaffa
Keesh
VJ
Wolfie

The first four scenes are set on the Friday night (or, technically, Saturday morning) of May half-term.

The final scene is everything after that.

I've kept the locations vague – an island, a city, the suburbs, the sticks – in the hope that you can pin them down in locations that work well for you. Feel free to personalise any references to particular places. Maybe you want all the settings to be in a small cluster – so that 3.00 a.m.'s suburbs are the outskirts of 2.00 a.m.'s city, for instance – or maybe you want them to be far-flung.

Even where a character's gender is specified, I originally wrote all these characters gender-blind, with the intention and hope that they could be performed in any combination. Any dialogue that seems to nail down a gender for a character can easily be cut or adapted as you see fit. The only thing I wouldn't change is that **VJ** *and* **Wolfie** *should be the same sex.*

A '/' denotes an overlap of interruption of the line.

1.00 a.m.

An island.

A music practice room in a school. **Epi**'s *in his dressing gown – it's probably pretty old and tatty – and he has an instrument of some sort. In my mind it's a cello but any instrument would work – he doesn't necessarily have to be very good at it.*

Epi *prepares to play – adjusting his music stand, posture, tuning, etc. – and then starts to play a tune. Once he goes wrong a few times and can't fix it, he gives up and starts playing random notes.*

Peebs *enters, boots caked in mud, carrying a holdall. He lingers by the door silently for a bit, listening, out of* **Epi**'s *sight.*

Peebs Nah that's *definitely* not right.

Epi Hey. Hi.

Sorry were you –

He notices **Peebs**'s *clothes.*

Epi – you weren't asleep.

Peebs It's early.

Epi *wavers for a moment between whether he should keep playing or say something else.*

Peebs You play that like every weekend, I can hear you from my room.

Epi Well. Yeah. I have to practise sometime.

Beat.

Er. Where's your room?

Peebs . . . Ketterley.

Epi Oh. Obviously. Yeah.

Peebs So on weekends I'm hearing you play – I don't know, whatever that was – and in the week I've got Skinny up there listening to hardcore trance while [he] revises.

Epi . . . I can shut the window if you want.

Peebs It's fine, it's better than the trance. Not that I've got anything against that stuff, just, you know. I wouldn't choose to revise to it.

Pause.

He takes off his boots and starts hitting the sides on the floor, or any other available surface, to get the mud off.

Epi *tries to do some quiet tuning of his instrument, but the noise of* **Peebs'** *boots is a bit too distracting.*

Peebs   What time have you got?

Epi   Huh?

Peebs   Time.

Epi   Um. One.

Peebs *makes a kind of 'hmm' sound.*

Epi   What?

Peebs   No, I've got the same.

Pause.

He starts bashing his boots again.

I swear it feels like it's morning already.

Epi   Yeah?

Peebs   Doesn't it feel like it should be later to you?

Epi   Maybe. I dunno.

Peebs did you . . . like, need something?

Peebs *(indicating his boot)*   D'you mind me doing this?

Epi   I mean. Not like this is my bedroom.

Peebs   I'll try and do it in the bin.

Pause as he finds the bin and start scraping the dried mud in there instead.

I'm having an operation on Monday.

Epi   . . . OK.

Peebs   And so I was meant to be going to Ash's for the weekend so I get in, like, two days of actual half-term cos I'm gonna have to stay in bed for the rest of it.

Beat.

Epi   Right.

Peebs   But Ash runs off really quickly after Chemistry and I'm, like, what the hell you're meant to be taking me back to yours – so I end up walking around on the pitch for like *hours* I swear, holding my phone like *this* to get a signal so I can call him – and when I get through [he's] like *hi, how are you* like a total freak – and he's already on the ferry – and for ages he actually pretends he's forgotten I was even meant to be staying.

Turns out his mum's banned anyone from coming over.

Wanna know why?

Epi   Why?

Peebs   House isn't clean.

Beat.

Epi   Really?

Peebs   Yep.

Epi   . . . but you wouldn't – care / about

Peebs   Oh. I know. I know. But.

He shrugs.

Epi   That's wank.

Peebs   Why do parents care about stuff like that? Like even if it was dirty enough for me to notice, which I bet it's not, like, she should see my room – who does she think I'm even gonna tell?!

Epi   Your mum.

Peebs   What, all the way over in Texas? Good luck.

He lies down on the floor in irritation, before popping back up and pulling a jumper out of his holdall. He puts it on and lies back down.

So, yeah, I'm actually just stuck here now.

And I saw Mr Marcello in the corridor like three times and every single time he's like 'ohhh here you are again' and it's like. Get away from me.

Epi   Oh. Yeah. This is why I hide out here.

Peebs   I can't believe he lives here out of choice. It's just weird.

Beat.

Epi Y'know, no one here even told me there was gonna be another person staying when you went full-time.

Peebs I'd say I'm shocked but that's like the least shocking thing I've ever heard.

Epi I kinda got – used to it being just me.

Peebs I'm never gonna be used to this. Everywhere's so quiet it's creepy, I tried to eat in the hall once and just wanted to throw something.

Sorry if you wanted the company.

Epi I don't eat there either.

Peebs Oh.

Epi I don't, like, sit there all pathetic on my own in the hall, why would I do that?

Peebs OK, OK.

Epi Like, you do know why I'm called Epi, right?

Peebs (*as if he's only just thought about it for the first time*)   . . . no.

Epi Cos back in Year 3 I was the only one in school with an EpiPen.

Peebs *laughs for a second, before saying:*

Peebs I forgot you've been here that long! No wonder you bloody live here, mate.

Epi Uh –

He decides not to take the bait there, and carries on.

Yeah, so they did, like, a whole long thing in assembly about all the things I'm allergic to and what to do if I went into anaphylactic shock.

So I don't eat in the hall even in the week. Way too many nut particles.

Peebs Is it just nuts?

Epi And, like, everything else pretty much. Fish and milk and eggs. And bee stings.

Peebs *Milk?*

Epi . . . a bit, yeah.

Peebs Have you ever eaten any of it by accident? And, like, your face swelled up or something??

The Small Hours   563

Epi   Uh, once. In the infant school. That's why they did the whole assembly thing.

Peebs   What was it like?

Epi   I mean. Like, horrible, I never want it to happen again, but it was kinda exciting. I had a bunk bed at hospital.

It'll be fine, y'know.

Peebs   What?

Epi   Your operation.

Peebs   You don't even know what I'm getting done.

And plus you hear all that stuff about people who the anaesthetic doesn't totally take for them and they can feel everything but they can't move or speak or let the doctors know or anything.

Beat. **Epi** *doesn't quite know what to say to that.*

Peebs   It's a cyst I'm getting removed.

Epi   Oh. Right. Jesus.

Peebs   Sounds so dramatic, it's meant to be really safe.

Epi   OK.

Peebs   But like I said, everyone says that.

Beat.

I had a dream that it, like, burst. My cyst. And I got a magnifying glass or something and looked inside and I could see all my flesh in layers and all this pus bubbling inside it like a volcano or something. And it had teeth.

Epi   Teeth?

Peebs   Yeah, like, all these little baby teeth around the edges?

Epi   That's gross.

Peebs   Yeah, I know.

Epi   What *is* a cyst anyway? Is it pus inside?

Peebs   I dunno, I think it's some kind of liquid. The doctor kept calling it a *sac* when he talked about it and that just really grossed me out so I think that's why I had the dream.

Epi   Y'know my dad had about five different operations last year. And he was actually pretty OK. Apparently they're, nurses are like trained to be really good before operations, especially if you tell them you're worried.

Beat.

Peebs   OK.

Epi   Dunno if that's helpful.

Peebs   I'm not actually worried.

Epi   You kinda sounded like you were.

Peebs   I'm not.

Just I can't believe I'm basically not gonna get a half-term now.

Epi   Maybe everyone will come and visit you.

Peebs   Would you come back here, of your own free will, once you got to the mainland for a week?

Epi   . . . maybe not.

Peebs   Yeah.

Pause.

Epi   What's Texas like?

Peebs   Hot. I can't really go out much there cos I burn really easily even with suncream.

I went to NASA last time though, that was cool.

Epi   You can drive when you're sixteen over there.

Peebs   Yeah.

Epi   Do you reckon if one of us got a car when we turn seventeen they'd let us keep it here? And like . . . go places?

Peebs   Where would you go though? The stone circles? Yaaaay. Not like I've seen those five million times already.

Beat.

Not sure what else to do, **Epi** *distracts himself with his instrument. He plays the song he was playing at the start of the scene – times it on his phone – and it only lasts about twenty seconds, if that. He looks at the timer, dispirited.*

Epi   I don't think I'm ever gonna finish this.

Peebs   What?

Epi   Composition unit. Like I thought I might get it done tonight cos I couldn't get to sleep, but. Three minutes is actually ages. Like if you actually time it, it's so long.

Peebs   Yeah.

So what're you gonna do?

Epi   I should probably just take some Sominex and try and get to sleep.

He starts to put his instrument away. Once he's finished and is about to leave:

Nice talking to you, Peebs.

Beat.

Peebs   Yeah. Yeah.

. . . might actually go for a smoke, thinking about it.

He starts pulling his boots on again.

They come out into the open air.

Peebs *starts to fish a cigarette out of a crumpled pack somewhere in his pocket.*

Peebs   Hang on, you're not allergic to smoke, are you?

Epi   . . . no.

Peebs   OK, just checking before you start, like, foaming at the mouth or whatever.

Epi   I don't have *rabies*.

Peebs (*laughing*)   Oh yeah! Yeah, I'm thinking of rabies.

Comfortable pause.

Where do your parents live again?

Epi   Er. China.

Peebs   Wow.

Epi   Yeah.

Peebs   . . . do you wish you'd moved there too?

Epi   Um. Kinda just think he should have stayed here in the first place.

Peebs   Yeah.

Same.

Beat.

If I have kids, I would never do that to them. Ever. Just fuck off and like . . .

He breaks off, surprised by himself. He's said all this with such force that both of them are a bit taken aback.

So he checks his phone, holding it out to try and find signal.

You probably wanna sleep.

Epi   I mean. Yeah, but.

If I don't sleep through tomorrow I might as well, I dunno – go down to the sea. Not that there's anything interesting out there but. Could try and flag down a ferry.

Peebs   Tomorrow?

Epi   Yeah.

Peebs   . . . All right. Let's do that.

Epi   OK.

Peebs   My door's the one right by the fire escape. Just bang really loudly if I don't hear.

Epi   OK. Yeah. I'll do that.

He leaves.

Peebs *tries again with the lighter – no dice. He sighs a bit, and plonks himself down.*

He might feel his cyst, wherever it is.

He checks his phone . . . nothing doing there either.

Time passes slowly.

2.00 a.m.

A city.

Red *and* **Jazz** *are walking together, eating chips.*

Red   You know who's banging now?

Jazz   Who?

Red   Col and Hannah.

Jazz   NO. Are you shitting me? Oh my God.

. . . I shared a *sofa* with them!

Red   What, at his house?

Jazz   Yeah!

Red   Covered in jizz now.

Jazz   NO. Oh my God. How did – this doesn't compute, this makes literally no sense to me.

Red   Yeah, but they don't know I know, they think it's some big secret, so – shh.

Jazz   Ugh. Sorry, I need to go and delete this whole conversation from my brain or I'm gonna have horrible disturbing dreams later.

Red   You're so welcome.

Beat.

Jazz   This is me.

Red   This is – oh OK.

I didn't know we were –

Wait, is your dad in?

Jazz   No, he's – on a date, I think.

Red   Oh. Right.

Can I see your digs?

Jazz   – sure. Yeah.

She lets **Red** *into her bedroom.*

Red   You got your own private loo?!

Jazz   Yeah.

Red   That's mad.

Jazz   Why?

Red   You don't even have to have, like, morning strategy now.

Jazz   Ohhh. Yeah, forgot about that.

Red   Give us a look then.

She checks out **Jazz**'s *ensuite.*

Red   How's Papa bear?

Jazz   Yeah, he's all right.

Red   Do you think he'd mind if I called him Papa bear?

Jazz   He'd probably think it was weird that you decided to start now.

Red *laughs.*

Red   Yeah.

On a date, eh?

Must be having a good night.

Jazz *shrugs.*

Pause.

Red   Where has he taken her, Pryzm?

Jazz   I don't, like, *ask* him what he's doing.

Red   I bet you if we go down there now – it's still open, we'll find them, like, plastered on the ground next to one of the ambulances.

Jazz *doesn't find this as funny as* **Red** *expects her to.*

Beat as **Red** *tries to think of something else to talk about.*

Red   You know the last time we saw each other was that time in Subway.

Jazz   – oh yeah!

Red   Six months ago.

Jazz   Was it actually six months?

Red   Yeah. It was November.

Jazz   Wow.

Red   I feel, like, completely different now.

Jazz   Your hair is different.

Red   Yeah. Shouldn't even be called Red any more.

Y'know, Mum says that if you and Milla still want her to cut your hair you can just pop round and she'll do it.

Jazz Would that – ?

Red Free, obviously.

I dunno, I think she'd like to see you.

Pause. She picks up a medal that's carefully nestled somewhere in **Jazz**'s *room.*

Red This is fun, when'd you win this?

Jazz Last term.

Red *puts it on.*

Red Does it suit me?

Jazz Um –

Red I'm kidding.

Takes it off, gives it back.

Still running then.

Jazz Yeah. Yeah. Mostly long distance now.

Red That's good.

Jazz I'm going to this sports camp thing for it.

Red Really? In summer?

Jazz Yeah.

Red OK.

Jazz The people who run it came to the, um, the event I won, and they asked if I wanted to come.

Red Oh, right.

Well done!

Jazz Thanks.

Red What do you do at camps like that? Just . . . train really hard all day?

Jazz I guess so, that's what they're for.

Red What do you do when it rains?

Jazz   Same thing.

Red   Can I come?

Beat.

Jazz   . . .

Red   You don't want me to. That's fine.

Jazz   No, like . . .

Why d'you say stuff like that?

Red   I dunno.

Jazz   You do, you always get this weird look. Like you know you're taking the piss.

Red   I think I just – really enjoy being all – you know how you sometimes get this vision of something you *could* do or say? And it's really rude or inappropriate?

Jazz   . . . yeah . . .

Red   I just do it. I can't help it. Like whatsherface, Tanya from year below was walking down the corridor this week balancing loads of things on her and I just had this vision of like – batting the stuff out of her hands.

So I just did it. And she was really pissed off about it, like, obviously, and on one hand I felt really bad cos it was such a dick move but then I also kinda couldn't stop laughing cos somehow I also found it really funny.

She might even laugh in the telling.

Jazz   And what happened?

Red   Nothing. Got put on report again.

Jazz   Oh. Right.

Red   What?

Jazz   Nothing.

Just thought you were getting better is all.

Red   Oh my God, Jazz. You literally sound like my teacher right now.

Jazz   All right, all right.

Red   Why do you think I wanna hear comments like that? From you?

Jazz   Red –

Red   No –

Jazz   C'mere –

Red   Oh my God – no – like – don't bloody *hug me* now –

Jazz   You wanna wear my medal? Will that help?

Red   Don't be stupid, I don't actually want it.

Jazz   Go on.

Red   No. Fuck off.

Jazz   Hey.

Red   No, just seriously do not touch me right now when I asked you not to touch me, OK?

Jazz   . . . you're a real dick you know that?

Red   Fucking –

Jazz   I'd forgotten what a dick you are / but you really are.

Red   You literally have no idea what you're talking about, you're not even around anymore so don't go fucking telling me *I'm* a dick all right – I am having to literally stop myself from laying into you right now so don't / *push* me –

Jazz (*hands up*)   OK! OK OK!

Pause.

Red   Oh my *days*.

I should probably go cos I still feel like I'm gonna punch something or – I'm just kinda (*does some sort of gesture to mean 'freaking out'*) right now.

Jazz   Maybe you need to – breathe –

Like really deep and slow – / like

Red   *I know how to breathe!*

Jazz *demonstrates.* **Red** *manages to join in.*

Pause.

Red   If you weren't family I would actually have hit you.

Jazz   Yeah, well, I'd probably have hit you back, wouldn't I?

Red   You'd have tried.

All that running and I swear you've not got any muscles.

Pause.

Jazz, I'm just telling you in advance I reckon I might need to vom in your nice toilet later.

Jazz   Oh. Was it the ke / bab?

Red   Dunno. Don't matter.

Jazz   D'you want some water?

Red *shakes her head.*

Pause.

Red   Milla's not here.

Jazz   Yeah, she's proper cabin crew now. So she's always in Dubai or asleep.

Red   Cool.

She's doing what she wanted.

Jazz   Yeah. They just wouldn't take her till she was twenty-one cos she wouldn't have been allowed to serve drinks.

'S really quiet with just me here though.

Red   Yeah. I bet.

Jazz, I don't get your dad. I don't get loving someone that much – and just . . . like a year ago today, I looked on my phone, a year ago today we were all watching *Gladiator* – you, me, Milla, my mum and your dad. And now it's a year later and everything's shit and I don't know why.

Jazz   Red . . .

Red   Why would he just cut and run. For no reason.

Jazz *shrugs.*

Red   Don't just shrug. Is that it, just –

She does a caricatured version of **Jazz***'s shrug.*

Jazz I dunno. Maybe you should talk to Milla about this.

Red Well I never see Milla anymore, do I, sounds like I'll never see her again at this rate, and I'm not talking to her, am I, I'm talking to you 'so I'm asking *you, Jazz*, what do *you* think?

Jazz But like. . .they're divorced. That's it. We can't, like, do anything about it, so it's not worth me thinking anything.

Red Really.

Jazz I dunno what you want me to say.

I mean – if I'm honest –

I kind of saw it coming.

Beat.

Red OK.

Jazz Sorry if that –

Red No, clearly I'm just stupid. Clearly.

Pause.

Why'd you see it coming?

Jazz Er.

Don't go mad when I say this, OK?

I, uh, saw my dad's porn.

Beat.

Red . . . right.

Right.

Jazz And, like, on its own that doesn't mean anything, like it's gross but, whatever, just – I borrowed his laptop for my PE presentation because it was when PowerPoint kept crashing on the main computer –

Red When? When was this?

Jazz Ages ago. I dunno. Like – September? I dunno. It was only the one time but it was like twenty sites of this . . . teen girl stuff.

*She sees **Red**'s reaction and backtracks.*

Nothing weird, not like, *kids* – Jesus – but like – 'barely legal' or whatever.

So.

Red   Shit.

Jazz   Mmm.

Red   You're really calm about this, mate, how are you more calm about this than about Col and Hannah?!

Jazz   Cos I've kind of bleached it out of my brain. I just don't think about it.

Red   That kind of.

Kind of puts everything in a different . . . light, I guess.

Pause.

Shit.

Jazz   I'm really sorry but – I have to get to sleep really soon.

I'm trying to get up early every morning to run.

Red   Where?

Jazz   Just around. Past the station, down to the green and back.

Red   OK.

Jazz   It's shit but. I kind of have to get in the habit, the camp people said I should.

Red   So what should I do?

Beat. **Jazz** *takes a bit too long to make the connection.*

Jazz   You can sleep here too if you want.

Red   Nah. It's fine.

Jazz   You can have Milla's bed.

Red   It's fine.

It doesn't count when I make you ask, y'know?

Jazz *tries to think of a helpful response but before she can:*

Red   Can I have some water before I go? Just in case I feel – [sick] again on the way back.

Jazz   Oh – one sec –

She finds her sports bottle and hands it to **Red**, *who takes a long slug.*

She holds on to the bottle for a moment, taking in the room again.

Red   My mum would *love* this place, y'know.

Beat.

Jazz   Yeah.

Milla's bed's still there. It's up to you.

Red   I'm just gonna stay here for like . . . five more seconds.

She stands there longer than that.

Time passes slowly.

3.00 a.m.

The suburbs.

Keesh *and* **Jaffa**. **Jaffa** *is playing a video game;* **Keesh** *is advising.*

Jaffa   Hang on, can I use my sniper here?

Keesh   Nah your play style's a bit – up close for a sniper. They take ages to reload as / well

Jaffa   OK, help! –

Keesh   Kite them. Kite them.

Jaffa   *How?*

Keesh   This way. No not – there are enemies that way – back to where you were at the start. You have to run or / they'll –

Jaffa *dies.*

Jaffa   *Nooooo.*

Keesh   Yeah. That happens.

Jaffa   I'm gonna be so annoyed if it takes me back like ten minutes . . .

He shakes his hands around, getting ready to play again while the game loads their last autosave.

OK. Cool.

Keesh   Right – so – this you can do.

Jaffa   Yeah.

A small silence as they're both concentrating, transfixed.

Keesh   You can / kite –

Jaffa   Yeah – I know –

Pause.

Keesh   Cos you don't wanna be using a pistol when you're right up close, you wanna switch to shotgun.

Jaffa   OK . . .

Keesh   And you wanna get into a rhythm of, like, shotgun, *bam*, once or twice, and then you *run away* and they have to chase after you while you cool down, cos otherwise they'll just melee on you, OK?

Jaffa   Right –

Keesh   So – close up – shotgun – RUN AWAY RUN AWAY –

Jaffa   I'm doing it, the controls are all – screwy –

Keesh   Yes! Yes! So just check there's nobody –

Jaffa   One more over there –

Keesh   – no don't bother with – just pistol him –

Amazing. OK so now –

Jaffa   Shh shh shh shh shh –

He reads or listens to something new happening in the game.

What does that mean?

Keesh   You can go back to the underground passage and save her or you can keep going this way and save Julius and he replaces Laya in your party.

Jaffa   Wait, seriously?

Keesh   Yeah, it's like the first big choice you have to make.

Jaffa   So if I go and help Laya I can't actually do the rest of the quest?

Keesh   Yeah.

Jaffa   And if I leave her she's dead? For real?

Keesh   Yeah.

Jaffa   For the whole game?

Keesh Yeah.

Jaffa Jeeeesus.

So what happens if I save her not Julius?

Keesh Nobody from his tribe will help you the whole rest of the game. They'll just get in your face about it.

Jaffa OK. Is that . . . how much help would they / actually

Keesh No no no I can't tell you, you just have to choose with what you know now.

A pause while **Jaffa** *mulls.*

Jaffa That's not a fair choice though. In real life there'd be a way to do both cos I could just / send –

Keesh Yeah but in real life you wouldn't be able to spend all this time thinking about it, you'd just have to decide in the moment, so it's not like they're going for realism. In real life no one would just come up and give you the choice between A and B.

Jaffa OK, here we go. Keesh, are you gonna – A) play video games all night or B) do your essay?

Keesh Oh my God just cos you got to a hard bit.

Jaffa *Keesh.* It's 3.00 a.m.

Keesh *looks at her watch, doesn't want to believe it, and compares it to* **Jaffa***'s. But they both say the same time.*

Keesh That did *not* feel like four hours.

Jaffa I know.

He gets his bag, and dumps out an improbable number of energy drinks.

Keesh Thing is though.

Jaffa What?

Keesh I have time, I've got the whole of this week.

Jaffa Yeah, except she wants you to post it to her for Monday.

Keesh (*knowing this is a pathetic excuse*)   I don't have a big enough envelope.

Jaffa *reaches inside his bag, brings out a big enough envelope.*

Jaffa I *brought* you a bloody envelope.

Keesh How did you do that?

Jaffa Magic.

He takes an energy drink and opens it.

Come on. Down it.

Keesh *reluctantly does the same.*

Keesh What's she actually gonna do though? Like, send bailiffs over? It's half-term.

Jaffa She will ring up your house. And she'll ring early enough that you're still asleep and your mum'll bring the phone to you in bed and you'll have to try and sound like you haven't just woken up. And that *never works.*

Keesh That just sounds kinda funny to me.

Jaffa And she'll use it as an excuse to dick on you when you get back.

Beat.

I promise you'll feel better once you do it.

Keesh Oh my God. Jaffa. Shut up. Look.

Beat.

This is gonna sound like an excuse.

Jaffa . . . right.

Keesh It's really hard to make myself start when I'll just put loads of effort in and then end up getting like four out of forty like last time. It's all too big and scary now.

You know she didn't even, like, ask me permission before she read all of it out to the class?

Jaffa She probably knew you'd say no.

Keesh Yeah. I shoulda stuck a copyright on it or something. Then I could sue her.

Beat.

They treat us like shit for being in bottom set.

Jaffa Keesh . . .

Keesh They do! You're not there, they treat us like shit. Or she does, at least.

And I wouldn't be so crap at it if she was a better teacher anyway. Like you remember when I went to go talk to her after we got results for the Russia paper –

Jaffa *Fuck me*, the Russia paper –

Keesh And she were, like 'you got the lowest result in the year, lower than the students who have, English as a second language' and I wanted to be, like, yeah, whose fault is that? It's not like they'd even have let me take History if they knew I were gonna do that bad.

And she's *so nice* to you.

Jaffa I know. It's crap.

But y'know my last report from her was literally copy–pasted from someone else's – she called me a she halfway through.

Keesh Really?

Jaffa Yeah. 'He is a pleasant and polite pupil who has made satisfactory efforts in History this term. He has learnt to explain her answers and develop them into an argument.'

Keesh 'Pleasant and polite'.

Jaffa Yeah, I *know*.

Keesh Could be worse, I was 'lively'.

Beat.

Jaffa You want me to put some bird poo in her pigeonhole?

Keesh *can genuinely consider this, or pretend to.*

Keesh Nah you're all right.

Jaffa Cos I could. Just write your essay, get a bird to do one on it, then attach a little note saying 'it's already been shat on, so you don't have to'.

Beat.

Keesh I just want one night not thinking about it, is all.

Jaffa Didn't you take the night off from it, like, every single night last week?

Keesh   Yeah but I were still thinking about it – so the week just ran away from me – and I had this, like, cold sweat on the whole time from thinking about it. Like feel my hand right now.

Jaffa   I'm not gonna feel your hand.

Beat.

I didn't go to Mog's thing tonight. Cos you said you wanted help.

Keesh   You can get off with Mog anytime though.

Jaffa   Yeah, I *definitely* can't.

Pause.

'Specially since now people will probably start going on again about *us* being together.

Keesh (*unable to help herself*)   I mean, if you keep bringing me romantic gifts like envelopes, what are people s'posed to think?

Sorry.

I can leave if you want.

Jaffa   Yeah, well, you're here now, aren't you.

Pause.

I'm gonna get some food.

He heads out.

Keesh *tries to get herself to focus on her history textbook, but gives up after a few moments and chucks it away angrily.*

She hears **Jaffa** *arguing downstairs with his mum. Freezes a bit to try and make out what they're saying but can't.*

She goes and retrieves the textbook, trying to smooth it out where it got creased. Near where it landed, she spots a framed photograph, lying face down. She stretches to pick it up and look at it – then laughs out loud.

Jaffa *comes back with a plastic bag and empties about five packs of strawberry sugar laces out of it.*

Keesh   Jaffa is that *you*?!

Jaffa   Oh – gimme that back.

Keesh   That is *priceless* – why've you got it up / here?!

Jaffa   *Give* it – my mum were up here last night being, like, 'Remember this little boy? What happened to him?'

Keesh   Why? I'd have thought she'd be, like, oh, you're doing so well.

Jaffa   I dunno. I think she thought I were just gonna stay a baby forever.

Keesh   Really?

Jaffa   Well. I think that's it. That's how I feel with the twins, I'm still surprised they can walk.

Keesh   Yeah that's creepy.

Beat.

Did we wake your mum up?

Jaffa   Er – yeah.

Keesh (*whispering*)   Sorry.

Jaffa   It's fine.

Keesh (*maybe even whispering still, in a big fake stage-whisper*)   I've like completely ruined your night.

Jaffa   No.

Beat.

Keesh   What's your mum worried about?

Jaffa   Uh.

Keesh   Is it to do with the time she was talking to Lou's mum and said she was worried I was rubbing off on you?

Jaffa   . . . I think she's just annoyed because the twins wake her up at like six every day anyway.

Keesh   Has she said anything like that to you about me?

Jaffa   She does like you, I promise. It's loads of other stuff too.

Keesh   . . .

She stares at **Jaffa** *like she doesn't believe him. Because she doesn't.*

But she lets it slide.

Keesh   OK.

She takes a moment looking at the photo, chewing on a strawberry lace.

I can't stop looking at your fringe!

Jaffa   Shut up.

Keesh   Is this actually from 2008?

Jaffa   Uh –

Keesh *turns the photo round to show* **Jaffa** *the date on the back.*

Jaffa   Guess so.

Keesh   Holy shit.

I don't even remember 2008. Or I sort of do but I mostly don't. It's just like bits and pieces and random moments, not a proper, like, story.

Jaffa   That's what's wrong with your history essays.

Keesh   Is it?

Jaffa   I dunno. Maybe.

Keesh   I'm worried about doing it and now I'm worried about seeing your mum in the morning too. She'll be mad I kept you up all night.

Beat.

Do you know what you're gonna choose?

Jaffa   Do you know what *you're* gonna choose?

Keesh   Yeah, well, there's a difference between this (*pointing at her essay*) and this. (*Pointing at the console.*)

Jaffa   ?

Keesh   *You* can always do another play-through after and make the other choice.

Time passes slowly.

4.00 a.m.

The sticks.

A house party.

VJ   Wolfie! Hide me.

Wolfie – I –

VJ You have to hide me from Tuss. Please. I'll explain later. Help me, Wolfie, you're my only hope.

Wolfie Upstairs loo – window in back – through that, onto the roof.

Beat.

Maybe lock it behind us.

And they're off. They rush through to the loo past various obstacles, and climb out of the window in a really convoluted, difficult way, maybe one having to push the other through.

But they make it, and they emerge onto the roof. **VJ** *tries to recover.*

VJ Oh my God. OK.

Wolfie VJ.

VJ Wow.

Wolfie VJ! Can you still hear Tuss?

They both freeze and listen.

VJ I think we're safe.

Beat.

I never even knew this existed.

Wolfie Yeah, I – I've come here a few times.

What's Tuss want with you?

VJ Uhhh – knows I'm at the point of embarrassing myself.

Wolfie Ah.

VJ I knew you wouldn't judge me. Don't want the same thing to happen again.

I just need to – like – sober up a bit. Fresh air is good.

Beat. She tries to make out the landscape, squinting.

You can't actually see anything.

Wolfie Yeah. I mean it'd just be trees anyway.

VJ Ugh. Yeah.

What time is it now?

Wolfie   Uh. Four. Ish.

VJ   First bus in – six hours.

I'm gonna have to stay awake or I'll just sleep through it.

Wolfie   My mum could give you a lift back with me.

I dunno, like, if you want.

VJ   Nah, don't worry. It's such an awkward place to get to.

Wolfie   I guess.

VJ   And I'm gonna have an amazing bus nap.

Beat.

Y'know, this conversation is like my last bit of human contact with a sane person for a week.

Wolfie   Is it?

VJ   Oh yeah. Once I get home, family time all the time.

Pause as **Wolfie** *visibly considers saying one thing – then changes her mind.*

Wolfie   I shoulda brought my jacket out here. I always forget cos I think it's gonna be warm.

I swear this is like the worst party so far. Ever since Lee did the shit in the bath I worry about someone doing that again.

VJ   Wasn't Lee.

Wolfie   Oh, *sure* –

VJ   Nah, he stepped up later when I had a fit about no one owning up and he was like 'VJ I'll clean it up but if I clean it up no one's allowed to say I did it' so I'm not gonna slander him.

Wolfie   Aw. OK.

So . . . we're staying up here till ten?

VJ   We should have got food, right?

Wolfie   I can go find all that cake you brought.

VJ   Nah. Stay here. Sit.

Wolfie *doesn't have to be told more than that.*

Pause.

VJ My mum always gives me so much stuff to bring cos she's worried I'll look, I dunno, ungrateful.

Wolfie I love your mum.

VJ *makes a long, sceptical 'hmmmmm' noise.*

Wolfie What?

VJ – no, nothing.

She just hates me hanging around and being under her feet but then if I want to go to a party so I can get *out* from under her feet she starts moaning about driving me places and makes all this cake for no reason cos she cares more about what people think of her as a mum than what I actually want.

Wolfie *You* didn't wanna come.

VJ Well. I wanted to be allowed to come. And even something this boring is better than staying home.

Wolfie Do you remember that time when Mac had a party and then afterwards sent us all like / this –

VJ Like a fucking *bill*! I know! And Alina left her purse behind and he took the money she 'owed' him out of it before giving it back to her.

Wolfie Did he actually?

VJ Yeah.

Wolfie What a prick.

VJ You know what he is?

Wolfie He's / rubbo.

VJ Rubbo. So rubbo.

I can't wait for the day I don't have to see any of them again.

Wolfie Really?

VJ *shrugs.*

Wolfie That's – Veej, that's really sad.

VJ No, I just – I don't actually think I'd hang out with most of them if we weren't. You know. Living here.

Wolfie   Right.

VJ   I don't mean you, but – most people here are just – kind of shit. Even my parents. Everything people care about is shit.

Wolfie   Err, like what?

VJ   Not you. But. They're fine just living here, in a place in the middle of nowhere where no one's actually doing anything, they're just *raising children*. They don't actually care about anything. And everyone we know is just gonna end up becoming their parents – or worse – and they don't think there's anything wrong with that.

Wolfie   That's their choice though.

VJ   I know. I know. But for me, personally, for *me*, like, the idea of staying here any longer than I have to or even coming back here ever is – feels like death to me.

Wolfie   OK. Wow.

VJ   Sorry. Bit morbid.

Wolfie   No I get it, I do get that, it's –

I think you're, I guess, you're clever and so it makes sense. That you feel like that.

VJ   You think I'm clever?

Wolfie   Err, you know you are.

VJ *bumps shoulders with* **Wolfie** *in a companionable way, as she gets a pen from her pocket.*

VJ   Ahh, Wolfie. You can stay.

She starts writing her name, doodling little drawings on the roof.

I dunno. Like . . . I think I just wanna do something different, I don't wanna do things the way everyone else is doing them but I don't know how and I don't know what I even mean.

Beat.

Wolfie   I – sometimes feel like –

I get this weird feeling that I've been in the same clothes so long that I'm bursting out of them like the Hulk and when I'm at school I'm like – huge and all of the Year 7s are miniature? And my arms are gonna have to start poking out of the windows and my head's gonna be mashed up against the ceiling cos I'm too – huge for all of it.

VJ *is silent, but in a way that means she gets it.*

Wolfie   I never talk about this.

VJ   Yeah?

Wolfie   Well, bit of a downer isn't it.

VJ   No. It's not.

Pause. She offers the pen to **Wolfie** *– who takes it.*

She writes her own name on the roof, and the date.

Finally – studiously not looking at **VJ** *–* **Wolfie** *calls* **VJ** *by her real name.* **VJ** *looks at* **Wolfie***, slightly surprised by this.*

VJ   Yeah?

Wolfie   Sorry I just was gonna say – earlier –

I think you're great, you know.

I've liked you for ages, I think you're brilliant.

Sorry.

Pause.

VJ   Right.

Wolfie   You're not . . .

I probably shouldn't have said anything.

VJ   No, it's fine.

Wolfie   I think I thought that maybe you thought, that time, when I was really drunk and I wouldn't talk to you, that you thought I was being a prick and I just wanted you to know that I wasn't, that I, um, that I actually really like you.

Beat.

Sorry I've just been building up to that for . . .

Huh.

Pause.

We good?

VJ   Yeah, of course! Of course we are.

She carefully envelopes **Wolfie** *into a hug.*

VJ   All right?

Beat.

Wolfie   Such a shit party.

VJ   I know. The fucking worst.

Pause. **Wolfie** *hears noises from inside the house.*

Wolfie   Are people leaving?

VJ   No. They're just waking up.

5.00 a.m. . . .

Jaffa   I just about make a decision, though I keep a save just in case
I wanna go back.

Peebs   Me and Epi wander round the beaches and the stone circles a bit.

Epi   It's kinda shit but kinda fun.

Wolfie   I kinda half do my homework and half watch TV even though
there's nowt on on Sundays –

Keesh   I just think it's not fair to have to wake up this early to go to
school.

Peebs   I know I should make a revision plan but then I look at all these
lovely months stretching out on the calendar, and . . .

Red   Prom is OK. Even though my mum nags at me for choosing the
wrong size shoes.

Wolfie   Results are . . . fine.

Epi   Sort of what I expected.

Keesh (*to* **Jaffa**)   That's the thing, I keep thinking about how I might
just never see you again after September.

VJ   After the first seminar I drag everyone to the pub with me cos I'm
like 'My people! People who are like me!'

Jazz *finishes a run, checks her stopwatch – her time isn't good enough.*

Jazz   Fuck.

Keesh   We try and have each other's backs all the time cos it's either us
against customers or us against the area manager.

Jaffa I'm lugging a load of legal texts through the snow and I just keep on going: two more years and this is done.

Epi I literally dream about exams now. I dreamt I was taking one and then actually had to wake up and go and take one.

They turn twenty-one.

Jazz I bust my knee – not allowed to run for months – and I have way too much time to think.

Wolfie Way too much time per job application, like, Jesus Christ.

Jazz And I start thinking, like, maybe this is a sign I should quit while I'm ahead.

Epi I needed a stamp, which feels so old-timey to say –

VJ We spend hours mapping glacial valleys –

Epi – and she peeled one off and stuck it on my nose –

VJ – but once it's dark I keep looking at the lake stretching out for miles –

Epi – and I could feel myself going really really red –

VJ – and I know it's dangerous, but doggy paddling into the pitch-black coldness of it is incredible.

Epi – and that's when I knew.

Keesh There are a few of us that, if we're all together when we're closing, we put on dance music when we clean –

Peebs My housemate and me message each other every morning like 'urrrrrrrrr I don't want to get out of bed' which is a weirdly fun ritual.

Keesh – and then I'll put the same song on my phone when I walk back – and the song'll follow me home – and put me to sleep.

Jaffa So I told myself: I work as hard as I can and either I A) get on a Legal Practice Course or B) I don't. And if I don't, I'll do something else.

Red I'm trying to keep up with things like laundry and stuff but I keep seeing things on my floor. I'm not sure what they are.

Jazz Milla really faintly tells me I'm being sensible, all the way from Abu Dhabi.

VJ This other geoscientist tells me I'm scaremongering and I have to stop myself snatching his stupid mug and smashing it over his head.

Wolfie   I'm just zoning out while my photocopies print and suddenly it hits me: I was really brave.

VJ   When I quit, on my last day I go and find that guy's mug – write 'PRICK' on the bottom of it in capital letters.

Wolfie   I spent so long thinking I shouldn't have said anything to her when actually I was really fucking brave.

VJ   And now I've left I wanna do something genuinely important to, like, justify that.

Jazz   I go and help my dad move house. Again. And after loads of comments about my knee –

Red   And the um the annoying thing is when I have to stop using any social media at all, because it's being monitored.

Jazz   – which I'd already asked him to shut up about – I just delete his number for a bit.

– We're looking for a donor and we want someone we know.

Peebs   I might have had too much to drink but that feels like something I could . . . definitely do.

Keesh   At least when we get made redundant, we all get made redundant together. The end of my last shift is 11.00 a.m. in the middle of July, and I buy myself a box of ice lollies and eat them on the way home.

Of course everyone's like 'this isn't the end for people working in retail' but. Kind of only a matter of time at this point.

Jaffa   The twins come visit me in London and I take the day off and I feel . . . I can't believe how much more energy they have than me. I sort of thought they'd get older but I'd stay the same age.

– If you don't come out of the road I'm gonna have to call someone.

Red   It's fine, I'm walking / to –

– You can't walk to Dover. / You can't walk all the way there.

Red   SSSSSHHHHHH. Shut up. Look – I just – I can't talk about it because / I'm being –

– I just need to – I just want to call someone to make sure you're safe.

I promise no one is listening to this.

Wolfie   I take myself to Spain and I take bottles of water and go on really long walks where I feel too . . . small for all of it.

Keesh   I go to see an eighteen and they wave me through and I have this amazing rush like I've got away with something – then I remember, I'm twenty-seven.

Peebs   I come and see her occasionally – not stepping on anyone's toes, but, occasionally – and when she was about four I held her up to the mirror and was like – look, OK, you can see you've got my nose, my face shape, my eye-crinkles.

Then I see her a year later and she's got none of those!

They turn thirty.

Epi   The day before I turn thirty my dad calls me and – well, tells me what the doctors have said, doesn't actually ask me to come but I – something comes over me and I know I have to step up.

Wolfie   When I shake her hand for the first time it's like – oh shit. That's it. That feeling again. Hello.

Epi   The whole thing lasts four months.

Wolfie   Settling in for the long run.

Epi   And then I'm ordering flowers, calling executors, selling his flat, closing the door for the last time and handing over the keys –

Wolfie   I'm terrified but really fucking happy to feel like this again.

Epi   – and I circle back to Heathrow.

Red   When I come home my mum's really happy to be able to give me a haircut, and I want to make a joke about keeping the scissors away but . . .

– What have you been up to since the last time I saw you?

Keesh   Oh. Hm. Er.

Well this morning I saw a really good dog.

Jazz   Hey.

Red *takes* **Jazz***'s hand, noting a ring.*

Jazz   Oh! Yeah. Um. A few years ago.

Jaffa   I buy my mum dinner for her sixtieth, which is great, I'm happy I can do that, and I feel genuinely grateful to her that she gave me so much help to get to that point.

VJ   It's not about not noticing anything day to day – that's not what it's about – like when you're in a plane you don't notice how fast you're going do you, you can only sense acceleration you can't sense velocity –

– V, I kinda just want to watch the film.

VJ   Sorry. It's just on my mind. I'll be quiet.

Red   I think you think I disappear when you don't see me. But I don't. Every second you live, when you're having your cup of tea in the morning and watching telly, I'm living that too. You just don't see it.

Jazz   OK.

– There's so much less money in that.

Jaffa   I know. But it's community-oriented.

And it's not that I don't like what I do, in loads of ways it's great, it's . . . just it's been years now, and . . .

I don't know why my feelings changed, but they did.

– . . .

Jaffa   Mum.

– What?

Jaffa   Are you angry with me?

– Of course not. Why would I be angry?

Jaffa   . . .

Keesh   I'm saving up. I'm trying to be really tight with myself and save it up right now.

VJ   Building a climate model for the next year is pretty straightforward.

Keesh   Cos I don't know what I'll need it for.

VJ   Building one for the next hundred years creates uncertainties.

Keesh   But if there aren't any emergencies I might be able to spend it on something good.

Jazz   You don't get it, like . . . the idea of having kids makes me feel terrified.

– Why?

Jazz   Loads of reasons.

– . . . so that's it, then.

Jazz   I'm sorry.

– What are you actually worried about?

Epi   Um.

I guess. That everything in the future will be just 'more of the same'. Or that things might get worse.

I don't think about it for a while and then a year's gone by and I'm the same. And then a year goes by and –

They turn forty.

Peebs   Jude corners me at her parents' wedding anniversary and asks what I do when I'm not visiting.

Jazz   This is what I do when I feel really pissed off and I need some space:

Peebs   I kind of scramble to think over the past month or year.

Jazz   I figure out a circular route that feels like it'll take a good long time.

Peebs   It feels like too much effort to explain tiny things that don't feel that important after they're done.

Jazz   But then every time I do it, it takes less time and the circle gets smaller.

Peebs   So I say, I deal with people's problems and then I mostly just go to the pub. And she doesn't respond to that, just keeps eating her candyfloss in a kinda sulky way.

Jazz   It takes less time to get back to the roads and squares I've already seen.

Peebs   She just says 'you've got fatter since last year', which, I almost wave my hands spookily and say 'IT'LL HAPPEN TO YOU TOO!' but I don't wanna give her a complex.

Jazz   Are you angry I didn't come and see you when you were – ?

Red   – oh.

No. You wouldn't have been allowed to.

It woulda been nice if you'd asked.

But it was a long time ago now.

– But what I mean is, how did you just break off from what you were doing like that? How were you brave enough?

Jaffa   Why are you asking me this?

– I dunno. I'm on a track and I feel like it's too late for me to do anything different.

Jaffa   You're *thirty*. Both of you are babies.

Red *takes* **Jazz***'s hand – no ring.*

Jazz   Oh – yeah.

Red   I'm sorry.

Peebs   Jude's doing a long-distance degree and when I'm invited over for Seder she won't shut up about asteroid probe-mining resources. And I love her but I *just don't find it interesting.*

Red   I held off for a while because I was worried I'd pass something on, but she's not me. She's herself. And the other two are so normal it's scary, so. What can you do.

Peebs   And then she glares at me and says 'oh well I expect that sort of response from people like you' and I'm sorry? People like me? I have no idea what the hell she means by that.

Keesh   . . . St Petersburg isn't as cold as I thought it would be.

They turn fifty.

VJ   One of my colleagues, one of my friends, we're troubleshooting some code and he makes me a cup of coffee just when I need it and . . . I don't know. I just look at him differently.

Epi   I go back to the island and sit on the beach near where my school used to be and take some pictures. And I have a conversation in my head with my dad about how he missed out by being in Beijing the whole time.

Jazz   Do you think it's our parents? Why it's both of us got divorced? And Milla?

Red   . . .

No.

Jazz   Do you want to go for a run?

A walk?

Red   Yeah, let's do that.

They turn sixty.

– Are you actually starting a herb garden? Both of you?

Wolfie   Well. It's what my parents did in *their* sixties.

– That's cos they were retired. And they didn't have to do it in a dome.

– (*to* **Epi***, about an instrument*)   You used to play, didn't you?

– Did you?!

Epi   Uhh. Yes.

Maybe he even plays a few notes again.

Still can. Still got the muscle memory.

Jaffa   The city I was born near declares bankruptcy and it feels like I just popped out to the shops, left the back door open, and came back to find everything burnt to the ground.

– Would you go back if you could?

Peebs   Um.

Hm.

VJ   OK, one of my conditions for staying in this is that we don't spend more than . . . twenty per cent of the time talking about our health. I don't want to be one of those people.

– You really don't want to hear about my back?

VJ   Oh go on then.

They turn seventy.

– I guess it must be scary for you to see so much changing.

Jaffa   Not really.

– No?

Jaffa   I've seen everything change before.

Red   I call my daughter because she's having a tough time with doing normal daily things – talk her through her laundry. And it hurts hearing her struggle, I understand it but my heart hurts for her. And then after I ring off my heart keeps hurting – a sort of stabbing pain – and I think – oh. I see.

VJ   Did I do all right?

– I think so.

They turn eighty.

Epi   I keep hearing flight announcements. And making sure I've got everything. For some reason I've got cash in my pocket even though it's been years since we used cash.

And when the plane comes I get on.

Wolfie   My grandson came up and said, there's going to be a generation ship and I want to go on it.

And I said, what?

Jazz   Most of the time . . . I don't notice . . . my knee. I don't know if it's stopped hurting . . . or if everything else has just caught up.

Wolfie   And he said, a generation ship, we'll go on it and have children and grow old and die on the way to a moon that can support life.

We're going to have a terrarium.

And I said, there's absolutely no way you're doing that, your dad would have a fit.

Although the next time he came he didn't mention it. So maybe I dreamt it.

Jaffa   I don't question when things are different – when someone I thought was alive is dead or someone I thought was dead is alive – I'm not exactly reliable.

Peebs   I probably would. Go back. For a day or a week or two, just out of curiosity.

They turn ninety.

Keesh   I can tell you where I was born and how I did at school and when I had my first child and when I worked at Sainsbury's and when I was unemployed and the time I went to Russia. But saying it now isn't the same as how it felt at the time. It's not everything.

– That makes sense.

Keesh   I would need more time to tell you everything.

– I think we have to wrap it up now.

Keesh   Don't worry. It was a big ask.

The End (*sort of*).

[... *I kinda like it if we leave the play there. I think it leaves us a long way from where we began, with the past irretrievably in the past, in the same way that time does. But like the characters, you too have a choice: A) leave it here, or B) go back to the start in the last few moments. In real life we don't get to go back, which is why I like option A. But this is theatre, not real life. And anyway, in* real *life it's only been, what, forty-five minutes? An hour? So if option A doesn't feel right . . .*]

Epilogue

Keesh *is finishing her essay, while* **Jaffa** *sits there timing her.*

Keesh   I hate you. I *hate* you. This is the worst thing I've ever done.

Jaffa   Five seconds.

Keesh *finishes her sentence, grimaces at the work one last time and folds the pages up.* **Jaffa** *holds out the envelope, and* **Keesh** *slots her essay into it.*

Jaffa   D'you feel better now?

Keesh   No. Come on, your end of the bargain, you've had ages to think.

Jaffa   All right.

He takes up the console, shows **Keesh** *what he's going to pick.*

Keesh   Cool.

Jaffa *drops his finger from a huge height to make one of the choices in the game.*

Jaffa   That felt a lot less . . . dramatic than I thought it was gonna be.

Keesh   Same.

She cracks open two energy drinks, offers one to **Jaffa**.

Keesh   Round 2?

Jaffa *takes it – they clink cans, take a long slug each and then go back to the game.*

The End (sort of).

The Small Hours

BY KATHERINE SOPER

Notes on rehearsal and staging, drawn from a workshop with the writer, held at the National Theatre, October 2018

How Katherine came to write the play

'I wanted to write about the differences between adolescence and adulthood and explore whether snapshots of our lives as adolescents can illuminate the people we eventually become, as well as the way time can feel like a wide, open expanse when you're young. Ultimately I wanted to write a piece that paid tribute to the small yet momentous events and choices we make as teenagers, while showing how these fit into a larger shape of a life. The idea which sparked writing this play was thinking about what I remembered from being young. I felt time went very slowly and I didn't have much agency, but now it's different. I can buy what I want, go where I want, I have more direction over my life. A year slips by without realising it. It's been a year and a half since I started writing this play but it feels like five minutes. For a young person, though, a year and a half feels like an odyssey. It is exploring how time passes and the way it speeds up as we get older.'

Katherine Soper, 2018

Approaching the play

Amy Hodge, the lead director, began by asking the group if they had specific things they'd like to cover in the workshop and the following list was created:

- How to work with a cast larger than the one specified of eight characters in the play
- How did Katherine imagine the last ten pages to look?
- Music ideas: sound world/genre
- Explore specifics in regards to staging
- Changing language in the play, i.e. swearing and slang specific to the area the play is set
- How to stage duologues with a larger cast

- Does the setting of the play matter?
- Time concept – is there a vision for how time flips back and forward?
- How can directors age the performers playing from sixteen to ninety years old?
- Are there any points in the play that Katherine does not want changed?
- Understanding specific language, e.g. 'bottom set', 'rubo'
- Discussing how to best portray the pornography scene in sensitive settings
- Punctuation and grammar, specifically in the second half
- Are there any specific cultural references?
- Themes – overall what is the play trying to say?
- How can directors get young people to be passionate about these characters?
- Characters are gender blind, but why is it important that VJ and Wolfie are the same sex?
- Does Katherine have any visions of specific characteristics?
- Transitions – changing hours into years and changing age; how do directors make that clear?
- The ending – what is the reason behind the alternative endings and what are Katherine's thoughts on whether we do or don't include it?
- What ideas/restrictions are there surrounding the different voices at the end?
- Is there any hesitation with regard to using technology on stage?
- What time is the play set? If it moves forward in time, does it start in 2018?

Amy summarised the questions by creating a list of subjects that the group would cover in the session to answer them:

- Character
- Setting
- World of play
- Production
- Practical – language/time
- Themes

Themes

The participants identified the following themes within the play:

Choices	Nostalgia	Relationships
Time	Dreams	Future
Circles of repetition	Gender identity	Feeling trapped
Growing up	Circles	Parental impact
Life	Death	Games
Mental health	Community	Aspiration
Love	Hopes/dreams	Isolation
Memories	Parenting	Relationships
Sexuality	Academic pressure	Hobbies
Family	Divorce	Isolation

Nostalgia, isolation, time and the absence of parents were themes that felt particularly pertinent. In every scene parents are absent. Amy suggested that it could be interesting for directors to ask their groups what they feel about their parents and to explore ways for them to examine how their perspective on themselves and their parents changes over time.

Dissecting the play: FACTS and QUESTIONS

Amy always starts a process with FACTS and QUESTIONS. This is a way to read the play that enables you to be detailed rather than interpretational. It gives directors a foundation and is really practical.

Purpose of exercise: To forensically consider the detail in what is written and from the detail find the answers of how to stage it.

EXERCISE: FACTS AND QUESTIONS – FIRST SCENE

Working through the first scene together the participants created a list of the FACTS:

- It is Friday night/Saturday morning 1.00 a.m.
- It is May half-term.
- They are in a music practice room.
- They are in a school.
- They are on an island.
- Epi is in a dressing gown.
- Epi plays an instrument (cello).
- Epi is practising a tune and playing random notes.
- There is Peebs.
- Peebs is wearing boots – they are muddy.
- Peebs is carrying a holdall.
- Peebs lives in Ketterley.
- Epi does not know where Peebs lives.
- There is music.
- There is Skinny who listens to hardcore trance music.
- The mud on Peebs's boots is dry.
- Peebs is having an operation on Monday.
- Peebs studies Chemistry.
- Ash studies Chemistry.
- People can go home at half-term to their family.
- Ash has gone home on the ferry.
- Peebs and Epi don't go home.
- Peebs had an expectation he was going to Ash's.
- Peebs has a phone.
- Peebs says he is messy.
- Peebs is not leaving for half-term.
- There is Mr Marcello – he lives on site.
- Peebs has been stuck here during previous holidays.
- Peebs used to go home sometimes.
- Epi used to be the only full-time border.
- Epi is called Epi because he uses an EpiPen.
- Epi has been here since he was age seven or eight.
- Epi had an allergic reaction at school – he's allergic to lots of things, including milk and eggs.

- Epi doesn't eat in the main hall
- Peebs is having a cyst removed.
- Peebs has heard stories about hospital and has had a nightmare about the cyst.
- Epi has a dad who had five operations last year.
- They are not seventeen but sixteen or younger.
- Last time in Texas Peebs went to NASA.
- There are stone circles on the island.
- There is isolation.
- Epi has access to Seminex.
- Epi studies music – he has a composition unit which has to be three minutes' long.
- Peebs smokes.
- There is rabies.
- Epi's parents are in China.
- There is a coast – they can access the coast.

From each FACT emerged a series of useful QUESTIONS:

- Why are they awake at 1.00 a.m.?
- What are they checking the time on?
- Why do they care about time?
- Have they got somewhere to be?
- Are they worried about being caught?
- Why have they got access to the music room?
- What sort of island is it – real or not?
- Where are we in the world
- What kind of school is it?
- Why is he in a dressing gown?
- How long has Epi played the cello for?
- Does he enjoy playing the cello?
- Who teaches him?
- If not a cello what instrument is it?
- What kind of tune is played?
- How good are they?

- Why doesn't Peebs walk straight in?
- How well do Epi and Peebs know each other?
- How often do they chat?
- Are they friends?
- How old are they?
- How bad are Epi's allergies?
- What is Epi's real name?
- From where is Peebs having a cyst removed?
- Is the cyst cancerous?
- Is the operation serious/not serious?
- Is it Peebs's first time in hospital?
- Why has Peebs had a nightmare about it?

DISCUSSION FOLLOWING THIS EXERCISE

Katherine explained that in her mind she imagined that Epi played a cello but that it could be any instrument. This choice can be determined by the musical ability of the person playing Epi.

From the list of facts, Epi is working on a music composition unit, which has to be three minutes' long; three minutes feels like a long time for him.

Deciding at what level Epi is studying music might give you an idea of what age the characters potentially are.

It's useful to ask what different instruments say about character and the world they inhabit. What is important about musical taste? What does that say about human beings? Classical music versus rock music versus hardcore trance – all of these genres say something about character and the school.

Discovering these details will enable the group to build character and relationships.

One of the FACTS is that Epi doesn't know where Peebs lives, so this is where the FACTS can help to answer some of the QUESTIONS, as companies work through the scene, step by step.

QUESTIONS that were asked around the fact that Peebs lives in Ketterley:

- What is Ketterley?
- What is the history of Ketterley?
- Is Ketterley a house within the boarding school?

Research idea

None of the companies taking part in the workshop had experience of boarding schools, so the world of the play was completely new to them. Amy suggested a task for companies might be to put 'Ketterley' into Google and see what comes up, alongside researching the structure of boarding schools. What are the young people's thoughts around boarding school? Is there an opinion of it being elitist/the best? Are they privileged if they are away from their families?

QUESTIONS that were added to this topic included:

- What does it mean to be in a house like Ketterley?
- What house is Epi in and how does that affect the relationship with Peebs?
- Peebs used to be part-time. Why? When did they become full-time?
- What is it like not to go home?

Katherine said that she wrote the play so that Epi used to be the only full-time boarder. Remembering the fact that Epi has been there since they were seven or eight indicates how Epi is living his/her life. It is interesting to consider what nostalgia is to a fifteen–sixteen-year-old. When you are fifteen or sixteen what do you remember about your primary school years? Nostalgia feels like one of the key themes in the play.

Working out the FACTS and QUESTIONS gives you the detail. The choices you make when answering the QUESTIONS need to unlock the most useful ideas for the scene; the answers affect how the actors play their parts.

For example, when looking at the fact that Epi's dad had five operations last year, could this mean that Epi is exaggerating? How believable is Epi? When rehearsing the scene, you could try it in different ways:

- You could try it with Epi really ill and Peebs really worried about the operation; notice whether this approach is helpful for the scene.
- Or you could try it with two people who are lonely – is it more helpful that Epi has no mates and falls back on these exaggerations to make up for not having any friends? You could look back to the list of FACTS and related QUESTIONS to see which ones could be useful in unlocking the scene. For example:

FACTS:

- Epi's parents live in China.
- Peebs's parents live in Texas.

- Peebs has a phone but can't get a signal.
- Peebs and Epi don't go home.
- Both have parents who live in a place they can't easily get to.

QUESTIONS:

- What are the characters' relationship with their parents?
- Why don't they go home?
- How alone/isolated are they?

Place

Katherine hasn't specified geographically where the play is set, so directors can connect it with what works for their group. Thinking about the isolation in this play might help generate ideas when thinking about a setting.

Remembering the FACTS related to geography:

- It is an island.
- There are stone circles.
- There is a coast.
- There is isolation.

And the QUESTIONS related to those FACTS:

- What are the stone circles?
- What do they mean?
- What do they say about time, is there a relationship?
- Is it just the school on the island or is there a village?
- How do you get off the island?
- Do they feel forgotten?
- Do they need rescuing?

The most essential dynamic is that Peebs and Epi are left alone in an isolated area.

Interrogating the scene using FACTS and QUESTIONS provides an opportunity to really gain an understanding of the scene and its subtext. It gives a director fuel to work with the play beyond simply reading it. It pulls you away from your own prejudices and opens out the search for what the writer has intended.

Amy suggested to the group that they might want to have a sense of the FACTS and answers to their QUESTIONS before starting rehearsals, or that this could be a process undertaken with the cast. In terms of answering the QUESTIONS, some are answered directly in the script, whilst others will need to be made up and some won't be answered until the rehearsal process is under way. How the QUESTIONS are answered and how the group interpret the FACTS will underpin the vision for the production.

Subtext

How does the language we use affect others? There is subtext in everything we do. The beauty of this play is that so much is in the subtext.

THE FIRST FOUR SCENES: THE MAIN EVENTS, BIG CHOICES, KEY CENTRAL MOMENTS, SUBTEXT

Thinking about the key moments, there is something about choice in all of them. They are useful ways into what the scene is all about. There's a core dynamic of two people being isolated, left behind and trying to find some solace from the other. There is a version of that in each scene to work towards.

First scene

The moment of connection on p. 563 is really important:

Peebs   Where do your parents live again?

Epi   Er. China.

Peebs   Wow.

Epi   Yeah.

Peebs   Do you wish you'd moved there too?

Epi   Um. Kinda just think they should have stayed here in the first place.

Peebs   Yeah.

Same.

Epi and Peebs both feel that their parents have left them. Peebs makes a choice to open up and Epi chooses to connect as a friend and go to the beach. Theatrically the scene is about two people struggling to connect in isolation and, for a moment here, they connect.

Second scene

Jazz and Red on p. 572. Jazz says they need to go to sleep and the beat after Red's line 'So what should I do?' is key. Red wants Jazz to make them an offer to sleep over. The beat is Jazz taking too long to answer.

There are lots of miniature moments building to this but this is the key one.

The point Katherine is making here is about the way people can experience things differently. A person can be in the same situation as another but be affected by it differently. She wanted to write the scene where one person needs something that the other person can't give them at that moment for whatever reason. It's something that she thinks happens in a lot of friendships.

Note: If the word 'jizz' is problematic for your setting, you could change the word to 'vomit'. As long as the spirit of the lines and what they are trying to do is still replicated.

Third scene

Keesh and Jaffa are talking overtly about choices. Playing the computer game vs doing the essay.

Jaffa wants to get Keesh to write the essay as they've ducked out of a party to get it done.

The key moment is on p. 579:

Keesh   What's your mum worried about?

Jaffa   Uh.

Keesh   Is it to do with the time she was talking to Lou's mum and said she was worried I was rubbing off on you?

Jaffa chooses not to say his mum doesn't like Keesh and Keesh chooses in that moment to keep the peace and talk about something else rather than challenge Jaffa about it.

Note: 2008 is mentioned when they look at the photograph – this date can be changed to reflect whatever year it was when they were five or six years old.

Katherine has deliberately chosen a fictional game for the characters to play rather than an existing reference.

Fourth scene

VJ and Wolfie – the whole scene is dancing around this key moment on p. 582:

Pause as **Wolfie** *visibly considers saying one thing – then changes her mind.*

VJ has a choice about how to respond. It has to be a confession where some vulnerability is at stake in confessing. She is scared to be that honest for whatever reason. Although the play does not explicitly state this, the subtext is that she loves her the way that teenagers love each other. VJ hears her but compassionately chooses to pretend not to hear.

A participant asked: 'Why it was important that VJ and Wolfie are the same sex?' Katherine replied that it is always terrifying to confess to someone that you care about them, but in this case it is terrifying because they are close friends. If it had been a boy and girl it probably would have come up sooner.

Katherine suggested that the groups might need to think about how best to convey the sexual/romantic subtext and the emotional connection – perhaps through prolonged eye contact/how they interact physically. Perhaps it is about exploring the inability to be totally normal around a person you have feelings for. Something physical that is completely ordinary when you are not romantically connected can feel incredibly loaded and weird when you are with someone you care about.

It is also important to invest in the background of their relationship, so the stakes are about losing a friendship, not just losing a potential lover.

In the first half of the play there is a sense that the relationships with parents are not good. In the second half things have been changed, brought back with a new lens. It might be helpful to join up those dots and track this progress of a shifting relationship.

Structure and form

The first four scenes feature four very different couples, all in different places with dialogue written in the form of duologues. The second half of the play looks and feels very different. It has a completely different style of writing with direct address and characters moving through time, with ages ranging from twenty-one to ninety years old. This has the potential to be very rich and a joy to stage, but without due diligence in preparation work, there is a risk it can become confused and look like a non-specific group of people talking to the audience. Katherine noted that there are a lot of deliberate formal dynamics that come into play.

The last ten pages

After reading the last ten pages Amy asked: 'What do we know? Mechanically, what's happening?'

- The characters are getting older.
- It's fast in pace.
- Transitions are instant.
- Time keeps moving forwards until the end.
- The plot follows several stories.
- There is no pattern – all the stories meld.
- Ages shift (there are choices here as to whether you specify/declare the age shifts).
- There is direct address (talking to the audience) except when there is a dash which represents different characters and when Jazz and Red are talking (the step-siblings).
- Sometimes scenes are interlinked, sometimes they are separate.

Discussion: How do you make the story clear? How to keep consistency and continuity?

The play starts as one thing and becomes something completely different. There is a danger it could feel like two different plays if it is not carefully crafted – that's the challenge.

Could technology help the audience to see the changing age? Maybe a sound world of a clock that starts slow and gets quicker? Or perhaps signposts are created using placards or projection?

Katherine has written characters' ages in as signposts and it could be amazing to see this integrated visually in some way.

The observation that time gets quicker is useful. As they get older there is less text as they are running out of time. This is where the form and content connects. The content of the play is saying time gets quicker and the form is doing the same.

The science of time

The science of time is a key theme and idea to consider when approaching *The Small Hours*.

When you are ten years old a year is a tenth of your life. As you get older a year becomes proportionally smaller, which is why it speeds up. So when you're a baby, a day is forever because you've only had a few of them.

As the play progresses, it feels like time goes more and more quickly but the characters slow down. They aren't moving as quickly as time is.

Some characters don't live until they are ninety. The way Katherine thought of it is that the last line a character has is when they step out of the world.

EXERCISE: EXPLORING PERCEPTIONS OF TIME

Amy suggested some methods through which the directors could explore the perception of time with their groups:

- You could ask your group to stop in silence to see what three minutes feels like.
- You could explore a physical sense of time with your cast – ask them to walk across the space in the time they think is a minute.
- You could ask them to write a letter to their younger selves at age seven or eight.
- Then ask them to write a letter to their future self.
- Then ask them to do this for another character in the play.
- Ask them to consider where they see themselves in ten years' time. Ask them to write another letter to their future selves about their aspirations for the future.

Explaining the form of the last ten pages

On p. 593, as an example, we can see that although Jazz and Peebs are talking at the same time they are not talking to each other. They are in different times and different places. Where the dialogue is sectioned off though they are in conversation with each other, so it's a bit like uniting meaning – like a mini-scene. There is a change in situation: a new place, a new time.

A dash (–) indicates another person.

Katherine wanted to create the sense that these things are happening at the same time and at specific, special moments. As an example, on p. 591, Epi and Wolfie are alternating between their special moments – two big things are happening:

- Epi is saying goodbye to their father for the last time.
- Wolfie is saying hello to the person they are about to spend the rest of their life with.

There is a relationship between these two separate things that is emotional rather than literal. It's a moment inviting thematic connections, comparisons, contradictions or contrasts.

Significant moments in the last ten pages

The end of the play does not have the same arc as the first four scenes because it's written in a completely different form.

Thematically and emotionally there are a few moments that stand out for Katherine:

- Epi being worried that everything will stay the same or get worse.
- Red having an episode of mental illness on p. 590 ('If you don't come out of the road', 'I promise no one is listening to this').

These are high stakes for Red. It is a scary moment for her. Katherine wanted to show that it does get bad but that you can get through it. Red is possibly sectioned after this.

Amy commented that is it useful to notice how intense and emotionally demanding these sections are. The back-story will be key for the cast to know who these people are and what their characters have been through.

The Jazz and Red conversations are still navigating their closeness or lack thereof. They are the only two who maintain a relationship in the last ten pages. This is because Katherine thought they were the two characters most likely to, because they had shared a family home for years.

Katherine introduced a useful word here: 'sonder' – meaning the profound feeling of realising that everyone, including strangers passed in the street, has a life as complex as one's own – populated with their own ambitions, friends, routines, worries and inherited craziness. The following text on p. 592 reflects this idea:

Red   I think you think I disappear when you don't see me. But I don't. Every second you live, when you're having your cup of tea in the morning and watching telly, I'm living that too. You just don't see it.

Keesh has the text at the end where she tries to sum up parts of her life. But it is a potted summary that is inadequate in the way that any summary of our lives would be inadequate. It is useful to consider who she is talking to and Katherine said that there is room for this moment to be more metaphorical rather than literal.

Characters exercise

All the characters have their own world to build. Starting with the character Peebs, looking just at the last ten pages of the play, the participants read all Peebs's lines aloud, as if it was a monologue. They repeated the exercise for each character.

Note: It's useful to apply the FACTS and QUESTIONS exercise to these created monologues, as there is a lot of detail to be found.

Circles

Katherine pointed out when working through Epi's journey that Epi says at the end he circles back to Heathrow. If you look for them, you will notice there are many references to circles and circling throughout the whole of the second half. It's connected to the idea that you go through each year and it's October again, the idea of repetition.

Amy asked the group: 'What do circles mean to you?'

- Bond
- Circle of life
- Closing the circle
- There are eight characters and if you turn eight on its side, it's infinity
- A circle brings people together
- You can see everyone in a circle
- A year is a circle
- It's the strongest shape

Reading Epi's journey through to the end Amy asked, 'Who is he talking to?' Could it be Mum, or a therapist? There are lots of options. It's interpretative and could be a decision you discover with your group.

Time: when the play is set

It's going to be important to focus on which year is the setting for the last ten pages.

Katherine said that there's something very compelling about going into the future but it shouldn't become a weird, sci-fi piece. Jaffa mentions 'the

town going bankrupt' that's happened in Detroit and a cashless society –
these things are happening. She thinks there is a way of representing the
future that focuses on the normal average human experience.

Staging ideas

Amy suggested a number of ways in which the groups could think about
staging their play:

- You could use a spotlight up and spotlight down on different
  characters.
- You could set it in the round with projection of a clock ticking on
  the floor.
- You could create a sundial on the floor.
- A large ensemble could be the characters represented by a dash (–).
- You could project newspaper headlines to show time passing.
- You could show photos of cast ageing.

Katherine said ideas that show the world changing but the characters only
responding to them as much as we do in life would be effective.

Duologues don't have to be two people on stage. There's fun to be had
in terms of how you present age through your production.

To bring this all together, there are three things to help:

1 Clarity of your characters' journeys
2 The form and content – using the themes to affect how you stage
   the play
3 How you track this idea of time changing

Why are there two endings?

A few participants said when they read early drafts that they wanted the
characters to go back to the start. Katherine thought this was an interesting
idea, but that it should be a conscious theatrical choice: 'you can't do it in
real life but you can in art'. So, if you do go back, do it knowingly, not
because it's a nice ending.

References

Katherine was inspired and influenced by the following:

TV/FILM

A documentary series called *Up*. It started in 1964 when the children were seven and they went back and filmed them every seven years till they were aged sixty.

The film *Boyhood*, directed by Richard Linklater and filmed over twelve years of a boy's life.

MUSIC

Pure Heroine, the debut album by New Zealand singer Lorde, written when she was fifteen to sixteen years old.

From a workshop led by Amy Hodge
with notes by Psyche Stott

Stuff

by Tom Wells

Vinny's organising a surprise birthday party for his mate Anita – she needs cheering up and Vinny can't think of any better way to do that. It's not going well. His choice of venue is a bit misguided, Anita's not keen on leaving the house and everyone else has their own stuff going on. Maybe a surprise party wasn't the best idea? A play about trying (but not really managing) to help.

Cast size
9

Tom Wells is a Hull-based playwright. His plays include: *Broken Biscuits* (Paines Plough/Live Theatre, Newcastle); *Folk* (Birmingham Rep/Hull Truck Theatre/Watford Palace Theatre); *Jumpers for Goalposts* (Paines Plough – Watford Palace Theatre and UK tour, 2013/14); *Cosmic* (Ros Terry/Root Theatre, East Yorkshire tour, 2013); *The Kitchen Sink* (Bush Theatre, 2011 – winner of the Most Promising Playwright, Critics' Circle Awards, 2011 and the 2012 George Devine Award); *Me, as a Penguin* (West Yorkshire Playhouse, 2009 and Arcola Theatre/UK tour, 2010); *About a Goth* (Paines Plough/Oran Mor, 2009). *Ben and Lump*, which he wrote as part of the Coming Up season (Touchpaper), was broadcast on Channel 4 in 2012; his play *Jonesy* was broadcast on BBC Radio 4; and he wrote words for the musical *Drip* (Script Club/Boundless), with music by Matthew Robins. He has also written pantomimes for the Lyric Hammersmith and Middle Child, Hull. He is currently under commission to the Royal Court Theatre and the National Theatre, and is writing a new play to be broadcast on BBC Radio 4.

Characters

Vinny – *fifteen, organising the party, has liked Anita for ages*

Frankie – *fifteen, Anita's best mate*

Matt – *sixteen, quiet, gay*

Magda – *fifteen, plays guitar a bit*

Stace – *fifteen, trying to be helpful*

Kate – *sixteen, actually helpful, doesn't say much but her facial
expressions are priceless*

Dani – *seventeen, Stace's cousin, just visiting*

AJ – *sixteen, aspiring graffiti artist, trouble*

Tez – *thirteen, aspiring Ravenclaw, not trouble*

Scene One

A hall.

It's scruffy – cardboard boxes, half-broken furniture hidden underneath dust sheets, that sort of thing – in need of a lick of paint and a good tidy-up, but welcoming too.

Vinny, **Matt**, **Kate**, **Magda**, **Stace** *and* **Dani** *are waiting in the dark.*

Frankie *walks in.*

Vinny *turns the lights on.*

Everyone   SURPRISE!

A moment.

Vinny   What d'you think?

Frankie   Yeah. No it was good. Yeah.

Vinny   I thought so.

Stace   Not scary?

Frankie   Not scary no. You could probably sound a bit more joyful.

Matt   We will.

Vinny   And we've got party poppers as well, but just, not for the practice run.

Kate   I did mime.

Frankie   Ace. Mega.

And maybe, also, you know . . .

She gestures at the general surroundings.

Make this a bit less bleak.

Vinny   That's what we're doing now, while you're picking Anita up.

Frankie   Right. Well. Best of luck. And I'll see you in like: twenty minutes?

Vinny   Keep in touch, keep texting, so we know what you're up to.

Frankie   I'm literally just walking to Anita's house then turning round and walking back with Anita.

Vinny   Still though.

Frankie *rolls her eyes.*

Magda   Is there more of a plan than that?

Vinny   Frankie's off now, to pick Anita up, get her to come here but not explain why.

Magda   How?

Frankie   I'll think of something.

Stace   D'you think that's enough?

Vinny   Good point actually.

Frankie   What d'you mean?

Vinny   Like you don't think it'd be good to have a ready-prepared reason.

Frankie   I think you've got bigger stuff to focus on, Vinny.

Vinny   Like what?

Frankie *looks round at the hall.*

Vinny   Fair enough.

Frankie   Laters.

She leaves.

Vinny   So, everyone else is getting here for half past, if they're coming, I don't know if they're coming.

Magda   Who else?

Vinny   Loads of her mates from other stuff, as in not school, stuff she just does.

Matt   Cool.

Vinny   Made a secret Facebook event, fifteen people have said 'maybe'. (/ 'interested')

Matt (*less convinced*)   Cool.

Stace   That's amazing.

Vinny   She's amazing.

Kate   Shall I check the big door's open, then, through there? Not just the side door. In case they're early and they don't know about the side door.

Vinny   Good thinking.

He looks at lots of keys.

It's probably, well, I don't actually know but it's one of these.

Kate *looks at the keys for a moment.*

A little sadly.

Kate   I'll try them all.

She leaves.

Stace   So it's us, Frankie, Anita . . .

Magda   And a load of randoms off Facebook we don't even know.

Vinny   And maybe AJ actually, still waiting on AJ.

Magda   AJ's coming?

Vinny   If he can get away. He's in a bit of trouble so, grounded actually so –

Stace   Again?

Vinny   His mum caught him practising graffiti in her garage.

Magda   Shit.

Vinny   Yeah it's properly bad.

Matt   Who practises graffiti?

Vinny   Not AJ, not anymore. His mum's not letting him near aerosols ever again.

Stace   What about deodorant?

Vinny   He's got to use roll-on.

Stace   What about squirty cream?

Vinny   Banned.

Stace *looks shocked.*

Vinny   But, she's got work this afternoon, left him at home with Tez, reckons he can, fingers crossed anyway, reckons he can slip past him, get here in time, bring a load of booze to make some sort of punchy cocktail thing, like a proper high school party, like in films. I got red plastic cups in case.

Magda   And he's definitely coming?

Vinny   Should be.

Magda *'s not keen.*

Magda   Right. Great.

Vinny   What's up with AJ?

Magda   He's a dick.

Vinny   Yeah, obvs, but apart from that.

Magda *and* **Stace** *look at* **Matt**.

Magda   Matt?

Vinny   Oh shit, course, cos of . . .

Matt   Shall we start doing party stuff?

Vinny   Mate, honestly, just don't worry about it, don't give it another thought.

Matt   Where's the balloons?

He looks for the packet of balloons.

Vinny   He said that actually.

Matt   Thought they were here somewhere.

Vinny   Said tell Matt it's totally fine, you don't need to feel awkward or embarrassed or anything.

Matt *stops looking for the packet of balloons.*

Matt   Um. What?

Vinny   Yeah, like he did tell me what happened, not in a bad way, he was dead nice about it, says he's really flattered actually, that you think of him like that, and if he was, you know, you'd probably be exactly his type and everything.

His words.

But at the same time it probably is best to just try and move past it, if you can, pretend it never happened.

Magda   Pretend what never happened?

Vinny   Not really up to me to say is it?

Matt Um. Maybe just say.

Vinny Oh. Well. Pretend Matt never asked him out.

Magda He didn't.

Vinny Yeah, AJ said you'd say that, and like loyalty's a really ace quality, Magda, so –

Magda What?

Vinny Just saying, AJ's offering Matt this white flag, being the bigger guy, he doesn't have to do that.

Magda He's lying.

Matt Please can we just . . .

It's fine.

Magda Really though?

Matt *nods.*

Stace Really?

Matt The important thing today is: Anita. We all get to see her, tell her we miss her, tell her she's ace, on her birthday. Maybe also have a dance.

Vinny Exactly. So if we can all just get in the party spirit.

Magda In here?

Vinny We'll make it look properly nice, properly birthday-y.

Matt There is balloons somewhere.

Stace I've got bunting.

Vinny And she'll be like amazed and delighted, completely amazed and delighted we've done this super mega immense thing for her.

Magda You have.

Vinny Well.

Magda I'd've probably just dropped a card round, had a chat.

Vinny Oh.

Magda In case she's not up for it. Partying and that. After the saddest month of her life.

Vinny Right. Um.

Magda   But then I'm not completely in love with her, trying to get out of the friend zone every minute for the past four years.

Vinny   If she's not up for it we can all just, everyone can just like finish their biscuits, go home.

Matt   There's biscuits?

Stace   I made biscuits.

She shows everyone a tin of home-made biscuits.

Have one.

Everyone takes one. **Dani** *looks at hers.*

Dani   Wow.

It sounds like the opposite of 'wow'.

Stace   This is Dani, everyone. My cousin.

Dani   Here for the weekend, hey.

Matt *is enjoying his biscuit.*

Matt   This is so nice.

Stace   I just thought, you know.

Vinny   D'you think it's bad then, if Anita's not up for it, just sending everyone home?

Stace   Well . . .

Dani   Yeah.

Vinny   I feel like they won't mind. They're used to more sort of structured extra-curricular activities anyway – orchestra, D of E.

Kate *comes back in.*

Kate   Everywhere's open now, big door and that.

She gives the keys back to **Vinny**.

Vinny   Cheers.

Stace   Biscuit?

Kate   I would absolutely love a biscuit.

She takes a biscuit, delighted.

Vinny   Better crack on with this bunting then.

Stace   Oh.

She is getting bunting out of her bag.

There's quite a lot.

It keeps coming.

Dani   There really is.

Stace   It's hard to figure out how much you'll need. And once you're going you can get a bit carried away.

Dani   A bit?

A moment.

Kate   I'll go find some steps.

She leaves again.

Matt *finds the packet of balloons.*

Matt   Balloons?

Vinny   Plan.

Matt *hands everyone a balloon to blow up.*

They blow them up.

In silence.

Making odd bits of awkward eye contact.

Vinny   You're all very quiet.

Matt   Um.

Vinny   What?

Matt   No, nothing, just.

Vinny   Out with it.

Matt   Well. Er.

Matt *doesn't know what to say.*

Magda   Let's be real for a minute, Vinny: this place is shit.

Vinny *'s balloon deflates.*

Dani   Ouch. Burn.

Stace   Magda.

628   Tom Wells

Vinny   Bit harsh.

Magda   It is shit though.

Stace   Just, doesn't seem like it'd be sort of the, the natural place for, I dunno.

Like I get it's a good place to meet and stuff, if you're organising something. Cubs maybe. The WI.

Vinny   It's the best.

Stace   But is it a good place for a, um . . .?

Vinny   Party, Stace. Say it with me: party.

Stace *looks around.*

Stace   If I'm honest, it isn't screaming party. As a place.

Magda   If anything, it's screaming: dogging.

Stace   Magda.

Dani   Yes! Exactly!

Like I've never been dogging or whatever but if I was looking for somewhere to do it, somewhere to dog, that car park . . . Perfect. Or the woods actually, the ones just behind, looked very doggy. Dogging-y.

Vinny   It is not the perfect place for dogging.

Dani   Oh, ok, interesting.

Stace   It actually is.

Vinny   What?

Stace   Read about it online, it's like a hotspot.

Magda   The car park or the woods?

Stace   Both.

Like, the car park, standard dogging, and then the woods round the back if you're after something a bit more, um, outdoorsy.

Vinny   How do you know this?

Stace   My gran was looking up picnic spots on TripAdvisor. It escalated.

A moment.

Kate *comes back in with some stepladders.*

Kate   Found these so . . . Bunting time?

Vinny   I'm not sure it is bunting time.

Kate   Come on, Vinny, it's always bunting time.

Stace   There's sort of three big bits, three separate strands.

She sorts the bunting into three piles.

Magda   Shall we put some through there, like the entrance as well?

Stace   Good plan.

Magda *picks up a pile of bunting, passes it to* **Kate** *and takes a pile herself.*

Magda   Right, someone else grab that, who's helping?

She marches out.

Matt *picks up the last pile of bunting and leaves.*

Matt   Vinny? In a bit.

Vinny *leaves as well.*

Kate, **Stace** *and* **Dani** *are left.*

Kate *has got one end of the bunting, near the steps.*

Stace *is trying to untangle the rest.*

Dani *rolls her eyes, and looks at her phone.*

Stace   It's got in a tangle.

Kate   D'you need a hand?

Stace   No it's, cheers, getting there.

It isn't.

Kate *comes to help.*

Kate   Can I maybe . . .?

Stace *hands the bunting over and* **Kate** *starts untangling.*

Kate   You hold this.

She passes **Stace** *an end then starts unwinding, walking away, untangling as she goes.*

Stace *looks at* **Dani**.

Stace It'll be alright you know. I'm sure it'll be alright.

A moment.

Dani.

Dani *looks up from her phone.*

Dani What?

Stace Just saying, like your mum and dad and that, I'm sure it'll be –

Dani I don't want to talk about it.

Stace Oh. Course.

A moment.

Kate *is still unravelling the bunting.*

Stace Dani's mum and dad are having some issues.

Dani I literally just said I don't want to talk about it.

Stace Oh, ok, sorry, soz.

Silence for a bit.

Kate *notices.*

Kate Nearly done.

Stace Cool. Cool cool cool.

Kate Three big loops?

Stace Definitely. I reckon. Dani? What d'you reckon?

Dani Yeah fine whatever.

Stace Ok this is no good.

She drops her end of the bunting, sits next to **Dani***.*

Kate *just carries on putting it up, by herself, with the stepladders.*

Stace We should definitely talk about it.

Dani Nothing to talk about is there?

Stace Well. I mean. That's not true actually.

Dani *looks resigned.*

Dani Just to get you up to speed, Kate: my family is literally falling apart. No biggie.

Kate   Oh.

Dani   Yeah it's pretty bad.

Stace   It'll be alright.

Dani   Let's not talk about it, then. Crack on with your bunting.

Stace   I think we should, I think we should talk about it.

Dani *sighs, looks at her phone again.*

Stace *looks at* **Kate** *for help.*

Kate *doesn't know what to say really.*

Kate   What's happened?

Stace   You probably should tell her.

Dani *looks at them both.*

Dani   All kicked off yesterday. TK Maxx.

Mum had this massive row with my dad about a spiralizer – she wants to make courgetti, he's not keen – next thing she's making me pack an overnight bag, jump in the car with her, driving halfway across the country so we can stay at Stace's mum's house. On a futon.

Kate   Oh.

Dani   I wouldn't mind but I was meant to be going to this really cool club night with my friend, we're on the VIP list, you go to a special chained-off area, gold chains, there's Prosecco, it's quite a big deal.

Kate   Oh.

Dani   And all the way over yesterday my dad's calling her, trying to, she's not picking up, she's like, 'Let him worry a bit, let him think about what he's done'. Mum reckons it goes a bit deeper than courgetti. 'The spark's gone,' she says. 'Leaves his pants everywhere, does crosswords in bed, doesn't see me for who I am anymore' – which is, apparently, an empowered, sexual being, and potential vegan. They're just treading water, Mum reckons, treading water till I get off to uni and there's no point anymore, is there? There's no point.

Kate   Oh.

Dani   And I am, like, 'Mum, I do not want to hear this, save it for'.

Her best mate Lorraine, not Lorraine Kelly.

But now my dad's texting, he's here, apparently, he's in town, looking for my mum, needing directions, I was, like, 'Dad, I would love to help but unfortunately I'm at a shit non-party with Stace's semi-mates in the middle of nowhere, bye'.

Stace   We can go back to ours now, find him. Help a bit.

Dani   So I can be there for the showdown? No thanks.

I mean I've literally spent the last seventeen years watching their marriage disintegrate – Mum's words, not mine – I know exactly what she'll be saying, like, 'Too little, Alan, too little too late', and he'll look all forlorn or whatever, probably cry a bit. Like he did in the middle of *Moana*.

I'd rather be here to be honest. Which is saying something.

Stace *doesn't know what to say.*

Kate   Um. Finished this.

Stace *looks at the bunting.*

Stace   Oh that looks – doesn't it, Dani? Looks ace.

Dani *doesn't say anything.*

Kate   It reminds me a bit of *Bake Off*.

Stace   I'm trying to make the world a bit more like *Bake Off*. Bunting, kindness, shortbread.

The others come back in.

Matt   Wow. Stace!

Stace   It was Kate really.

Magda   Awesome.

Kate   Go team.

Vinny   Yeah it's. . .

He can't quite muster enough enthusiasm.

Not quite the hip sixteen-year-old urban party vibe I was imagining but, yeah.

Colourful.

Magda   Anita isn't hip. Or urban. I'm fairly sure she's not even up for a party but –

Vinny   Course she's up for it.

Nobody agrees.

Anyway, it's a surprise, you don't get a choice if you're up for it or not, do you? You just get it. And then you deal with it. Like life.

Magda   Had quite a lot to deal with though hasn't she, just lately, don't you think?

Vinny   Which is why she deserves a party.

Magda   Ok.

Vinny *gets a text.*

Vinny   Frankie's just going past Morrison's. T-minus fifteen minutes. We should crack on. What else needs doing?

Dani   Drinks?

Vinny   AJ's sorting drinks, he says.

Magda   Music?

Stace   Yeah, music.

Vinny   Shit.

Magda   What?

Vinny   Forgot about music.

Dani   There's no music?

Stace   I'm sure we can just, we've got phones, there might be some speakers somewhere.

Dani   Who has a party without music?

Stace   Dani.

Dani   Seriously though.

Vinny   You're right.

Stace   Magda's got her guitar. Maybe we can have some actual music.

Vinny   The guitar's here?!

Magda   Don't.

Stace   Maybe we can have some actual real-life music. Maybe that's cool and better than remembering to bring speakers.

Magda   I only know one song.

Vinny   Come on then, let's hear it.

Magda *picks her guitar up.*

Magda   Thing is, I should explain: I was thinking, like, what d'you get Anita for her birthday, she's had a properly shit year, but also, it is her birthday so, something special, obvs.

But then I've got like thirty-seven p, in the world, which does limit my options a bit.

To, like, a Freddo.

So then I started thinking about my actual skills, decided: write her a song, just write her a song, just do it.

Stace   No way.

Vinny   This is immense. Isn't it though? Immense.

Matt   I've just got her some Skittles. A medium bag. That's it.

Kate   She does like Skittles.

Magda   And this might be awful. I just . . . You'll tell me, if it's bad? Then I know before I try and sing her it, ruin her day?

Vinny   Deal.

Magda   Ok. Ok.

She gets ready to play.

Before I start –

Vinny   Mate, just play it.

Magda   No, I just, I should explain that, I know I'm not like the best singer in the world.

And in terms of the guitar I only know three to four chords, depending if you count D seven, so also not that good.

And then this is only the first song I've ever written, so bit of a work in progress.

Dani   Can't wait.

Stace   Dani.

Dani   What? I can't.

Magda   It's called 'Stuff'.

She sings.

   Shit stuff happens
   Sometimes shit stuff happens
   Happens to you
   Shit stuff

   But good stuff also happens
   Sometimes good stuff also happens
   Hopefully
   That's enough.

She stops.

That's it.

Vinny   One word: phenaynay.

Dani   Not a word.

Stace   Magda!

Magda   It's not phenaynay.

Vinny   It flipping is.

Dani   What's phenaynay?

Stace *shrugs.*

Magda   As I was singing it I was like: Magda, this is actually worse than you originally thought, lesson learnt, stop singing.

On the plus side: it's not long.

Matt   Catchy though.

Stace   Really catchy. Also, you know: true. Sometimes shit stuff does happen. Good stuff too, obvs.

Magda *smiles.*

Magda   Well. Cheers.

You're my mates and you're fibbing but.

Stace   Oh, Dani, no.

Dani *'s getting a packet of cigarettes out.*

Dani   I'll breathe out the window, no need to freak out.

She opens the window.

Stace   No it's not –

You just, you can't.

Magda   We don't smoke. Any of us. It's like a thing we don't do.

Dani   I'm not asking you to smoke.

Magda   We're anti-smoking, strongly.

Dani   I'm anti-singing, strongly. Didn't stop you.

Magda *looks a bit hurt.*

Magda   Put this away then.

She starts putting the guitar away.

Stace   She doesn't mean it.

Magda   Stace?

She looks at **Stace** *to encourage her to say something to* **Dani***.*

Stace   Um. You can't actually do that here, Dani. It's just, like, even the packet –

Dani   Just a packet.

Stace   Got all the stuff on about, you know . . .

Dani   What?

Magda   Well. Cancer.

Dani   So?

Stace   Oh it's my fault really, I haven't explained properly about the party and that, Anita and the party and everything. And the thing is I'm sure when you meet her you'll like, you'll get on so well cos you're both funny in the same way, a bit, like, quite a spiky way that's maybe a bit tough, a bit harsh or something, and also she's sort of unexpectedly glamorous compared to, compared to us, really, so I think you'll be a good, um, but, thing is, about Anita is she's sort of a bit straightforward about stuff, a bit zero tolerance about stuff she really believes in and one of the things she really believes in is like not –

Dani   I'm not asking for permission.

Stace   No but, I know but –

Dani   Don't need anyone's permission.

Stace   Of course but just –

AJ *crashes in, with* **Tez** *following.*

AJ   Alright, losers!

You lot know Tez, following me everywhere, won't piss off.

Tez   Hey.

AJ *holds out a fist to* **Vinny**.

AJ   Fist bump, Vinny.

Vinny *fist bumps* **AJ**.

AJ   Fist bump, Magda.

Magda *fist bumps* **AJ**.

AJ   Mega. Fist bump, Stace.

Stace *fist bumps* **AJ**.

AJ   Fist bump, Matt.

No?

Little fist bump?

Little fist bump for AJ?

Matt, *a little wary, fist bumps* **AJ**.

AJ   Wahey!

Whoa, who's this?

Dani   Dani, here for the weekend.

She holds her fist out, bored.

Stace   My cousin.

AJ   Great, what d'you think you're doing?

Dani   Fist bump.

AJ   Not that hand, that hand.

He points at the cigarettes.

Dani   Oh for –

AJ   What?

Dani   Why are you all having a go? People smoke. Like millions of people. Admittedly I'm amongst a level of geek I haven't encountered for a while but still –

AJ   Are you actually thick?

Dani   What?

Stace   AJ, it's –

AJ   Today specially.

Stace   I haven't said yet.

Dani   What?

AJ   Oh shit, sorry, didn't realise.

He is apologetic.

We should get you up to speed.

Can I just – ?

He takes the cigarette, still not lit, and indicates the packet.

Dani's *not sure what's going on. She holds it out.*

Dani   Oh.

AJ   Cheers.

He puts the cigarette back in the packet, then takes it, chucks it out the door. As far as he can.

AJ   There. Better.

Dani   Oh no you didn't.

AJ   I did.

Dani   You didn't just do that.

AJ   I'd do it again.

Dani *looks at* **Stace**.

Dani   What is happening?

AJ   Anita's dad just died of lung cancer. Bit insensitive to start lighting up at her party. Just saying.

Stace   We've not really seen her since, not properly.

Apart from we went to the funeral but.

I should've explained.

Dani   Probably, yeah.

Stace   Sorry.

A moment.

Dani   For the record, throwing somebody a birthday party when their dad just died is really weird.

AJ   Yep.

Dani   And organising it in a really depressing place and also dogging hotspot, that is also weird.

AJ   Forgot about the dogging.

Vinny   My dad's the caretaker, so it's free.

Dani   You are all just so weird.

AJ   Yep.

Dani   And annoying.

AJ   Yep.

Dani   Those cigarettes cost like seven quid.

AJ   I'll give you seven quid. To leave.

Dani   Fine.

AJ looks in his wallet.

AJ   Well, I haven't got seven quid, we'll have a whip round.

Dani   Probably just go to be honest.

Can't have chucked them that far.

Great mates you've got, Stace. This wasn't a pleasure.

Also (*to* **AJ**) your hair's shit.

Stace   Dani, please, don't just –

Dani   Watch me.

She storms off.

AJ   Laters.

Vinny   AJ, mate.

AJ   What?

Like, I can get on with most people but she is just an absolute bellend.

Stace   She's having a bit of a weekend.

AJ   Also, she is so wrong about my hair, I can't even.

Tez   Really?

AJ   Shut up.

Stace   I better go after her.

AJ   Why?

Magda   Well, she's not from here and she's just disappeared, by herself, into a renowned dogging hotspot, as night falls.

Stace   Don't.

Magda   D'you want a hand?

Stacey   It's fine.

Vinny   What about the party?

Stace   Be back in a sec.

Vinny   But –

Stace *leaves.*

AJ   People.

I do not understand people.

Tez   Understatement.

AJ   Shut up, you're not even invited.

Tez   And you're grounded, so.

AJ   'You're grounded, so.'

Tez   You're grounded, and I'm meant to be keeping an eye on you. Only reason I'm here.

No offence, everyone.

Kate   None taken.

Tez   I'm just doing what I have to do, for Mum, following you everywhere, making sure you don't start doing more flipping graffiti –

AJ   Wasn't even graffiti. Not graffiti if it's in your mum's garage is it?

Tez   Well, I hope you were practising for something a bit more public, otherwise it's just sad.

Matt   Go, Tez.

AJ   He's showing off.

Tez   I'm not showing off.

AJ   Worried Mum'll get mad I got out the house, blame him, cancel his trip to Harry Potter world.

Tez   Well, yeah.

AJ   Such a dick.

Tez   I just really like Harry Potter. I'm just –

AJ *gets* **Tez** *in a headlock.*

AJ   A dick? Thought so.

Tez   Ow.

AJ   Say it, say it and I'll let you go.

You're a dick.

Magda   AJ.

AJ   Say you're a dick.

Say it.

Vinny   AJ, he's going red.

AJ   Say you're a dick and I'll let you go.

Tez   No.

AJ   Fine, you're not a dick, my mistake.

Tez   Thank you.

AJ   You're a Slytherin.

Tez *fights back.*

Tez   Shut up!

AJ   That's what a Slytherin would say.

Magda   AJ, just –

AJ   I've seen you, Tez. Chatting to snakes, disrespecting house elves –

Tez   Muggle.

AJ   Hating on muggles.

Matt   Let him go.

AJ, let him go.

He touches **AJ** *on the arm.*

AJ *stops.*

AJ   Fine.

He lets **Tez** *go.*

AJ   Wriggle out. (*Quietly.*) Slytherin.

Matt   Enough.

Tez *smiles.*

Tez   Ravenclaw respect.

Matt *and* **Tez** *fist bump.*

AJ   Since when are you the Sorting Hat?

Magda   AJ, you know so much about Harry Potter. Like a disarming amount.

AJ   Shut up.

Vinny *gets a text.*

Vinny   Ten minutes. Frankie's picked Anita up. They're heading back.

Kate   Great.

Vinny   Stay calm, everyone, it'll probably be fine.

AJ   Drinks?

Vinny   Said you'd bring them.

AJ   I have done. Relax.

He starts getting bottles of spirits out of his bag. There's a lot.

Tez   You're kidding.

AJ   Pretend you can't see.

Tez *sighs.*

Stace *arrives back. She looks quite flustered.*

Stace   Oh, um.

Magda   Stace are you ok?

Matt   What's up?

AJ   Where's the dickhead?

Stace   That's the thing: I was just, I was wondering if you lot might've seen her? Cos, like, I haven't. Can't find her. Bit worried now.

Kate   She's not been back.

Magda   What happened?

Stace   Just must've legged it down there, into the woods, looking for her ciggies and then now I can't . . . Like I'm sure it's fine and everything, I'm sure she's just, but, thing is: I'm actually not sure it's fine. Getting quite dark now and, you know . . .

Kate   Have you rung her?

Stace   Straight to voicemail.

Magda   We'll help.

Stace   Thank you.

Magda   If we all just spread out a bit, look for her. Does that sound . . .?

Kate *nods her approval.*

Stace   She's probably gone back to mine, I do know that, it's probably stupid.

Magda   We'll come now.

AJ   Maybe go in twos, cos of the dogging.

Vinny   So like: me and you Stace, Kate and Magda, AJ and Tez. Matt can wait here in case she comes back.

AJ   I'm not helping.

Vinny   What?

AJ   No offence, Stace, I just can't be arsed looking for her.

Stace   That is a bit offensive.

AJ   Come on, mate. If I find her I'll only tell her where to go again. I'm not the man for the job.

Stace   Fair enough actually.

AJ   I'll wait here, look after everyone's stuff. And someone better be here in case these randoms from her youth orchestra start arriving.

Vinny   They're not coming are they?

Kate   Not what matters just now.

Vinny   Fair.

Stace   Right. Well. Be nice to her if she turns up.

AJ   Maybe.

Tez   I'll be nice to her.

AJ   Go find her then.

Tez   Can't, can I? Keeping an eye on you.

AJ   And can I just say what a great job you're doing? Mum'll be so pleased I've got out the house, turned up at a party with all this booze, and this –

He shows **Tez** *a can of spray paint he's got in his bag.*

Tez   What? How?

AJ   Probably take you to Harry Potter world on a broomstick.

You go find her. Make a three with them or something.

Me and Matt'll hold the fort.

Matt   Um. What?

AJ   Just saying, we'll stay here, sort out this punch, everyone else can go find what's-her-name, Dani.

Tez   Nah.

AJ   It's basically the Triwizard Tournament, Tez, you'll love it.

Magda   Again. So much detail.

Tez   Um.

If you're sure?

AJ   Course I'm sure.

Tez   I was asking Matt.

Matt *shrugs, nods.*

Tez   Ok then.

Vinny   Ace, right, if we all go different ways, have a good look round, meet back here in five?

Vinny, **Tez**, **Stace**, **Kate** *and* **Magda** *leave.*

Matt *looks at* **AJ**.

AJ *is lining up bottles of booze.*

There's a big bowl to mix the punch stuff in.

He examines some rum.

He stops.

Matt *is looking at him.*

AJ   What?

Matt   Nothing.

Silence.

AJ *sniffs the rum. Tries a bit. Pours the bottle into the bowl.*

Matt   Um. What is actually going on?

AJ *shrugs, smiles.*

AJ   Mixing this aren't I?

Making it all nice.

Why?

Matt *shrugs.*

A moment.

AJ *opens a bottle of vodka. Sniffs it. Shrugs and pours it in.*

AJ   Fun.

Matt *is still looking at him.*

AJ   Also I was thinking it'd be good to chat.

Matt   Right.

AJ If that's ok.

Matt I mean, I guess.

AJ I guess.

Matt Don't.

AJ Ok.

Soz.

Still mad at me, then.

Matt I wasn't mad at you.

AJ You are now.

Matt Cos you lied about me. Told Vinny I tried it on with you.

AJ I know, I panicked.

Soz.

A moment.

Matt I'm not mad at you.

AJ It's just: you seem mad.

Matt Cos you're infuriating.

AJ See?

Matt Look, just say it, whatever it is you're wanting to say, say it, and then, I dunno.

AJ Ok.

Ok then.

He pours whisky into the bowl.

D'you want some of this? It's horrific.

Matt Don't change the subject.

AJ I suppose just, what I'm wondering is: are you sure?

Matt Um.

AJ Just in case you're not sure.

About like, you know.

What I was saying before, about us two, like –

Matt Is this, um. Are you kidding?

AJ *shakes his head.*

Matt Oh.

Yeah I'm, I'm pretty sure yeah.

AJ Ok.

Cool.

Ok.

Matt Maybe time for a mixer, d'you think? Something soft. Mixer time.

AJ Fine. Ok.

Matt Are you ok?

AJ Maybe Coke? Sprite? D'you want some?

Matt AJ.

AJ What?

Matt Are you ok?

AJ Yeah, yeah, course.

Matt Ok.

AJ Maybe Fanta.

He pours some Fanta into the bowl.

It's just, I do actually think . . .

Like we do have a proper laugh and that, and like, I dunno.

We are the only gays so . . . Like at school so . . .

Matt Exactly.

AJ What d'you mean?

Matt It's not like we're a good fit or anything – we're just the, the only ones. That we know of.

It's like, isn't it, like pandas?

AJ What you on about pandas?

Matt   Everyone's always having a go at pandas, in zoos, getting really wound up about pandas. Cos they're endangered but also they're just not in a rush. At all. And the zookeepers go on the news saying they've done everything they can think of, flown in this panda from a different zoo to try and breed, make a baby panda together, but nothing's happening. And the zookeepers are all making out it's really frustrating and that. But I just think: fair enough. There's loads of things you might be looking for in a mate sort of thing. It's not enough that you're just both pandas.

AJ   Right.

Matt   You're not even out.

AJ   You're still a virgin.

Matt   And you just got crabs off some lad off the internet.

AJ   Worth it.

Matt   Was it?

AJ   Course.

Fun.

And then, bit itchy.

And then I went to the clinic, got some cream. No biggie.

Matt   Does sound fun.

AJ   Plus the cream they give you, you've got to put it everywhere, hair, body, face, got coconut oil in, made my skin look properly nice. Everyone was like, 'AJ, you look immense'. I was, like, 'Cheers, I've had crabs'.

Matt *smiles.*

AJ   See?

We have a laugh.

Matt   Yeah.

Yeah.

He smiles at **AJ**. *Looks down.* **AJ***'s still smiling.*

Matt   Feel like we're mates, is the thing.

Feel like maybe that's worth more than, I dunno. At the moment, anyway.

Like having someone else who sort of, gets it. A bit.

AJ   Oh I'm getting it.

Matt   Not like that just.

Makes me feel a bit, I dunno. Braver or. Not as lonely.

AJ   Ok.

Yep.

But like, definitely not . . .

Matt   Yeah. No. If that's . . .

AJ   Course it is. Course.

Just like checking in.

He stirs the punch a bit.

Kate *comes in.*

Matt   Have you found her?

Kate   No. We're spreading out a bit now, going into the woods properly. Stace is quite anxious. I've come in search of torches.

Matt   Oh, um.

He and **Kate** *look through various boxes, and pull out quite strange stuff.*

Maybe the leftovers of a jumble sale or something.

AJ *goes back to making punch.*

Kate   I'm not sure this is working.

Matt   Is there a cupboard anywhere? Or a drawer in the kitchen bit or something?

Kate   I've already looked.

Matt   Don't know what to say then really.

Kate *looks thoughtful.*

Kate   All we've got to do is think like a torch.

Matt   Um.

Kate   Think like: if I was a torch, where would I be?

Matt   Oh. I don't know. Sorry.

Kate *looks forlorn.*

AJ   What about your phones?

Kate   Pardon?

AJ   You've probably all got torches on your phones.

Kate *thinks about this.*

Kate   Good point.

She leaves.

Matt *looks at* **AJ** *making punch.*

AJ *stops and smiles.*

Matt   What?

AJ   Just thinking: you're probably right and everything. Mates, et cetera. But just thinking: we should probably get off a bit now to make sure?

Matt *laughs.*

AJ   What?

Matt   You're amazing.

AJ   Think about it though. They always, in films they always talk about not fitting together that well, like you just did, but then they try it and a switch just sort of flicks on, suddenly they're just at it, all the time, it's immense.

Matt *shakes his head.*

Matt   That's just films, I think.

AJ   Oh.

Probably.

Yeah.

Matt   Mates is better.

AJ   Really?

Matt   Really.

He smiles.

Keep imagining, we're like properly old, twenties, we're off out dancing, you're pulling this lad –

AJ   At least one.

Matt   Oh.

AJ   Five or six, probs.

Matt   I've spotted someone nice who I've seen about a bit, but he's maybe a bit shy or something.

AJ   Right.

Matt   Like a socially awkward hunk – broad shoulders, cable knit – which I think is probably my type.

AJ   Loser.

Matt   And we're just, like, I dunno, you're downing shots, I'm not, knowing we've got this night out in front of us, where fun stuff happens, for both of us, even though we've got quite different ideas of what fun is.

AJ   I'll be shagging.

Matt   Probably.

AJ   You'll be drinking tea, thinking about haikus.

Matt   Exactly.

Keep thinking about that.

And, like, I'm really glad we're mates.

Even though it's just sort of, early days or whatever.

I'm really glad you told me and that.

I'm really glad.

AJ   I'm really glad.

Matt   I am.

AJ   Dickhead.

Matt   Cos it's good to have mates who are like you isn't it? But then it's also good to have mates who are really different.

AJ   I guess.

Matt   And I just think, I'm a Ravenclaw. My mates are all Ravenclaws. So it's nice to have a mate who's something different. My first Gryffindor.

AJ   You think I'm . . .?

Matt   Jumps headfirst into stuff. Thinks it's all about him. Quite annoying . . . Classic Gryffindor.

AJ *smiles.*

AJ   I'll take that.

Matt   Thought you might.

He smiles.

There's like a youth group in town, Wednesday nights.

AJ   A youth group? Seriously.

Matt   Been wanting to go for ages but, not quite managed it.

AJ   Next Wednesday?

Matt *smiles.*

Matt   Go on then.

AJ   Sorted.

He smiles.

Maybe some of them'll be up for it.

Matt   Tell them your crabs story, icebreaker, see what happens.

AJ   Will. Do.

He smiles.

Dani *bursts in.*

Dani   Fucking hell.

Matt   Dani – you ok?

Dani   Tell me this has booze in.

She is scooping a big red cupful of punch.

Matt   Oh, um –

AJ   Tons, mate.

Dani *has started to down it.*

AJ   Wow.

That is actually impressive.

Dani   If you'd just seen what I'd seen, you'd be necking this too, I promise.

The others arrive back.

Matt   What's going on?

Stace   Oh, um, yeah.

Dani   Don't you dare say a thing.

Any of you.

She gets more booze.

Stace   Right. Ok.

She zips her mouth shut.

Matt   Seriously, um.

Stace   Thing is –

Dani   Shut it.

Stace *shuts up.*

Matt   Are you all ok?

Magda   Bit traumatised

Tez   Bit?

Vinny   I feel weird.

Matt   What's happened?

Dani   I said shut it.

AJ   Somebody has to tell us.

Nobody does.

I can put Tez in another headlock if you like, it's really easy.

Tez   You're two years older and you drink protein shakes.

Kate   Dani?

Everyone looks at **Dani**.

Dani   Ok, here's the deal:

I'll tell you, I'll say it once, and then we never talk about it again.

AJ   This gets better.

Dani   Deal?

Matt   Deal.

Dani   Fine. So.

You chucked my cigarettes, out there, that general direction. Yeah?

AJ   Yep.

Dani   I went to get them back. Ended up rummaging around in the, undergrowth, bracken is it? Doesn't matter. Found them.

So far so normal.

Took a while.

And I was like, in my head I was like: fine. Just smoke here.

Thought I'd just hide, there's like these two trees together with a gap in the middle, smoke, calm down. So I'm sat there thinking: one cigarette, one lovely cigarette, really like enjoying each drag, thinking that'll put the jumped-up little shit – that's you by the way –

AJ   Obvs.

Dani   That'll put the jumped-up little shit –

AJ points to himself, proudly.

Dani   – back in his place. Restore a bit of order, in my head, self-esteem, et cetera. Thought I'd really enjoy it.

But then . . .

Matt   What?

Dani   It's actually too awful.

AJ   What? Tell us . . .

Dani   Gradually started to realise I wasn't . . . alone.

AJ is grinning.

AJ   Shit. The bed.

Matt   Bit spooky.

Dani   Stace, maybe you could . . .?

She goes to get another drink.

Stace   You sure?

AJ   Stace, don't leave us hanging.

Dani *nods and turns away, dramatically.*

Stace   So, um, at this point, we're all of us out looking for Dani. She's not answering her phone, not in the car park, I've come back in and got you lot, we've headed into the woods. Kate's suggested phone torches but they actually make everything seem creepy, bit horror film, low-budget, so we turn them off and just use natural night vision.

Vinny   The moon.

Stace   Exactly. And people say, don't they, if one sense is not as good, the others get stronger, and I think that's what must've happened cos suddenly we can all hear this, like, quite quiet sort of, um, grunting.

AJ   No way.

Stace   Yeah just like . . .

She grunts.

AJ   Please let this be what I think it is.

Stace   Creep up to this clearing, and we can see Dani in between these trees, but she's like gesturing like: stay back, stay away.

But we don't.

Creep up, really quietly, and then . . .

AJ   Then . . .?

Stace   Feels wrong to sort of.

Matt   Please just tell us.

Stace   The thing is it is quite bad.

Dani   Quite bad?

Vinny   We can't ever unsee it. You have to remember that. Dani especially.

AJ   Unsee what? Just say it.

Tell us.

A moment.

Kate   Dani's mum and dad were dogging.

AJ   What?!

Magda   Yeah.

AJ   WHAT?!

Kate   Dani's mum and dad.

Having sex.

In the woods.

And we all saw.

Including Dani.

AJ   You are kidding me. You are having me on.

Stace *shakes her head.*

AJ   Literally now? Literally out there now?

Stace   Well, they've finished now. We waited till they'd, um, till the end before we, yep.

Kate   We didn't like to disturb them.

AJ   This has to be karma, has to be.

Magda   How?

AJ   She's a total dick to us, goes outside, ends up watching her mum and dad dogging.

Dani   Alright.

Stace   I didn't know Uncle Alan had it in him.

Dani   *Alright.*

Matt   But actually, it's nice isn't it? In a way.

They're, you know.

They're sort of, friends, again.

Marriage-wise – back on track.

Stace   It's true, Dani. One less thing.

Dani *gives a massive thumbs up.*

Dani   Time to move on, I think.

Vinny *gets a text.*

Vinny   This is officially our one-minute warning.

Everyone springs into action.

Stace   Argh!

Magda   Can't believe it's happening.

Matt   And we're all here.

Stace   And the bunting's up. Cheers, Kate.

Vinny   Frankie says not to jump out but I just think we have to really, don't we? It's a surprise – we have to.

Matt   Party poppers, party poppers.

He hands everyone a party popper.

AJ   Right, gang. Positions.

Everyone gets in position.

And . . .

He turns the light off.

A moment.

Stace   This is the most excited I have ever been in my whole entire life.

AJ   You ready, mate?

He punches **Vinny** *on the shoulder.*

Vinny   Yeah.

Well. Sort of.

AJ   What?

Magda   Vinny, you've done it. Enjoy it. Come on.

Vinny   Yeah. Yeah.

Matt   Vinny, are you ok?

Vinny *doesn't say anything.*

Stace   What's up?

Vinny   No, nothing it's . . .

Magda   Vinny. Seriously.

Vinny   Well, I guess.

Um.

Honestly?

And I know it's quite a weird time to tell you this but.

I'm quite worried.

AJ   What you on about?

Vinny   I just think: all the stuff everyone said, about how it's not exactly a good place for a party, and how Anita's probably not really feeling like a party anyway, cos, like, she just lost her dad and everything, how it's actually quite a poorly judged thing to do, how we're quite weird for doing it, I'm just starting to think like: yeah.

Magda   Now? You're thinking that now?

Vinny   Yeah.

Cos it is a really weird idea – it is though – probably be a disaster, or maybe make Anita more upset than she already is, and it's sort of dawning on me what a massive, massive, massive mistake it was, and that I'm just like completely an idiot.

Cos, sort of, I wouldn't make her sadder for the world.

Not for the world.

Just wanted to do something nice for her, something, I dunno. But stuff escalates doesn't it? Gets a bit out of hand and everyone else brings all their mess to it as well, before you know it . . .

Feels like that's what's happened here, a bit. A lot.

AJ   They're coming.

Vinny   Ok, ace.

They all crouch down waiting for Anita and **Frankie**.

Frankie *opens the door.*

Frankie   Um?

Everyone jumps out, lights on, party poppers.

Everyone   SURPRISE!

Frankie   Said don't do that.

Vinny   What?

Frankie   Don't, I said. Don't jump out.

In my text.

Vinny   Where's Anita?

Frankie   Not here is she. Which is why I was like . . .

Vinny   What?

Frankie   Yeah. Slight change of plan.

Vinny   *Slight?*

Frankie   Thought it'd be better to just explain it face to face.

AJ looks at his party popper.

AJ   But I've popped.

Vinny   I don't get what's happened.

Frankie   Basically, she's gone home.

Cos, she didn't want to come out in the first place, like leave the house at all, which we knew might be a bit of a problem, we did say didn't we, but I convinced her in the end, I was just like let's go for a walk, a birthday walk, told her about my pedometer, how I'm meant to get ten thousand steps, she was like ok, so we did.

Vinny   That is good actually.

Frankie   Yeah, so the plan's working. But then she wanted to go the other way, she was like I'd really like to just wander round town a bit, the shops, maybe have a hot chocolate, so I had to be like: no, it's your birthday, we need trees. Birthday trees.

Magda   Is that a thing?

Frankie   I was improvising. Stroke panicking. And she was like, um, ok? And then we got out here and she was just asking me, Frankie, where are we actually going, they're not even nice trees, they've got some sort of leaf disease it's weirdly sad – which is true, have you seen, all these little black spots it's properly rank – so I just thought: be honest. Come clean.

So I said the reason we're here is everyone's doing you like a little birthday party, they just wanted to see you, and we didn't think you'd come if we told you so. And Vinny's dad gave him the keys to the hall for free. Thought it might be nice to be all together, have some cake, with your mates who you haven't seen for a bit.

But, in the end: no.

You could see it meant a lot to her, but just . . .

Magda   No.

Frankie   I mean she's not here is she so.

Vinny   Right.

Frankie   Said to say cheers and everything though.

And she's looking forward to seeing everyone.

Just quietly.

When she's ready.

Not today but.

Cos I guess it's like her first birthday without her dad and everything.

And I guess we're used to seeing her quite in charge and stuff, but she's not quite in charge just now.

Her mum's still in a bit of a state, think she feels a bit weird leaving her.

And she's still in a bit of a state also, I reckon. Never said that obvs but. But it turned out she was still in her PJs underneath her hoody, so.

I just thought it was leisure wear. Hard to tell sometimes isn't it? Post-onesie.

Vinny   Right.

I mean it was a shit idea, so.

Magda   Not that shit.

Vinny   You literally said this place was shit.

Magda   Yeah but not the, the thought's not shit. The thought's decent.

Matt   Worth a try, wasn't it?

AJ   Definitely, mate. What he said. Definitely.

A moment.

Vinny   Might as well go then.

Don't think anyone else is coming anyway.

Kate   Might be a few. It's only just time.

Vinny *slumps.*

AJ   Mate.

Vinny   I just.

I really really like her.

AJ *hugs him.*

AJ   I know.

Vinny   And I miss her.

AJ   Course you do.

Vinny   Just wanted to make her feel, I dunno.

Not better.

Just maybe, I dunno.

Maybe a bit less shit?

Stace   It's a really nice thought, Vinny.

Dani   Like so misguided but.

Stace   Dani.

Dani   Yep, soz.

Vinny   I can't believe you made all those biscuits.

Stace   It's fine.

Vinny   And Kate put up the bunting.

Kate   I enjoyed it.

Vinny   Magda wrote a song.

Magda   It's nothing.

Vinny   And Matt bought those Skittles.

Matt   Just a medium bag.

Frankie   Whoa. Back up.

Vinny   What?

Frankie   Magda wrote a song? For Anita?

Magda   Didn't have money for a prezzie so I just thought . . .

Frankie   What kind of song?

Magda   Um. Short?

Stace   And good.

Magda   Ish.

Frankie   Right, I might have a plan.

Vinny   What?

Frankie *gets one of the dust sheets off the pile of boxes.*

Frankie   We can nick this can't we?

Vinny   I guess. What's . . .?

Frankie   Just need some paint.

AJ *fishes a spray can out of his bag.*

AJ   Frankie, mate, I thought you'd never ask.

Frankie   Alright, Banksy. Ready?

Scene Two

Lights up on everyone.

The audience are the other people who've turned up for Anita's party.

Frankie, **Kate**, **Vinny**, **Magda**, **Matt**, **AJ**, **Tez**, **Stace** *and* **Dani** *stand at the front, and talk to us directly.*

Vinny   Um, hey, everyone. Hey.

Just to say: thanks so much for coming.

I was worried no one would turn up, but then everyone's turned up, so . . .

Nearly everyone.

Um, Frankie?

Frankie   Yeah.

I guess the sort of headline news is: Anita's not here.

I know. Anti-climax. But that's just, that's just what's going on.

She sends her love though and, she is alright, and I'm sure she'll be back sort of out and about soon, just she maybe wasn't quite ready for sort of, partying today.

So, yeah.

We're basically, we're sending you all home. Soz.

Vinny   Sorry.

Frankie   But before you go . . .

Magda's written this song for Anita, and I had a thought, maybe if we like all sang it together, and recorded it – Vinny's off to record it on his phone – then he'll send it to Anita so she knows we're all thinking of her and that.

He doesn't mind if it uses up all his data.

Vinny   I don't.

Frankie   He reckons Anita's worth it.

Vinny   She is.

Frankie   So we've got the words here –

The gang hold up the sheet, with the lyrics painted on.

– and then Magda'll sing it so you know how it goes. Magda?

Magda *sings.*

Shit stuff happens
Sometimes shit stuff happens
Happens to you
Shit stuff

But good stuff also happens
Sometimes good stuff also happens
Hopefully
That's enough.

Frankie   Ready, Vinny?

Vinny's *recording. Thumbs up.*

Frankie   Everyone? 1, 2, 3, 4.

Everyone sings.

Shit stuff happens
Sometimes shit stuff happens
Happens to you
Shit stuff

But good stuff also happens
Sometimes good stuff also happens
Hopefully
That's enough.

Stuff

BY TOM WELLS

Notes on rehearsal and staging, drawn from a workshop with the writer, held at the National Theatre, October 2018

How Tom came to write the play

Tom wanted to write about friendship and love and teenagers encountering love for the first time. The play is a focused idea of what the characters want but they bring their 'mess' along too. 'It's a celebration of that mess.' The teenagers think they have done a good job in setting up a party. They have brought things to dress the space to make it their own version of good, although in reality it probably isn't good.

The play is also about adults being flawed. The characters learn that grown-ups, who are usually the ones to resolve problems, have their own problems and mess. The idea of dogging within the play ties into the idea that parents' solutions are not always the best – in this case it might be slightly misguided but they're just trying to do the right thing to save their marriage. 'It's like coming up with the wrong answer to the right question.'

Lead director James Grieve said that what makes Tom's plays so special is how he 'shines a light on the micro events in people's lives'; events that feel massive to the people involved but not necessarily to the outside world. Tom doesn't write plays like *Antony and Cleopatra* where the characters rule nations and fight wars; but for the characters within Tom's plays, they themselves feel as big as Antony and Cleopatra. James stated that it is worth remembering that good plays should take place in the most extraordinary moments of characters' lives. A useful exercise could be to ask your young people: 'Why are these forty-five minutes in these characters lives extraordinary?', 'Why isn't the play set at Anita's dad's funeral?' or 'Why isn't this set around the previous encounter between AJ and Matt?' When unpicked, these are micro but extraordinary moments for everyone in the play.

Approaching the play

James noted that Tom writes plays about people who aren't normally seen on stage. You should work towards engaging your actors to find performances true to people who aren't always in the spotlight.

James suggested starting the rehearsal process with a read-through to ensure everyone in the company has a similar understanding of the text. The next step would then be to allow the actors to ask any questions they had about the play to clear up any misunderstandings. Some questions that arose from the workshop were answered as follows:

Q   What does 'phenaynay' mean?

A   It's not a real word; it's adapted language from the word *phenomenal.*

Q   What is the club that AJ and Matt refer to?

A   A confidential club for teenagers of the LGBT+ community.

Q   How long is 'a moment'?

A   A breath, long enough to notice no one talks – how long it takes for the thought to land.

Exercises for use in rehearsal

ADJECTIVE EXERCISE

James encouraged participants to think of three adjectives to describe the play. The group came up with the following adjectives: awkward, messy, characterful, sincere, amusing, realistic, challenging, affectionate, reassuring, nervous, bantering, rallying, truthful, friendly delicate, life affirming, innocent, cathartic, hopeful, funny realistic, relatable, gentle, sarcastic, heart-warming, insightful, vulnerable, engaging, relevant, realistic, inclusive, real, uplifting, searching, lost, optimistic, natural, bonding, togetherness, broken, honest, hope, acceptance, anxious, thoughtful, witty, supportive, genuine, poignant, touching, human, radiating.

With your company, doing a mood board, a word cloud (an image composed of words used in the play, in which the size of each word indicates its frequency/importance) or anything visual that feels in and of the world of the play could be useful early in rehearsals.

An extension task could be to discuss what the play isn't. Examples given were: cynical, draining, aggressive, dull, dark.

OBJECT ASSOCIATION

The characters in the play want to make something nice for Anita so they hand-make things; actors could do the same – e.g. they could bring in a piece of music or item that reminds them of the play or the characters and could share this with the rest of the group.

WRITE A SYNOPSIS OF THE PLAY IN 140 CHARACTERS,
I.E. A TWEET.

Actors might find this harder to do than they would with plays they know
well, e.g. *Hamlet*. It also might be harder to synopsise a multi-character
play. Does it start from Vinny's perspective of throwing a party? Or Dani
and her parents? Each starting point is a different route into the play.
James's tip is to start with 'A group of friends . . .' or something of that
nature as there is no one protagonist of the play.

DISCUSS THE THEMES OF PLAY

You could brainstorm with your group what they think the themes of the
play are and write them on A3 paper to put up in the rehearsal room. This
could be a useful framework to go back to. They may even be useful
further along the process if any issues arise – solutions can sometimes be
found in these early brainstorms.

The group came up with the following themes: love, unrequited love,
friendship, loss, insecurity, fear, teenage-hood.

It can be helpful to get a visual sense of what the play is. An extension
task could be for companies to draw an image that represents some of the
themes or scenes or moments from the play.

IMPROVISATIONS

You could set up some improvisations to explore character, relationships
and/or events that are not in the play but inform the action. James suggests
that being specific with instructions will allow it to feel safer for the actors
to explore; e.g. give a place, time and character objective.

Suggestions for improvisations:

- Park bench – improvise a conversation with characters on a park
  bench.

- You could improvise historical events in characters' lives, e.g. a
  previous encounter between AJ and Matt, Anita's dad's funeral.

- You could improvise the whole play without the script.

UNITING

Uniting is different for every director and there is no one right way to go
about it.

James's definition of a unit is: a fundamental change within a scene,
where once an action has occurred or piece of dialogue delivered, the play

can't go back to what it was before that moment happened; for example a character making an entrance or exit.

Uniting can be a useful rehearsal tool as it breaks the play down into manageable chunks. It is also helpful as a way to know what to rehearse and with whom if you don't have all your actors available for every rehearsal. Uniting is also beneficial as it means actors read the play a few times, subsequently becoming more familiar with the text. Having a list of all the units gives a good map of the events of the play. James's tip is to name units from the dialogue within them that best summarises the unit.

The group worked through the first few pages of the script, breaking the scene into units through discussion. This is what they decided. Your group may discover something different.

Unit 1 ('Surprise!') ending on p. 622 after Frankie exits.

Unit 2 ('Made a secret Facebook event') ending on p. 623 after Kate exits.

Unit 3 ('AJ's coming?') Ending on p. 625 after Stace's line 'Really?'.

Unit 4 ('get in the party spirit') ending on p. 626 after Vinny's line '. . . D of E'.

Unit 5 ('It's screaming: dogging') ending on p. 628 after Kate's re-entrance.

Unit 6 ('Bunting time?') ending on p. 629 after Matt's exit line 'In a bit'.

Unit 7 ('my family is literally falling apart') ending on p. 632 when the others return.

Unit 8 ('phenaynay') ending on p. 635, just before Stace says 'Oh, Dani, no'.

Unit 9 ('a thing we don't do') ending on p. 637 when AJ enters.

FACTS AND QUESTIONS

Creating a list of FACTS and QUESTIONS within each scene can be useful to bring clarity to actors and directors, and ensure everyone has a mutual understanding of the world of the play. The answers to the questions will impact on actors' decisions about how they play the characters. These lists might also be helpful for the director when giving notes to actors later down the line and can even help solve problems in tech and early performances.

James mentioned that Katie Mitchell is famously known to use this technique in her rehearsal room as detailed in her book *The Director's Craft*.

A short example of what James and the group came up with:

FACTS	QUESTIONS
They are in a hall	What type of hall? Where is it?
There are particular items in the hall	What colour paint on walls?
The characters are waiting in the dark	How welcoming is the hall?
Vinny made a secret Facebook group	Why are they there?
Others have been invited	What are they waiting for?
Vinny has keys for the hall	How long have they known each other
They are waiting for AJ	How much in advance did they plan this?

Characterisation

James reminded the group that the play is naturalistic and actors should be encouraged to celebrate the nuanced, delicate, naturalistic characters. James also discussed how character work can give actors a distilled sense of themselves and their place in the world. The group collectively suggested the following activities:

- Character lists: ask actors to go through the text and write lists using the following headings – what characters say about themselves; what they say about others; what others say about them.

- You could also ask them to consider subtext: how characters feel inside and what they say outside.

- Hot seating: this is where an actor sits in character and others in the group ask them questions about their lives.

- Acting off the ball: passing a ball around in a scene to indicate who has possession of the moment. Remind actors they are all contributing to a line even when silent.

- Status/stakes games using pack of cards, where the number on the card determines the status of the character.

- Creating and playing 'top trump' cards.

- Get the cast to create social media profile posters for their characters.

- Write career advice to each character.
- Ask actors to consider what animal their character would be. How might this inform their physicality?
- Actors could tap out their character's rhythm.
- Where is a character's centre? You could invite actors to discover which body part the character leads from physically?
- You could then physically explore the combination of a character's rhythm with their centre.

Accents

Tom stated that the play is not located anywhere specific, so any accents are fine. Although Dani is 'an outsider' she doesn't need to have a different accent.

Production, staging and design

Tom and James suggested the play can be performed, and lends itself well, to any configuration. The more immersive the better, but be mindful of audience interaction; e.g. perhaps audience blowing up balloons could detract from the action onstage – protect the integrity of the scene. It is fine if you wish to have the characters milling about the stage during pre-set and if you have a space where exits and entrances aren't possible, it is fine to have actors standing in neutral on the outskirts of the space.

SET

The play is set in a scruffy village hall; it is well used but not decaying. It has been there a long time and has lots of things lying about from various clubs who use the space. It's not a cool space by the characters' standards. James and Tom stated that if you have a less than desirable venue, you can use that to your advantage; you don't need much to make the play work as long as there is clarity of story and ideas. Tom encouraged directors to allow their young people the opportunity to make the bunting – the more homemade looking it is, the better. James suggested that there are great opportunities for characters to utilise junk as furniture, such as exercise bikes, space hoppers, crates. The DIY element of the setting is to be embraced.

LIGHTING

A basic wash is fine if that is all that is available to you. Front lighting could also help. The space should feel stark and bright like an old community hall. The play is set in the evening around dusk, possibly between May and September.

COSTUME

The characters probably wear jeans, T-shirts, hoodies, etc. They are not dressed up even though it's a party. Vinny may have made a bit more of an effort. Allowing young actors involvement in costume is advised – they might know best.

MOVEMENT

The play doesn't require any complex movement. Ensure each character's physical journeys in the staging are clear.

The 'shit stuff happens' song

It is important to Tom that Magda's song is sung and played live by the actor playing Magda and should remain as written. Magda needs to make herself vulnerable; this gesture is how she shows her love. She isn't great. The song can't be too impressive. The chords used could be D7, G, C. Tom references Grace Petrie who self-declares her work not good or complex but makes good music. The song at the end of the play should leave the audience feeling joyful. You are welcome to be creative with the song, incorporating vocal harmonies and rapping, while the audience should be encouraged to sing along!

Gender

Tom stated that it is important to observe the following regarding gender:

- Any actor can play any character – but *Matt and AJ must be male characters.*
- If Vinny is female, then Anita has to be male; i.e. Vinny is heterosexual. It's fine to change Anita's name to match gender.

- If you must change characters' names, then you can, but stay truthful to the intention of the name; e.g. Stace shouldn't be a Theodore.
- It's fine to change pronouns within the text to suit any character gender changes.

Big casts

James made a few suggestions for companies bigger than nine:

- Rehearse two separate casts who perform on different nights.
- Have an understudy cast.
- Build a company, e.g. designers, stage management, operators.
- Act One could be played by one cast, Act Two by another, as long as you find a way to keep the storytelling clear.

Suggested references

Actions: The Actors' Thesaurus by Marina Calderone

The Director's Craft: A Handbook for the Theatre by Katie Mitchell

From a workshop led by James Grieve
with notes by Lakesha Arie-Angelo

Participating Companies

20Twenty Academy
Abdabs Youth Theatre
Aberconwy
Aberdeen Academy of Performing
  Arts College
Aberystwyth Arts Centre Youth
  Theatre
Acorn Young People's Theatre
act 2 academy
ACTAcademy UK
Acting Up!
Actors Workshop
ACTS
All the Arts Theatre School
AllStars Theatre Company
Alnwick Playhouse Youth Theatre
Alumni
Anglo European School
Ardclough Youth Theatre
Ark Helenswood Academy
Arts1
artsdepot Performance Company
ArtsEd Skills Academy
Astor Youth Theatre Company
Atlantic Coast Theatre
Aylward Academy
Barbara Priestman Academy Theatre
  Company
Barton Peveril
BDC Company
Bedford College
Bedlington Academy Performance
  Group
Berzerk Productions
Bilborough Sixth Form College
Bishops High School
Blaze Youth Theatre
Blueprint
Bolingbroke Academy Theatre
  Company
Bolton Sixth Form College
Boomsatsuma
Borders Youth Theatre

Bridgend College
Brighton College
Brookfields SEN School
Burnage Academy for Boys
Burntwood School
Caithness Young Company – Eden
  Court/Lyth Arts
Calderdale Theatre School
CAM Theatre Company
CAPA College
CAPA College Dance Company
Cast Youth Theatre
CASTEnsemble
Cavendish School
CAYT – Crescent Arts Youth Theatre
Cheltenham Youth Theatre
Chichester Festival Youth Theatre
Christopher Whitehead Language
  College and Sixth Form
CHSG Players
Church Stretton School
Cockburn Company
Cockburn John Charles Academy
COLAI Players
Corn Exchange Newbury Youth
  Theatre
Cramlington Youth Dramatic Society
  (CYDS)
Cranford Community College
Creatio Arts
Culloden Academy Youth Company
Curious Connections
Dalton Theatre Company
De Warenne Academy
Delanté Détras Theatre Company
Dimensions Performance Academy
Diocesan School for Girls
Dorchester Youth Theatre
Drama Lab
Dudley College Performing Arts
Dukies Youth Theatre
Dumfries Youth Theatre
Eastern School of Performing Arts

Easy Street Theatre Company
ECMT
Eden Court CREATIVE – Lochaber
   Youth Theatre
Eden Court Youth Theatre
Fallibroome Academy
Fire & Steel Theatre Company
Fisher Youth Theatre Group
Flying High Young Company
Forest Hill School
Fortrose Academy Youth Theatre
Fred Longworth High School
Garrick Young REP
Gateshead College
GEMS Wellington Academy Sixth
   Form Theatre Company
George Dixon Academy
Glasgow Acting Academy SCIO
Gloucestershire College
Grand Young Company
Griese Youth Theatre
Gulbenkian
Hackney Shed Collective
Halesowen College
Hall for Cornwall Youth Theatre
Hayworth Players
Hex Harts Theatre Company
Holy Trinity Catholic School
Hornsea School and Language College
Hunterhouse College
Huntingdon Youth Theatre
Identity School of Acting
Ignite
Ilkley Players Greenroom
In Yer Face Productions
Invicta Grammar School
Kildare Youth Theatre
Kingham Hill School
King's Theatre Company
Kings Youth Theatre
Kingsford Community School
Kingsley Bideford Community
   Theatre Company
Knightswood Secondary School
Knox Academy
Knutsford Academy Young Actors

Lakeside Youth Theatre
Lambeth College
Lammas/Norlington
Lightcliffe Academy
Lincoln Young Company
Lister Community School
LOST Youth Theatre Company
LUMOS THEATRE
M6 Youth Theatre
MAAD (Matthew Arnold Amateur
   Dramatics)
Mark Jermin Stage School
Masque Youth Theatre
MATE Productions
Matravers School
Meridian School
Mill Hill County High School
Millburn Academy Drama Club
Milton Keynes Theatre
Mishmak Youth Theatre
Monaghan Youth Theatre
Monoux College
Montage Theatre Arts
Mount Temple Comprehensive School
Mr. Sands Youth Theatre
Mulberry Schools Trust
New College, Swindon
New Vic Youth Theatre
NHC Actors
Nicholas Chamberlaine School
NMPAT – Young Actors Company
Norden Farm Youth Theatre
North Durham Academy
Norwich School
Norwich Theatre Royal
Nottingham College Actors
Nu.Dynamic Theatre Company
Nuffield Southampton Youth Theatre
NYTP
Oaklands
Oldham College
OP and MCS Company
Orange Tree Theatre Young Company
Ormiston Rivers Academy
Outwood Academy, Hemsworth
Oxford High School

PACT
Page2stage Youth Theatre
Patrician Youth Centre
Perfect Circle Youth Theatre
Perth High School
Pike and Musket
Playacting Youth Theatre
Pomegranate Youth Theatre and
   Gekkota Arts
PQA Maidenhead
Prendergast Players
PRO:Jections Theatre Company
Pump House CYT
Queen Anne's School
Queens Hall Youth Theatre
Queen's Park High School
Queen's Theatre Cut2 Company
Queensbridge School
R&D: Connect
Rainham Mark Grammar School
Rare Studio Liverpool
Ravens Wood School
Reed's School
RHSC Drama Club
Ringwood School
Rotherham College
Roundwood Park School
Royalty Theatre Youth Academy
RR6
Ruislip High School
Sandbach School Theatre
Sandwell College Young Directors
SAS Productions
Scarborough Sixth Form College
See&Eye Theatre
Sgioba Drama Òigridh Inbhir Nis
Shadow Syndicate
Shakespearia
Sheffield People's Theatre
Sherborne Girls
Sherman Youth Theatre
SHS Acting Company
Sir Henry Floyd Grammar School
SLT Youth Theatre
South Hunsley School
Southwark Playhouse Young Company

Spotlight Drama Youth Theatre
Spotlight UK
SpringBoard Theatre Company
SRWA theatre company
St Anselms, College
St Gabriel's
St John Plessington Catholic College
St John's and King Richard's
St Mary's Calne
St Saviour's and St Olave's School
St Thomas More Catholic High School
St Brendan's Sixth Form College
St Ives School Youth Theatre
Stag Youth Theatre
Stagecoach Chelmsford
Stagecoach East Kilbride
Stagecoach Huddersfield
Stagedoor
Stockport Academy
Stockport Garrick Youth Theatre
Stonar School
STORE ROOM YOUTH
   THEATRE
Story Makers
STP Company
Stratford School Academy
Suffolk New College Performing
   Arts
Sundial Theatre Company
Surbiton High School
Sweet Pea Theatre
TBTL Young Company
The Actors Centre Theatre Company
The Blue Coat School Oldham
The Boaty Theatre Company
The Bourne Academy
The Burgess Hill Academy
The Canterbury Academy
The Chantry School
The Cobham Players
The College Merthyr Tydfil
The Customs House Youth Theatre at
   Jarrow School
The Drama Studio
The Garage Theatre Company
The John Fisher School

The John Lyon School
The Lowry Young Company
The Oaks Academy
The Petchey Academy
The Plough Youth Theatre Seniors
The Shed
The Upstarts
The Young Rep Acting School
The Young Theatre
Theatre Royal Stratford East Youth
  Theatre
Theatre Unboxed CIC
Thomas Rotherham College
Through The Wardrobe: Children's
  Theatre Company
Tiptoe School of Performing Arts
Tobacco Factory Theatres YTM
  Perform
TPS
Tracing Steps
Trinity Youth Theatre
Unlimited Theatre
UROCK Theatre Company
Urswick Youth Theatre
Vandyke Upper School
Wallington County Grammar School

Walsall College
Warminster School
Warwick Arts Centre Connections
  Company
Weavers Academy
West End Classrooms
West London Free School
West Yorkshire Drama Academy
Westborough High School
Westfield Arts College
White City Youth Theatre
Wildcats Theatre School
Wildern School
Windsor College
Winstanley College
Woodrush High School
Woolwich Polytechnic School
Worlds End Productions London
Worthing College
Yate Academy
YDA – Young Dramatic Arts Theatre
  Company
Yew Tree Youth Theatre
Young and Unique@ CCC
Young Lyric
Youth Arts Centre

Partner Theatres

Aberystwyth Arts Centre
The Albany, London
artsdepot, London
Bristol Old Vic
Bush Theatre, London
Cast, Doncaster
Chichester Festival Theatre
Derby Theatre
Eden Court, Inverness
The Garage, Norwich
HOME, Manchester
The Lowry, Salford
Lyric Hammersmith, London
Lyric Theatre, Belfast
Marlowe Theatre, Canterbury
Northern Stage, Newcastle
North Wall Theatre, Oxford
Norwich Playhouse
Nottingham Playhouse
Queen's Theatre, Hornchurch
Royal & Derngate, Northampton
Sheffield Theatres
Sherman Theatre, Cardiff
Soho Theatre, London
Theatre Royal Bath
Theatre Royal Plymouth
Theatre Royal Stratford East, London
Traverse Theatre, Edinburgh
Warwick Arts Centre
York Theatre Royal

Performing Rights

*Application for permission to perform, etc. should be made
before rehearsals begin to the following representatives:*

For *Class*
United Agents
12–26 Lexington Street
London W1F 0LE

For *The Sad Club*
42MP
Palladium House
7th Floor
1–4 Argyll Street
London W1F 7TA

For *Flesh, Chaos* and *Stuff*
Casarotto Ramsay & Associates Limited
Waverley House
7–12 Noel Street
London W1F 8GQ

For *Variations*
Curtis Brown Group
Haymarket House
28–29 Haymarket
London SW1Y 4SP

For *Salt*
Berlin Associates
7 Tyers Gate
London SE1 3HX

For *Ageless* and *The Small Hours*
The Agency
24 Pottery Lane
Holland Park
London W11 4LZ

Copyrights

National Theatre Connections Team 2019

Kirsten Adam	*Connections Producer April 2019 onwards*
Holly Aston	*Connections Producer November 2017–March 2019*
Arianne Welsh	*Connections Assistant Producer March 2019 onwards*
Adele Geddes	*Connections Assistant Producer March 2015–February 2019*
Carmel Macaree	*Connections Administrative Assistant*
Tom Lyons	*Dramaturg*
Alice King-Farlow	*Director of Learning*
Paula Hamilton	*Deputy Director of Learning*
Virginia Leaver	*General Manager*

Workshop notes edited by Kate Budgen
With special thanks to Conor Hunt, former Connections
Administrative Assistant

The National Theatre

National Theatre
Upper Ground
London SE1 9PX
Registered charity no: 224223

Artistic Director
Rufus Norris
Executive Director
Lisa Burger